READINGS ARE WRITINGS

READINGS ARE WRITINGS

A Guide to Reading and Writing Well

Jan Youga
Mark H. Withrow
Janis Flint-Ferguson

Prentice Hall, Upper Saddle River, New Jersey 07458

Library of Congress Cataloging-in-Publication Data

Youga, Janet Martha.
 Readings are writings : a guide to reading and writing well / Jan
Youga, Mark H. Withrow, Janis Flint-Ferguson.
   p.   cm.
  Includes index.
  ISBN 0-13-097882-5 (pbk.)
   1. English language—Rhetoric.   2. Reading (Higher education)
 3. College readers.   I. Withrow, Mark H.   II. Flint
 -Ferguson, Janis   III. Title.
 PE1408.Y58 1996   95-15721
 808'.0427—dc20   CIP

Editorial/production supervision: *Harriet Tellem*
Acquisitions editor: *Alison Reeves*
Assistant development editor: *Kara Hado*
Editorial assistant: *Kane Tung*
Manufacturing buyer: *Lynn Pearlman*
Cover design: *Wendy Alling Judy*

 © 1996, by Prentice-Hall, Inc.
Simon & Schuster/A Viacom Company
Upper Saddle River, New Jersey 07458

Printed in the United States of America
10 9 8 7 6 5 4 3 2 1

ISBN 0-13-097882-5

Prentice-Hall International (UK) Limited, *London*
Prentice-Hall of Australia Pty. Limited, *Sydney*
Prentice-Hall Canada Inc., *Toronto*
Prentice-Hall Hispanoamericana, S.A., *Mexico*
Prentice-Hall of India Private Limited, *New Delhi*
Prentice-Hall of Japan, Inc., *Tokyo*
Simon & Schuster Asia Pte. Ltd., *Singapore*
Editora Prentice-Hall do Brasil, Ltda., *Rio de Janeiro*

CONTENTS

PART FOUR   **PERSUASIVE DISCOURSE**   **205**

Chapter 9   **Reading Persuasive Discourse:**
                   The Reader/Writer Relationship   207

Chapter 10   **Writing Persuasive Discourse   225**

PREFACE TO TEACHERS

Like many other readers, this book was born out of a search for a good textbook. As each of us faced teaching English Composition year after year, we would share our opinions about readers, searching for one that reflected the way we taught writing. Most textbooks simply did not work for us and when we found ourselves celebrating even partial successes, we decided it was time to write one ourselves—one that would contain not only what we knew about reading and writing techniques but also what we knew about how students learn to write and what motivates them to love and appreciate writing. We came up with several principles on which this book is based.

Students Need to See Reading and Writing Connections

This book emphasizes the close connection between good reading and writing skills, that *readings are writings and that writers are readers*. We want students to develop an appreciation for the writing techniques used in the readings, and to see their own writing as something others would genuinely want to read. Throughout the book, we have encouraged students to examine how the readings reflect writers at work and how their own writing will appear to a reader. We have also pointed out connections between the skills used for each activity and how a greater facility with language will increase their ability to complete successfully both reading and writing tasks.

Students Need Tools to Work With

While our ultimate goal in a college writing course is to enable students to write college-level analytical essays, this is a high-level skill that builds on a variety of other reading, writing, and thinking skills. Most of our students are not well prepared for this kind of writing, and we have found that we get the best analytical writing from them when these other skills have been carefully developed:

> When students know how to *read critically* and have a variety of reading strategies available to help them in this process;
>
> When students understand *writing as a process*;
>
> When students have developed enough fluency to express themselves confidently, to understand the role their own *voice* and the knowledge they have gained from experience play in their writing;
>
> When students have developed the ability to *express their ideas and opinions* clearly and to take the responsibility of ownership for these ideas, knowing how to support them well;
>
> When students have learned the influence of *audience* in writing, the need to take their readers' stance into account so that they keep listening to the writer's message; and
>
> When they have learned to sift through *gathered information*, separating main ideas from details, recognizing biases, identifying strong support, and practicing incorporating this support into their own positions.

Students Need a Developmental Framework

We have found that students progress more rapidly in our courses if they see that the reading and writing skills they learned for the first assignment are being used in the second, if there is a clear sense of progression. In this book, the progression is from personal to more objective, academic writing.

We begin with teaching students how to write about their personal experiences, *Expressive* writing. We want them to have a chance to work on expression and style while writing about subjects they are familiar with—their own lives and experiences and the lessons they have learned. This writing also emphasizes the importance of voice and the power of capturing the personal and the human experience in a unique way.

After they have learned to tell a good story using a strong voice, we then teach them how to use this experience to support an opinion. The narrative skills are put to use as the stories become illustrations and examples, and the voice becomes a tone of conviction powerfully asserting the validity of an idea.

We teach this skill in the section of the book on *Affirming* writing. While this may not be a familiar term to teachers, the kind of writing it represents—opinion pieces, position papers, editorials—is. We have included this section for two reasons. First, we found that it was a natural progression from expressive writing. After students have shared their personal experiences, we then ask them to explain how these experiences have shaped their thoughts, beliefs, and convictions.

Second, we found that this type of writing served as a natural bridge to *Persuasive* writing. We found that students struggled with persuasion because it involves both expressing an opinion in a powerful way and convincing someone else that this stance is true and should be adopted. The dual focus of clearly expressing one's own stand and having to accommodate the needs of a skeptical or even antagonistic audience was difficult for most students. So, we divided this task into two: learning to express one's opinion in a strong, convincing way and then learning to accommodate the needs of an audience which disagrees. Thus, the movement of the book from Expressive to Affirming and then to Persuasion.

The next section of the book focuses on *Informative* writing, which tries both to review and build on the skills in the previous sections. For example, it allows students to practice sharing what they know and have learned from personal experience and from holding certain convictions, while learning to shape these lessons for particular audiences. At the same time, it leads them away from personal writing to the more objective, critical stance of academic prose. The rhetorical strategies they are now familiar with are discussed in terms of options available to writers: Voice may range from personal to objective; audiences may be friendly, supportive, antagonist, or critical; support may come from experience, original research, or the library. The analytical essay, then, is taught as the end of a continuum of writing ranging from the most personal to the most objective, and which involves selecting particular options (e.g., third-person point of view, outside research, a critical stance, logical organization) from a wide range of stylistic choices.

In other words, throughout the book students are guided from being able to express their own experiences in a powerful way to being able to take on a more scholarly, critical stance.

There is a parallel progression in the readings based on the intimacy or distance of the reader/writer relationship. The readings, then, also move from the most personal to the most objective and academic, both within each section and from one section to the next.

Students Need Good, Challenging Models

The professional readings in this book were chosen for their quality and diversity. We looked for essays that we felt were both timely and timeless and that would engage students in the process of discussion and analysis. We have focused on critical reading skills and provided continual practice of these reading strategies throughout the book.

Students Need to Be Encouraged

As teachers, we are continually amazed at the dedication of student writers who have something important to say and who are ready to put in the time and effort necessary to say it well. That dedication is evident in the *student samples* in this book. These essays are used to illustrate writing techniques throughout the book, and we have included the students' entire composing processes in the chapters devoted to writing. We want these essays to celebrate the successes students have achieved in writing courses and to encourage other students to put in the time and energy it takes to develop their potential and experience this success themselves.

These five basic principles form the organizational framework for this book:

Part One   Demonstrates the connection between reading and writing. It introduces students to basic critical reading strategies and to the writing process. Each strategy and stage of the process is explained and students are shown how each contributes to more effective reading and writing.

    Part Two   Focuses on *Expressive Discourse* and a close, personal reader/writer relationship. It encourages students to appreciate voice in writing and to work on fluency. It also emphasizes the importance of narrative skills in creating good examples and introductions for other types of papers and of careful thought and reflection in all writing. Within this section the *Anecdote*, the *Narrative*, and the *Reflective Essay* are discussed.

    Part Three   Focuses on *Affirming Discourse* and a supportive but less personal reader/writer relationship. It encourages students to express their opinions and to understand the need for explaining and supporting their assertions. This section allows students to practice expressing their views in a compelling way. Within this section the *Opinion Essay*, the *Position Paper*, and the *Editorial* are discussed.

    Part Four   Focuses on *Persuasive Discourse* and the complexity of the reader/writer relationship that develops when an audience is skeptical or antagonistic to the writer's ideas and must be convinced of their validity. It introduces students to the idea of ethical, emotional, and logical support (Aristotle's ethos, pathos, and logos), and proper documentation is illustrated. Within this section *Evaluation, Argumentation,* and the *Proposal* are discussed.

    Part Five   Focuses on *Informative Discourse* and the most objective and distant reader/writer relationship. Conventions of academic writing are discussed as are the uses of original and secondary research. Within this section *Observation, Explanation,* and *Critical Analysis* are discussed.

    Part Six   In the final section of the book, we have again emphasized the close connection between reading and writing by selecting essays in which both student and professional writers discuss how reading and writing have influenced their lives. We want students to understand that these two skills have the power to greatly influence others and that they, too, have the power to touch someone else with their words.

Within all the chapters, good reading techniques are emphasized through the professional samples, and writing techniques are focused on through the student samples.

We want to thank the students who have contributed to this book. Specifically, we wish to thank the students from Columbia College in Chicago, Illinois; Gordon College in Wenham, Massachusetts; Illinois State University in Normal, Illinois; and Keene State College in Keene, New Hampshire. Special thanks go to Elizabeth Eckert and Todd Craig who created essays especially for this book.

We also wish to thank Becky Pierson and Gabe Wettach, our administrative assistants, and our colleges for their faculty development support. Special thanks to the students in Jan's Fall 1993 English Composition classes at Keene State College and Janis' Fall 1994 Core Writing classes at Gordon College with whom we piloted this book and who gave us valuable feedback on the essays. Thanks also to Elizabeth McMahan for her sage advice and southern hospitality, to Rex and Laura for their infinite patience with us, to Mary Ballou for her good advice, to Alison Reeves and Kara Hado for their guidance and faith in this project, and to Harriet Tellem for her work on the book.

Thank you to our reviewers: Nancy Gilman, Salem State College; Douglas D. Hesse, Illinois State University; Lea P. Jacobson, Memphis State University; Joyce Kinkead, Utah State University; Jim Moody, South Suburban College; Patrick J. McMahon, Tallahassee Community College; Kathy Jean Nontangasa Dickison, Lexington Community College; Maureen Potts, University of Texas at El Paso; Audrey J. Roth, Miami-Dade Community College; Betty Ann Sisson, Oklahoma State University; and Clifford W. Young, Miami-Dade Community College.

Jan Youga
Mark H. Withrow
Janis Flint-Ferguson

ACKNOWLEDGMENTS

Diane Ackerman, "The Psychopharmacology of Chocolate" from *A Natural History of the Senses* (pages 153–57) by Diane Ackerman. Copyright © 1990 by Diane Ackerman. Reprinted by permission of Random House, Inc.

Mary Field Belenky, et al., "To the Other Side of Silence" in "Background of the Study" from *Women's Ways of Knowing*. Copyright © 1986 by Basic Books, Inc. Reprinted by permission of BasicBooks, a division of HarperCollins Publishers, Inc.

Louise Bernikow, "Confessions of an Ex-Cheerleader," *Ms. Magazine*, October 1973. Permission granted by *Ms. Magazine*, copyright © 1973.

Robert Bly, "The Hunger for the King in a Time with No Father," from *Iron John* (pp. 92–97), © 1990 by Robert Bly. Reprinted by permission of Addison-Wesley Publishing Company, Inc.

David Carlin, Jr., "Not by Condoms Alone: Society and the AIDS Epidemic" reprinted by permission of COMMONWEAL FOUNDATION.

Lorene Cary, "Welcome to St. Paul's" from *Black Ice* by Lorene Cary. Copyright © 1991 by Lorene Cary. Reprinted by permission of Alfred A. Knopf, Inc.

William Jefferson Clinton, Inaugural Address, January 20, 1993. Copyright © 1993 by William Jefferson Clinton. Reprinted by permission of the author.

Diane Cole, "Don't Just Stand There," *New York Times*, April 16, 1989. Reprinted with permission from Diane Cole.

David Daniels, "College Lectures: Is Anybody Listening?" reprinted with permission of the author.

Annie Dillard, "Mother," and "Reading is Subversive," pages 110–17 and 182–84 from *An American Childhood* by Annie Dillard. Copyright © 1987 by Annie Dillard. Reprinted by permission of HarperCollins Publishers, Inc.

Elizabeth Eckert, "To Enter As a Child" reprinted by permission of *Campus Life*.

Barbara Erenreich, "Teach Diversity—with a Smile." Copyright © 1991 by Time, Inc. Reprinted with permission.

Peter Elbow, "Desperation Writing" pages 60–64 from *Writing Without Teachers* by Peter Elbow. Copyright © 1973 by Oxford University Press, Inc. Reprinted by permission of Oxford University Press, Inc.

Endicott College Viewbook. Reprinted with permission of Endicott College, Beverly, MA.

Robert Fulghum, "Laundry" from *All I Really Need to Know I Learned in Kindergarten* by Robert Fulghum. Copyright © 1986, 1988 by Robert Fulghum. Reprinted by permssion of Villard Books, a division of Random House, Inc.

Carol Gilligan, "Images of Relationship," reprinted by permission of the publishers from *In a Different Voice* by Carol Gilligan, Cambridge, Mass.: Harvard University Press, Copyright © 1982 by Carol Gilligan.

Ellen Goodman, "Women Divided: Family or Career," *The Boston Globe*, 1994. Copyright © 1994, The Boston Globe Company. Reprinted with permission of The Washington Post Writers Group.

Dick Gregory, "Not Poor, Just Broke," from *Nigger: An Autobiography* by Dick Gregory. Copyright © 1964 by Dick Gregory Enterprises, Inc. Used by permission of Dutton Signet, a division of Penguin Books USA Inc.

Gregory H. Hemingway, "To Make Papa Proud," from *PAPA: A Personal Memoir*. Copyright © 1976 by Gregory H. Hemingway. Reprinted by permission of Houghton Mifflin.

Indigo Girls, "Virginia Woolf," from *Rites of Passage*. Words and music by Emily Saliers © 1992 EMI VIRGIN SONGS, INC. and GODHAP MUSIC. All Rights Controlled and Administered by EMI VIRGIN SONGS, INC. All Rights Reserved International Copyright Secured. Used by Permission.

Andrew Kimbrell, "The Male Manifesto," *The New York Times*, June 4, 1991. Copyright © 1991/1993 by The New York Times Company. Reprinted by permission of the New York Times Company.

Lawrence L. Langer, "The Human Use of Language" by Lawrence L. Langer. Copyright © 1977 by Editorial Projects in Education, Inc. Reprinted by permission of the author.

Anthony Lewis, "Abroad at Home/Their Brutal Mirth," *The New York Times*, May 20, 1991. Copyright © 1991/1993 by The New York Times Company. Reprinted by permission of The New York Times Company.

Malcolm X, "Coming to an Awareness" from *The Autobiography of Malcolm X* by Malcolm X, with the assistance of Alex Haley. Copyright © 1964 by Alex Haley and Malcolm X and copyright © 1965 by Alex Haley and Betty Shabaz. Reprinted by permssion of Random House, Inc.

Margaret Treece Metzger and Clare Fox, "Two Teachers of Letters," *Harvard Review* 56:41, (1986) 349–354. Copyright © 1986 by the President and Fellows of Harvard College. All rights reserved.

Horace Miner, "Body Ritual Among the Nacerima," reproduced by permission of the American Anthropological Association from *American Anthropologist 58.3 (1956): 503–7. Not for sale or further reproduction.*

Donald Murray, "The Inglorious Terrors of War" *The Boston Globe*, January 8, 1990. Copyright © 1990 by Donald Murray. Reprinted by permission of the author.

Donald Murray, "Reading as a Reader," excerpt from *Read to Write, A Writing Process Reader*. Copyright © 1986 by Holt Rinehart and Winston Inc. Reprinted by permission of the publisher.

Robert M. Pirsig, "Quality," excerpt from *Zen and the Art of Motorcycle Maintenance*. Copyright © 1974 by Robert M. Pirsig. Ill: Copyright ©. By permission of William Morrow & Company, Inc.

Joseph M. Queenan, "Too Late to Say 'I'm Sorry,' " (*Newsweek* "My Turn") © 1987 by Joseph Queenan. Reprinted by permission of the author.

Anna Quindlen, "Public & Private/Death Watch" *The New York Times*, May 16, 1991. Copyright © 1991/1993 by The New York Times Company. Reprinted by permission of The New York Times Company.

Ishmael Reed, "America: The Multinational Society" from *Writin' is Fightin'* by Ishamel Reed. Copyright © 1983, 1988 by Ishamel Reed. Originally appeared in *San Francisco Focus*. Reprinted with the permission of Atheneum Publishers, an imprint of Macmillan Publishing Company.

A.M. Rosenthal, "No News From Auschwitz," August 31, 1958. Copyright © 1958 by The New York Times Company. Reprinted by permission.

Laurence Shames, "The Eyes of Fear" reprinted by permission of Sterling Lord Literistic, Inc. Copyright © 1982 by Laurence Shames.

Daniel Shanahan, "A Proposal for a Multilingual America," *Chronicle of Higher Education*.

Part One

READING
AND WRITING
CONNECTIONS

When we read we bring to this task a unique self—all of our past experiences, knowledge, feelings, beliefs, biases, all that encompasses who we are. At the same time, reading a text changes this self; it may increase our knowledge of a subject, reinforce our beliefs, or challenge the way we think. This altered self is then brought to the next reading experience and further changes occur within us.

We undergo a similar process when we write. As we struggle to create good pieces of writing, we make discoveries about ourselves and our topic. As we strive to articulate our ideas, they are reinforced or challenged, and these changes in the way we think, in turn, influence subsequent writings.

One of the reasons that reading and writing are such powerful agents for change is that they are *activities* we engage in. We are not reading if we are just moving our eyes across the page, nor are we writing if we are simply copying words from a book. Reading means comprehension; it means we are actively engaged in making sense out of the words in front of us, in understanding someone else's thoughts. And writing means communication, expressing our ideas in a way that someone else will understand. Reading is the process we go through that enables us to comprehend a text, and writing is the process we go through that enables others to comprehend our text. This active involvement in the process of *making meaning* for ourselves and others, like any other experience we have, naturally affects us. We come to a better understanding of both ourselves and the people we want to reach with our words.

The reading and writing processes, then, are closely connected in that they both influence who we are and how we learn. As readers and writers we are ever-changing and ever-expanding, and so, as we continue to read and write, a spiral of growth is set into motion.

But this ability to understand and to be understood, like any other activity, takes practice, especially since reading and writing are complex processes. For example, good readers know how to prepare themselves to read a text by using prereading strategies, how to monitor their comprehension while they read, and how to reach a final goal of understanding. Similarly, good writers have many ways in which they prepare themselves to write, many strategies for revision, and ways to determine when they have produced a successful final copy.

In the first two chapters we will review the skills that good readers and writers use in these processes and show how both the reader and the writer travel down paths with similar landmarks.

Chapter One

READING AS A PROCESS

Have you ever found yourself on page 34 of a text and suddenly realized that the last thing you remember reading was on page 31? For three pages your eyes have been moving steadily from one word to the next, but your mind was disconnected from the page. And since doing eye exercises is not reading, you were forced to go back to page 31 and try again.

We all have had this experience of drifting away as we read; it is an easy thing to do, especially when there are distractions around us competing for our attention. While this happens even to the best readers, there are strategies you can use that will keep you from wasting so much time backtracking. In the rest of this chapter, we will discuss these strategies using the essay "To Make Papa Proud" by Gregory Hemingway to illustrate effective reading techniques.

DETERMINING YOUR PURPOSE

Why are you reading this essay by Hemingway? The most likely answer is that your teacher is requiring it. That, then, is your motivation for getting through the piece. But what are you trying to get out of it? That may seem like a strange question, but having a clear purpose for reading is a key element for success because you do not read everything in the same way.

For example, when you get mail, you do not give the same attention to junk mail as to personal letters or bills. Each of these gets a different kind of reading, and the difference is determined by the purpose. You read a personal letter from home with great care because your purpose is to find out the family news and to know that you are loved and cared about. The cursory reading of junk mail (if you read it at all) is to find out as quickly as possible if you have the slightest interest in the subject. Similarly, you do not read a textbook chapter on which you will be tested in the same way that you read a mystery novel or *TV Guide*. In other words, you vary your rate of reading and the care with which you approach the text according to your purpose for the task.

Reading for Pleasure or for Information

Generally, reading can be divided into two broad purposes: reading for pleasure and reading for information. You are reading for fun when you pick up the latest Stephen King novel, for example, and you are reading for information when you find yourself hiding in an isolated corner of the library cramming for a test.

Your purpose for reading is not determined by the kind of text you are reading. For example, even though novels are written to be enjoyed, when one of them is assigned for a class, the purpose in reading is no longer just "fun" because you are thinking of the book in terms of some kind of evaluation—an essay test, an analytical paper, a list of quotations to identify. This experience is not the same as sitting in front of a fire and selecting that novel as an enjoyable way to spend an evening. Students also sometimes find that even if they are not being evaluated but are told by their teachers to read a book for pleasure, just the fact that it is required somehow takes all the fun out of it. They still find themselves reading for information, anticipating that they will be held accountable for it in some way.

So, again, besides the fact that it is required, why are you reading Hemingway's essay? Will you be tested on it and therefore need to know plot, characters, setting, and significance? Or are you being asked to read it because it's an interesting story and an enjoyable piece of writing? You probably can't answer these questions since the purpose for reading within a classroom context is generally determined by the teacher. You might ask your instructor!

GETTING READY TO READ

Have you ever noticed how you decide which magazine to read while you're biding your time in a waiting room? Or have you ever noticed how easy some material is for you to read while other reading seems so difficult? Or have you ever been reading something and suddenly realized how the ideas in this piece related to your own thoughts on the subject?

In all of these situations, you are relying on something called *prior knowledge* to aid you in reading. You will usually select a magazine based solely on the title because from the words *Sports Illustrated* or *Ms.* you can predict what the articles will be about and that they will interest you. You find some material easy to read because you already know a good deal about the subject and so the context is familiar to you. Your reading is also greatly aided by your ability to make connections between ideas you've already thought about and the new information the reading is providing. Your prior knowledge, then, about the words in a title or the subject or ideas presented becomes the foundation on which you build your comprehension of the new text.

For example, if you had looked at the title and the subheads of this chapter before you began reading, you could probably have predicted a good deal about the contents. If your past experience has made you aware of strengths and weaknesses in your own reading process, your knowledge of these skills is probably making comprehension even easier. And if you have already studied something about the reading process, you are probably using that knowledge right now as a basis for understanding the information presented here.

Prior knowledge, then, is a key to getting the process of reading off to a good start. The more you think about and prepare for the reading, the easier it will be.

Using Background Information

To see how this process works, let's do some prereading before you look at the selection in this chapter. Just before the essay, you will find the following background information:

TO MAKE PAPA PROUD
Gregory H. Hemingway, M.D.

This episode from Gregory Hemingway's memoir relates an incident that happened while Gregory (also called Gig) and his father, Ernest Hemingway, were spending a summer in Havana, Cuba, during the days before Castro. Gregory was eighteen and had just decided to follow in his father's footsteps and become a writer.

Perhaps the first item of note in this background paragraph is who Gregory's father is. Most of you have probably read something by Hemingway: *The Old Man and the Sea, A Farewell to Arms,* or perhaps "The Snows of Kilimanjaro." Even if you have never read anything by Hemingway, most of you would recognize him as a famous writer. Perhaps the second item of note, then, is that Gregory is a doctor, as indicated by the M.D. after his name, and therefore did not choose his father's profession even though at eighteen this was his goal. And yet you are meeting Gregory not as a physician but as a writer because he has chosen to record his memories of his papa; so in that sense, he has followed in his father's footsteps.

These conclusions derived from the background will be helpful in understanding the piece. But looking at background is a step many readers skip. It seems "easier" just to go directly to paragraph 1 and start, and sometimes this direct approach will not hamper you. But usually, when you skip over important information, you find yourself backtracking, having to search for something you obviously missed. In this case, for example, you would not know who "Papa" was. And so, the easier route would actually wind up making the reading harder since this information is crucial for understanding the piece.

Developing an Interest in the Reading

Besides prior knowledge, the most important element in reading success is interest. As you undoubtedly know, it is very difficult to comprehend and to focus on material in which you have no interest. One way to spark an interest in any topic is to see how the topic relates to you. For example, look at the title, "To Make Papa Proud." Without knowing anything else about the selection, you can help prepare yourself for it by relating that title to your own life.

Prereading journal   Write about a time when you did something just to make someone—a parent, a teacher, a camp counselor, a friend—proud of you. Describe what you did, why it was important to impress this person, whether you succeeded in making this person proud of you, and how you felt about it afterward. Consider how far you would go to make someone proud of you. Now keep this experience in mind as you read about Hemingway's attempts to please his father.

Establishing a personal connection to a subject provides you with an extra motivation for reading. It makes you care more about what the author has to say because you can see how it relates to your own life. This approach may sound rather self-centered, but if you really *cannot* see, on your own or with the help of someone else, how a text relates to you—by giving you pleasure, by providing you with a different point of view, by helping you gain knowledge of something you value or insight into something that concerns you—you will find it difficult if not impossible to understand it.

As you may have already learned, this lack of interest is often what keeps students from passing certain courses. They have not yet understood on their own or had anyone successfully explain to them why they should care about chemical formulas or poetic meter or ancient philosophies. The fact that a lack of interest can have such a devastating effect on learning shows how crucial a factor it is. Taking the time to establish an interest in the topic, then, is time well spent.

READING ACTIVELY

As noted earlier, it is easy for your mind to drift while reading, especially if other things—how much pressure you're under to finish reading, the great time you had the night before, the warm sunlight streaming through the window—are competing for your attention. The key to avoiding this drifting is to remain actively engaged in the reading while you do it: to be aware of what you are comprehending, to note what you don't understand, to discover what you can relate to, and to keep track of what you might need to know later. Good readers monitor their progress, often by keeping a pencil at hand while they read to mark significant or favorite passages and to write questions or connections in the margins. This practice of "reading with a pencil" is a good habit to develop as it will help keep you alert and focused.

Monitoring Your Progress

you read as and when you reread it no next

Only you can know if you are comprehending a text and how secure you are in that understanding. But sometimes you think you understand something and then you get to class and hear other students or the teacher discussing the piece and you wonder if you got the assignment wrong. Did they read the same thing you did?

Yes. But what has probably happened is that you have "cheated" a little in monitoring your comprehension. You read the piece and assumed you understood it, but you never challenged yourself in any way to find out if that were really true. The following techniques will help you to assess your comprehension more honestly.

Steps to help monitor Reading comprehension

Annotating the text. This technique takes some practice but once you master it, it works very well for any text. You can begin by turning all the headings and titles of the piece into questions and your reading then becomes a search for answers. For example, you could keep in mind while you read this essay that you are really trying to find out if Gregory made his papa proud.

In addition, you can monitor your progress by asking yourself questions as you read, by noting words you don't understand, and by underlining ideas you like or respond to in some way. To help you with this technique, the Hemingway essay has been *annotated* with questions and comments in the margins. This is a technique that you should try to develop for yourself as you work your way through other texts.

Also while you read keep in mind the background information we discussed and your own memory from the prereading journal you did.

TO MAKE PAPA PROUD

Gregory H. Hemingway, M.D.

This episode from Gregory Hemingway's memoir relates an incident that happened while Gregory (also called Gig) and his father, Ernest Hemingway, were spending a summer in Havana, Cuba, during the days before Castro. Gregory was eighteen and had just decided to follow in his father's footsteps and become a writer.

HF—novel by Mark Twain. *Portrait*—difficult novel by James Joyce. Why is Gregory reading these writers?

That summer in Havana I read papa's 1 favorites, from *Huckleberry Finn* to *Portrait of the Artist as a Young Man*: like him, I sometimes had two or three books going at the same time. Then papa steered me to the short story masters, Maupassant and Chekhov. "Don't try to analyze—just relax and enjoy them."

How would you feel if you were given a task and told not to expect your work to be any good?

"Now," papa said one morning. "Try writing 2 a short story yourself. And don't expect it to be any good."

How does Gig's attempt to write seem to be going so far?

I sat down at a table with one of papa's fine- 3 pointed pencils and thought and thought. I looked out the window, and listened to the birds, to a cat crying to join them; and to the scratch of my pencil, doodling. I let the cat out. Another wanted in.

Note references to Papa's pencils and Papa's typewriter.
List the ways Papa responds to Gig's writing. Which response

I went to papa's typewriter. He'd finished 4 with it for the day. Slowly I typed out a story and then took it to him.

Papa put his glasses on, poured himself 5 another drink, and read, as I waited. He finished it and looked up at me. "It's excellent, Gig. Much better than anything I could do at your age. Only change I'd make is here," and he pointed to the

<table>
<tr><td>

is most impor-
tant to Gig?

Why would Papa
describe writing
as a lottery when
he admits it is a
skill that takes
study and disci-
pline?

What is your
reaction to
Papa's speech?
Why do you
think he goes on
and on about
how hard writing
is? How do you
think Gig is feel-
ing during this
speech? How
would you feel if
you got an A+
on a paper and
the teacher
talked on and
on about previ-
ous students?

</td><td>

line about a bird falling from its nest and find-
ing, miraculously, that if it flapped its wings, it
wouldn't crash on the rocks below.

"You've written . . . 'All of a sudden he real- 6
ized he could fly.' Change 'all of a sudden' to
'suddenly.' Never use more words than you have
to—it detracts from the flow of action." Papa
smiled. I hadn't seen him smile at me like that
for a long time. "But you've won the lottery, pal.
Writing takes study, discipline, and imagination.
You've shown me with this that you have the
imagination. And if you can do it once, you can
do it a thousand times. Imagination doesn't
leave you for a long time, maybe never.
Dostoyevsky was fifty-seven when he wrote *Crime
and Punishment.*

"God, I used to get sad in Key West when 7
people sent me their work and I could tell after
reading one page that they didn't have it and
never would. I answered every goddamn letter,
usually saying that writing well was mainly a mat-
ter of luck, that to be given a great talent was like
winning a million-to-one lottery; and if you
weren't blessed, all the study and self-discipline in
the world wouldn't mean a thing. If their letter
had something like 'Everybody says I'd make a
great engineer but what I really want to do is
write,' I'd answer, 'Maybe everybody isn't wrong
and you'll probably make an excellent engineer
and then forget all about writing and be delight-
ed you never went into it.'

"I wrote hundreds of letters like that and I 8
was getting a dollar a word in those days.

"Later, when there were even more letters, I 9
shortened my answers to 'Writing is a tough
trade. Don't get mixed up in it if you can help it.'
They probably thought, 'That conceited son of a
bitch probably hasn't even read my stuff. But
because he can write, he makes a big exclusive
thing of it.'

</td></tr>
</table>

What kind of a teacher do you think Papa would be?
How does this feeling about his skill compare to his comment about imagination in paragraph 6? Note the casual reference to Papa's third drink.
How does this paragraph relate to Papa's smile in paragraph 6? What does it say about their relationship?
Turgenev: famous Russian writer. Why did Gig plagiarize?

"The important thing is, Gig, that now I can 10 teach *you* because you have the tools. And, in all immodesty, I know a lot about the trade.

"I've wanted to cut down for a long time. 11 The writing doesn't come so easily for me anymore. But I'll be just as happy helping you as doing it myself. Let's have a drink to celebrate."

Only once before can I remember papa 12 being as pleased with me—when I tied for the pigeon-shooting championship. And he was confident that there was another winner in the family when I entered the short story for a school competition and won first prize.

Turgenev should have won the prize. He 13 wrote the story. I merely copied it, changing the setting and the names, from a book I assumed papa hadn't read because some of the pages were still stuck together.

I didn't feel like a winner and wondered 14 how long it would be before papa found out that the only creative contribution I had made to the story was to alter "suddenly" to "all of a sudden."

Fortunately I wasn't around when papa dis- 15 covered my plagiarism. It got back to me that someone asked him if his son Gregory wrote. "Yes," he replied, with gusto and sparkle, flashing that "say cheese" smile he sometimes affected. "Gregory writes an occasional bad check." And, of course, everyone laughed.

Someone in that crowd might have thought, 16 "What a brutal bastard to make such a callous wisecrack about his son. I guess all those stories I've heard about him being a hard-shelled bully are true."

How did Gig help make his father hard-shelled?

Hard-shelled, yes, but I helped make that 17 shell.

Summarizing the main point While you are reading, in addition to asking questions, you need to keep trying to determine the main point of the essay. Many readers interpret "main point" to be plot (what happened) or subject matter (what the piece is about). So, if you were asked what the point of Hemingway's essay is, you might answer, "It's about some guy who plagiarized" or "It's about plagiarism." If you then went to class and the discussion about main point started to revolve around father–son relationships and the extent to which someone will go to win approval, you might well wonder if you had read the same text as your classmates.

In trying to determine the main point, it may help you to consider more than just what the piece is about. Just as it helps comprehension to determine your purpose for reading, it can also help if you consider the author's purpose for writing. Why do you think Hemingway remembered this incident? Why was it significant to him? What was he trying to say about his father? About himself? About their relationship? In other words, while the essay *is* about some guy who plagiarized, you can push yourself further in articulating your understanding of the piece. First of all, the "guy" has an identity, both a name and a relationship that is significant—he is Gregory, Ernest Hemingway's son. Second, he had a reason for plagiarizing which can be discussed both in terms of the title (making his papa proud) and in terms of that relationship (father–son, parent–child, teacher–student, coach–novice).

As you formulate your ideas about the main point, then, think both about what you understood from the piece and what you think the writer was trying to tell you. And while you might be able to express your basic understanding of the piece through the words, "It's about some guy who plagiarized," you will need to go beyond that to explain why Hemingway wrote the essay.

If you are having difficulty determining the main point of an essay, try these three steps to summarize it:

1. List the *main topic of each paragraph* in the essay.
2. Condense this list by *lumping together paragraphs with similar ideas* so that you are left with a shorter list of what seem to be the several key points in the piece. At this stage, these key ideas can be put into your own words to form a *summary paragraph*.
3. To find the main idea, look at this condensed list and search for the *common thought* or thread that holds them together. What is the author saying about these key ideas?

In the Hemingway essay, for example, after listing the main point of each paragraph, the list could be condensed to the following points:

> Gig obediently follows the orders of his father to read and write (paragraphs 1–4).
>
> Hemingway provides feedback focused on how rare writing talent is (paragraphs 5–11).
>
> Gig's plagiarism is explained as an attempt to win his father's approval (paragraphs 12–14).
>
> Hemingway jokingly responds to Gig's plagiarism, and Gig seriously responds to his father's joke (paragraphs 15–17).

In looking at this list, plagiarism certainly emerges as a topic, but two out of four of the items on the list concern Gig's actions in response to his father, rather than in response to his own desires and interests. And Hemingway's reaction in the other two items is callous in some way, "hard-shelled" as Gig puts it, not acknowledging Gig's needs as a son. Yet even in the end, it is Gig who accepts the responsibility for his father's response.

In other words, a list such as this clearly indicates that plagiarism is only a part of what the essay is about. If you take the time to do this kind of summarizing activity, you are less likely to miss out on the full meaning of the piece.

Mapping it out   Another way in which you can check your understanding of a text is to create a visual representation of it. This method is particularly effective if you are a visual learner and having a picture of something in your mind helps you to remember it. "Reading maps" take various shapes. Some are like lists—outlines of main ideas or arguments, comparisons of different theories or the positions of different authors, recurring patterns of a text. Others are more imaginative and include diagrams of text structure or drawings of symbols and images. Whatever form they take, these visual representations of the written text can help you to memorize information or discover meaning.

For example, let's look at a thematic map, one that captures the meaning of the piece, for Hemingway's essay.

A map such as this one communicates a number of key ideas in the piece. First, by his place at the top of the drawing and by the size of the lettering, Papa's position as a famous writer is made clear. Putting young Gig on the road to this famous writer shows that he wants to follow in the footsteps of this celebrity. In addition, the famous writer is his father and so this road shows Gregory's personal desire to make his papa proud. In the process of trying to please his father he has failed—symbolized by the F's—except for once when he won a pigeon-shooting contest and now with the story. The Dead End sign shows how the story led to failure again when the plagiarism was discovered.

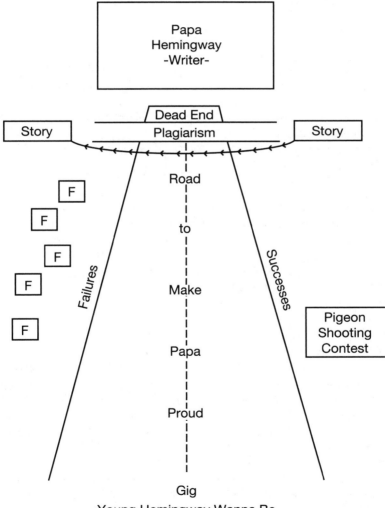

Other types of reading maps emphasize the main point by putting a word such as "pride" in a central box and then showing how all the other ideas in the piece revolve around it:

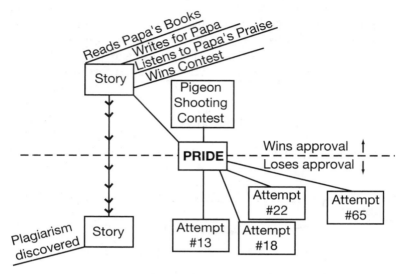

Reading maps can also help you determine the organization of a piece and develop your critical thinking skills by plotting out each major idea or premise and then analyzing this development to determine if it is logical. Whatever kind of drawing you make, the map can help you hold the essay—its meaning, its ideas, its organization—in a single picture.

REREADING

Why would you reread something you have already read? Sometimes it is for pleasure, just as you might see a movie you like more than once. Sometimes you reread because you are confused and need to go back to increase your understanding, as when you reread material before a test. You may also realize later that something you read has become very important to you and you go back to find out why.

As with your first reading, you need to reread with a purpose and this purpose will determine your reading strategies. If you are trying to study for a test, for example, you will probably pay close attention to chapter summaries. If you are rereading for pleasure, you may savor it this time, lingering over your favorite passages, since you are not rushing ahead to find out what happens.

And in terms of pleasure, it is only after you have read a text and understood its main point that you are in a position to really appreciate it in terms of how well it was written. You can go back and see how you were being carefully and deliberately led to the ending of the piece. You can see how certain events or lines were emphasized and others diminished. You can see how characters or ideas were developed and how certain writing techniques were used. In other words, you can not only determine the meaning of a piece but also discover how that meaning was conveyed. These techniques that you observe in other writers will help you to appreciate the fine craft of writing and then become methods you can use in your own writing. Rereading, then, is an important strategy because it increases the value of the selection for you both as a reader and as a writer.

In the Hemingway essay, for example, a crucial event in the story takes place in paragraphs 3 and 4. It is at this point that Gig struggles to write a story, wrestles with his desire to please his father, contemplates his own talent or what he probably sees as a lack of talent, stalls and stalls, finally decides to plagiarize, selects the story, and copies it. But all of this internal struggle is left out. All we, as readers, know at this point is that he thought for a while and typed out a story. The real significance of the little activities in paragraph 3, the fact that these insignificant actions are masking a momentous decision, is kept from us until paragraphs 12 and 13. Only then do we find out how much Gig has struggled to please his father—and how little he has succeeded—and that he chose to plagiarize in a desperate attempt to win his father's approval. The real significance of the event slowly unfolds for us and this unfolding helps to sustain our interest in the piece. Imagine how different it would be if Gig had started this story, "One summer in Havana I disappointed my father by plagiarizing a story from Turgenev."

CHECKING YOUR UNDERSTANDING

It is always interesting to listen to the comments people make as they leave a movie theater. Nearly everyone will have some evaluative comment ranging from "What a great film!" to "Well, that was a waste of time." In addition, people will start recalling scenes they liked best or offering their own opinions about how something might have been done better. Often, someone else in the party will disagree and a little debate will ensue with both sides defending their stands and offering evidence from the movie to support their claims.

Discussing the Reading

Conversations such as the ones that occur about movies also happen around readings and are one of the best ways for you to determine if you have really understood something because they force you to articulate your thoughts, feelings, and opinions about it. This can also be part of the pleasure of reading—sharing these responses both with others who agree with you and share your appreciation and with those who disagree but help you see a perspective you may have missed. This is why teachers usually encourage class discussion of a reading; it helps you to check your comprehension of the piece and encourages you to share your ideas with others.

However, many students find entering into class discussions difficult. Even students who can chatter away about the relative quality of *Deep Space Nine* versus *Star Wars: The Next Generation*, citing detailed examples of character strengths and flaws, recalling plot twists that captured the imagination or seemed too far-fetched, and critically analyzing the logic of the medical or technical advances portrayed on the show, fall silent when these same discussion skills are needed to analyze an essay in class. This silence has many causes: shyness in front of strangers, fear of the teacher's judgment, apathy about the reading, or simply not seeing that the skills called for are variations of the same ones used in daily discussions with friends.

However, since discussions are often required and affect students' grades, since they reflect a natural part of our daily lives even when they occur in the more artificial classroom setting, and since they are an integral part of many professions, it is advantageous for you to learn how to participate in them.

You can build confidence in your ability to participate in several ways. First, *listen to yourself when you are having those critical conversations with friends* about TV shows or arguing over which movie to rent or presenting a proposal for how to spend spring break. Unless some form of coercion enters the discussion as when someone says, "We're going to Florida because it's my car," these conversations can provide you with practice time. In class the range of listeners will be wider and you may not feel as confident about the topic, but you can still use those same skills of stating and defending a position.

Second, you can practice for the discussion by *talking to someone about the reading before class*. Once you know that someone else had the same questions or came to the same conclusions, you may feel more confident bringing these points up to the larger group.

Third, *listen carefully to how your teachers usually begin discussions* and try to plan something to say. For example, if your teacher always starts with a broad question such as, "So, what did you think about this reading?" or "Did you enjoy this essay?" you can plan a response ahead of time. In the same way, if the teacher usually asks about organization, language, or the writer, you can pay particular attention to these as you read.

Finally, if you are nervous about being asked questions, *come to class prepared to ask a question* yourself. Asking a good, thoughtful question about a reading gets you talking out loud to the group and can prove that you read the essay as much as an answer can.

Answering Textbook Questions

In addition to *annotating* the text yourself so that you have notes about your own questions, thoughts, and observations, you might also find it helpful to pay attention to any *questions that are provided in the textbook*. Text questions often give clues as to the meaning of the piece and indicate the direction in which the discussion might go.

The following questions, for example, will help you to articulate your understanding of the Hemingway essay.

Checking Your Understanding

1. Describe the father–son relationship that is revealed in this story. What is Gig confessing about this relationship? Why would he want to tell this story since it is not a positive reflection on either him or his father?

2. How did you respond to the two men in this essay? Did you side with either of them or feel more drawn to one than the other? Why?

3. Plagiarism is a serious offense—it is stealing. While Gregory clearly makes a choice to do this, there are ways in which his father is contributing to the pressure he feels to cheat. In the academic world, why do students plagiarize? What personal motivations might they have? How might outside factors contribute to the pressure students feel to cheat?

In addition to understanding the reading, you should also look at the questions to help you understand how the piece was written, to examine aspects of style such as voice, audience, organization, use of details, and word choice. These stylistic choices a writer makes are called "rhetorical strategies," and they will help you appreciate how the piece is written as well as what it says.

Examining Rhetorical Strategies

1. Between paragraphs 3 and 4, Gig makes the decision to plagiarize, then sits down and copies the Turgenev story. Write a brief journal entry in which you recreate the thought process that led Gig to the decision. Be sure to reveal how his relationship with his father influenced his plagiarism.

2. While this story captures a writing failure for Gregory, he is not a failure as a writer. He failed in his attempt to imitate his father's skill as a short story writer, but he succeeded in writing a critically acclaimed nonfiction memoir about his life. How is writing fiction different from writing nonfiction? Why might one form be easier for some people? Are there any ways in which this true story about Gig's life is similar to a short fiction story?

You will find questions that will help your comprehension and help you appreciate the writer's style throughout this book.

THE RECURSIVE NATURE OF READING

Even though we have discussed reading in terms of stages, pre-reading, reading, and rereading do not occur in a straightforward, linear fashion. The reading process is *recursive*. For example, you may reread passages that are difficult or that you really like before you have finished reading the whole piece. And you may stop in the middle of a piece to look up the definition of a word that is a crucial part of the background information you need. You may pause in your reading because a particular line reminds you of an experience you have had and you take a minute to reflect on it. You may find a line in the piece that would be a perfect quotation to use in a paper you are working on and stop to make note of it.

In other words, it is important to remember that good reading skills involve more than just moving your eyes from one word to the next and that a variety of skills may be employed at any time in the process. You will also need to discover through trial and error which strategies work best for you. Just remember that your reading should be purposeful—try to discover what the writers felt was so important that they just had to write it down and share it with you.

A SUMMARY OF READING STRATEGIES

1. Determine your *purpose*. Know why you are reading the piece.
2. Tap into your *prior knowledge* of the topic. Think for a minute or briefly write down what you already know about it.
3. Try to establish some *interest* in the reading by relating it to your life.
4. Read any *background information* provided on the essay or the author.
5. Make use of any *comprehension aids* the text itself may provide: introductions, summaries, subheadings, and questions.
6. Monitor your progress while you read by *reading with a pencil* in hand and noting questions, thoughts, definitions, connections to other readings, patterns in language or organization, and both key and weak ideas or arguments in the essay.
7. *Summarize* the main point of the essay. State what the essay is about and identify the author's purpose in writing it.
8. Make a *reading map* of the essay.
9. *Reread* when necessary for comprehension or to note the writing techniques being used.
10. *Discuss* the essay with someone to check your comprehension.

And remember that any of these strategies may prove helpful at any time in your reading process.

Chapter Two

WRITING AS A PROCESS OF READING AND REVISING TEXT

Just as good readers use a variety of skills to comprehend a text, so writers use various techniques to produce a comprehensible text. And, as we said earlier, there are similarities between these two processes. Both involve determining a purpose, preparing for the activity, re-seeing the text, and monitoring comprehension.

DETERMINING YOUR PURPOSE

As in reading, one of the keys to successful writing is having a clear sense of purpose. What are you trying to accomplish? What effect are you trying to have on your readers? While there are many ways to answer those questions, in this book we are focusing on four specific purposes that cover a wide range of writing: expressive, affirming, persuasive, and informative.

Expressive writing is personal writing in which the authors are trying to express something about who they are and how they came to be that way. *Affirming* writing is also personal but focuses on the writer's opinions rather than experiences. In *persuasive* writing the author goes one step further, not just expressing personal opinions, but trying to make other people adopt them, to change the reader's mind or behavior or attitude. And in *informative* writing, the author focuses on communicating information, sharing knowledge. While these aims can be defined and distinguished from each other, they are not like a row of sealed boxes, absolutely separated from each other. The aims overlap and you will be able to use the skills you learn in one kind of writing in all the other writing you do.

The best way to understand these aims and the differences among them as well as to see how these purposes overlap is to watch how a piece of writing changes as the author's purpose does. So let's explore each aim further by examining four versions of the same essay, each written with a different purpose in mind.

Eckert wrote one version of the essay you are about to read as an assignment in a writing class. The essay was then entered into a contest, which it won, and was published in *Campus Life* magazine. Eckert then revised the original essay three times so as to illustrate each of these aims.

CORAL REEF

Elizabeth Eckert

Expressive Purpose

Personal writing which reveals the writer's thoughts, emotions, and experiences is often called *expressive.* In its most extreme form it is found in diaries meant only for the writer's eyes to see. In this form, the author and the audience are the same and so the writing is intensely personal. In fact, if the writer even suspects that someone else might see it, some form of censorship or shorthand is usually used for protection. Personal letters and narratives, on the other hand, are also forms of expressive writing, but they are written for others to read. The writer will deliberately shape a memorable personal experience, for example, so others can appreciate the story and share in the event.

However, even though this writing has an audience outside of ourselves, we still *envision our readers as being friendly and receptive.* When we write a letter to family or share a past experience with a new friend, we don't expect our writing to be criticized. We don't expect our family to say, "Why in the world is this person writing to us?" or the new friend to say, "That's a stupid story. Tell me something more interesting." So while we, as writers, can learn the skills we need to tell our stories effectively, we still expect these personal expressions to be received as they are given—in the spirit of friendliness and sharing.

Eckert's purpose in this piece is to share her first experience snorkeling around a coral reef. In this brief narrative, she describes how she felt and what she saw, shaping her story to make us experience this with her.

Expressive Version

I balanced myself on the side of the crazily swaying boat, checking and readjusting each strap and buckle for the last time. It was like sitting on a wall between two worlds. The ocean lay inscrutably behind me, now and again sending up promises of cool sparkling spray that glimmered on my sun-parched skin, inviting it to a deeper relief that waited below.

I wondered what those shielding waves hid beneath 2
them.

But now I was ready. With one deep breath I hurtled 3
myself backward over the side into the arms of the waiting
ocean. There was a moment of confusion as I tumbled
through the water, but soon the sea gently righted me, the
bubbles cleared before my mask, and I could see for the first
time the alien landscape of the tropical coral reef.

At first, the only thing my stunned mind could register 4
was color. An explosion of gold and pink and white and
green and blue burst on my unsuspecting eyes—hues and
intensities I'd never seen before, incarnated in unearthly
shapes and forms my landworn mind couldn't begin to comprehend. I floated there, limply, as my brain tried to piece
together some coherent image out of the flood of new information pouring into my head.

My bursting lungs finally brought me out of this state of 5
near paralysis, frantically affirming that I was the foreigner.
My brain began to clear as I drew a deep breath of comfortingly familiar oxygen.

A few strong kicks of my fins and I began to glide slow- 6
ly over the surface of the coral reef, hungrily devouring each
new detail.

I watched as a sea snail wended its way slowly over the 7
rough terrain. As I dove down for a closer look, I spotted a
pair of sullen eyes staring at me from a darkened recess.
Suddenly, all three feet of a shy, sharp-toothed moray eel shot
out and away, in search of a quieter, less threatening place to
rest.

There were tiny, stinging noctiluca that illuminated the 8
water at night with an eerie glow. Deadly, blood-red scorpion
fish covered with hundreds of stinging spines, and mysterious
manta rays that glided along the bottom like devil-shaped
clouds. Delicate, striped angel-fish trailing their wing-like fins
behind them, and beak-nosed parrot-fish the color of rainbow sherbet.

I was nearly overwhelmed by the strange unearthly beau- 9
ty all around me. The closer I looked, the more I saw. The
detail seemed infinite: worlds within worlds within worlds.

I emerged from the water, as from a baptism. The very 10
air tasted stronger on my tongue. I looked at the people

around me on the boat, familiar faces, and wondered why I never realized how beautiful they were. And when I finally stepped back on land, I noticed I was looking at the grass in amazement.

I had regained wonder.   11

Affirming Purpose

In *affirming* discourse, the writing moves into the realm of opinion and the writer's purpose is to share a point of view with others. Many affirming pieces begin with personal experience and explain how the writer's opinion grew out of that experience; thus, in writing affirming discourse, you will often find narrative skills helpful and stories being used as examples to support the writer's point of view.

In addition, affirming discourse has a similar audience to that of expressive writing in that the readers are *friendly, receptive readers who agree with the writer* and want to hear someone else express opinions and ideas that affirm what they believe. We all like to hear our own opinions expressed well by someone else and to have our beliefs reinforced by others. Thus, you will generally find believers in church on Sunday, feminists at NOW meetings, and anti-abortionists at Operation Rescue. This writing is, then, an exchange of ideas among friends of similar persuasion, and they often provide us with additional or updated information that we can use in explaining our views to others.

This next version of Eckert's essay is the original, which was published in *Campus Life*, a magazine read primarily by Christian high school and college students. Her audience, then, is made up of readers who already agree with the basic tenets of faith expressed in the piece: her assertion that God exists and that the beauty found in nature is a reflection of God's glory. She has no need to hesitate in this expression of faith or to try to persuade her readers of its validity because she knows they already agree with her and will see this as a simple reminder to appreciate what God has given them.

Notice how much of her own story is used and reshaped to support her opinion in this piece. Also notice the shift from past to present tense now that she is not simply recalling the event but commenting on it.

Affirming Version

I am balancing myself on the side of a crazily swaying 1
boat, checking and readjusting each strap and buckle for the
last time. It's like sitting on a wall between two worlds. The
ocean lies inscrutably behind me, now and again sending up
promises of cool sparkling spray that glimmer on my sun-
parched skin, inviting it to a deeper relief that waits below.

I wonder what those shielding waves hide beneath them. 2

But now I'm ready. With one deep breath I hurtle 3
myself backward over the side into the arms of the waiting
ocean. There is a moment of confusion as I tumble through
the water, but soon the sea gently rights me, the bubbles clear
before my mask, and I can see for the first time the alien
landscape of the tropical coral reef.

At first, the only thing my stunned mind can register is 4
color. An explosion of gold and pink and white and green
and blue bursts on my unsuspecting eyes. Hues and intensities I've never seen before, incarnated in unearthly shapes
and forms my landworn mind can't begin to comprehend. I
float there, limply, as my brain tries to piece together some
coherent image out of the flood of new information pouring
into my head.

It is my bursting lungs that finally bring me out of this 5
state of near paralysis, frantically affirming that I am the foreigner. My brain begins to clear as I draw a deep breath of
comfortingly familiar, everyday oxygen.

A few strong kicks of my fins and I begin to glide slowly 6
over the surface of the reef, hungrily devouring each new
detail.

All reef life lives on or around the huge, twisted, 7
labyrinthian mass of rock-like dead coral. The living coral
grows upon it in delicate, filigreed fans, intricate branches
and flower-like bouquets. Thousands of tiny coral animals
live in each one of these, their feathery arms looking like
snowflakes on the smooth stony surface of their fantastic
houses as they extend them out to feed. Beside them the
long, thin tentacles of the sea anemone gently wave in the
unseen currents, waiting for some unsuspecting creature to
wander too near his hundred poison-tipped arms. Astounded, I watch as a small, bright yellow and blue fish swims

straight into the center unscathed. It is a clownfish, the sea
anemone's only friend, who brings him tasty morsels in
exchange for his many-armed protection.

Nearby a sea snail, bearing its extravagantly ornate, 8
pink-pearly portable fortress upon its back, wends its way
slowly over the rough terrain. As I dive down for a closer
look, I spot a pair of sullen eyes staring at me from a darkened recess. Suddenly, all three feet of a shy, sharp-toothed
moray eel shoot out and away, in search of a quieter, less
threatening place to rest.

The amount and variety of life living on this one hunk 9
of reef is overwhelming. There are crazily shaped Christmas
tree worms and electric-colored sea slugs, making their
homes in the crevices and cracks. There are soft, bulbous
sponges and ghostlike, pulsating jellyfish. There are impossible sea cucumbers, long black sausages that squirt out their
intestines at me if I pick them up. They don't mind; they can
grow new ones.

There are tiny, stinging noctiluca that illuminate the 10
water at night with an eerie glow. Deadly, blood-red scorpion
fish covered with hundreds of stinging spines and mysterious
manta rays that glide along the bottom like devil-shaped
clouds. Long, tube-like trumpet fish and 300-pound Mola-
molas—huge spherical fish that live at the mercy of the currents, because their fins are too tiny to propel their bulk.
Delicate, striped angelfish trailing their wing-like fins behind
them, and beak-nosed parrot-fish the color of rainbow sherbet.

The closer I look, the more I see. The detail seems infi- 11
nite: worlds within worlds within worlds.

The whole of the reef is cloaked in a silence that fills my 12
ears with its grandeur. Everything here moves with fluid grace
and majesty to the primal pulse of the sea.

I am nearly overwhelmed by the strange unearthly 13
beauty all around me. It's like nothing I've ever seen. I feel as
if I am re-learning what childhood was like, when everything
was fresh and new and miraculous.

Miraculous. I am in the midst of a miracle. I see, as I 14
must have sometime long ago, before the first time I was ever
bored, the fingerprints again. His fingerprints. His mind.

I emerge from the water as from a baptism; my eyes 15
reborn. The very air tastes stronger on my tongue. I look at

the other people around me on the boat, familiar faces, and wonder why I never realized how beautiful they were before. When we step back on land, I notice I am looking at the grass in amazement.

I have regained wonder.   16

Creation had been shouting his glory, but I had become 17 too accustomed to the sound to hear it.

Persuasive Purpose

At the point when writers begin to envision an audience that no longer agrees with the ideas being expressed or the position being taken, they must shift into a *persuasive* stance. At this point, *the reader is no longer assumed to be friendly and may in fact be reluctant or even hostile.* Success in persuasive writing means using strategies to keep readers interested and receptive to the message. Unless they keep reading, there is no chance of changing their minds or behaviors.

In Eckert's persuasive piece, she is speaking (directly through the use of "you") to someone who is reluctant to try snorkeling because of the potential dangers involved. To allay these fears, she carefully explains to her readers what will happen to them and what they are likely to see. Through her vivid description, she makes the deep appear inviting instead of threatening. She essentially takes the dive with her readers, and like a gentle, knowledgeable guide, reassures them of the safety of the venture. She also promises that the outcome of this dive will make it all worthwhile.

Persuasive Version

The first time someone suggests you try putting on a 1 mask and snorkel and exploring the wonders of the deep, two disparate images will keep popping into your mind: one being that of the noble-looking deep sea divers you watched on the old Jacques Cousteau shows, who frolicked harmoniously with the exotic sea life, the other that of those scenes from *Jaws* where the Great White shark turns unsuspecting swimmers into after-dinner mints.

The reality, however, will be like nothing you could 2 have ever anticipated. Your trip underwater will be neither a Disneyesque communion with nature nor a terrifying encounter with its more malevolent forces, but a baptism of sorts. Explore those depths once and you will never see the world in quite the same way again.

You will hurl yourself backward over the side of the boat   3 into the arms of the waiting ocean. There will be a moment of confusion as you tumble through the water, but soon the sea will gently right you, the bubbles will clear before your mask, and you will see for the first time the alien landscape of the tropical coral reef.

At first, the only thing your stunned mind will be able   4 to register is color. An explosion of gold and pink and white and green and blue will burst on your unsuspecting eyes. Hues and intensities you've never seen before, incarnated in unearthly shapes and forms your landworn mind can't begin to comprehend.

Most likely, you will have to float there limply a   5 moment, as your brain tries to piece together some coherent image out of the flood of new information pouring into your head. Then, with a few strong kicks of your fins, you will begin to glide slowly over the surface of the reef. It will be a sensation much akin to that of flying—very silent, graceful flying. The vast array of detail to absorb will astound you.

All reef life lives on or around the huge, twisted,   6 labyrinthian mass of rock-like dead coral. The living coral grows upon it in delicate, filigreed fans, intricate branches and flower-like bouquets. Thousands of tiny coral animals live in each one of these, their feathery arms looking like snowflakes on the smooth stony surface of their fantastic houses as they extend them out to feed. Beside them the long, thin tentacles of the sea anemone will wave gently in the unseen currents, waiting for some unsuspecting creature to wander too near to their hundred poison-tipped arms. You may watch, astounded, though, as a small, bright yellow and blue fish swims straight into the center of the animals unscathed. It is a clownfish, the sea anemone's only friend, who brings tasty morsels in exchange for their many-armed protection.

The amount and variety of life living on this one hunk   7 of reef will be overwhelming. You will see crazily shaped Christmas tree worms and electric-colored sea slugs, making their homes in the crevices and cracks. There will be soft, bulbous sponges and ghostlike, pulsating jelly fish. You might even see a sea cucumber, a long black sausage-looking animal that will squirt out its intestines at you if you pick it up, and escape, none the worse for the wear. They can grow a new digestive system like a starfish grows new arms.

The closer you look, the more you will see. The detail 8 will seem infinite: worlds within worlds within worlds.

The whole of the reef will be cloaked in a silence that 9 will fill your ears with its grandeur. Everything there will move with fluid grace and majesty to the primal pulse of the sea. The strange, unearthly beauty will be overwhelming. It will be like nothing you've ever seen. And, for a moment, you may feel as if you are remembering what childhood was like, when everything was fresh and new and miraculous. You will begin to see as you did long ago, before you learned to be bored.

If you are like me, you will emerge from the water as 10 from a baptism; your eyes reborn. The very air will taste stronger on your tongue. You will look at other people, familiar faces, and see that they are beautiful. And when you step back on land, you might just look at the grass in amazement.

So, do not expect to go underwater and not be 11 changed.

If you take a deep breath and dive under, you will 12 regain that which you thought you had lost forever.

You will regain wonder.   13

Informative Purpose

Finally, when the message itself becomes the writer's focus and less attention is given to the writer's personal experiences or opinions, the purpose becomes *informative—* focused on the information being provided. In its extreme form, it is *the least personal kind of writing with no intrusion by the writer and no explicit acknowledgment of the audience* (although all writing is meant to be read by someone and so follows conventions that allow the writer to be understood). Encyclopedias are a good example of this kind of distant prose focused on communicating information. However, most informative writing involves someone in authority sharing information with someone who needs it. It may therefore be addressed to a very specific audience and the expert role of the writer may be acknowledged.

In Eckert's informative essay, which she has composed as a script that would accompany a filmstrip, her role is that of distant authority, describing exactly what people viewing the filmstrip are seeing. She relates some of the information to her audience, but she has removed herself and her own personal experience and opinions from the writing. As a teacher might do during a slide lecture in a classroom, she focuses on the information about the reefs that her audience should know. Paragraph breaks indicate where the slide would change.

Informative Version

The coral reefs that exist in the warm waters of the trop- 1 ics are some of the most remarkable, complex, and beautiful ecosystems in the world.

They stand like oases or islands of life in oceans that are 2 otherwise like deserts, relatively devoid of living things.

The reason for this is that tropical waters contain very 3 little oxygen, a substance that is necessary for practically all organisms to sustain life. This is because in the warmer climates where these oceans exist, their waters stay at an almost constant temperature.

In colder climates, where the days are much warmer 4 than the nights, the sun will warm the top layer of the ocean. At night, this layer will cool until it is actually colder than the layer beneath it. Since warm water rises and cold water sinks, the top layer will move downward and the next layer move upward, creating a mixing action which draws more oxygen into the ocean.

Thus, colder oceans have enough oxygen to support 5 massive amounts of life. Giant schools of fish and great forests of plant life can live there comfortably, because there are enough resources for all.

In tropical climates the nights are not cold enough to 6 cause the layers of water to mix. Less oxygen is drawn in, which limits the amount of life that can be supported. If you have ever gone swimming in a tropical ocean, you will have noticed how white and sandy most of the seafloor is. This is because almost nothing lives there. But nature has designed a solution to this problem in the form of the coral reef.

In this aerial view of a tropical ocean, most of what you   7
see are vast stretches of clear blue water that go straight down
to white sandy bottoms. The dark forms you see, which look
a bit like islands underwater, are nature's solution to the limited oxygen supply. They are the coral reefs.

Coral is not a kind of rock, as some people assume   8
when they first see it. It is a tiny living animal, which lives in
a house it makes for itself out of calcium carbonate it extracts
from the sea. Here you can see the tentacles of one of these
animals stretching out to feed. At the center of these tentacles is a mouth into which the coral draws the food it catches. Usually, the coral eats tiny organisms, which it can sting
and kill, or pieces of dead animals.

When predators approach, the coral animal can draw   9
itself into its house, where it is relatively safe.

Coral comes in a great variety of shapes and colors. A   10
few of them are the staghorn coral . . .

the spiky coral . . .   11
and the brain coral.   12

These animals live in vast colonies. Over thousands of   13
years as the old coral die and form a hard stony foundation,
and new ones build on top of them, giant reefs are formed.
Waves break upon these reefs and churn the water, bringing
much needed oxygen into the water. Because of this, and
because of the shelter the reef provides, many other kinds of
animals and plants make their homes there and form a complex and interdependent society.

Thus the coral reefs become colonies where many   14
species exist in cooperation using and recycling the limited
resources at hand.

In these four versions, we can see how Eckert's purposes
change from sharing her personal experience with the coral reef
to instructing others in some basic information about the reef
itself. Between these, she shares a point of view about the reef and
persuades others to try the snorkeling experience. In other words,
based on her knowledge of reefs, Eckert can write a variety of
papers for many different readers. In addition to those illustrated
here, she could write a letter to a friend about her trip, an editorial about coral reef damage, instructions for first-time snorkelers,
a research paper on the moray eel, or an annotated bibliography

of essential reading for snorkelers. Which format and approach she picks depends on what her purpose is and who her readers are.

In addition, these essays show how, while four different purposes can be identified, the skills used in writing these papers overlap. There is a large expressive element in Eckert's affirming essay because she uses her personal experience to support her opinion. She also draws on this positive experience with and opinion about snorkeling to convince others to try it. And her observation skills, knowledge, and experience all help her to provide accurate information. In others words, while you are focusing on the writing skills of each aim, you will be increasing your facility with all of them.

GETTING READY TO WRITE

Sometimes you will be uncertain about what your purpose is before you begin writing. You may have a topic you want to pursue but you aren't sure what approach you want to take. In this case, your purpose will take shape as the paper does.

But often *the purpose is determined by the task at hand.* Whether it's an advertising executive preparing a major presentation for a client, a social worker filling out a case study report for the agency, a minister writing the required Sunday sermon, or a student writing a paper for class, the purpose is often dictated to the writer by the nature of the assignment. And the writing will not be successful unless the writer understands the requirements of the task at hand.

To illustrate how trying to complete a required task works in shaping a piece of writing for a reader, we will follow the process of a student, Chad Adams, as he responds to the first assignment in his writing class.

TWO

Chad Adams

Adams' Assignment

When Adams wrote his essay "Two" he was responding to the following assignment:

We are, each of us, multifaceted. We have certain qualities, characteristics, interests, hobbies, loves, hates, commitments. But these did not develop in a vacuum. All along the way events and people have been influencing us, pushing us, encouraging us, or even steering us clear of certain experiences. Sometimes we accept the influence as offered. Other times we rebel and are influenced by trying hard not to be.

To begin this assignment think of aspects of yourself that are important to you: your honesty, your diligence, your love of nature and our delicate environment, your interest in football, basketball, soccer, your choice of a major, your hopes for a future job, your idea of true friendship, your faith in something, your fascination with dogs or cats or tropical fish, your commitment to family or independence or success.

Now select one of these that has a good story behind it that helps to explain where this part of yourself came from. You might, for example, tell us about the first time you discovered an interest in your major or the day you bought your first tank of fish. You may tell about meeting someone you admired and wanted to be like. Or maybe you can recall a time when your honesty or some other characteristic was tested and you found out how much a part of you it was.

Your assignment is to recreate that event for us. You are not just to tell us about what happened, but actually to put us there experiencing it with you. Where were you? Who was there? What happened? How did you react?

Also, the influence on you should be clear through the telling of the story. No canned conclusions that say, "the significance of this event for me was . . . ." Just tell the story vividly and let that experience reveal the way it affected you.

Adams has been instructed to tell a personal story so his purpose will be expressive—it will focus on the writer and his life. But which story in his life should he choose to write about?

The assignment offers some guidance in helping him select one. First, he must think about his qualities, characteristics, interests, hobbies, loves, hates, commitments. Second, he must match these up with the events in his life and eliminate those that do not have a story behind them because the assignment is asking for a narrative not an explanation. Third, he must make sure that the story is a good one that will illustrate the influence without his having to explain it explicitly. Adams tackles these steps one at a time.

Adams' Prewriting

Tapping into your *prior knowledge* is just as important before you write as it is before reading. In this prewriting stage you are trying to get something down on paper. You may be making a list of possible topics, jotting down all the ideas you have on the subject, using a list of questions to stimulate your thinking or just freewriting on the assignment to see what comes out. Whatever method you use, you are trying to gather together all the information that applies to the task.

Sometimes, this prior knowledge comes from within, as when you write a personal essay based on your experience. Prewriting might then consist of *brainstorming* a list of all the interesting experiences you can remember and might want to write about, or it might mean taking one experience and jotting down everything you remember about it. Or you may make a visual representation as we discussed when reading "To Make Papa Proud" in Chapter One. You might put your main idea in the center of the page and visually organize your thoughts and events around it. When used as a prewriting technique, this is called *clustering*. All of your experiences or memories will not become part of the paper. At this stage, you are just discovering your options.

Other times, the prior knowledge will not be what you already know but what you need to know before you can write. You may need to conduct *original research*, gathering data through questionnaires, surveys, or interviews. Or you may need to do some *library research*. In this case, your prewriting may consist of analyzing and synthesizing—weeding out and pulling together—the material you have accumulated. In any case, using your prior or gathered knowledge is a preparatory step.

Because Adams is drawing from personal experience, his approach was to brainstorm a list of his characteristics and interests:

> Adjectives about me: tall, blonde, changing, friendly, sometimes outspoken
>
> Likes: chocolate, honesty, computers, programming, quiet, contemplation, family, hoops
>
> Dislikes: loud people, beets
>
> Values: honest, friendly
>
> Commitments: Shirley, school, family
>
> Hobbies/interests: computers, cards, fantasy, sci-fi

After creating this list of possible topics, Adams moved on to the next requirement—selecting those that he could tell a good story about. He listed four: computers, Shirley (his fiancée), family, and hoops. And after looking over this list, he quickly settled on "hoops." But basketball had been a major part of his life in high school, so he started to brainstorm about good basketball stories and immediately came up with a list of eight different options. From this list he settled on one entry, "last game sophomore year—Richmond" and started to jot down a fourth list of ideas for the paper. Finally, after these four brainstorming sessions, Adams was ready to write.

WRITING A DRAFT

Although Adams had a host of good basketball stories he could write about, he did not want to write a typical basketball story about how he had scored the winning basket just as the final whistle blew. Effective and true as he knew these stories could be, he wanted something that would show how very much a part of his life the sport was. For this reason, he decided to focus on the game he *didn't* get to play.

Adams' First Draft

Of course you know that everything that a high school 1
sophomore believes has to be true. As a sophomore in a small
school in northern New Hampshire, not really looking to the
future at the time, my attitude toward classes was, "Well, at
least they are something to tide me over until basketball practice." With this in mind I muddled through my classes,
excelling in the ones I really liked, and running the edge on
the ones I didn't. The most anxious time for a student cruis-
ing under this philosophy is REPORT CARD time. For me
this was often a time of long lectures by my step-father, a
quarter of which I actually might listen to. This would then
be followed by an admonition to do better, to study harder,
and to apply myself.

"After all, college is in only three years and if you want 2
to get into one you have to start applying yourself now." Well,
naturally, three years to a sixteen year old is nearly a quarter
of his/her life . . . classes could wait. I just never really found
a reason to try. There was no real impetus for me to really put
my nose to the proverbial grindstone.

One of the greatest things about playing basketball is 3
away games. You ride on a bus for a half an hour to an hour
with fifteen of your closest friends, not to mention all of the
cheerleaders and the women's team, and get to be as rowdy
as you want. The especially good games were the ones played
at the far distant schools. We played two games in Canada,
the best of which was against Richmond. For this game we got
to leave school at noon, and had time to go buy all of our
assorted food for the trip before the bus left at 1:00.

Well, this fine January day dawned bright and clear. The 4
roads were good, and the Richmond game was scheduled for
that afternoon. The only black mark against it was the fact
that we had to pick up our report cards before we left for the
bus. This meant that tomorrow would be lecture day.

The bell rang at noon. Forty students rushed to their 5
lockers. Forty students rushed to the office to get their report
cards. Forty students shoved them into pockets to get them
out of the way. Then comes the shopping, the walk to the
gym and finally . . . the moment of truth. I pulled the by now
wrinkled piece of yellow paper out of my pocket and looked.

"History: C– . . . well, I can live with that. Geometry: B+   6
. . . excellent! Biology: A . . . another excellent! French: F . . .
uh oh, that's not good at all. Well, as long as there isn't ano
. . . Oh, my God! English: F." Two F's. Two F's means, according to the people who make the rules, ineligibility for high
school sports. Have you ever had the feeling that your world
has just been turned upside-down? My head spun. It couldn't
be. I looked again, praying that I had seen wrong. It still said,
in two glowing red letters, "Your season is done, stupid."

I was completely at a loss. Walking the line was one   7
thing, but this DEFINITELY didn't qualify. What do I do?
What do I do?! I'll go talk to Coach! Maybe there is some way
around it. I went and stood in the doorway to his office. He
asked me what was up and I held up two fingers. I felt really
stupid, but I couldn't make myself say it.

"Two?" he said. "What about two?" I looked at him real-   8
ly ashamed.

"I got two F's." I could see the thoughts as they rolled   9
through his head. Then a look of resignation settled on his
face. I felt my heart crash through the floor.

"You know what that means, don't you?" I nodded.   10
"Well, go to your teachers tomorrow and make sure there
wasn't any mistake, and other than that I don't know what to
say. You can come with us today, but I can't let you play, we
could be disqualified." I nodded and turned to leave. It's too
bad guys aren't supposed to cry, this seemed like a good time.

"Oh, and Chad?" I turned and looked back. "I assume   11
this won't happen again."

"Not in a million years." I knew in my heart that those   12
were five words I would never betray.

REVISING FOR READERS

Adams' process in revising his essay was one of distilling. Adams
asked over and over again, "What do my readers need?" He finally decided that they needed a lot less than he originally thought
and that the extra information he was providing was more like
excess baggage than essential items for this trip down memory
lane.

After writing the first draft, Adams identified his problem: "The beginning seems too long to me. I realized that I needed to set the background and tone for the actual plot, but it almost seemed excessive to me and I can't tell what to cut." Adams wants to tell too much because he doesn't know what his readers need to understand the situation.

With the help of a conference with his teacher, Adams came to see the problem with the paper as one of *focusing*. Adams needed to identify his main point in terms of what he wanted readers to understand. This was easy for him: He wanted us to feel how devastated he was when he realized he couldn't play.

But paragraphs 1 and 2 focus on Adams' not being a very good student and being warned by his step-father that this would cause problems for college. Neither Adams' step-father nor ruined college plans have anything to do with the story that follows or with his main point. He quickly realized the first two paragraphs could be cut. In fact, he realized that paragraph 3 actually sounded like another introduction.

But the next three paragraphs didn't please Adams either. They did not capture the excitement he was feeling and seemed to contain too much general information about away games and the weather. He was afraid readers would get bored instead of feeling his anticipation.

But in addition to seeing what needed to be changed, Adams also recognized that the best part of the piece was "the suspense part where I rush out of the school, report card in pocket (crumpled) and then finally get to look at it." This part he knew he wanted to keep.

So, Adams tried to re-see his draft and select what he felt was essential for the reader.

Adams' Final Draft

Richmond. One of the most important games of the 1 regular season, one of the games we waited all season for and it was today! For this game we got to get out of school early . . . what could be better? Well, I guess they could have waited until tomorrow to give us our report cards.

The bell rang at noon. Forty students rushed to their 2 lockers to dump their books. No one studied on an away trip; it just wasn't done. Forty students rushed to the office to get their report cards. Forty students shoved them into pockets to get them out of the way. Then came the shopping—junk food for the trip there, grinder for the trip home, and lots of soda. Then the walk to the gym and finally . . . the moment of truth. I pulled the wrinkled piece of yellow paper out of my pocket and looked.

"History: C– . . . well, I can live with that. Geometry: B+   3 . . . excellent! Biology: A . . . another excellent! French: F . . . uh oh, that's not good at all. Well, as long as there isn't ano . . . Oh, my God! English: F. Two F's."

Two F's means, according to the people who make the   4 rules, ineligibility for high school sports. My head spun. It couldn't be. I looked again, praying that I had seen wrong. It still said, in two glowing red letters, "Your season is over, stupid."

I was completely at a loss. My attitude toward classes   5 had always been "they keep me busy until practice." As a result I tended to be a borderline student. What did it matter? College was still three years away. There was just no impetus to put my nose to the proverbial grindstone.

But walking the line was one thing. This was different.   6 What do I do? What do I do?! I'll go talk to Coach! Maybe there is some way around it. I went and stood in the doorway to his office. He asked me what was up and I held up two fingers. I felt really stupid, but I couldn't make myself say it.

"Two?" he said. "What about two?" I looked at him, my   7 expression filled with shame.

"I got two F's." I could see the thoughts as they rolled   8 through his head. Then a look of resignation settled on his face. I felt my heart crash through the floor.

"You know what that means, don't you?" I nodded.   9 "Well, go to your teachers tomorrow and make sure there wasn't any mistake. Other than that I don't know what to say. You can come with us today, but I can't let you play because you could disqualify the whole team." I nodded and turned to leave. It's too bad guys aren't supposed to cry because this seemed like a good time.

"Oh, and Chad?" I turned and looked back. "I assume   10 this won't happen again."

"Not in a million years."   11

CHECKING YOUR READERS' UNDERSTANDING

Adams has made some serious improvements in this draft in terms of focusing and eliminating unnecessary background. From the first paragraphs he is trying to create the excitement of the Richmond game and forty students trying to prepare for the trip. As he said in his comments on the paper: "I think the opening paragraph sets the excitement quickly. Big Game Today! This should make people want to go on to find out what happens in the Big Game." He has selected the most important information from the opening of the previous draft—how he viewed classes as something to tide him over until practice—and has integrated that into his thoughts after he reads the report card. He has also collapsed the general information about away games in paragraphs 3 and 4 of the first draft into the opening paragraph on the importance of Richmond. Thus, it only takes us two paragraphs to get to the heart of the story.

He has kept this heart, the best part of the first draft, intact except for eliminating his last sentence because he felt it was repetitious and less powerful than his actual words to the coach.

What Adams realized was that he was trying to tell us everything and that the extra information was actually detracting from rather than enhancing his story. By using the first two paragraphs to build up tension, he could highlight his disappointment and we would understand what a loss this was for him.

In addition to these large changes, Adams has reread the piece and edited it for clarity. For example, in paragraph 2 of his final draft, he has kept the repetition of "forty" but has now incorporated into this paragraph phrases that provide the background about away games (studying and food for the road) that he had taken out.

While this is a small change, such *editing is absolutely essential to good writing*. If a piece is well written each change, even just a word substitution, can affect the entire piece. Adams cannot simply remove paragraphs of background without carefully checking each missing sentence to see what information he is no longer providing and to design a way to include anything that is still necessary.

At this stage, Adams is also reading to make corrections and choices, such as where to paragraph. He decides, for example, to make what was paragraph 6 in the first draft into paragraphs 3 and 4 in the final in order to emphasize the moment of reading the grades. He hopes this emphasis will let the impact that the grades had on him produce a similar impact on his readers.

THE RECURSIVE NATURE OF WRITING

While Adams actually did write and then revise, the process was not as linear as it may seem. While constructing the first draft, he was already mulling over different approaches. As his first draft shows, he really did start the paper twice, creating two separate introductions.

In other words, writing, too, is recursive. Prewriting strategies may come in handy any time in the composing process when we get stuck and need to regroup. Editing may start with the first word we write down if we cross it out for a better one. We may write our introduction last—after we have found out what we really wanted to say. Like reading, writing is a dynamic process, and we need to adjust it to suit our individual needs.

A SUMMARY OF WRITING STRATEGIES

1. Determine your *purpose* for writing. Reading the assignment carefully or analyzing the writing task at hand will help you.
2. Make use of helpful *prewriting* techniques such as brainstorming, outlining, clustering, or research.
3. Do a first *draft* to get your ideas down and to explore possible approaches to the task.
4. *Revise* with your readers' needs in mind. What do they need to know and what effect do you want this writing to have on them?
5. *Reread and edit* to be certain that your readers will understand the piece and be able to follow it as you want them to.

And remember that any of these strategies may prove helpful at any time in your writing process.

Part Two

EXPRESSIVE DISCOURSE

All writing is communication. We have ideas we want to share and we need to express them in such a way that they will be understood by others. Sometimes what we really want to share is ourselves—some event we have experienced that has helped to shape us, some person we have known who has influenced us, some observation we have made that is significant to us. This type of personal writing is called *expressive discourse.*

In expressive writing, writers recreate in words some special part of their lives and that recreation is so vivid that we can see and feel what the writers saw and felt. We are invited into the writer's life to witness part of what has shaped that person's identity.

These expressions of personal experience come in a variety of forms. They range from the most intimate recordings of feelings found in diaries and personal letters to very polished personal essays. In more intimate recordings, the relationship between the writer and the reader seems very close while in more reflective essays, the writer seems to be more distant. Sometimes we, as readers, are being invited to relive an experience and other times to step back and reflect on the meaning of some event. In the examples you will read in the following three chapters, you will see a wide range in this reader/writer relationship, from intimate to almost philosophic. But the heart of all of these expressive pieces is the same—the personal experience and voice of the writer.

Chapter Three

READING EXPRESSIVE DISCOURSE: THE READER/WRITER RELATIONSHIP

As readers, we approach expressive texts expecting to receive a personal message from the writer. If the writing is successful, we are able to relate to what the writer has gone through, to feel a common bond of human emotion, even if we have never actually gone through this experience ourselves. In other words, this reading is closely identified with the idea of reading for pleasure we discussed in Chapter One because we are reading to hear about an interesting part of someone's life.

We approach this kind of reading, then, as willing listeners, ready to learn something about the author, about life, or about ourselves. We are essentially being entertained by good stories and interesting anecdotes. We are drawn to the text by its emotional intensity, cleverness, or fascinating details that make us really feel the experience. As we read, we look for things that we can relate to and for clues that help us better understand the writer. We try to appreciate the writer, the experience itself, and how the story is told to us.

In expressive discourse, there is a special relationship between the writer and the reader because of the use of the first-person pronoun, the "I," which is a characteristic feature of expressive writing. In addition, the "I" is understood to be the author, not a fictitious narrator as in literature. This means that we, as readers, are being spoken to directly by the writer, who is sharing a true story with us.

This closeness creates a special bond between writer and reader that we would never feel while reading an encyclopedia or even a novel where we know that none of the events really happened and none of the characters really existed. It is a special invitation to enter into someone's life, to walk with them awhile, and to leave them feeling a little less like a stranger.

There are many types of expressive writing, but often this type of writing describes a significant and influential event or person the writer cannot forget. Sometimes this event is recreated so vividly that we are invited to experience it with the writer as it is recreated in words, just as sometimes the significant person is described so vividly we feel we have just met that individual. Other times, we are invited to step back a little and to reflect on the meaning of the writer's experiences. As readers, we are asked to become a little more distant and invited not just to experience but also to contemplate the significance of the experience in our own lives.

The following three essays will illustrate examples of the reader/writer relationship in expressive writing. The first is an anecdote, the second an autobiographical narrative, and the third a reflective essay.

ANECDOTE

LAUNDRY

Robert Fulghum

In Robert Fulghum's humorous book *All I Really Need to Know I Learned in Kindergarten*, he often stops to talk to his readers directly. He uses not only "I" in these passages, but also "you," and it is clear that he means us, the readers.

In this kind of expressive writing, the bond between reader and writer is so close the writing is almost a conversation. We are addressed directly, our thoughts and reactions are anticipated and commented on; our attention is drawn to events that the writer does not want us to miss or wants us to interpret in a particular way.

In other words, our reading is guided, almost as if the writer took us by the hand and led us through the experience. And we respond not only to what happened but also to the writer's interpretation of the events and of our anticipated reactions. It is like traveling with a chatty cousin who not only explains everything we see and do, but tells us how we should react to each sight and experience. It might be annoying, if the writer were not so sincere and, in this case, endearing.

The voice used in this kind of writing is crucial for its success. The writer must create an atmosphere in which we feel that we are being spoken to directly. Fulghum achieves this by being casual in his style. We almost feel as if he quite literally stops talking, looks right at us, and says, "You can't always explain everything you do to everybody, you know."

This intimate kind of writing also often occurs in situations where the writer and the reader are the same. When we keep a diary or personal journal, for example, we essentially are chatting with ourselves about events and feelings and often commenting on them—chiding ourselves for being so foolish about something or congratulating ourselves for getting something important done. When we return to the diary as a reader, we do so to discover ourselves as we were at the time of the writing and to review the events of our lives, in the same way that we read Fulghum to discover who he is and what he has experienced.

Anecdotes often appear as *illustrations* or *examples* in longer pieces of writing. When a difficult idea needs to be explained or a situation needs an illustration, anecdotes often provide those specifics that can help readers comprehend an abstract situation more fully. In essays in later chapters you will often find anecdotes occurring after the words "for example." They can also serve as very effective introductions that get readers immediately involved in an issue by personalizing it through a brief story or scenario.

Prereading Journal

We all have things that we are in charge of in our homes or at work or among our friends that we take pride in because we know we do them well. Perhaps you're the one who always sets up the new electrical gadget in the house or who works with difficult customers or who plans how you and your friends will spend the weekend. Describe an incident when you were called upon to carry out these duties and found it more challenging than usual.

Background

Although Fulghum has worked as a salesman, a minister, and a cowboy, he describes himself as a philosopher about "ordinary things." This selection from Fulghum's book, subtitled "Uncommon Thoughts on Common Things," reminds us of the basic tenets of life: Share everything. Play fair. Don't hit people. Put things back where you found them. Flush. Warm cookies and cold milk are good for you. In this essay he deals with another of life's little kindergarten maxims: Clean up your own mess.

During Reading

While you read, note any place in the text where you feel Fulghum is speaking directly to you as a reader.

Reading Selection

I am in charge of the laundry at our house. I like my 1
work. It gives me a sense of accomplishment. And a feeling of
involvement with the rest of the family, in a way. And time
alone in the back room, without the rest of the family, which
is also nice, sometimes.

I like sorting the clothes—lights, darks, in-betweens. I 2
like setting the dials—hot, cold, rinse, time, heat. These are
choices I can understand and make with decisive skill. I still
haven't figured out the new stereo, but washers and dryers I
can handle. The bell dings—you pull out the warm, fluffy
clothes, take them to the dining-room table, sort and fold
them into neat piles. I especially like it when there's lots of
static electricity, and you can hang socks all over your body
and they will stick there. (*My wife caught me doing this once and
gave me* THAT LOOK. *You can't always explain everything you do to
everybody, you know.*)

When I'm finished, I have a sense of accomplishment. 3
A sense of competence. I am good at doing the laundry. At
least that. And it's a religious experience, you know. Water,
earth, fire—polarities of wet and dry, hot and cold, dirty and
clean. The great cycles—round and round—beginning and
end—Alpha and Omega, amen. I am in touch with the GREAT
SOMETHING-OR-OTHER. For a moment, at least, life is tidy and
has meaning. But then, again . . .

The washing machine died last week. Guess I over- 4
loaded it with towels. And the load got all lumped up on one
side during the spin cycle. So it did this incredible herky-
jerky, lurching dance across the floor and blew itself up. I
thought it was coming for me. One minute it was a living
thing in the throes of a seizure, and the next minute a cold
white box full of partially digested towels with froth around
its mouth, because I guess I must have fed it too much soap,
too. Five minutes later the dryer expired. Like a couple of
elderly folks in a nursing home who follow one another
quickly in death, so closely are they entwined.

It was Saturday afternoon, and all the towels in the 5
house were wet, and all my shorts and socks were wet, and
now what? Knowing full well that if you want one of those
repair guys you have to stay home for thirty-six hours straight

and have your banker standing by with a certified check or else they won't set foot on your property, and I haven't got time for that. So it's the laundromat over at the mall.

Now I haven't spent a Saturday night in the laundromat 6 since I was in college. What you miss by not going to laundromats anymore are things like seeing other people's clothes and overhearing conversations you'd never hear anywhere else. I watched an old lady sort out a lot of sexy black underwear and wondered if it was hers or not. And heard a college kid explain to a friend how to get puke off a suede jacket.

Sitting there waiting, I contemplated the detergent 7 box. I use Cheer. I like the idea of a happy wash. Sitting there late at night, leaning against the dryer for warmth, eating a little cheese and crackers and drinking a little white wine out of the thermos (*I came prepared*), I got to brooding about the meaning of life and started reading the stuff on the Cheer box. Amazing. It contains ingredients to lift dirt from clothes (anionic surfactants) and soften water (complex sodium phosphates). Also, agents to protect washer parts (sodium silicate) and improve processing (sodium sulfate), small quantities of stuff to reduce wrinkling and prevent fabric yellowing, plus whiteners, colorant, and perfume. No kidding. All this for less than a nickel an ounce. It's biodegradable and works best in cold water—ecologically sound. A miracle in a box.

Sitting there watching the laundry go around in the 8 dryer, I thought about the round world and hygiene. We've made a lot of progress, you know. We used to think that disease was an act of God. Then we figured out it was a product of human ignorance, so we've been cleaning up our act—literally—ever since. We've been getting the excrement off our hands and clothes and bodies and food and houses.

If only the scientific experts could come up with some- 9 thing to get it out of our minds. One cup of fixit frizzle that will lift the dirt from our lives, soften our hardness, protect our inner parts, improve our processing, reduce our yellowing and wrinkling, improve our natural color, and make us sweet and good.

Don't try Cheer, by the way. I tasted it. It's awful. (*But my* 10 *tongue is clean, now.*)

Checking Your Understanding

1. Explain why Fulghum enjoys this tedious chore of doing laundry.

2. Kindergarten is a place where learning and play are perfectly meshed. What does Fulghum learn while doing laundry and how does he make this chore fun?

Examining Rhetorical Strategies

1. Describe the reader/writer relationship in this piece. How did being spoken to directly make you respond to Fulghum and his philosophic ramblings about Cheer?

2. Select the paragraph you found the most entertaining. What writing techniques did Fulghum use to hold your attention?

3. At one point, Fulghum waxes philosophical about laundry as a "religious experience." How does his style at this point reflect the wanderings of his mind on this subject?

AUTOBIOGRAPHICAL NARRATIVE

CONQUERING THE STREETS OF MEMPHIS
Richard Wright

One of the most common forms of expressive writing is the autobiographical narrative in which we are told a story. The level of intimacy established in a narrative varies depending on the style of the author and the kind of story that is being told, but our presence as readers is definitely acknowledged in several ways.

First, the writer is careful to give us all the *background information* that we need to understand the story and enough of the *setting* so that we can picture the scene in which the action takes place. On the other hand, these details are selective—we are given only the information we need for this particular incident to make sense.

Second, and closely connected to background, is *plot*. We are listening to a good story and most of these narratives could begin with the familiar, "Once upon a time." Our relationship to the writer is that of attentive listener—we gather round to hear a good tale of joy or woe. But the writer must choose a focus for the tale. While it is only a little piece of the writer's life, it must still feel as if it were a self-contained story with a beginning and an end. The author must decide where to start, what to tell, and what to leave out so that we find the plot interesting and intriguing.

Third, the *significance* of the story for the author is usually clearly indicated in some way. Our attention is drawn to the meaning of the experience for the writer so that we gain some insight into the "I" telling the story. Often this significance is not stated explicitly; we are left to figure out the meaning on our own. But when a story is told well it is not difficult to see why the author remembered it and wanted to share it.

Finally, when a writer wishes to establish a closer relationship to the reader, greater *involvement* can be encouraged by making us feel as if we are "right there" as the writer suffers or laughs or falls or climbs or blushes or blusters. Through vivid description and dialogue we are made to feel as if we have gone through this experience with the writer. In this way, we are not just drawn in by a good plot but also by the way this plot unfolds.

In other words, whether we are being addressed directly or not, we are still being led through the reading because the author is recreating the story from a particular point of view. The author determines how much of the story to tell and when and how to reveal details. The writer may also manipulate our emotional response by making us feel the experience as it happens or by creating suspense and using vivid details. Our reactions and needs, then, are being anticipated, so that we experience this event in just the way the writer wants us to.

Prereading Journal

In this reading, Wright has to conquer his fear of the gangs he faces on the streets of Memphis. Consider a time when you were afraid or nervous about something that was about to happen. How did you conquer your fear? Did you force yourself to go through it or were you forced by someone else? How did you feel once the dreaded experience was over?

Background

Richard Wright is an African-American writer perhaps best known for his novel *Native Son*. The following selection is from his autobiography *Black Boy*. Wright recalls his childhood growing up in a tenement in Memphis and how he had to assume adult responsibilities around the house when the family was abandoned by his father.

During Reading

As you read this story, notice the elements of a narrative that were just discussed:

> What background is provided and what is the setting (context, time, place)?
> What happens (plot)?
> What is the significance of this event for Wright?
> How does Wright get us involved in the story?

Reading Selection

Hunger stole upon me so slowly that at first I was not   1
aware of what hunger really meant. Hunger had always been
more or less at my elbow when I played, but now I began to
wake up at night to find hunger standing at my bedside, staring at me gauntly. The hunger I had known before this had
been no grim, hostile stranger; it had been a normal hunger
that had made me beg constantly for bread, and when I ate a
crust or two I was satisfied. But this new hunger baffled me,
scared me, made me angry and insistent. Whenever I begged
for food now my mother would pour me a cup of tea which
would still the clamor in my stomach for a moment or two;
but a little later I would feel hunger nudging my ribs, twisting
my empty guts until they ached. I would grow dizzy and my
vision would dim. I became less active in my play, and for the
first time in my life I had to pause and think of what was happening to me.

"Mama, I'm hungry," I complained one afternoon.   2

"Jump up and catch a kungry," she said, trying to make   3
me laugh and forget.

"What's a *kungry?*"   4

"It's what little boys eat when they get hungry," she said. 5

"What does it taste like?"   6

"I don't know."   7

"Then why do you tell me to catch one?"   8

"Because you said that you were hungry," she said,   9
smiling.

I sensed that she was teasing me and it made me angry. 10

"But I'm hungry. I want to eat."   11

"You'll have to wait."   12

"But I want to eat now."   13

"But there's nothing to eat," she told me.   14

"Why?"   15

"Just because there's none," she explained.   16

"But I want to eat," I said, beginning to cry.   17

"You'll just have to wait," she said again.   18

"But why?"   19

"For God to send some food."   20

"When is He going to send it?"   21

"I don't know."   22

"But I'm hungry!" 23

She was ironing and she paused and looked at me with 24
tears in her eyes.

"Where's your father?" she asked me. 25

I stared in bewilderment. Yes, it was true that my father 26
had not come home to sleep for many days now and I could
make as much noise as I wanted. Though I had not known
why he was absent, I had been glad that he was not there to
shout his restrictions at me. But it had never occurred to me
that his absence would mean that there would be no food.

"I don't know," I said. 27

"Who brings food into the house?" my mother asked 28
me.

"Papa," I said. "He always brought food." 29

"Well, your father isn't here now," she said. 30

"Where is he?" 31

"I don't know," she said. 32

"But I'm hungry," I whimpered, stomping my feet. 33

"You'll have to wait until I get a job and buy food," she 34
said.

As the days slid past the image of my father became 35
associated with my pangs of hunger, and whenever I felt
hunger I thought of him with a deep biological bitterness.

My mother finally went to work as a cook and left me 36
and my brother alone in the flat each day with a loaf of bread
and a pot of tea. When she returned at evening she would be
tired and dispirited and would cry a lot. Sometimes, when
she was in despair, she would call us to her and talk to us for
hours, telling us that we now had no father, that our lives
would be different from those of other children, that we
must learn as soon as possible to take care of ourselves, to
dress ourselves, to prepare our own food; that we must take
upon ourselves the responsibility of the flat while she worked.
Half frightened, we would promise solemnly. We did not
understand what had happened between our father and our
mother and the most that these long talks did to us was to
make us feel a vague dread. Whenever we asked why father
had left, she would tell us that we were too young to know.

One evening my mother told me that thereafter I would 37
have to do the shopping for food. She took me to the corner
store to show me the way. I was proud; I felt like a grownup.

The next afternoon I looped the basket over my arm and went down the pavement toward the store. When I reached the corner, a gang of boys grabbed me, knocked me down, snatched the basket, took the money, and sent me running home in panic. That evening I told my mother what had happened, but she made no comment; she sat down at once, wrote another note, gave me more money, and sent me out to the grocery again. I crept down the steps and saw the same gang of boys playing down the street. I ran back into the house.

"What's the matter?" my mother asked.   38

"It's those same boys," I said. "They'll beat me."   39

"You've got to get over that," she said. "Now, go on."   40

"I'm scared," I said.   41

"Go on and don't pay any attention to them," she said.   42

I went out of the door and walked briskly down the side-   43
walk, praying that the gang would not molest me. But when I came abreast of them someone shouted.

"There he is!"   44

They came toward me and I broke into a wild run   45
toward home. They overtook me and flung me to the pavement. I yelled, pleaded, kicked, but they wrenched the money out of my hand. They yanked me to my feet, gave me a few slaps, and sent me home sobbing. My mother met me at the door.

"They b-beat m-me," I gasped. "They t-t-took the m-   46
money."

I started up the steps, seeking the shelter of the house.   47

"Don't you come in here," my mother warned me.   48

I froze in my tracks and stared at her.   49

"But they're coming after me," I said.   50

"You just stay right where you are," she said in a deadly   51
tone. "I'm going to teach you this night to stand up and fight for yourself."

She went into the house and I waited, terrified, won-   52
dering what she was about. Presently she returned with more money and another note; she also had a long heavy stick.

"Take this money, this note, and this stick," she said.   53
"Go to the store and buy those groceries. If those boys bother you, then fight."

I was baffled. My mother was telling me to fight, a thing   54
that she had never done before.

"But I'm scared," I said.   55

"Don't you come into this house until you've gotten   56
those groceries," she said.

"They'll beat me; they'll beat me," I said.   57

"Then stay in the streets; don't come back here!"   58

I ran up the steps and tried to force my way past her   59
into the house. A stinging slap came on my jaw. I stood on the
sidewalk, crying.

"Please, let me wait until tomorrow," I begged.   60

"No," she said. "Go now! If you come back into this   61
house without those groceries, I'll whip you!"

She slammed the door and I heard the key turn in the   62
lock. I shook with fright. I was alone upon the dark, hostile
streets and gangs were after me. I had the choice of being
beaten at home or away from home. I clutched the stick, crying, trying to reason. If I were beaten at home, there was
absolutely nothing that I could do about it; but if I were beat-
en in the streets, I had a chance to fight and defend myself.
I walked slowly down the sidewalk, coming closer to the gang
of boys, holding the stick tightly. I was so full of fear that I
could scarcely breathe. I was almost upon them now.

"There he is again!" the cry went up.   63

They surrounded me quickly and began to grab for my   64
hand.

"I'll kill you!" I threatened.   65

They closed in. In blind fear I let the stick fly, feeling it   66
crack against a boy's skull. I swung again, lamming another
skull, then another. Realizing that they would retaliate if I let
up for but a second, I fought to lay them low, to knock them
cold, to kill them so that they could not strike back at me. I
flayed with tears in my eyes, teeth clenched, stark fear making me throw every ounce of my strength behind each blow.
I hit again and again, dropping the money and the grocery
list. The boys scattered, yelling, nursing their heads, staring
at me in utter disbelief. They had never seen such frenzy. I
stood panting, egging them on, taunting them to come on
and fight. When they refused, I ran after them and they tore
out for their homes, screaming. The parents of the boys
rushed into the streets and threatened me, and for the first
time in my life I shouted at grownups, telling them that I
would give them the same if they bothered me. I finally

found my grocery list and the money and went to the store. On my way back I kept my stick poised for instant use, but there was not a single boy in sight. That night I won the right to the streets of Memphis.

Checking Your Understanding

1. What was your reaction to the violence in this story? Why does his mother tell him he has to fight now although she has never encouraged him to do it before?

2. How does Wright triumph over his fear? How did his triumph compare to what you felt when you conquered yours?

Examining Rhetorical Strategies

1. How does Wright make you feel as if you are "right there" with him during this piece? What techniques does he use to get you involved in the story?

2. Wright begins this piece with a scene about hunger. How does he relate this introduction and the idea of "hunger" to his fight with the gangs?

REFLECTION

THE PERFECT PICTURE
James Alexander Thom

Often authors use expressive writing to examine their lives or the human condition. These personal reflections are not egotistical; these writers see themselves and their lives as being representative in some way of the lives of many people and use their experience to reflect on some larger issue. In Alexander Thom's essay on the media, for example, he is commenting on the way that news reporting has become sensationalized to the point that "human suffering has become a spectator sport." How much of a person's personal life, especially a personal tragedy, should be subjected to the scrutiny of the public has long been debated. While the debate is a longstanding one, Thom feels his personal experience will add something to the discussion.

Although the basis for the writing is still personal and the writer still uses "I," the reader is asked not only to become engaged in the story, but then to reflect on the larger issues involved. We are invited to listen to the writers as they try to make sense out of the issues in their lives. If our lives are similar to theirs, we are aided in coming to terms with who we are. But even if our lives do not have some direct parallel— we are not reporters, for example—we are still invited to reflect on how we view human tragedy and on the ethical issue Thom faced: Would we have taken the perfect picture even at someone else's expense?

As readers, then, we must take a more reflective stance. We are not being led through the piece as directly as we are in narratives. Instead, understanding the meaning of the piece requires more work on our part, more analysis of the whole situation. In the case of Thom's essay, we are asked to reflect on how we make moral decisions.

Prereading Journal

Sometimes we are faced with hard decisions, moral dilemmas that make us think very seriously about right and wrong. The pressure to make such decisions sometimes comes from peers or authority figures and sometimes from within us. Think of a time when you have faced a moral dilemma and had to make a decision about what to do. Describe the circumstances surrounding the dilemma and how you came to a decision about it.

Background

Thom has been a professional essayist, novelist, journalist, editor, and as this essay indicates, a police reporter. This essay first appeared in the August 1976 edition of *Reader's Digest* and describes an incident that took place fifteen years earlier when Thom was called to the scene of an accident at which he was expected to play the role of the "good reporter."

During Reading

Keep note of what things the writer does that mark him as a "good reporter" and what things make him wonder if he is suited for the profession.

Reading Selection

It was early in the spring about 15 years ago—a day of pale sunlight and trees just beginning to bud. I was a young police reporter, driving to a scene I didn't want to see. A man, the police-dispatcher's broadcast said, had accidentally backed his pickup truck over his baby granddaughter in the driveway of the family home. It was a fatality.   1

As I parked among police cars and TV-news cruisers, I saw a stocky, white-haired man in cotton work clothes standing near a pickup. Cameras were trained on him, and reporters were sticking microphones in his face. Looking totally bewildered, he was trying to answer their questions. Mostly he was only moving his lips, blinking and choking up.   2

After a while the reporters gave up on him and followed the police into the small white house. I can still see in my mind's eye that devastated old man looking down at the place in the driveway where the child had been. Beside the   3 house was a freshly spaded flower bed, and nearby a pile of dark, rich earth.

"I was just backing up there to spread that good dirt," 4 he said to me, though I had not asked him anything. "I didn't even know she was outdoors." He stretched his hand toward the flower bed, then let it flop to his side. He lapsed back into his thoughts, and I, like a good reporter, went into the house to find someone who could provide a recent photo of the toddler.

A few minutes later, with all the details in my notebook 5 and a three-by-five studio portrait of the cherubic child tucked in my jacket pocket, I went toward the kitchen where the police had said the body was.

I had brought a camera in with me—the big, bulky 6 Speed Graphic which used to be the newspaper reporter's trademark. Everybody had drifted back out of the house together—family, police, reporters and photographers. Entering the kitchen, I came upon this scene:

On a Formica-topped table, backlighted by a frilly cur- 7 tained window, lay the tiny body, wrapped in a clean white sheet. Somehow the grandfather had managed to stay away from the crowd. He was sitting on a chair beside the table, in profile to me and unaware of my presence, looking uncomprehendingly at the swaddled corpse.

The house was very quiet. A clock ticked. As I watched, 8 the grandfather slowly leaned forward, curved his arms like parentheses around the head and feet of the little form, then pressed his face to the shroud and remained motionless.

In that hushed moment I recognized the makings of a 9 prize-winning news photograph. I appraised the light, adjusted the lens setting and distance, locked a bulb in the flashgun, raised the camera and composed the scene in the viewfinder.

Every element of the picture was perfect: the grandfa- 10 ther in his plain work clothes, his white hair backlighted by sunshine, the child's form wrapped in the sheet, the atmosphere of the simple home suggested by black iron trivets and World's Fair souvenir plates on the walls flanking the window. Outside, the police could be seen inspecting the fatal rear wheel of the pickup while the child's mother and father leaned in each other's arms.

I don't know how many seconds I stood there, unable 11
to snap that shutter. I was keenly aware of the powerful storytelling value that photo would have, and my professional conscience told me to take it. Yet I couldn't make my hand fire
that flashbulb and intrude on the poor man's island of grief.

At length I lowered the camera and crept away, shaken 12
with doubt about my suitability for the journalistic profession. Of course I never told the city editor or any fellow
reporters about that missed opportunity for a perfect news
picture.

Every day, on the newscasts and in the papers, we see 13
pictures of people in extreme conditions of grief and despair.
Human suffering has become a spectator sport. And sometimes, as I'm watching news film, I remember that day.

I still feel right about what I did.   14

Checking Your Understanding

1. Do you feel Thom was a "good reporter?" How would you feel about
    what Thom did if you were his boss on the newspaper? If you were
    a member of the little girl's family? What is the difference between
    Thom's taking the picture and his writing the essay? Is the essay also
    an intrusion on the "poor man's island of grief?"

2. How would you describe your relation to the writer? How was Thom
    able to make you care about this issue of how human suffering is
    handled by the media? What would you identify as his contribution
    to this discussion?

Examining Rhetorical Strategies

1. Assume Thom took the picture and rewrite paragraph 11 from the
    moment the flash goes off. In your revision show what Thom was
    expecting to happen that, in the original version, made him decide
    against taking the picture. Keep your style in this paragraph as
    much like Thom's as possible.

2. How does Thom make you *see* his dilemma exactly the way that he
    saw it? What role does the camera play in his explaining his decision?

A SUMMARY OF EXPRESSIVE READING

As we have seen in the above examples, there are several crucial
elements in expressive discourse.

First, expressive pieces are based on the *personal experience* of
the writer and are written in the *first person* ("I"). As we read them

we hear the writer's *voice* and come to know the writer better. This personal interest often gets us involved in the piece.

Second, expressive pieces vary in terms of the *reader/writer relationship*. In some pieces we are almost participating in a dialogue in that we are addressed directly (as "you") and our reading is guided by the writer. In other, more reflective pieces, we are expected not just to get involved in the story but to reflect on the human significance of the larger issue it represents.

Third, the primary purpose of our reading is to hear about the personal experience of the writer. However, most expressive pieces have some relevance for our own lives, too. We can *relate* to the writer, to the experiences, to the type of life the author lived, or to the general ideas raised in the piece. This connection to the piece often helps us to reflect on our own lives.

Fourth, the success of expressive pieces depends on how well the authors achieve their goal of *sharing a part of themselves*. We should be able hear the writer's voice, to be drawn into a good story, to feel an invitation to reflect on the issues raised by the writer's life experience.

And finally, expressive pieces are dependent on the *quality of the writing*. These pieces are made to be enjoyed; we should feel invited, welcomed, involved, entertained, challenged by the fact that the writers have expressed a part of their personal lives in words. When a writer succeeds in capturing the truth of the human experience with all its emotion, this type of writing can be the most powerful and beautiful of all nonfiction prose.

Chapter Four

WRITING EXPRESSIVE DISCOURSE

"Write about a significant experience in your life," the teacher says, and at first the task seems easy. After all, you simply need to select some past event and write down what happened. You have many events to choose from so that if you get stuck on one, you can simply switch to another without being forced to go back to the library to do more research. If you pick the right event, you should have plenty of details to choose from; if you need more, you can add more information, provide more background, write more about what happened afterward or about how you have changed as a result of the experience. But writing about yourself, writing expressive discourse, is not always as easy as it seems. In fact, it can be the most difficult kind of writing you do.

DETERMINING YOUR RELATIONSHIP TO YOUR READERS

One aspect of expressive writing that makes it difficult is that it is so personal. Sometimes it is easier and more comfortable to hide behind the causes of the American Revolution or the migratory habits of the blue heron than to explain who you are.

Because expressive writing is so personal and so revealing, you may find yourself spending some time thinking about how you want to present yourself. Do you want to come across as warm and friendly or as rather distant or perhaps even critical? Do you want to sound confident and sure of yourself or hesitant and maybe a little confused? Charming and inviting or straightforward, take-it-or-leave-it? In other words, what kind of *voice* do you want to use and what kind of a relationship do you want to have with your readers?

Robert Fulghum's voice, for example, is quite chummy; there is little or no distance between him and his readers. Richard Wright speaks with an urgency that puts us right on the streets with him, feeling his fear, his hunger, and his victory. James Alexander Thom also lets us experience his story with him, but through the lens of a camera and the invitation to reflect on what invading someone's privacy means. In writing expressive discourse, then, you will need to consider how you want to appear to your readers, to relate to them, and what voice you want to use to speak to them. What impression are you trying to make?

SELECTING A FOCUS

Expressive writing is also complicated because you do have so much material available to you. While this may keep you from running out, it also means you will need to be selective about what you choose to use.

Selecting a Topic

Your life is probably filled with little gems that would make great stories—learning to ride a bike, accidents and mishaps of all sorts, deaths, weddings, school days, moves. But to create a good expressive piece, you need to select your topic carefully. Consider the following:

Is this a story that you can tell well? Some stories will seem great in your memory, but as soon as you try to tell them you realize that "you had to be there" to appreciate them. You will need to be able to tell this tale in such a way that we will feel as if we had been there.

Do you remember enough about it?   Often you will recall some incident from your childhood and you may even be able to embellish it a bit with details supplied by others, but to recreate it would be difficult because you were so young when it happened that the story is vague in your memory. It's better to select something you remember well and can recall vividly so you can make it vivid to others.

Do you remember too much about it?   You also need to be careful about the flip side of the problem. Some stories are too complicated and involved to be adequately contained in one essay. Be careful to choose something that is manageable, not a story with several subplots and a cast of thousands.

Is this something you are willing to share?   Some events in our lives are very powerful and emotional stories, but the thought of sharing them with someone else makes us uncomfortable. If you select such a topic, you will find yourself holding back on information or on the emotions involved and so the very aspects of the story that would make it powerful will be lost. If you pick something very personal make sure you can commit to telling the story honestly and effectively.

Is it something too generic?   Just as some subjects are too personal to share, other topics are so common as to seem trivial. Perhaps prom night or coming to college are truly significant events to you, but they will seem like everyone else's prom night or college move unless you find a unique angle to take on the story. While people will enjoy a plot they can relate to, they also need to be able to see why this was significant to you and what was special about it. Make sure the unique aspect of your story is clear.

Narrowing Your Topic

Even after you have narrowed your options down to just one story, you still have a number of decisions to make. Remember that you are trying to *recreate* the event for your readers. You will need to consider how much you need to tell your readers for them to understand what happened. How much background should you provide? Where should you begin—and end, since your life story is still going on? Should you use dialogue or just explain what people said since sometimes the exact words are hard to remember? How much description should you use? Does every person involved in the story need a special introduction or can several be lumped together? Would readers need a sense of the whole building in which an event happened or would just the most important room be enough?

Making these decisions depends on your establishing a *focus*, a *main point* around which your story revolves. Ask yourself what the *heart* of your piece is, the one moment without which there would be no story. Once you are sure of this central point, then select the details that will support and enhance that moment. You must choose your details carefully so that your readers can see clearly what you want to share with them.

MAKING IT SIGNIFICANT FOR YOUR AUDIENCE

One of the most deflating responses a writer can get to a personal story is "So what?" Your readers have listened attentively, but they can't figure out why you told them about this event. So that you do not experience this response, you need to make sure that your story has *significance*, that your readers not only know what happened but also why you want to share this particular experience with them. As Chapter Three pointed out, readers of expressive writing approach the text expecting to receive a personal message from the writer; as writers of expressive discourse, then, you must be sure that you have a personal message to share.

However, making the significance of your story clear does not mean that you need to hit your readers over the head with it. It may be tempting to add a sentence such as "What I learned from this experience was . . ." or "The lasting effect that this person had on my life was . . ." to make sure that readers will understand exactly what your message is, but this kind of ending does more harm than good. If you have told the story well or created a vivid portrait, this kind of ending is not only unnecessary, it also insults your readers' intelligence. A reflective comment at the end can be effective, as it is in Thom's essay, but it is best to keep it short lest it lead readers away from the personal focus. In most well-written pieces the message is clearly communicated *through the telling* of the story.

Readers understand the significance because they clearly see why you can't forget this memory.

ORGANIZING YOUR THOUGHTS

If you are writing a narrative, the most common form of organization is chronological and this will probably work well for you. A pattern such as the one Richard Wright used is often effective:

1. The author sets the scene and puts the event within context;
2. The events of the story are presented in the order in which they occurred; and
3. The author steps back and briefly comments on the significance of the event.

Because this pattern presents the story clearly and is easy to follow, it is an obvious choice to use for a narrative. But you need to remember that it is a *choice*. The events did happen in a certain order, but you do not have to write your paper in that same order. You may find, for example, that you want to start in the middle of the piece and use *memory* or *flashbacks* to fill us in on background information. Or you may wish to weave the necessary background into the story through *description* or *dialogue*. You may also find that the paper works best if you do not tell just one story but instead take a more reflective look at *several incidents* that illustrate some pattern in your life. In all of these cases, though, you will probably still find it helpful to begin with the chronological framework. From there you can consider different options as you revise.

Notes on the Anecdote

Remember that a close reader/writer relationship is crucial in this form of writing. You may even be addressing the reader directly. Your *voice* must be personal and in fact should really show some of your personality. Your overt role as guide in this kind of writing means that you can lead us in the direction you want to go and explain the connections of any tangents. However, the freedom of this chatty style can be deceiving. You will need to *be firm about what your point is* and through your story and comments make that point clear to your readers. (While Fulghum's essay in

Chapter Three may seem to ramble, he uses religious images and the idea of goodness throughout to hold his piece together.)

When you use the anecdote as an illustration, there should be no doubt as to why you told this story. An introduction or example, no matter how entertaining or moving, must still clearly serve to support the point of the paper.

Notes on the Autobiographical Narrative

Your narrative will have three parts: *background information,* the *story* itself, and the *significance* of the event in your life. When constructing your essay, you need to think about *balance.* Most of the paper should be the telling of the story.

When you think about the background information you need to provide, *measure it* in relation to the story itself. If you find that we need a good deal of information to understand your story, you should consider ways to mete it out so your paper is not top heavy with introduction and we do not get bored trying to figure out why we are being given so much information. Using memories, flashbacks, and interspersing background into the plot will help you.

During the recreation of the event, *weigh* each detail against the main point of the piece. Consider if a particular description contributes to our understanding of the piece. Is it helping us relive the event with you? You may find it helpful to use a clustering exercise to check the connection of each part of your story with the main point.

If you find yourself needing to explain why this event was meaningful to you after you have told the story, consider whether you have made the emotion within the story vivid enough. If you have, we should be able to feel the significance without your spelling it out. A brief comment might be desirable, but should not be necessary.

Keep the focus of the piece on the story and keep the weight of the background information and the explanation of the significance in check.

Notes on the Reflective Essay

All of the advice for writing a narrative holds true for the reflective essay. You will still need to select a good story or several good incidents and tell them well, in a way that makes us feel their power. However, the purpose of this essay is not just to recreate a memory and make us feel the significance of this event for you. In reflective essays, the focus is on the *human significance* of the event, how your personal experience reflects a larger human concern.

Reflective essays, then, are like invitations first to relate to a personal story and then to see this narrative in a larger context. Readers need to see the connection between what happened to you and what happens to others or to what is happening in the world. As a writer you will need to both draw readers into your personal story and then pull back from that personal engagement to a more reflective stance that lets you comment on its significance for others.

Alexander Thom's essay, for example, is not just about a personally significant experience on the job, but about the human dilemma of moral choice and our growing indifference to human suffering. That is his reflective message about the story. Your essay will also need to explain how your personal story illustrates the importance and validity of your reflective message. Be sure you select background, details, and a main point that all lead to and support your reflection.

THE WRITING PROCESS AT WORK

While all these decisions about voice, focus, significance, and organization may seem overwhelming, fortunately they all do not have to be made before you start writing. Most writers, in fact, try out one approach and then as they write, they discover how to make the story more effective. This often takes place with the help of drafts, as we discussed in Chapter Two, and is recursive: We write down our memories, we read what we have written, looking for potential papers, then we choose one and start shaping our text. At this stage we often must go back and search our memories for more information, evaluate what we come up with, and continue writing and shaping. Slowly, we figure out how to make the story we have in our memories meaningful to others.

In the next few pages, we will watch one student go through this process of creating a meaningful story, looking over his shoulder as he works. In "First Goal" you will see Rob Ness doing serious revision in terms of the four elements we have just discussed.

FIRST GOAL

Rob Ness

Background

Ness was a first-year student when he wrote this essay for the first assignment in his writing class. After completing a brainstorming list in which he was asked to divide his life into several large categories and list major events that had happened within each time frame, Ness decided to write about an incident that had happened to him in Korea, where his father was stationed at a military base. The soccer game described below was played when Ness was attending Seoul American High School.

First Draft

1   A light drizzle drifted down soaking everything and everyone. The first half and most of the second trudged by leaving the game scoreless.

2   "Ness! Prepare to go in for Eric." Immediately I began restretching my muscles. The starting right-wing had just signaled for a breather.

3   My coach called me to his side. Moments later, "Subs" rang out. As I sailed in I tagged hands with Eric. My thoughts blurred with excitement and anxiety. With the throw-in, the left-wing shot up the left sideline. I sprinted up the right sideline, keeping pace with the play.

4   Stopping at the corner of the eighteen, I watched the melee that soon occurred on the opposite corner. The opposing goalie moved in to take control.

5   Suddenly, there it was, ambling along the six yard line unconcerned with the tangle of legs it had left behind. Without a thought, I moved in. Contact and the ball hummed past the fingertips of the scrambling goalie. The net pulsed.

6   Accustomed to missing, I stood dazed with disbelief. Reality set in when the left-wing slammed into me in celebration. The game ended without any further points being scored.

Writer's comments   I picked this story because it was the most memorable highlight of my soccer career. The best part of it was moments after I scored a goal. It stunned me. At least that's what I'm trying to convey. Organizing the paper so that it remains clear and understandable is where I need help.

Teacher's comments   This is a very good start. There are some nice images in here like the way you describe the ball. But you've said this was the highlight of your soccer career, and yet when I read this I feel sometimes as if you are left out of it a little too much. How did you feel as you were stretching? Was it unusual for you to be called into a game? Did you feel uninvolved with all that was happening on the field, like the ball would never come to you? Another thing that is making me feel distant from this is that last paragraph. It sounds very formal. Can you loosen it up? And can you also mention that it's a soccer game?

Analysis

Ness' story and comments clearly show his *purpose*—he wants to recreate that memorable event and he wants us to experience it as he did. He also has identified the most important moment for him, the *focus* and heart of his piece— when he realizes what he did and is stunned by the outcome. He recognizes, however, that the *organization* may not be strong. He is, of course, following the usual organization for a narrative, taking us chronologically from the beginning to the end of the game and providing two sentences of back-ground, first about the weather and then about the lack of goals scored. But he is wondering if there isn't a better way to cover this material.

The teacher's comments are aimed at making Ness think more about the *relationship he wants with the readers*. He is keeping us at arm's length both with his lack of involve-ment in the piece and with his slightly formal style. To believe that this really was a crucial event for him, we need to feel it as he did, not be kept at a distance. In addition, the language and the pace of the piece need to reflect the excitement and chaos of the moment, and not sound reserved.

As you will see, Ness was able to revise his text and do a final draft that captured the moment in a much more imme-diate way and that drew the reader into the game with him.

Final Draft

"Ness! Prepare to go in for Eric."   1

A light drizzle was drifting down onto the playing field 2
at Seoul American High School soaking everything and
everyone. Surprised at hearing my name called by the coach,
I leapt to my feet and began to restretch my bench-stiffened
muscles. Though my body was soon limber, my mind
remained tense with anticipation. The starting right-wing
had just signaled for a breather.

This soccer match had been expected to be a blowout 3
in our favor. But the first half and most of the second had
trudged by leaving the game scoreless. As a bencher I normally didn't get any playing time unless our team was winning by three or more points.

But my coach called me to his side and moments later, 4
"Subs!" rang out. As I sailed onto the field, I tagged the hand
of the exhausted right-wing. My mind was a blur of excitement and anxiety as I watched the game resume with a throw-
in. Mark, the left-wing, skillfully brought the ball to the
ground and sped down the left sideline. I sprinted down the
right side keeping pace with the play.

We stopped at the corner of the eighteen yard line, 5
and I helplessly watched the melee that was taking place in
the opposite corner. The opposing goalie moved in to take
control.

Suddenly, there it was, ambling along the six yard line, 6
unconcerned with the tangle of legs it had left behind.
Without a thought, I moved in, head down and leg cocked.
All that was there was the ball, the goal, and me. Contact. I
glanced up as the net pulsed.

I stood dazed with disbelief. I had always missed that 7
shot during practice. The spell that held me was broken
when Mark slammed into me in celebration.

Five minutes later Eric was again ready to play. As I 8
approached the bench, I was unable to stifle the widening
grin on my face. I had no reason to—I had just scored the
first goal of my high school career.

Another wave of wide grins struck me as the referee's 9
whistle let loose four shrill blasts signaling the end of the
game. The score remained one to zero.

Analysis

The first major change we sense in this piece is our own involve-ment—we are "right there" with him from start to finish. This is accomplished mainly through Ness' own involvement; he puts him-self and his feelings into the piece and does not back away at the end.

From the new opening line of dialogue we are invited onto the field with Ness. He keeps us with him by letting us in on how he's feeling: He's a bencher who seldom gets to play; he feels help-less as he watches the melee on the field; he can't control his smiles at the end. And he has integrated the background informa-tion (including what kind of game is being played) into the story rather than tacking it on at the beginning. Finally, he has made the moment that he identified as crucial, his stunned feeling after the ball goes in, a paragraph of its own for emphasis.

In addition, the story is made more enjoyable by Ness' style. He chooses words like "melee," "trudged," "bench-stiffened," and "pulsed" which carry emotional power as well as accurately convey meaning. He also does an excellent job of describing the ball and his body in paragraph 6. Emphasizing "contact" by making the word a sentence on its own and using "the net pulsed" instead of saying that the goal was scored are also effective.

With these changes, then, Ness is able to bring us into the story as he wanted and to make us see why this moment was "the most memorable highlight" of his soccer career.

Exercise

To practice doing a narrative out of the usual chronological order, try rewriting the opening of Ness' piece making the first line:

"Subs!" or
"My mind was a blur of excitement and anxiety as I watched the game resume with a throw- in."

Consider how you could provide the necessary background from one of these two starting points.

WRITING FOR READERS

Ness wrote a first draft that simply recorded what he could remem-ber. But as he revised, he began to consider (1) how he wanted his readers to feel and respond to the experience and (2) how he could shape the experience so that it would have this desired effect. The revision, then, was done purposefully so that his piece of writing would also be an enjoyable piece of reading for someone else.

STRATEGIES FOR WRITING EXPRESSIVE DISCOURSE

The assignment Review the *purpose* of the assignment. Remember that expressive writing is personal. You will need to select a topic that is a meaningful part of your life, that reveals who you are in some way.

Prewriting Select your *subject* carefully. Since each day of your life could present you with a possible topic for this assignment, you will need to select one that is worth telling about both for you and for your readers. It can be very helpful to do some brainstorming of significant events and people in your life and then decide which have a good story behind them that you would enjoy recreating for readers.

Drafting While you are writing, keep the following four goals discussed in this chapter in mind:

1. Determine your relationship to your readers. Consider what kind of *voice* you will use. What kind of person were you at the time of this incident? Do you need to reflect a child's way of thinking, the voice of a rebellious teenager, the insecurity and uncertainty of someone in the middle of one of life's big decisions? What impression do you want to give your readers about who you are?
2. Select the *focus* of your subject carefully. Many events and people in your life have significance for you and would be worth writing about, but you need to be careful about which you select. Consider:

    Is the subject something that can be covered adequately in one paper? Do you have enough material? Do you have too much?

    Can you speak about this subject honestly and genuinely convey its significance without feeling uncomfortable? If your topic is common to most people, what unique angle will you take on it to keep from being generic?

What is the main point or heart of your piece? Do all the details you have picked support and enhance this central idea?

3. Make the *significance* clear to your readers. How would they answer the question "So what?" What is your personal message to them? Remember you do not need for this message to be stated explicitly, but if you do not, the significance needs to be clear through your vivid recreation of the event or person.

4. *Organize* your thoughts. Most expressive pieces are narrative in structure and thus are organized chronologically. Even if you want to focus on your relationship with someone, you will likely recall events that happened when you were together. Remember that the order in which you put events is a matter of *choice* and you may use techniques such as flashbacks to help you shape the event so the most important moment receives the utmost attention.

Editing   As you edit pay particular attention to the following aspects of expressive writing:

A good, consistent voice
Vivid description and perhaps dialogue
An interesting plot with a clear chronology of events
Good character descriptions
Clear personal significance
A main point around which all the other details revolve

Chapter Five

FURTHER EXPRESSIVE READINGS

The readings contained in this chapter illustrate a wide variety of reader/writer relationships, ranging from the intimate relationship established in the student essay, "Night Sounds," to the distant, more reflective and literary voice of free-lance writer Laurence Shames in his essay, "The Eyes of Fear."

PROFESSIONAL ESSAYS AND READING TECHNIQUES

The five professional samples focus on reading techniques. Each sample includes a suggestion for a prereading journal, a during reading activity, and questions for after reading that will help you to understand the reading and appreciate the rhetorical strategies the author used in writing the essay.

MOTHER

Annie Dillard

Prereading Journal

Think about a unique characteristic of one of your relatives or friends, something she or he says or does all the time: your mother's favorite bit of advice, your uncle's knack for telling long stories, your sibling's favorite way of getting on your nerves, how your best friend shows concern for you. Describe a brief scene you remember that illustrates this characteristic.

Background

Dillard is an essayist whose nonfiction works include *An American Childhood* from which this selection is taken. In this book she describes her early life growing up in Pittsburgh. This chapter from the book concerns her mother—both her character and her influence on her daughter.

During Reading

Dillard divided this essay into sections indicated by the space breaks. In each section she provides *anecdotes* about her mother. Keep track of what characteristic of her mother she is highlighting through each little story.

Reading Selection

One Sunday afternoon Mother wandered through our 1 kitchen, where Father was making a sandwich and listening to the ball game. The Pirates were playing the New York Giants at Forbes Field. In those days, the Giants had a utility infielder named Wayne Terwilliger. Just as Mother passed through, the radio announcer cried—with undue drama— "Terwilliger bunts one!"

"Terwilliger bunts one?" Mother cried back, stopped 2 short. She turned. "Is that English?"

"The player's name is Terwilliger," Father said. "He 3 bunted."

"That's marvelous," Mother said. " 'Terwilliger bunts 4
one.' No wonder you listen to baseball. 'Terwilliger bunts
one.' "

For the next seven or eight years, Mother made this sur- 5
prising string of syllables her own. Testing a microphone, she
repeated, "Terwilliger bunts one"; testing a pen or a typewriter, she wrote it. If, as happened surprisingly often in the
course of various improvised gags, she pretended to whisper
something else in my ear, she actually whispered, "Terwilliger
bunts one." Whenever someone used a French phrase, or a
Latin one, she answered solemnly, "Terwilliger bunts one." If
Mother had had, like Andrew Carnegie, the opportunity to
cook up a motto for a coat of arms, hers would have read simply and tellingly, "Terwilliger bunts one." (Carnegie's was
"Death to Privilege.")

She served us with other words and phrases. On a 6
Florida trip, she repeated tremulously, "That . . . is a royal
poinciana." I don't remember the tree; I remember the thrill
in her voice. She pronounced it carefully, and spelled it. She
also liked to say "portulaca."

The drama of the words "Tamiami Trail" stirred her, we 7
learned on the same Florida trip. People built Tampa on one
coast, and they built Miami on another. Then—the height of
visionary ambition and folly—they piled a slow, tremendous
road through the terrible Everglades to connect them. To
build the road, men stood sunk in muck to their armpits.
They fought off cottonmouth moccasins and six-foot alliga-
tors. They slept in boats, wet. They blasted muck with dyna-
mite, cut jungle with machetes; they laid logs, dragged
drilling machines, hauled dredges, heaped limestone. The
road took fourteen years to build up by the shovelful, a
Panama Canal in reverse, and cost hundreds of lives from
tropical, mosquito-carried diseases. Then, capping it all,
some genius thought of the word Tamiami: they called the
road from Tampa to Miami, this very road under our spinning wheels, the Tamiami Trail. Some called it Alligator Alley.
Anyone could drive over this road without a thought.

Hearing this, moved, I thought all the suffering of road 8
building was worth it (it wasn't my suffering), now that we
had this new thing to hang these new words on—Alligator
Alley for those who liked things cute, and, for connoisseurs

like Mother, for lovers of the human drama in all its boldness and terror, the Tamiami Trail.

Back home, Mother cut clips from reels of talk, as it 9 were, and played them back at leisure. She noticed that many Pittsburghers confuse "leave" and "let." One kind relative brightened our morning by mentioning why she'd brought her son to visit: "He wanted to come with me, so I left him." Mother filled in Amy and me on locutions we missed. "I can't do it on Friday," her pretty sister told a crowded dinner party, "because Friday's the day I lay in the stores."

(All unconsciously, though, we ourselves used some 10 pure Pittsburghisms. We said "tele pole," pronounced "telly pole," for that splintery sidewalk post I loved to climb. We said "slippy"—the sidewalks are "slippy." We said, "That's all the farther I could go." And we said, as Pittsburghers do say, "This glass needs washed," or "The dog needs walked"—a usage our father eschewed; he knew it was not standard English, nor even comprehensible English, but he never let on.)

"Spell 'poinsettia,' " Mother would throw out at me, 11 smiling with pleasure. "Spell 'sherbet.' " The idea was not to make us whizzes, but, quite the contrary, to remind us—and I, especially, needed reminding—that we didn't know it all just yet.

"There's a deer standing in the front hall," she told me 12 one quiet evening in the country.

"Really?"   13

"No. I just wanted to tell you something once without 14 your saying, 'I know.' "

Supermarkets in the middle 1950s began luring, or 15 bothering, customers by giving out Top Value Stamps or Green Stamps. When, shopping with Mother, we got to the head of the checkout line, the checker, always a young man, asked, "Save stamps?"

"No," Mother replied genially, week after week, "I build 16 model airplanes.' " I believe she originated this line. It took me years to determine where the joke lay.

Anyone who met her verbal challenges she adored. She 17 had surgery on one of her eyes. On the operating table, just before she conked out, she appealed feelingly to the surgeon, saying, as she had been planning to say for weeks, "Will

I be able to play the piano?" "Not on me," the surgeon said. "You won't pull that old one on me."

It was, indeed, an old one. The surgeon was supposed 18 to answer, "Yes, my dear, brave woman, you will be able to play the piano after this operation," to which Mother intended to reply, "Oh, good, I've always wanted to play the piano." This pat scenario bored her; she loved having it interrupted. It must have galled her that usually her acquaintances were so predictably unalert; it must have galled her that, for the length of her life, she could surprise everyone so continually, so easily, when she had been the same all along. At any rate, she loved anyone who, as she put it, saw it coming, and called her on it.

She regarded the instructions on bureaucratic forms as 19 straight lines. "Do you advocate the overthrow of the United States government by force or violence?" After some thought she wrote, "Force." She regarded children, even babies, as straight men. When Molly learned to crawl, Mother delight-ed in buying her gowns with drawstrings at the bottom, like Swee'pea's, because, as she explained energetically, you could easily step on the drawstring without the baby's notic-ing, so that she crawled and crawled and crawled and never got anywhere except into a small ball at the gown's top.

When we children were young, she mothered us ten- 20 derly and dependably; as we got older, she resumed her career of anarchism. She collared us into her gags. If she answered the phone on a wrong number, she told the caller, "Just a minute," and dragged the receiver to Amy or me, say-ing, "Here, take this, your name is Cecile," or, worse, just, "It's for you." You had to think on your feet. But did you want to perform well as Cecile, or did you want to take pity on the wretched caller?

During a family trip to the Highland Park Zoo, Mother 21 and I were alone for a minute. She approached a young cou-ple holding hands on a bench by the seals, and addressed the young man in dripping tones: "Where have you been? Still got those baby-blue eyes; always did slay me. And this"—a swift nod at the dumbstruck young woman, who had removed her hand from the man's—"must be the one you were telling me about. She's not so bad, really, as you used to make out. But listen, you know how I miss you, you know where to reach me, same old place. And there's Ann over there—see how she's grown? See the blue eyes?"

And off she sashayed, taking me firmly by the hand, and 22 leading us around briskly past the monkey house and away. She cocked an ear back, and both of us heard the desperate man begin, in a high-pitched wail, "I swear, I never saw her before in my life. . . ."

On a long, sloping beach by the ocean, she lay 23 stretched out sunning with Father and friends, until the conversation gradually grew tedious, when without forethought she gave a little push with her heel and rolled away. People were stunned. She rolled deadpan and apparently effortlessly, arms and legs extended and tidy, down the beach to the distant water's edge, where she lay at ease just as she had been, but half in the surf, and well out of earshot.

She dearly loved to fluster people by throwing out a 24 game's rules at whim—when she was getting bored, losing in a dull sort of way, and when everybody else was taking it too seriously. If you turned your back, she moved the checkers around on the board. When you got them all straightened out, she denied she'd touched them; the next time you turned your back, she lined them up on the rug or hid them under your chair. In a betting rummy game called Michigan, she routinely played out of turn, or called out a card she didn't hold, or counted backward, simply to amuse herself by causing an uproar and watching the rest of us do double takes and have fits. (Much later, when serious suitors came to call, Mother subjected them to this fast card game as a trial by ordeal; she used it as an intelligence test and a measure of spirit. If the poor man could stay a round without breaking down or running out, he got to marry one of us, if he still wanted to.)

She excelled at bridge, playing fast and boldly, but 25 when the stakes were low and the hands dull, she bid slams for the devilment of it, or raised her opponents' suit to bug them, or showed her hand, or tossed her cards in a handful behind her back in a characteristic swift motion accompanied by a vibrantly innocent look. It drove our stolid father crazy. The hand was over before it began, and the guests were appalled. How do you score it, who deals now, what do you do with a crazy person who is having so much fun? Or they were down seven, and the guests were appalled. "Pam!" "Dammit, Pam!" He groaned. What ails such people? What on earth possesses them? He rubbed his face.

She was an unstoppable force; she never let go. When we moved across town, she persuaded the U.S. Post Office to let her keep her old address—forever—because she'd had stationery printed. I don't know how she did it. Every new post office worker, over decades, needed to learn that although the Doaks' mail is addressed to here, it is delivered to there. 26

Mother's energy and intelligence suited her for a greater role in a larger arena—mayor of New York, say—than the one she had. She followed American politics closely; she had been known to vote for Democrats. She saw how things should be run, but she had nothing to run but our household. Even there, small minds bugged her; she was smarter than the people who designed the things she had to use all day for the length of her life. 27

"Look," she said. "Whoever designed this corkscrew never used one. Why would anyone sell it without trying it out?" So she invented a better one. She showed me a drawing of it. The spirit of American enterprise never faded in Mother. If capitalizing and tooling up had been as interesting as theorizing and thinking up, she would have fired up a new factory every week, and chaired several hundred corporations. 28

"It grieves me," she would say, "it grieves my heart," that the company that made one superior product packaged it poorly, or took the wrong tack in its advertising. She knew, as she held the thing mournfully in her two hands, that she'd never find another. She was right. We children wholly sympathized, and so did Father; what could she do, what could anyone do, about it? She was Samson in chains. She paced. 29

She didn't like the taste of stamps so she didn't lick stamps; she licked the corner of the envelope instead. She glued sandpaper to the sides of kitchen drawers, and under kitchen cabinets, so she always had a handy place to strike a match. She designed, and hounded workmen to build against all norms, doubly wide kitchen counters and elevated bathroom sinks. To splint a finger, she stuck it in a lightweight cigar tube. Conversely, to protect a pack of cigarettes, 30 she carried it in a Band-Aid box. She drew plans for an over-the-finger toothbrush for babies, an oven rack that slid up and down, and—the family favorite—Lendalarm. Lendalarm was a beeper you attached to books (or tools) you loaned friends. After ten days, the beeper sounded. Only the rightful owner could silence it.

She repeatedly reminded us of P. T. Barnum's dictum: 31 You could sell anything to anybody if you marketed it right. The adman who thought of making Americans believe they needed underarm deodorant was a visionary. So, too, was the hero who made a success of a new product, Ivory soap. The executives were horrified, Mother told me, that a cake of this stuff floated. Soap wasn't supposed to float. Anyone would be able to tell it was mostly whipped-up air. Then some inspired adman made a leap: Advertise that it floats. Flaunt it. The rest is history.

She respected the rare few who broke through to new 32 ways. "Look," she'd say, "here's an intelligent apron." She called upon us to admire intelligent control knobs and intelligent pan handles, intelligent andirons and picture frames and knife sharpeners. She questioned everything, every pair of scissors, every knitting needle, gardening glove, tape dispenser. Hers was a restless mental vigor that just about ignited the dumb household objects with its force.

Torpid conformity was a kind of sin; it was stupidity 33 itself, the mighty stream against which Mother would never cease to struggle. If you held no minority opinions, or if you failed to risk total ostracism for them daily, the world would be a better place without you.

Always I heard Mother's emotional voice asking Amy 34 and me the same few questions: Is that your own idea? Or somebody else's? "*Giant* is a good movie," I pronounced to the family at dinner. "Oh, really?" Mother warmed to these occasions. She all but rolled up her sleeves. She knew I hadn't seen it. "Is that your considered opinion?"

She herself held many unpopular, even fantastic, posi- 35 tions. She was scathingly sarcastic about the McCarthy hearings while they took place, right on our living-room television; she frantically opposed Father's wait-and-see calm. "We don't know enough about it," he said. "I do," she said. "I know all I need to know."

She asserted, against all opposition, that people who 36
lived in trailer parks were not bad but simply poor, and had
as much right to settle on beautiful land, such as rural
Ligonier, Pennsylvania, as did the oldest of families in the
finest of hidden houses. Therefore, the people who owned
trailer parks, and sought zoning changes to permit trailer
parks, needed our help. Her profound belief that the country-
club pool sweeper was a person, and that the department-
store saleslady, the bus driver, telephone operator, and
house-painter were people, and even in groups the steel-
workers who carried pickets and the Christmas shoppers who
clogged intersections were people—this was a conviction
common enough in democratic Pittsburgh, but not altogether common among our friends' parents, or even, perhaps,
among our parents' friends.

Opposition emboldened Mother, and she would take 37
on anybody on any issue—the chairman of the board, at a
cocktail party, on the current strike; she would fly at him in a
flurry of passion, as a songbird selflessly attacks a big hawk.

"Eisenhower's going to win," I announced after school. 38
She lowered her magazine and looked me in the eyes: "How
do you know?" I was doomed. It was fatal to say, "Everyone
says so." We all knew well what happened. "Do you consult
this Everyone before you make your decisions? What if
Everyone decided to round up all the Jews?" Mother knew
there was no danger of cowing me. She simply tried to keep
us all awake. And in fact it was always clear to Amy and me,
and to Molly when she grew old enough to listen, that if our
classmates came to cruelty, just as much as if the neighborhood or the nation came to madness, we were expected to
take, and would be each separately capable of taking, a stand.

Checking Your Understanding

1. Explain how the mother's behavior made Dillard able to take a stand. How did her mother encourage critical thinking and independence?
2. How do you think Dillard feels about her mother now? What makes you think so?

Examining Rhetorical Strategies

1. Which of the anecdotes in the essay do you find most amusing or outrageous? Why? What techniques is Dillard using to create the humor in this section?

2. In what way do you feel Dillard has been influenced by her mother? How do her mother's characteristics or lessons show up in Dillard's writing style?

3. We all have had funny things happen to us—bizarre events or coincidences, hysterical mishaps, funny surprises. Following Dillard's example, recreate a funny or outrageous moment from your life. Make it clear what aspect of your character your description is illustrating.

NOT POOR, JUST BROKE

Dick Gregory

Prereading Journal

Look at the title of the essay. What would be the difference between telling someone you were "poor" and saying that you were "just broke?" How would it change that person's image of you?

Background

Dick Gregory is a comedian and a political activist. In this excerpt from his autobiography, *Nigger*, published in 1964, Gregory, like Dillard, creates a portrait of his mother through a series of brief stories he remembers about her. Through this portrait, he explains what it was like to grow up poor and black in a time of segregation.

During Reading

Note the contrasts between Momma's life with the white folks and Momma's life with her own children.

Reading Selection

Like of lot of Negro kids, we never would have made it 1 without our Momma. When there was no fatback to go with the beans, no socks to go with the shoes, no hope to go with tomorrow, she'd smile and say: "We ain't poor, we're just broke." Poor is a state of mind you never grow out of, but being broke is just a temporary condition. She always had a big smile, even when her legs and feet swelled from high blood pressure and she collapsed across the table with sugar diabetes. You have to smile twenty-four hours a day, Momma would say. If you walk through life showing the aggravation you've gone through, people will feel sorry for you, and they'll never respect you. She taught us that man has two ways out in life—laughing or crying. There's more hope in laughing. A man can fall down the stairs and lie there in such pain and horror that his own wife will collapse and faint at the sight. But if he can just hold back his pain for a minute she might be able to collect herself and call the doctor. It might mean the difference between his living to laugh again or dying there on the spot.

So you laugh, so you smile. Once a month the big gray 2 relief truck would pull up in front of our house and Momma would flash that big smile and stretch out her hands. "Who else you know in this neighborhood gets this kind of service?" And we could all feel proud when the neighbors, folks who weren't on relief, folks who had Daddies in their houses, would come by the back porch for some of those hundred pounds of potatoes, for some sugar and flour and salty fish. We'd stand out there on the back porch and hand out the food like we were in charge of helping poor people, and then we'd take the food they brought us in return.

And Momma came home one hot summer day and 3 found we'd been evicted, thrown out into the streetcar zone with all our orange-crate chairs and secondhand lamps. She flashed that big smile and dried our tears and bought some penny Kool-Aid. We stood out there and sold drinks to thirsty people coming off the streetcar, and we thought nobody knew we were kicked out—figured they thought we *wanted* to be there. And Momma went off to talk the landlord into letting us back in on credit.

But I wonder about my Momma sometimes, and all the 4 other Negro mothers who got up at 6 A.M. to go to the white man's house with sacks over their shoes because it was so wet and cold. I wonder how they made it. They worked very hard for the man, they made his breakfast and they scrubbed his floors and they diapered his babies. They didn't have too much time for us.

I wonder about my Momma, who walked out of a white 5 woman's clean house at midnight and came back to her own where the lights had been out for three months, and the pipes were frozen and the wind came in through the cracks. She'd have to make deals with the rats: leave some food out for them so they wouldn't gnaw on the doors or bite the babies. The roaches, they were just like part of the family.

I wonder how she felt telling those white kids she took 6 care of to brush their teeth after they ate, to wash their hands after they peed. She could never tell her own kids because there wasn't soap or water back home.

I wonder how my Momma felt when we came home 7
from school with a list of vitamins and pills and cod liver oil
the school nurse said we had to have. Momma would cry all
night, and then go out and spend most of the rent money for
pills. A week later, the white man would come for his eighteen
dollars rent and Momma would plead with him to wait until
tomorrow. She had lost her pocketbook. The relief check was
coming. The white folks had some money for her. Tomorrow.
I'd be hiding in the coal closet because there was only supposed to be two kids in the flat, and I could hear the rent man
curse my Momma and call her a liar. And when he finally went
away, Momma put the sacks on her shoes and went off to the
rich white folk's house to dress the rich white kids so their
mother could take them to a special baby doctor.

Momma had to take us to Homer G. Phillips, the free 8
hospital, the city hospital for Negroes. We'd stand on line
and wait for hours, smiling and Uncle Tomming every time a
doctor or a nurse passed by. We'd feel good when one of
them smiled back and didn't look at us as though we were
dirty and had no right coming down there. All the doctors
and nurses at Homer G. Phillips were Negro, too.

I remember one time when a doctor in white walked up 9
and said: "What's wrong with him?" as if he didn't believe that
anything was.

Momma looked at me and looked at him and shook her 10
head. "I sure don't know, Doctor, but he cried all night long.
Held his stomach."

"Bring him in and get his damned clothes off." 11

I was so mad the way he was talking to my Momma that 12
I bit down too hard on the thermometer. It broke in my
mouth. The doctor slapped me across the face.

"Both of you go stand in the back of the line and wait 13
your turn."

My Momma had to say: "I'm sorry, Doctor," and go to 14
the back of the line. She had five other kids at home and she
never knew when she'd have to bring another down to the
City Hospital.

And those rich white folks Momma was so proud of. 15
She'd sit around with the other women and they'd talk about
how good their white folks were. They'd lie about how rich
they were, what nice parties they gave, what good clothes they

wore. And how they were going to be remembered in their white folks' wills. The next morning the white lady would say: "We're going on vacation for two months, Lucille, we won't be needing you until we get back." Damn. Two-month vacation without pay.

I wonder how my Momma stayed so good and beautiful   16
in her soul when she worked seven days a week on swollen legs and feet, how she kept teaching us to smile and laugh when the house was dark and cold and she never knew when one of her hungry kids was going to ask about Daddy.

I wonder how she kept from teaching us hate when the   17
social worker came around. She was a nasty bitch with a pinched face who said: "We have reason to suspect you are working, Miss Gregory, and you can be sure I'm going to check on you. We don't stand for welfare cheaters."

Momma, a welfare cheater. A criminal who couldn't   18
stand to see her kids go hungry, or grow up in slums and end up mugging people in dark corners. I guess the system didn't want her to get off relief, the way it kept sending social workers around to be sure Momma wasn't trying to make things better.

I remember how that social worker would poke around   19
the house, wrinkling her nose at the coal dust on the chilly linoleum floor, shaking her head at the bugs crawling over the dirty dishes in the sink. My Momma would have to stand there and make like she was too lazy to keep her own house clean. She could never let on that she spent all day cleaning another woman's house for two dollars and carfare. She would have to follow that nasty bitch around those drafty three rooms, keeping her fingers crossed that the telephone hidden in the closet wouldn't ring. Welfare cases weren't supposed to have telephones.

But Momma figured that some day the Gregory kids   20
were going to get off North Taylor Street and into a world where they would have to compete with kids who grew up with telephones in their houses. She didn't want us to be at a disadvantage. She couldn't explain that to the social worker. And she couldn't explain that while she was out spoon-feeding somebody else's kids, she was worrying about her own kids, that she could rest her mind by picking up the telephone and calling us—to find out if we had bread for

our baloney or baloney for our bread, to see if any of us had gotten run over by the streetcar while we played in the gutter, to make sure the house hadn't burnt down from the papers and magazines we stuffed in the stove when the coal ran out.

But sometimes when she called there would be no 21 answer. Home was a place to be only when all other places were closed.

Checking Your Understanding

1. Do two brief character descriptions or drawings of Momma. Base one on how you feel she would look at home with her children and the other on how you feel she would look at the white folks' house. Support your description with evidence based on the contrasts you noted while you read.

2. Momma is trying to raise her children in the best way she knows how. Describe that way. What are Momma's values? What does she work for and how does she want her children to turn out? What sacrifices does she make to achieve her goals?

3. Explain Gregory's last line. Why was home a "place to be only when all other places were closed?" How do you think Gregory's Momma would feel about that statement?

Examining Rhetorical Strategies

1. Gregory provides many contrasts between the white folks' lives and his own. Assuming the role of the "white lady" who employed Momma, explain in her *voice* and from her point of view what Momma's two lives are like.

2. How would you describe the tone of voice Gregory uses in this essay? How does that tone support Gregory's message? Contrast this tone with that of Dillard's in describing her mother. How do the tones of these two authors reflect their experiences, their main points, and their different social backgrounds?

WELCOME TO ST. PAUL'S

Lorene Cary

Prereading Journal

Try to remember what was it like the first time you left home—to visit relatives on your own, for example—or a time when you had to move. Describe what it felt like to say good-bye to your family or friends.

Background

This *narrative* essay is from Cary's book *Black Ice* in which she describes her life at St. Paul's, an elite private prep school. In it she describes many events that reflect a typical adolescent girlhood, but she also captures the unique experience of a young African-American woman trying to find her way in an environment which has not yet shed its all-male, all-white history. This scene describes Cary's arrival on campus with her parents.

During Reading

Keep a list of your impressions about this school from the way Cary describes the setting. Also keep in mind the other elements of a narrative in this story: plot, significance, and audience involvement.

Reading Selection

My family and I stood in the Rectory just a year and 1
a half after Lee's first tea. Unlike her, I was armed with the experience of a proper, on-campus interview, and I was escorted by attractive young parents and a cuddly kid sister. Unlike Ed Shockley, I was not afraid that the white boys were going to catch me alone in the woods one night and beat me up. But for the first time, I had a whiff, as subtle as the scent of the old books that lined the wall, of my utter aloneness in this new world. I reached into myself for the head-to-the-side, hands-on-hips cockiness that had brought me here and found just enough of it to keep me going.

My dormitory was around the corner from the Rectory, 2
over a bridge and across the road from the library. Inside, just
off the common room, steps led to the open doorway of the
housemaster. He, too, was on hand to greet us.

I wasn't sure about Mr. Hawley. He had a round face 3
whose top half was nearly bald and whose bottom half was
covered over with a full, tweed-colored beard. Between the
top and bottom halves a pair of glasses perched on a small
nose and caught the light. He made a funny face when he
spied my sister: "And look what you brought along! We've got
a couple of those creatures running around somewhere. I'll
see if they've been run over yet by some station wagon gone
berserk."

I was later to learn that all the intelligence and will, all 4
the imagination and mischief in that face was revealed in the
pale eyes behind the glasses, but on this first meeting, I could
only bring myself to concentrate on the beard and the Kriss
Kringle mouth.

Mr. Hawley, it turned out, had family in Philadelphia, so 5
we talked about the city, and my parents described for him
just exactly where we lived.

Like other St. Paul's buildings, the Hawleys' house had 6
alcoves, staircases, and a courtyard, that presented to me a
facade of impenetrable, almost European, privacy. The
housemaster's home was directly accessible from the dormitory, but only by going from the vestibule into the common
room, then up stairs, through a heavy wooden door, into a
hallway, and another, inner door. Once in the living room, I
could see through the windows that we were across the street
from the gray granite library, but I would not have known it
had the drapes been pulled. The architecture that I so
admired from the outside did not yield itself up to me from
within as I had expected. I now felt disconcerted, as I had in
the Rectory. Mr. Hawley wanted to know just how far one
would drive along Baltimore Pike to get to Yeadon, and I,
standing in his living room, had no idea where his kitchen
might be.

Mrs. Hawley, a short, soft-spoken woman, appeared 7
from the rear hallway. Like her husband, she said ironic
things, but more gently. Startlingly blond children came with
her, one peeking from behind her skirt.

Mr. Hawley directed us to my room and showed my 8
father where to park by the back door so that we could
unload more handily. We carried my things up from a base-
ment entrance. Doors whooshed open and closed as other
girls and their families came and went, and the halls echoed
with the sounds of mothers' heels.

My room faced east. In the afternoon it seemed dull 9
and empty and dark.

"This'll be lovely when you get it all fixed up," my moth- 10
er said, by which I assumed that it looked dull to her, too.

Fine dust had settled contentedly over the sturdy oak 11
bureau and cloudy mirror, over the charming, squat little oak
desk and chair and in the corners of the closet. White people, as we said, were not personally fastidious (any black
woman who'd ever been a maid could tell you that, and some
did, in appalling detail, so I'd heard stories). I was determined to give the place a good wash.

The casement windows matched those elsewhere on 12
campus. My father opened one, tightened the wing nut to
hold the sash in place, and stood looking out into the mead-
ow. Then he peeked into the room next door, which was still
empty, and recalled how, at Lincoln University, the first students to arrive scavenged the best furniture in the dormitory.
"If there's any furniture you don't like, better speak now," he
joked. "I guess you wouldn't want to do that here."

I checked the room next door, and pronounced, with 13
laughter but not conviction, that I'd gotten a fair bargain.

The room seemed crowded with all of us about. I found 14
myself chattering on, very gaily, about where I would put my
things. What with the windows at one end, the narrow bed
against one wall, the bureau, the desk, the radiator, the closet, the door leading into the next room, the door leading in,
and the economy of my possessions, there were few options,
realistically, for interior design.

Still, I could not stop buzzing. So long as we stood 15
crowded together in the room, my sister jumping on the
naked mattress, my mother wondering about smoking a cig-
arette, my father by the open window clenching his jaw and
rubbing the back of his neck, and me burbling and babbling
as if words were British soldiers marching in pointless
columns, bright and gay, with flags and bright brass buttons

on crimson-colored breasts, on and on and on into battle; so long as we had nothing to do except to wait for the next thing to do; so long as the intolerable closeness remained and the intolerable separation loomed to be made, so long would this adrenaline rush through me, anarchic, atavistic, compelling.

16 Outside the move-in continued. Convinced that I was missing yet another ritual of initiation, I ran down the hall to check the bulletin board. As I stood reading, an Asian boy propelled himself into the vestibule. He introduced himself without smiling and asked me my name. Then, addressing me by the name I gave, he asked whether or not I lived in Simpson House.

17 "Listen," he said. "There's a girl upstairs. She's just moved in. Her name is Fumiko, and she's from Japan. She can hardly speak any English at all. She understands a lot, but she really needs someone to go and make her feel welcome."

18 "Do you speak Japanese?"

19 "Of course not." (He was Chinese-American.) He appeared to be reevaluating me. "Look, is anyone else around?"

20 "I don't know. I've just arrived myself."

21 "Well, welcome! Look, we've been helping her, but she needs a girl in her own house, and guys can't come in. Maybe you can tell some of the other girls. Really, she's only just come to the country."

22 Reluctantly, I agreed. I went to the room on the second floor that the boy had described, and found her. I introduced myself. We tried hard to pronounce each other's names, and we laughed at our mistakes. Fumiko was taller than I. She kept suppressing bows. We agreed to meet again later.

23 I returned to my family much calmer than I'd left, and I told them about my new friend. Now my mother seemed agitated. Just before we left for dinner, she began to tell me what items of clothing should go into which drawer.

24 "You always put underwear in the top. See, it's the shallowest one. Big, bulky things like sweaters and jeans go down at the bottom. But, now, please don't just jam your things in. I don't want you walking around here with stuff that's all jerked up."

25 "I know where things go."

"Listen. Skirts, your good pants, all that stuff needs to   26
be hung up. Let's see how this is packed." My mother
unzipped one of the suitcases on the bed. "You know, maybe
you might want us to take this big one home. I can't see
where you have room to store it."

I watched my mother lift layers of underwear delicately   27
from their berths. Her hands, precise, familiar, called up in
me a frenzy of possession. "I've got all night to unpack," I
said. "Please don't. I should do that."

"I'll just help you get started. Lord, I hope you don't   28
start putting together any of those crazy outfits you concoct
at home. I know you think that stuff looks cute, but it doesn't.
You didn't pack any of those fishnet stockings, I hope." Mama
selected a drawer for panties and one for bras and slips. I'd
brought a girdle—hers, of course—that was hidden in the
next layer.

"I *really* want to do that myself."   29

"I'm not taking anything away from you." Her voice   30
rose with maternal indignation.

"Let the child do it herself," my father said.   31

I knew that they were going to fight. It would be a silent   32
fight, because we were, even in this room, in public, so long as
we were on school grounds. I did not see how we would avoid it.
We'd been cooped up together, as my parents called it, all day.

Then my mother laughed. "All right, all right, I was just   33
getting you started," she said. "You'd think I was doing something wrong."

We left for dinner, and I closed my door.   34

Checking Your Understanding

1. What does Cary mean when she says "so long as the intolerable
    closeness remained and the intolerable separation loomed to be
    made, so long would this adrenalin rush through me?" How does
    this feeling compare to the ones you described in your journal
    about your first leaving?

2. What role does Fumiko serve in this story? What effect does she have
    on Cary's emotional state? What events or people helped you to set-
    tle into the new environment you described in your prereading?

Examining Rhetorical Strategies

1. Describe this scene either from the mother's or the father's *point of
    view*. What are they thinking? How are they feeling as they settle
    their daughter into her new home?

2. As a scholarship student, Cary is very comfortable in the academic
    world. But St. Paul's is a far cry from the schools of Philadelphia
    where she was raised. Look at the way in which she describes the set-
    ting and list words Cary uses to emphasize this difference between
    her old and new life.

CONFESSIONS OF AN EX-CHEERLEADER

Louise Bernikow

Prereading Journal

Discuss a group you were part of as a teenager that has had a lasting effect on you. The group might have revolved around some activity—a sports team or a community theater group. Or it might have been a group that helped shape your character and personality or that helped you discover an ability or talent you didn't know you had or that helped you survive the often difficult social situations teens face. Explain both the group and how you think it has affected you.

Background

This *reflective* essay appeared in the 1973 issue of *Ms.* magazine. Bernikow is reflecting on her high school days in the late 1950s: how she won her place among the school's elite—the cheerleading squad—and the effect it had on her, an effect she still feels sixteen years later. Notice how her reflections on her own life are shared by others who also played "the only game in town."

During Reading

While you read, keep track of how Bernikow makes herself into a cheerleader.

Reading Selection

The trick is to be up in the air with a big Ipana smile on 1
your face, touching the heels of your saddle shoes to the back of your head, bending your elbows as close as you can get them behind you. This makes your short red dress rise, revealing a quick glimpse of thigh and underpants. It also makes your 16-year-old tits, aided and abetted by stuffings of cotton or the professional padding of Maidenform, stick far out.

I am doing this of my own free will on a spring after- 2
noon in Madison Square Garden. The year is 1957, halfway between my sixteenth and seventeenth birthdays. I have

aimed at, plotted and waited for this moment. It is living up to my expectations. The Garden is crowded. This is the play-off game for the New York City championships: Forest Hills against Boys High.

The old Madison Square Garden smells like a locker 3 room, which is what makes it such a triumph that I find myself the center of attention in it. I am a star at last on male turf. There are 10 of us at halftime in the middle of the wooden floor with all the lights out except for the spotlight shining on us. I turn my face upward into the smell of sweat, into the applause and whistles dropping like confetti from the tiers of spectator seats above me.

Tip of my head to Maidenform padding to saddle- 4 shoed toes, dizzy with ecstasy, I go into the first cheer.

WE GOT THE T-E-A-M   5

I shake my shoulders and wiggle my ass.   6

IT'S ON THE B-E-A-M   7

I do some chorus-girl high-kicking, wiggle and shake a 8 little faster, and smile my smile a little bigger.

COME ON, FOREST HILLS, SKIN 'EM ALIVE!   9

Up in the air, head back, back arched, trembling all 10 over. I hit the ground squarely on my feet and run off to the sound of thunderous applause. The team emerges for the second half.

I am a cheerleader.   11

Forest Hills is defeated. I am sitting in the ladies' room, 12 having changed the short red dress for a gray flannel skirt and button-down pinstripe shirt. The Garden is dark and silent. The cheerleaders are dark and silent, too. We are all quietly weeping. When we leave the ladies' room to meet the team in the corridor, each of us embraces each of them. I move from one boy to another, despondently hugging. No funeral has brought more grief.

On the way home, I see the *Daily News* centerfold pho- 13 tograph of the Forest Hills cheerleaders. We are lined up like chorus girls, grinning, shoulders back. I feel as though I am looking at faded glory. When I get home, the telephone is ringing. My mother answers and says it is for me. I can tell from her face that she does not recognize the voice, and she hovers near my shoulder, monitoring me.

"Hello?"   14

There is no sound on the other end, then there is heavy   15
breathing, then faster huffing and puffing. I am terrified. I
hang up.

"Who was that?"   16

"No one."   17

And not until 16 years later do I understand the con-   18
nection: obscene phone calls are the other side of the cheerleader glory.

Glory. I was hell-bent on glory when I started high   19
school. On my awkward first day, I saw that cheerleaders were
the queens of the school, and I determined to become one.

Forest Hills was a "rich" neighborhood, but not every-   20
one at the high school was rich. I wasn't. In fact, I didn't live
in Forest Hills at all, but in Kew Gardens Hills, on the other
side of the tracks. I always felt like an outsider. When I
became a cheerleader, every time I put on that red dress and
went out there to jump and shout, every time I looked at the
gold megaphone on my charm bracelet and every time I
walked through the corridors of the school knowing fresh-
men and sophomores were whispering and pointing with
envy, I thought that I had managed, by hook and by crook, to
wiggle my way into the ruling class.

Methodical, ruthless, ambitious, and manipulative, I   21
studied the way "in" and discovered that, since cheerleaders
chose their replacements, I had to learn how to charm
women. Everything else in my life had depended on charming men and I, the original all-time Daddy's Little Girl, had
that one down pat; but women?

Sororities were the key. Although they were officially   22
outlawed, sororities ran things. The school cafeteria had special tables by custom for each sorority. As a sophomore, I
would walk by those tables on my way to the nonspecial area
where nobodies like me downed egg salad and Oreo cookies.
I studied the sorority girls.

At night, I stood before the mirror "doing" my hair as I   23
had seen it on the girls at those tables. I studied *Mademoiselle*
and *Glamour*, full of girls who looked like cheerleaders, and
there I discovered that fuzzy hair was my problem. Fuzzy
Jewish hair. The girls in *Mademoiselle* had sleek blonde hair.
Not me. The most popular cheerleaders at Forest Hills had
sleek blonde hair. Not me.

I pin-curled as per instructions, every night, half going 24
left and half going right. Still, in the morning, I combed it
out to find kinks and fuzz. Somehow, in spite of it, I was
"rushed" by sororities and, in blue serge Bermuda shorts and
pink knee socks, was accepted.

I discovered how you charm women: you imitate them. 25

From Nora I picked up the names of painters and 26
"acquired culture"; from Ellen I got my taste in plaid pleated
skirts; from Arlene I saw how to bite my lower lip cutely. I was
a sorority girl. I felt myself on shaky ground, always, but I
hung in there, selling bananas on the streets of Manhattan as
a "pledge," making the carfare back to Forest Hills where I
joined my "sisters" who had dumped me off without a penny.
We had an initiation ceremony; the fraternity boys came over
afterward.

Two sorority sisters were cheerleaders. When "tryouts" 27
time came, they taught the cheers to those of us who were
going to try. We practiced all the time. I did cheers in my
sleep and on the bus and in the shower. My family went nuts
from the "Yea, Team" thundering from my bedroom.

"I wanna use the bathroom," my brother pounded at 28
the door.

"Forest Hills—Forest Hills—THAT'S WHO!" I 29
screamed from within, my teeth all freshly Ipana white.

If I made cheerleaders, my mother would stop clicking 30
the hall light off and on when I came home from a date and
"lingered" in the hall.

If I made cheerleaders, boys would arrive in rows and 31
rows bearing tennis rackets, basketballs, baseball gloves, and
fencing masks to lay in tribute at my feet.

If I made cheerleaders, Jimmy Dean and Marlon 32
Brando would fall in love with me.

If I made cheerleaders, my hair would be straight. 33

Many tried; few were chosen. A jury of gym teachers 34
and cheerleaders watched as we, with numbers on our backs,
went through the cheers. I was Number Five. Something of
the Miss America pageant in all this and something of the
dance marathon. Girls were tapped on the shoulder and
asked to leave the floor.

What were the criteria? I have gone over the old pho- 35
tographs in vain. They do not say. It was not "looks," for even by

fifties standards, the cheerleaders were not the best-looking
girls. My own photograph shows an ordinary middle-class
Jewish girl. Her hair is short and flipped-up, with bangs. Her
large nose has a bump on it. (I resisted the nose-job binge my
friends went on. I have no idea where I got the courage.) She
is wearing dark-red lipstick and her eyebrows are heavily lined.
She looks older in the high school yearbook than she does now.

It wasn't looks that made a cheerleader, but "personali-   36
ty" or a certain kind of energy. Something called aggressive-
ness. Or bitchiness. Or pep.

Pep is what happened in American history before *vigah*,   37
but it only applied to females. Pep was cheerfulness. It mys-
teriously resided in the Ipana smile. "Weird" or "eccentric"
girls, moody girls or troublemaking girls did not have pep.
We who had it became cheerleaders, committing ourselves to
a season of steady pep, bouncy activity, and good clean dis-
positions.

I do.   38

We played some humid swimming meets in Far   39
Rockaway and Flushing, tottering at the edge of the pool and
getting our hair all fuzzy, but basketball was the main attrac-
tion. (There was no football. Rumor said a boy had once
been killed on the field and the sport discontinued.)
Cheerleaders as a group were married to the basketball team
as a group. We played wife.

Our job was to support the team. We were the decora-   40
tive touches in the gyms they played. We had some "prestige"
in the city because the team was good that year. They had a
little of our prestige rub off on them, too, for Forest Hills was
known for the good-looking stuck-up bitches there. We
learned to cater to the boys' moods, not to talk to Gary after
he had a bad game (he would glower and shake us off), and
yet to *be* there when he or Stanley or Steve came out of the
locker room all showered and handsome. We were there for
them always, peppy and smiling. Boys had acceptable temper
tantrums on the court, but cheerleaders never did. We were
expected to be consistently "happy," like the Rockettes at
Radio City Music Hall.

We were the best athletic supporters that ever lived.   41

We paired off, cheerleader and basketball player, like a   42
socialite wife and corporation executive, leading lady and

leading man. My social life was defined by my "status." I only went out with jocks. "Who's *he*?" or "What a creep!" applied to boys who wore desert boots or girls who were "brains." We knew kids "like us" in other middle-class ghettos in the city, and we stayed away from the Greek and Italian kids in our school, from "rocks" like Howie and Dominic who played cards and drank and "laid girls," and from girls like Carole and Anita whom we called "hitter chicks" and who, we whispered, went all the way.

Cheerleaders had a reputation for chastity. No one ever 43 said it, but we all understood it. On top of the general fifties hangups about sex, cheerleaders had a special role to play. Vestal virgins in the rites of puberty. Jewish madonnas.

Half the time, in real "civilian" life, I had to keep 44 pulling those gray flannel skirts down, making sure "nothing showed," keeping my legs crossed. I would have been incarcerated on the spot by my mother if, one morning, I refused to layer the top of my body with a bra and all its padding followed by a slip followed by a blouse. Even if I were to evade Mother, my peers would have condemned me as a "slut" if I appeared less dressed.

The other half the time, as a cheerleader, I dropped a 45 skimpy red costume over only bra and panties and got out there in the middle of a gym full of screaming spectators to wiggle my hips all over the place.

What does it do to the mind of a 16-year-old girl to be 46 Marilyn Monroe one moment and Little Goody Two-Shoes the next? I don't know, but it sure wasn't sane.

For weeks before we went, the word was whispered from 47 ear to ear among us: *Jamaica.*

Jamaica High School was the first "away" game we went 48 to in my senior year. The word was full of terror. Jamaica had black kids. Forest Hills High School had been redistricted every year and there were *no* blacks in the school. Aside from the rocks and hitter chicks, nearly everyone was white, middle class, and Jewish. We held mirrors up to each other and told each other we were very heavenly and the whole world was like us, except we never really believed it. We called Manhattan "New York" or "The City." It was as far away and glamorous to us as it was to Clarence in Peoria or Pat in Kansas. Our mothers wouldn't let us go there.

I confess: when I left the Forest Hills ghetto for the first 49
"away" game, I, Princess of the Pom-Poms, Our Lady of the
Saddle Shoes, Culture Queen, carried with me, hidden in my
purse, a menacing kitchen knife. For protection.

Every time I say "sure" when I mean "no," every time I 50
smile brightly when I'm exploding with rage, every time I imagine my man's achievement is my own, I know the cheerleader
never really died. I feel her shaking her ass inside me and I hear
her breathless, girlish voice mutter "T-E-A-M, Yea, Team."

God knows, I tried hard to kill her. Forest Hills had a 51
history of sending its red-skirted stars bouncing off for the
big league at Cornell, and it looked for a few months just
before I turned 17 as though I might follow their saddle-
shoed footsteps, but something happened. I went to Barnard
College instead.

Barnard was another kind of game, requiring a differ- 52
ent kind of coin to play. No points there for having been a
cheerleader. It was no longer a high-priced commodity, but
now a social deficit. I, alert to the winds of change and being
a good mimic, buried my cheerleader past. Fast.

"What did you do in high school?"   53
"I wrote poetry."   54
"I was in the theater."   55
"I listened to jazz."   56
And the cheerleader stayed buried until recently, when 57
I had a series of strange revelations:

Beautiful, exotic Janet, painter-poet, was a cheerleader
in Connecticut.

Acid-freak Nina, unwed hippie mother, was a cheerleader in Ohio.

Elegant Susan, theatrical and literary, was a cheerleader
in Philadelphia.

Shaggy Bob, radical lawyer, was a basketball player at
Midwood.

Junk dealer Joe was on the Bayside team.

I am not alone.

It *was* the only game in town for middle-class kids in the
American fifties.

The world is full of us.

T-E-A-M.

Yea, Team!

Checking Your Understanding

1. What is Bernikow confessing? What is the main point of her piece? Why do you think she feels the desire to confess?

2. How does the way Bernikow was shaped by her peers compare to the way you were influenced by your group? Why did she try to kill the cheerleader she had taken such pains to create? Did you ever try to free yourself of the influence of your group?

3. Reread paragraph 50 which begins "Every time I say 'sure' when I mean 'no,' . . . " Explain what Bernikow is trying to say about herself in this passage. Do you think that men in the fifties were taught to say "sure" when they meant "no?"

Examining Rhetorical Strategies

1. Map out the differences between Bernikow's life as a cheerleader and what she calls her "civilian" life. Make sure that your map includes the details she uses in the essay to characterize each of her lives.

2. Identify the tone of this essay. What kind of voice is coming through in this piece? How does this voice match Bernikow's message?

THE EYES OF FEAR

Laurence Shames

Prereading Journal

Several recent books have explored the idea that many people, especially men, are afraid of intimacy. Explain what the word "intimacy" means to you and what an intimate relationship would entail. Why might this kind of relationship be frightening for some people?

Background

Shames is a free-lance writer. This *reflective* essay first appeared in the "Ethics" column in *Esquire* in 1982, a magazine which has a predominantly male professional readership. Shames explores the idea of "strength" and what kinds of tests in life really prove "what we're made of."

During Reading

Shames uses Big Brother's method of control from George Orwell's *1984* to begin and end this piece. Keep track of what he is saying about the book and then determine how this relates to Arty's situation.

Reading Selection

Remember how they did it in *1984?*   1

They studied you until they'd learned your deepest   2
fear—rats, bats, darkness, whatever—and then they used that fear to turn you. The premise was that while human beings might be expected to behave with some degree of dignity and moral sense under normal circumstances, they'd crumble when confronted with their personal demons; courage and resolve would slip away, and people would become abject, malleable, capable of any sort of betrayal.

A sobering proposition—but one that, in Orwell's night-   3
mare world, proved only too accurate. How about in our world?

We, too, occasionally have our worst fears thrown in our   4
face, are confronted with situations in which the choice is between staring down our private bogeymen and skulking

away in safe but ignoble retreat. True, most of us will never have to deal with the primordial horror of having rodents nibble at us, but we will face other fears: the fear of intimacy, which, for many of us, is truly scarring and which can lead us to be dishonest, unfair, and self-defeating in our relationships; the fear of taking an uncharted course in a career—a fear that can turn us into morally hollow yes-men or cause us to be untrue to our real ambitions; and, in every aspect of our lives, the basic fear of change—a timidness about growth and risk that, in the long haul, can make us bitter, disappointed, and mean.

Consider, for example, the fear of intimacy. Intimacy 5 offers itself as one of life's great comforts, but for all its tender appeal, many of us find it terrifying. And not without reason: intimacy means reckless self-exposure, a bold baring of the soft white underbelly, an offering of the jugular. It demands more trust than many of us grow up believing the world deserves. Yet few of us choose to be hermits or celibates; the difficulty, then, is in reconciling our need for closeness with our fear of it. And, ethically, the danger is that we may go halfway, then balk, inevitably hurting people in the process, deceiving them without intending to, being helplessly dishonest to others because we're being untrue to ourselves.

In college I hung around with a group of guys for 6 whom meeting women was a major preoccupation. Some of us liked having one girlfriend at a time, in a sort of puppy-love version of what has come to be known as serial monogamy. Others preferred to juggle several entanglements at once, with results that ranged from the comical to the cruel. Then there was this fellow I'll call Arty. Arty had a style all his own. Forward, eccentric, and dapper, he insinuated himself into the favor of more young ladies than any of us could win. Yet he never seemed the slightest bit entangled. He was the consummate hit-and-run man, as adept at ending things as at starting them.

For a while, of course, this capacity of his impressed 7 the rest of us no end. Compared with the blistering pace of Arty's escapades, our humble efforts seemed sluggish and mundane. Gradually, however, even to us die-hard adolescents, it became clear that the fellow had a problem. His fear of getting close to women was so pronounced that it led him to all sorts of caddish behavior. Whatever his intentions may have been, he ended up misleading every woman he met, and he left behind, if not exactly a string of broken hearts, then certainly a number of ladies who had good reason to feel baffled, angry, and used. Arty was a classic case of a guy letting himself be bullied into shabbiness by his fears, not even truly enjoying his encounters because they were laced with so much anxiety. After a while, the rest of us didn't know whom to feel sorrier for—the women who crossed Arty's path, or Arty himself. *They* were victimized by Arty's fear only once; *he* was doomed to repeat the pattern again and again.

After college, some of us old friends stayed in touch, 8 staging informal reunions at various taverns in the cities where we'd ended up. True to form, we'd still discuss, among other things, our dealings with women, but the emphasis was different now. In spite of ourselves, we were getting serious. We were at the age when the question of marriage was beginning to bear down on us with the slow portentousness of a distant but oncoming train. We'd flirt with the subject and sometimes make goading conjectures about who would be the first to take the plunge. There was no consensus on this point; as to who would be the *last,* however, there was general and confident agreement.

We were wrong, of course. Arty was the first of us to 9 wed. To me, this was more than a surprise; it represented a moral victory of a high order.

I still remember when he told me of his plans. The rev- 10 elation literally took my breath away. This was *Arty*—the guy so scared of closeness that he'd hardly leave an imprint on a paramour's pillow. But people change—or *can* change. "Look," Arty said to me, "don't you think I know what I've been doing all these years? I've just been jerking around, wasting everybody's time, acting like the kind of person I really hope I'm not. I've got to take the chance and try to be different. I think I've found someone who understands how tough it's gonna be for me and who'll be able to handle it, and I've got to take a shot."

That was around three years ago, and Arty and his wife 11 are still fighting the good fight against Arty's fear of intimacy. It hasn't been easy. It's not the sort of fear you stand up to once and conquer; it requires a more durable sort of courage, the sort that renews itself every day.

Arty—so he admits—is still clutched at times by the old 12 terrors; he clams up, broods, gets moody and aloof. His wife, when frustrated, throws tantrums. The two of them have been known to make scenes and to indulge in extended sulks. Yet, beneath the turbulent surface of their marriage, there is a true adventure going on.

It's an adventure whose basis is a moral contract, a 13 mutual pledge not to retreat into halfheartedness. And while the contract's demands are unyielding, its rewards are rich and irreplaceable. "I no longer try to get away with the sort of evasions that I never *wanted* to get away with in the first place," Arty says. "Marriage is like boxing: you can run but you can't hide. Sooner or later, you're going to end up in a clinch—and it's in the clinches where you learn the most about yourself, where your strength is really tested."

But the challenge of marriage is one that Arty still wonders 14 if he's equal to. "You know," he said to me a while back, during a particularly bumpy phase, "I didn't exactly pave the way for this. I mean, I'd always been too scared even to really have a girl-friend, and all of a sudden this little voice starts telling me that maybe I should take this giant leap all the way to marriage, and I *listen*. Maybe it was just a crazy thing for me to do."

I disagreed with him, and told him so. To me, it was his 15 finest hour. Because if duking it out with our personal demons is full of potential pitfalls, it also offers opportunities for real self-transcendence, for genuine heroics. Where's the virtue, after all, in taking a stand when we're *not* afraid? What's the value of a moral contract that doesn't cost us anything?

Big Brother, in his perverse wisdom, was correct in his 16 assumption that every person has his private fear, his exposed nerve. But it doesn't take an all-seeing autocrat to discover that vulnerable point and to probe it—the circumstances of ordinary life will do that just as well. The way we hold our ground when that sensitive place is tweaked, when that anxiety-drenched sub-ject is foisted on us, is the surest test of what we're made of.

Checking Your Understanding

1. What was Arty's deepest fear that he had either to face or to be con-quered by? When Arty chooses marriage, why does Shames think

this is Arty's "finest hour"? Do you think the women Arty has known would agree with Shames' judgment?

2. Reflect a little more on the idea of intimacy in your culture and on your definition of intimacy. Do you agree with Shames that intimacy is "a moral contract" or a way of "taking a stand?" Do you think society encourages or values intimacy? Do you feel you have been taught how to be intimate? If so, where did your models come from? If not, do you wish you had had good models to follow?

Examining Rhetorical Strategies

1. Either describe an "Arty" you have known or describe what an experience with an Arty is like from the *point of view* of one of the women "victimized" by his fear.

2. Look again at the framing device Shames uses of *1984*. Explain why this is an effective analogy to use to describe Arty's situation.

STUDENT ESSAYS AND WRITING TECHNIQUES

In this section we will highlight four student essays. All of these essays were written in response to assignments in various expository writing classes.

In discussing these essays we will focus on writing for a reader. The introduction to each essay gives background on what the writer was trying to accomplish. The "Thinking About Writing" section draws attention to writing techniques the authors have used successfully to draw their readers into the piece. Finally, you are invited to try your hand at producing expressive papers through the suggested writing assignments.

NIGHT SOUNDS

Matt Hillas

Background

In this essay, Hillas' desire was to recreate a short, but intensely painful scene from his childhood. It was an event that Hillas had never tried to write about before. But he felt that since the situation at home with his parents was now so healthy, he had healed enough in the ten years since the incident to try to recapture his feelings. As you read, notice how Hillas tells this story from the point of view of the nine-year-old boy.

Reading Selection

Dad's angry voice from the living room jolted me 1 awake. I lay in my bed, motionless, waiting for the usual tirade to stop.

They had been drinking heavily as usual, Mom more 2 than he. At the age of nine, I had been used to these nightly battles for as long as I could remember: Mom and Dad would argue over dinner for a few hours until Mom would eventually retreat to sleep it off, and the house would finally settle down enough so I could get some sleep.

But not this night. 3

Mom's voice intermingled with Dad's. Apparently, nei- 4 ther of them felt tonight's clash at the kitchen table was finished. Dad's voice was getting louder and rougher, and I knew he was really angry. I clutched the sheets, terrified, not knowing what to expect.

I heard a choked scream from Mom—a guttural sound 5 you hear when someone loses their balance—and then a body landing hard onto the living room rug.

"Drunken bitch!" Dad screamed at the top of his lungs. 6 I heard him go downstairs to the garage, open the door to one of the cars, and slam it shut. He started it and pumped the accelerator repeatedly, revving the engine higher and higher each time. He finally reversed it and tore out onto our street. A few seconds later, I heard the distant sound of squealing tires as he rounded a corner too fast in his haste to get away from his own house.

Crying, I got out of bed, opened the door, and stepped out 7 into the hall. I should have been afraid for Dad and the condition he was in while driving, but at the moment, I was thinking only of Mom and how badly she might have been hurt by him.

Looking into the living room, I could see Mom on all 8 fours on the living room rug by the coffee table. She was crying as well.

I ran over to her and helped her to her feet and we 9 hugged each other, each of us still crying. I walked her the short distance to the door of their bedroom and she pulled away from me. "Go to bed," she whispered gently, almost tenderly: "Go to bed." I waited until she was inside and the door had closed behind her before I crept back to my bed alone.

Thinking About Writing

While all the action of this story is happening in the living room and outside the house, we get most of the scenes only from the limited view of nine-year-old Hillas. We hear only what he can hear from his bed—the angry voices, the choked scream, the body landing, the revving engine, and the tires squealing. Then at the end, we get a brief picture of his interaction with his mother before he is left alone. What does this structure say about Hillas' role in this story? How does this point of view help get us involved in the story even though we are not viewing it from where most of the action is taking place? How would the story be different if we did not begin with Hillas in bed listening to the sounds in the living room but instead were given the background of the home situation?

Writing Assignment

Select a childhood memory and recreate the story from the point of view you had then. Try to capture the world as you saw it as a child. You might select a childhood game that now strikes you as remarkably dangerous but which then just seemed like great fun. Or you might talk about the loss of a pet turtle or chameleon which seemed tragic at the time. Or perhaps you witnessed, as Hillas did, an adult tragedy that you only vaguely understood.

Whatever the event, try to capture the experience as you had it then, from your limited or innocent point of view.

GREATER VICTORIES

H. Galen

Background

Galen has written a poignant tale of life behind the fine-trimmed lawns of D.C. suburban homes. Galen deftly combines humor with pain, innocence with age, in her story of two adolescent girls' survival in a dysfunctional home. While you read, notice the relationship between the two sisters and how Galen makes you see how close they are. Also watch how the details of the home situation are slowly unveiled as the story proceeds.

Reading Selection

At three-o-clock in the morning, she remembers.   1

Right when everything else is nice and peaceful . . . the   2
day's work is over, homework done. We're sitting sprawled at
the kitchen table, sharing a beer. Holly has her chin cradled
in her hands, staring over the half-full dixie cup in a kind of
a trance. My head is laid down on the coolness of the table
top and my eyes are shut, resting against a heavy weight of
fatigue. After a day like we've had—a week like we've had—
the silence is incredible.

The clock ticks and the air conditioner hums. For   3
about four minutes the world is blissfully—truly miraculous-
ly—silent.

Then, Holly startles out of her daze and twists around   4
in her chair to look at the calendar near the phone. "Oh no,"
she moans.

My head stays down on the table, and my speech sounds   5
blurry from tiredness, "Oh no, what?"

"Oh shit. Oh *no.*" She covers her face with her hands   6
and arches her head back with despair. "I need *brownies.*"

Still, my head stays on the table—I am two thirds asleep,   7
and it takes me a minute to get the gist of what she is saying.

I need brownies. Brownies. *Brownies?*   8

"For CHEERLEADERS . . ."   9

For cheerleaders. The bake sale for the cheerleaders.   10
It's this big thing, every year—the junior high bake sale, host-

ed by the mothers of the cheerleaders—to raise funds for their uniforms. All the mothers bake brownies and Rice Krispie treats and cookies and zucchini bread cupcakes with little toothpick emblems stuck in them . . . And all the room mothers, plus about half the P.T.A. come in and help sell. It's really a big deal. They started announcing it way in advance. We've had the notice pinned up to our refrigerator with tacky little alphabet magnets for weeks.

Of course, *our* mother is not going to be making any- 11 thing for the occasion. Because our mother has been locked in her room for six straight days, drinking vodka. And it's been all we could do to keep the house running normally, groceries in the refrigerator, and the social services out of our business, without worrying about a stupid pan of brownies.

I look at Holly out of the corner of my eye. She is peer- 12 ing anxiously into the cabinet over the dish drainer, to see if my mom still has any cookbooks. Her face is a study in thirteen year old panic.

I am a little wider awake now, and all kinds of obnox- 13 ious things I could say to her are running through my brain. *IT'S THREE IN THE MORNING . . . I don't know how to cook either . . . And you can't wait till the last minute like this. I have a chemistry test tomorrow. Besides, this was your responsibility, not mine. Your school, not mine . . . your brownies, not mine. Don't be looking at me to . . . to . . .*

But I know it's hopeless. She needs brownies. It's all 14 part of the package, being a cheerleader—good grades, popularity, gymnastic talent, light blue eyeliner, Reeboks, perfect hair, straight teeth, and . . . brownies. And whatever else they want, when they want it. There are only 8 varsity cheerleaders in the whole junior high. It's a privilege you don't fool around with.

She is straining on tiptoe, about to knock herself 15 unconscious, pulling *The Joy of Cooking* towards her, with two fingers. Clouds of dust are rising from the pages and the book is tipping over the shelf's edge, about to crash right down on her head. You really have to admire that kind of determination.

My tirade fizzles and dies before it escapes from my 16 mouth. After all, it's not *her* fault the week has been like this.

I dive for the cookbook.   17

* * * * * * * * * * * *

Three-forty-five a.m.   18
"Okay, so we have enough eggs. Then I just need vanil- 19
la, and we can start."
"We don't have any vanilla."   20
"Look in the pantry. We must have vanilla. Everybody 21
has vanilla. Everybody in the western world has vanilla in the
cupboard."
I look again, spinning the turntable. Nutmeg, cinna- 22
mon, onion salt, . . . food coloring, birthday candles . . .
"There's no vanilla in here, Holly."   23
"Are you SURE? Did you LOOK?"   24
I fold my arms and look at her. Annoyance is rising to 25
irrational hatred inside my head. *I must try to keep calm. I must
remember, I am the adult in this situation. It is three in the morning.
What matters here is one thing only. The birth of a pan of brownies.
Nothing else.*

I exhale slowly. "*Yes,* Holly. You look *too* if you want. 26
There is no vanilla in . . . the . . . cupboard."

Holly folds her arms across her chest, and her nostrils 27
flare slightly. Deliberately she walks past me, climbs up onto
the counter, and with rigid control, opens both the cupboard
doors widely. She proceeds to scan the entire contents with a
stare that could wither plants. But alas, no vanilla.

I try not to look smug. I try to be charitable. I do not say 28
"I told you so." Only, "Well, it probably doesn't really need it
anyways. How much could one teaspoon of something matter?"

Holly slowly turns to look down at me sideways from the 29
counter. Her eyes are half-closed rageful slits. Outrage and
fatigue boil inside my head, dissolving my previous attitude
of silent martyrdom. My fists clench, and everything in me
tenses to scream back at her . . . *Fine, then—**I'm** going to bed.
These are not **my** brownies.*

But then I notice she is getting all teary eyed.   30
And something about the way she is pushing her feath- 31
ered hair back from her face . . . Something about her skin-
ny knees, kneeling on top of back issues of the *Washington
Post*, on top of some grungy potholders on the countertop,
reminds me that she is, after all, only thirteen.

Remorse-stricken, I hastily rummage through the 32
pantry until I come up with an old honeybear honey-squeez-
er. A little crystallized but still functional. "Look, Hol," I tell
her sensibly—"Look, we can just use honey. It's pretty much
the same thing as vanilla. I'm sure it will work fine. I'm totally sure. Julia Child does this all the time."

She doesn't answer me, but climbs carefully over the 33
toaster and off the counter and blows her nose.

We start over.   34

* * * * * * * * * * * *

Four seventeen a.m.   35

The brownies are in the oven. We decide to go in the 36
livingroom and paint our nails as long as we are awake. Holly
has a new color—iridescent lavender, it's called "Periwinkle
dream." I paint hers and she paints mine. I blow on mine so
they'll dry faster.

They are perfectly smooth. Flawless. Too bad, because I 37
probably won't be going to school tomorrow—there's no way
I'll be able to get out of bed in the morning . . .

Holly looks up, suddenly. "Do you smell smoke, or is 38
that just the nail polish remover?"

* * * * * * * * * * * *

Quarter to five in the morning.   39

Pan of brownies #2 is in the oven. Pan of brownies #1, 40
soaking in the sink—charred among stacks of still unwashed
supper dishes. The smoke detector is in stifled, quiet fragments in the rocking chair, where we threw it after knocking
it from the ceiling with a baseball bat. My body has reached
a point where it's stopped even asking for sleep. We are
munching on a couple of chocolate hunks Holly chiseled
from the center of the first pan, where it wasn't so burnt.
They taste kind of funny, like pollen or something . . .

In a sleepy reverie, we have slidden down to the 41
linoleum floor in front of the oven, and are watching the
progress of the second batch through a tinted window.

"Do they look okay to you?"   42

"I guess so . . . I've never made them before."   43

"They look okay to me . . ."   44

"Well, if they're not, I hope the whole damn P.T.A. 45
chokes on them."

"Yeah," says Holly, giggling . . . "Screw the P.T.A. . . ."   46
We laugh, dizzily, and slide a little further down on the   47
linoleum.
The first slanting sunlight peeks through the slats on   48
the kitchen window blinds.

* * * * * * * * * * * * *

Six fifty a.m.   49
The sun has risen to its place behind a humid curtain   50
of rainclouds, and the kitchen is filled with dingy morning
light. Drifting down the stairs is the furious roar of a blow
drier and three competing clock radios. I am fiddling with
the coffee pot, trying to figure out how the paper filter is supposed to crunch in there.
My little brother has woken up with the flu. My mom is   51
showing no signs getting out of bed. I am trying not to think
about my chemistry test.
A few minutes later there is a thundering noise on the   52
stairs and Holly comes racing through the kitchen in her uniform, like a blaze of red, white, and blue enthusiasm. Her
backpack is slung over one shoulder. She doesn't have time
for breakfast. She is late . . .
"Have a great day at the office, honeybunch," I say,   53
handing her the brownies. "I hope they don't poison the
P.T.A."
Her whole face lights up with a teary warmth that the   54
morning lacks, and she hugs me tightly. Then she flares her
nostrils and arches her eyebrows:
"*Screw* the P.T.A. . . ."   55

* * * * * * * * * * * * *

Standing in the window, I watch her back, as she march-   56
es determinedly down the driveway. The brownies are tucked
neatly under one arm. Her hair blows gently, fluffily in the
humid wind, and her head is held high.
I glance across the street at the neighbors' houses, with   57
their well-trimmed lawns . . . I hope they are watching. She is
beautiful, flawless, perfect. Even if the rest of us don't get to
school today, she will. She will get there, and she will represent us. Holly, the cheerleader. Holly, the beautiful and
brave. Loved by the P.T.A. and the whole community.
Undefeatable. Victorious.

My head is beginning to swim, and I feel irrationally 58
proud. Almost giddy. Sinking into a chair, I lay my head down
on the kitchen table and shut my eyes, imagining how it will 59
be when the P.T.A. lady asks her if her mom sent anything
over for the bake sale.

"Of course," she will say, elegantly . . .   60

It is definitely one of our greater victories.   61

Thinking About Writing

Galen has organized this paper into a series of brief episodes.
What effect does this organization have on you as a reader? How
does this accumulation of brief scenes allow you to understand
what the home situation is like?

Also, this piece is written in present tense, not the past tense
writers usually use for narratives. How does this help to bring you
into the story?

Galen is able to capture in this piece both the innocence of
adolescence and the very adult problems and challenges the two
girls need to handle. What images does she use to show both of
these worlds?

Writing Assignment

There are moments in our lives when we have to, as Galen
says, be "the adult in this situation." We are called upon to behave
in a responsible way, to know what to do in a difficult situation,
when deep inside we really feel completely at a loss. Perhaps
friends come to us for advice and actually expect us to know what
they should do. Or we find ourselves accepting a challenge we
thought we would never be able to handle. We act on a conviction
we have and see that we can stand up for what we believe. We try a
new activity and are thrilled at our success. In these moments, we
often grow up suddenly and find strength and wisdom we didn't
know we had.

Describe one of these moments in your life, one of your own
"Greater Victories."

You might wish in this story to try some of the writing techniques that Galen uses: present tense, dialogue, episodes, or weav-
ing the background into the story.

BOOMER

Tim Clark

Background

In this essay about attending his first baseball game, Clark describes "one of my most vivid memories as a child. I had a great childhood," he said, "yet many of the details seem a little fuzzy. This memory is not." For him, the essay really captured "so much of what I am and how I feel about baseball." As you read, notice the vivid descriptions of Boomer, the stadium, and the game. Also notice how Clark switches from first to third person in the last scene.

Reading Selection

They called him "Boomer." Full name, Ron Bloomberg. 1 He wasn't the best player on the 1975 New York Yankees, but he was easily my favorite. For one thing, he was always filthy. I could relate to that. In nearly every picture of me taken between the ages of four and ten, I look like I just got dragged through the neighborhood mud puddle. Boomer was the same way—shirttail hanging out, pants that were always more than a little baggy in the crotch, raggy socks bunched loosely around his ankles. Compared to the rest of the Yankees with their brilliant pinstripes and glistening black spikes he was a misfit. To me he was a demi-god.

My father grew up in Jersey City. He ate, slept and 2 dreamt about the Brooklyn Dodgers. The Bums of Ebbets Field. More often than not, when the Dodgers were at home, he would skip school and take the train to Brooklyn where he would work the turnstiles. After the third inning, he was allowed to watch the rest of the game for free from the bullpen bleachers. Some of the players recognized him and called him "Patty." He still has a box of old baseballs, the white horsehide faded and hardened with age, signed "To Patty" from a long list of Dodger heroes. It nearly killed him when the Dodgers moved to Los Angeles in 1957. It nearly killed him a second time when all three of his sons became die-hard Yankee fans.

I remember the day clearly: The drive from our home 3
in Connecticut with my dad and two older brothers to the
fabled Bronx battlegrounds—the old Yankee Stadium, the
House that Ruth built. The ride up the long escalator to the
mezzanine. The warm air carrying with it smells of steamed
hot dogs, pretzels and beer. The long walk through the tunnel that led to section G. Coming out of that dark tunnel and
seeing before me the greenest grass on the face of the planet, contrasted with the rich brown, freshly watered clay
infield. It was my first big league game and it literally took my
breath away.

I watched in silent awe as the pre-game batting practice 4
and infield drills were perfectly executed before my eyes.
Such precision, like soldiers displaying arms of leather and
wood. I was entranced as the game progressed, and I remember valiantly trying to keep score while stuffing my face with
one Yankee Frank after another.

Sixth inning. Runner on first. Yanks down by one. A 5
left-hand batter stands in, jaw stuffed with a huge hunk of
chewing tobacco, a scratched and faded blue helmet jammed
over a head of dirty blond hair that hung limply out the sides,
and the characteristic baggy socks. The Boomer.

The noise of the stadium seemed to fade, then disap- 6
pear. A little blond kid with his very own faded blue Yankee
helmet and an old baseball glove that hung limply off of
hands only five summers old sat tensely on the edge of his
blue folding seat. At the sound, he did not jump like his
brothers, or look at his dad or the now familiar hot dog ven-
dor in front of him. He did not move. His shining green eyes
were instead fixed on the tiny white streak that soon disappeared into the left field stands . . . Gone. It was no longer
silent.

Later that day, outside the players' entrance, a brilliant 7
white baseball was handed gently back to a little blond kid
with hands barely large enough to grasp it. His face shone
brightly as he read the inscription signed in a loose, flowing
style. It read, "Timmy—I hit it for you—Boomer."

Thinking About Writing

Clark paints a very vivid portrait of this memory through
carefully crafted descriptions: The Yankees wear "brilliant pin-

stripes and glistening black spikes"; the "white horsehide" of Patty's baseballs is "faded and hardened with age"; the air in the stadium smells of "steamed hot dogs, pretzels and beer." What effect does all this detail have on you as a reader?

Also, in the last paragraph, Clark looks back at himself as the "little blonde kid" receiving the ball from his hero. He pulls away from the first-hand experience and watches himself as a child receiving that ball. Why do you think Clark did this? How would the essay have been different if he had kept that paragraph in first person?

Writing Assignment

We are all influenced by people in our lives: parents, relatives, friends, teachers, coaches, heroes. Select one person who has had a lasting effect on you and describe that person so that your readers will meet her or him. Try to incorporate a specific scene that will show this person's character rather than just giving a list of attributes. Include as much detail in this scene as you can so that we experience your interaction with this person as you did.

FALL

Todd Craig

Background

Craig, an intense observer of his natural surroundings, wanted to do a descriptive paper about fall. But he was aware of how common this topic is. How many ways are there to say that the leaves change color? So, Craig wanted to try a completely different approach. Notice how, even though we do get a description of the leaves, Craig gives this piece a unique twist and takes an original approach to the topic.

Reading Selection

By the end of summer, roughly mid September, you begin to sense that autumn is finally coming. The first few dry, clear days make you swear it's October and there are more leaves on the ground than on the trees. You look about you. No brilliant colours yet. No rich crimson or that nostalgic dirty terra cotta. No rusty oranges or beautiful sun drenched golds. Still the same end of the summer olive. The nights begin to cool, however, and the sun sets more south each day. The days roll by slowly and the leaves begin to turn. Somewhere around there's a rake. 1

You wait for a few minutes. Door wide open. Not a peep of anyone anywhere. Then you hear a chain collar coming down the stairs. Chink, chink, chilinking. He saunters into the kitchen and notices the open door and you waiting. He waits. Nothing happens. He looks at you and you look back at him. The door slams behind you as you take off running after him. Running and calling at the top of your lungs. You find him in the backyard by the road. He sees you and takes off. He turns and barks. You bark back and run. He takes off after you. You yell and holler as he growls and yaps. He's "it." You're "it." He's "it." You're "it." 2

All afternoon you raked and raked. The skin between your thumb and fingers is raw and there's a blister. Three or four huge piles are now scattered everywhere. You tell yourself not to fall over the rake. But where is it? 3

You run as hard as you can then dive into a pile. Here 4
he comes. Mouth open wide. He's bouncing and bobbing
and his trailing tail wags like mad. You throw the biggest armful of leaves you can at him. He halts. Confusion then bark-
ing then a dive for your body. He's got your arm good but you
pull him down and wrestle in the leaves until you're exhausted. You fall over on your back and he watches you. Nothing.
Still nothing. Finally he realizes you're tired and eases up.
You grab him, pull him down and hold him close.

Clouds roll by underneath a steel sky. There's a chill in 5
the air. Frost tonight. The white oak still has a load of leaves
in it. More raking and more blisters next weekend. But you
don't mind. It's only once a year that autumn comes and the
trees turn colours you never thought possible. The sun is soft-
er in the afternoons and the evenings darken sooner. The air
is brisk and chilly once more. Just like you remembered.

It's getting darker. Someone in the house turned the 6
porch lights on.

You can feel his heart beat and he's still panting. You 7
scratch his belly and blow on his ears. He shakes his head.

You take off running and he follows you. Another wres- 8
tle in a pile of leaves and you're after him, constantly nipping
his tail with your hands and still yelling and hollering. He
halts, turns, and barks and takes off before another armful of
leaves is heaved at him.

It's getting darker still, almost night time. Now he's 9
after you. Around the trees, to the stone wall and the porch
and back. Harder and harder you run. Your lungs hurt. You
fall over the rake and land painfully on the ground. He barks
and comes after you. It really hurts. He waits. You stay there
a few minutes thinking about autumn and trees and what it
must be like in the urban areas where they have no yards. No
leaves. No need for rakes. No romps in the evenings. Dogs on
leashes.

Mom calls for dinner and you run down to the house. 10
He meets you at the door and you crash back into the
kitchen, both of you panting.

Thinking About Writing

We said earlier that the first-person pronoun is a characteristic of expressive writing. And yet this expressive piece uses the sec-

ond-person pronoun, "you." While Craig is still telling us a story that happened to him, he is using the "you" as a device to make us feel that we are there with him, waiting for the dog, running through the yard, throwing the leaves. Does this technique make you feel more or less involved than if he had used "I?"

Writing Assignment

Try your hand at describing something from a unique point of view. For example, you might describe your favorite place but how it looks after something wonderful has happened or something tragic. Or you might describe a person, your father, for example, the first time you realized that parents are human, too, and not invincible as we often imagine them to be. Or you might try, as Craig does, to invite us to experience a place or time by taking us through it with you. Whatever you choose, try to make your unique perspective on this come through.

Part Three

AFFIRMING DISCOURSE

In Part Two we discussed writing with the goal of sharing personal experiences with readers. We now move from expressive discourse to *affirming discourse*. Because our opinions often grow out of our own experiences, the division between expressive and affirming discourse is gradual rather than clear-cut. The pieces in this section begin with writers using personal experiences to explain and support an opinion. They then move to the use of arguments and information which lay the groundwork for persuasion—the next type of writing we will discuss. In terms of audience, the readings in this section progress from writing directed at readers who already agree with us but who want additional support, to readers who are sympathetic toward our opinion, yet who are still formulating a firm opinion about the issue at hand.

As readers, it's natural for us to be drawn to texts that support our existing ideas and beliefs. We all like positive reinforcement, even if we are already secure in our position. During an election, for example, we are often drawn to editorials with titles that suggest support for a candidate we already endorse or an issue on which we have already staked out a firm position.

In affirming discourse, writers share their opinions on topics that they feel strongly about. The sharing may take the form of a story relating an experience that led to the formation, evolution, or reevaluation of the opinion. As in expressive writing, the sharing of the opinion may reveal much about who the author is and how this identity was shaped. Whether the support for the author's position comes from a personal experience, a memorable observation, or relevant information, we get a good feel for why the author has arrived at the position being supported and so tend to appreciate the author's justification for taking that position.

This supporting of a position invites the reader to see the substantiation and validity of the author's point of view. While we are not asked to change our own opinions, we should leave the reading with a respect for the thoughtful reasoning that has led the author to embrace the position being shared. If we were originally drawn to the piece because we were looking for reinforcement of our own ideas, we often leave the reading with a sense of connectedness to the author due to the common ground we share.

Chapter Six

READING AFFIRMING DISCOURSE: THE READER/WRITER RELATIONSHIP

As readers, we approach affirming texts expecting to receive an opinion from the writer, to read about an issue about which the writer has firm ideas and beliefs. If the writing is successful, we are able to appreciate the logic and thoughtfulness of the writer's position. When the affirming discourse relies heavily on expressive writing we often learn how the writer came to embrace the opinion being shared.

Unlike expressive discourse, this reading is often identified with both being pleased and being informed because in reading affirming discourse our previous assumptions or points of view may be supported by expressive and informative writing alike. The expressive aspects may infuse the piece with emotional power that supports the writer's position. The informative aspects may infuse the piece with a logical appeal that supports the writer's position.

We approach this kind of reading, then, as willing listeners, anxious to have our own ideas and opinions supported by an author; our ideas are already assumed to be valid and desirable (or at least potentially valuable and desirable, if we find that we are neutral or ill informed on the topic). We are drawn to the text by such things as its power, logic, thoughtfulness, and attention to details that clarify or reinforce our preconceived notions.

As we read, we look for things that we can relate to and agree with. It is easy to appreciate well-considered support for positions that in some ways mirror our own. For example, if we live near a once beautiful forest that has been harvested by clear cutting, we may very well be receptive to a piece of affirming discourse critical of this practice. On the other hand, if we are the son or daughter of a logger who has lost employment due to government regulations restricting clear cutting, we may be much more receptive to a piece criticizing such regulations.

The following three essays will illustrate examples of the reader/writer relationship in affirming writing: an opinion essay, a position paper, and an editorial.

OPINION ESSAY

HAUNTED BY THE INGLORIOUS TERRORS OF WAR
Donald M. Murray

One kind of reader/writer relationship in affirming discourse grows out of an explanation of a personal opinion or belief. By explaining a belief that we feel others may not understand or accept, we hope to justify that belief for both our readers and ourselves. Often writers may not have a firm grip on the reasons for a personal opinion until they express in writing the experience or experiences that served to shape that opinion.

In his powerful account of the horrors of war, Donald M. Murray shares some traumatic personal experiences that served to shape his beliefs about the inglorious nature of combat. He shares his own story to explain his position that, as the Gulf War approaches, it is time for veterans to remind those who make war of its ignoble realities.

Could Murray's position be supported without the expressive aspects of his writing? Possibly. He could attempt to lay out the coldly logical reasons for dispelling myths of glorious combat. But such an essay would focus on the "what" rather than the "why" of the position. Murray's powerful expressive writing draws us into why he feels so strongly about the tendency to glorify war. His personal experiences and observations, the private and powerful aspects of his support, are what draw us into the essay and move us to appreciate his opinions.

Prereading Journal

Sometimes we base our ideas and opinions not on personal experience or observations but on false assumptions and unsubstantiated generalizations. We might see a filmed version of an historical event or a televised docudrama and think that we possess all the information we need to form a thoughtful opinion on the subject. Often, we receive additional information—whether we are seeking it or not—that forces us to reexamine the assumptions we had considered to be valid. Think of a time when you found yourself reconsidering an opinion you held. Describe the experience that led you to reconsider your position on the subject.

Background

This opinion piece first appeared in the *Boston Globe* on January 8, 1990, just prior to the outset of the Gulf War. Murray uses elements of expressive writing to lend support to his personal opinion that war should not be looked at as a glorious solution to world problems. Now a retired professor of English at the University of New Hampshire, he has published articles and books on the teaching of writing and has won the Pulitzer Prize for editorial writing.

During Reading

Keep note of anything Murray shares about his infantry experiences that conflict with or reinforce your assumptions about war and combat.

Reading Selection

I am haunted, as I am sure many other over-60 former 1 infantrymen are, when I am assaulted by the boasts of our political leaders, Arab and American. The ghosts of those who died in our war—World War II—rise and stand beside me, and we remember our private terrors in combat.

I look at our young soldiers with a particular tender- 2 ness, and the braver their before-their-first-battle statements sound, the more I am touched by their innocence. I know how long it will last.

It doesn't take days or hours or minutes to become a 3 veteran, but only seconds after a stranger shoots at you.

I was no reluctant soldier. I wanted to go to my war, to 4 take part in history, to prove myself in battle. I volunteered for the paratroops, and I am sure that my letters home were brave—and innocent. I would not dare read them now.

I suspect there are many reasons so many of us, over 5 60, do not speak of our combat experiences. We do not think anyone who has not been in combat will understand, we do not want to contaminate this unexpected life we live with the cynicism and the anger at our leaders that we felt in combat, and we are ashamed of what happened to us under fire.

6 The president, an officer who flew in combat in my war, speaks of a quick war, an efficient, well-planned operation.

7 I cannot speak of his war in the air or the war at sea. I salute those who died in those wars, but my memories these winter mornings are the memories of an infantryman.

8 I have jokingly said that if you want to know what combat is like, take a couple of dozen 11-year-olds on an overnight and then add live ammunition. But it is not funny.

9 I never had the feeling in combat that anyone knew what was going on. This is the perspective of a private, groveling in the mud, trying to understand the incoherent commands of terrified and usually half-crazy, sometimes more than half-drunk officers.

10 I sometimes think we measure happiness by the amount of control we can exercise over our lives. As a private in the infantry you have no control over your life. If you eat or what, if you sleep and when, if you go to the bathroom and how, if you live or die depends on the whim of young men who usually come from a better social class—officers are gentlemen, but are usually unprepared for combat.

11 It is a world without reason, and all of today's nightscopes, fancy gadgets and War College desert tactics will not change the way individual soldiers—and you are never as alone as you are in combat, despite all the movies—will feel under fire.

12 We called for down artillery on the enemy across the ridge and the shells fell on us. I was asleep when one of our tanks backed across the legs of the soldier sleeping beside me. Our planes bombed and strafed our positions.

13 A lieutenant, waving a .45 caliber pistol, ordered us to charge a hill against German artillery protected by entrenched machine-gun positions. We did not mutiny; we just watched as one German sniper hit him in the forehead, and I remember that we cheered. This was not history-book war.

14 Later, a sergeant led us behind the position, and we captured it.

A colonel ordered one of our regiments to attack on a   15
foggy winter night. His soldiers fought with efficient bravery
and in the morning realized that their heroic enemy was
American, a regiment in the same division.

I assume that the letters to their survivors did not say   16
the men were killed by American soldiers, and I would not be
surprised if that terrible night was laundered in the official
records.

I learned by cynicism. The next morning I drove the   17
officer investigating the action up the road over which our
regiments fought, forcing the jeep over the bodies of men
whose names I knew.

We were told the colonel was sent back to England and   18
promoted to general. That may not be true, but we believed it.

At times we hated our own officers more than we hated   19
the enemy. In fact, as reunions with former enemies—
German or Japanese or Vietnamese—have shown, combat
veterans often have felt a deep companionship for the men
who, as youths, were ordered into battle against us.

History books and films refer to "Blood and Guts"   20
George Patton. We said, "His guts and our blood."

Our soldiers in Saudi Arabia, if they go into battle—and   21
I certainly hope they do not—will find combat irrational, terrifying and never glorious.

Some say it is unpatriotic to speak of war as I do here,   22
an insult to brave Americans who died for our country. But I
believe I speak for them. Our leaders need to know the true
price of Kuwaiti oil, of supporting governments that do not
even believe in the most elemental rights of women.

Most old veterans are silent, but I will speak of my war.   23

I survived combat because I gave up all hope of living.   24
Knowing I would die, I tried to die well.

But the conditions of dying make that difficult. I wore   25
the skin off my hands digging into the ground under shell
fire. I ran to fight another day. I found it easy to shoot to kill.
I mistreated prisoners so they would talk.

I was one of the official heroes in the 82d Airborne who   26
marched in the victory parade down Fifth Avenue. But I
knew, as we passed the reviewing stand and the bands played,
that I messed my pants from terror, as most of us did, not

once but many times, and wore the same pants and under-pants from December until March.

I hear the politicians speak, and I smell the terrible 27 sweet smell of the dead and the stink of my own fear from 46 years ago.

That is what we, the over-60 infantrymen, do not 28 remind the old men who make the war in which young men die. It is time we speak.

Checking Your Understanding

1. Murray says that it is time for the over-60 infantrymen to speak. Why do you think Murray felt it was necessary for these veterans to share their stories as America was preparing to go to war? Who might most need to listen to the stories these veterans would be able to tell?

2. Why is it important that the United States government consider the implications of "supporting governments that do not even believe in the most elemental rights of women"?

3. Murray says that the inglorious terrors of combat he shares are not "history-book war." How and why might historical texts perpetuate false assumptions and incomplete accounts concerning war? What kinds of stories of the invasion of Panama and of the Gulf War will we probably never hear?

Examining Rhetorical Strategies

1. Which image was most effective in making you, as a reader, receptive to Murray's message? Did the effectiveness come from the style, the content, the emotions?

2. What is Murray's thesis? What specific support does he provide for this thesis?

POSITION PAPER

AMERICA: THE MULTINATIONAL SOCIETY
Ishmael Reed

Another kind of reader/writer relationship is established when we read affirming discourse that reinforces a position or belief we already hold. Sometimes we catch ourselves nodding in agreement and thinking, "That's exactly what I've always thought, but never could find the right words."

Affirming discourse that reinforces an existing position or articulates a vague but powerful feeling we have about a topic can be very pleasurable reading. It is natural to desire confirmation of our ideas and beliefs. It is comforting to know that we are not alone, that others embrace the same position that we do.

The tone for this kind of affirming writing varies greatly. It can take the form of a gentle reminder or it can possess all the bluster and emotion of a pep rally. The appropriate tone for sharing a position with those already in full agreement—head nodders—depends on why our belief needs to be reinforced. Maybe the author has had an experience that reinforced a belief she had let gather dust in a far corner of her mind; maybe the author has some new information that reminds him why he feels so strongly about his position. Reed is reaching out to readers who wish for North America to become "a place where the cultures of the world crisscross." By sharing recent or renewed realizations with a sympathetic audience, authors of the position paper reinforce our existing beliefs without our having to go through similar experiences or uncover similar support.

Prereading Journal

Think about an aspect of your home town that reflects the multinational nature of our society. Describe this aspect in enough detail so that readers visiting your home town for the first time will have a clear sense of what they will find. For example, you could describe a Chinese restaurant or a Hispanic Arts Festival.

Background

In addition to the collection of essays from which this piece is taken, *Writin' Is Fightin': Thirty-Seven Years of Boxing on Paper* (1988), Ishmael Reed has published novels and poetry. His position here is defended through both personal experience and historical interpretation. He also uses information from other sources, quotes from experts in academia that both agree and contrast with his own.

During Reading

Reed mentions numerous ethnic and cultural groups in his essay. Keep track of them and list some of the assumptions you make and/or stereotypes that you associate with each group.

Reading Selection

At the annual Lower East Side Jewish Festival yesterday, a Chinese woman ate a pizza slice in front of Ty Thuan Duc's Vietnamese grocery store. Beside her a Spanish-speaking family patronized a cart with two signs: "Italian Ices" and "Kosher by Rabbi Alper." And after the pastrami ran out, everybody ate knishes.

—*New York Times*, June 23, 1983

On the day before Memorial Day, 1983, a poet called 1 me to describe a city he had just visited. He said that one section included mosques, built by the Islamic people who dwelled there. Attending his reading, he said, were large numbers of Hispanic people, forty thousand of whom lived in the same city. He was not talking about a fabled city located in some mysterious region of the world. The city he'd visited was Detroit.

A few months before, as I was leaving Houston, Texas, I 2 heard it announced on the radio that Texas's largest minority was Mexican-American, and though a foundation recently issued a report critical of bilingual education, the taped voice used to guide the passengers on the air trams connecting terminals in Dallas Airport is in both Spanish and English. If the trend continues, a day will come when it will be difficult to travel through some sections of the country without hearing commands in both English and Spanish; after all, for some Western states, Spanish was the first written language and the Spanish style lives on in the Western way of life.

Shortly after my Texas trip, I sat in an auditorium located on the campus of the University of Wisconsin at Milwaukee as a Yale professor—whose original work on the influence of African cultures upon those of the Americas has led to his ostracism from some monocultural intellectual circles—walked up and down the aisle, like an old-time Southern evangelist, dancing and drumming the top of the lectern, illustrating his points before some serious Afro-American intellectuals and artists who cheered and applauded his performance and his mastery of information. The professor was "white." After his lecture, he joined a group of Milwaukeeans in a conversation. All of the participants spoke Yoruban, though only the professor had ever traveled to Africa.

One of the artists told me that his paintings, which included African and Afro-American mythological symbols and imagery, were hanging in the local McDonald's restaurant. The next day I went to McDonald's and snapped pictures of smiling youngsters eating hamburgers below paintings that could grace the walls of any of the country's leading museums. The manager of the local McDonald's said, "I don't know what you boys are doing, but I like it," as he commissioned the local painters to exhibit in his restaurant.

Such blurring of cultural styles occurs in everyday life in the United States to a greater extent than anyone can imagine and is probably more prevalent than the sensational conflict between people of different backgrounds that is played up and often encouraged by the media. The result is what the Yale professor, Robert Thompson, referred to as a cultural bouillabaisse, yet members of the nation's present educational and cultural Elect still cling to the notion that the United States belongs to some vaguely defined entity they refer to as "Western civilization," by which they mean, presumably, a civilization created by the people of Europe, as if Europe can be viewed in monolithic terms. Is Beethoven's Ninth Symphony, which includes Turkish marches, a part of Western civilization, or the late nineteenth- and twentieth-century French paintings, whose creators were influenced by Japanese art? And what of the cubists, through whom the influence of African art changed modern painting, or the surrealists, who were so impressed with the art of the Pacific Northwest Indians that, in their map of North America, Alaska dwarfs the lower forty-eight in size?

Are the Russians, who are often criticized for their 6 adoption of "Western" ways by Tsarist dissidents in exile, members of Western civilization? And what of the millions of Europeans who have black African and Asian ancestry, black Africans having occupied several countries for hundreds of years? Are these "Europeans" members of Western civilization, or the Hungarians, who originated across the Urals in a place called Greater Hungary, or the Irish, who came from the Iberian Peninsula?

Europe is complex

Even the notion that North America is part of Western 7 civilization because our "system of government" is derived from Europe is being challenged by Native American historians who say that the founding fathers, Benjamin Franklin especially, were actually influenced by the system of government that had been adopted by the Iroquois hundreds of years prior to the arrival of large numbers of Europeans.

Western civilization, then, becomes another confusing 8 category like Third World, or Judeo-Christian culture, as man attempts to impose his small-screen view of political and cultural reality upon a complex world. Our most publicized novelist recently said that Western civilization was the greatest achievement of mankind, an attitude that flourishes on the street level as scribbles in public restrooms: "White Power," "Niggers and Spics Suck," or "Hitler was a prophet," the latter being the most telling, for wasn't Adolph Hitler the archetypal monoculturalist who, in his pigheaded arrogance, believed that one way and one blood was so pure that it had to be protected from alien strains at all costs? Where did such an attitude, which has caused so much misery and depression in our national life, which has tainted even our noblest achievements, begin? An attitude that caused the incarceration of Japanese-American citizens during World War II, the persecution of Chicanos and Chinese-Americans, the near-extermination of the Indians, and the murder and lynchings of thousands of Afro-Americans.

Virtuous, hardworking, pious, even though they occa- 9
sionally would wander off after some fancy clothes, or ren-
dezvous in the woods with the town prostitute, the Puritans
are idealized in our schoolbooks as "a hardy band" of no-
nonsense patriarchs whose discipline razed the forest and
brought order to the New World (a term that annoys Native
American historians). Industrious, responsible, it was their
"Yankee ingenuity" and practicality that created the work
ethic. They were simple folk who produced a number of good
poets, and they set the tone for the American writing style, of
lean and spare lines, long before Hemingway. They worshiped
in churches whose colors blended in with the New England
snow, churches with simple structures and ornate lecterns.

The Puritans were a daring lot, but they had a mean 10
streak. They hated the theater and banned Christmas. They
punished people in a cruel and inhuman manner. They
killed children who disobeyed their parents. When they came
in contact with those whom they considered heathens or
aliens, they behaved in such a bizarre and irrational manner
that this chapter in the American history comes down to us
as a late-movie horror film. They exterminated the Indians,
who taught them how to survive in a world unknown to them,
and their encounter with the calypso culture of Barbados
resulted in what the tourist guide in Salem's Witches' House
refers to as the Witchcraft Hysteria.

The Puritan legacy of hard work and meticulous 11
accounting led to the establishment of a great industrial society; it is no wonder that the American industrial revolution
began in Lowell, Massachusetts, but there was the other side,
the strange and paranoid attitudes toward those different
from the Elect.

The cultural attitudes of that early Elect continue to be 12
voiced in everyday life in the United States: the president of
a distinguished university, writing a letter to the *Times*, belit-
tling the study of African civilizations; the television network
that promoted its show on the Vatican art with the boast that
this art represented "the finest achievements of the human
spirit." A modern up-tempo state of complex rhythms that
depends upon contacts with an international community can
no longer behave as if it dwelled in a "Zion Wilderness" surrounded by beasts and pagans.

When I heard a schoolteacher warn the other night 1£
about the invasion of the American educational system by
foreign curriculums I wanted to yell at the television set,
"Lady, they're already here." It has already begun because the
world is here. The world has been arriving at these shores for
at least ten thousand years from Europe, Africa, and Asia. In
the late nineteenth and early twentieth centuries, large numbers of Europeans arrived, adding their cultures to those of
the European, African, and Asian settlers who were already
here, and recently millions have been entering the country
from South America and the Caribbean, making Yale professor Bob Thompson's bouillabaisse richer and thicker.

One of our most visionary politicians said that he envi-
sioned a time when the United States could become the
brain of the world, by which he meant the repository of all of
the latest advanced information systems. I thought of that
remark when an enterprising poet friend of mine called to
say that he had just sold a poem to a computer magazine and
that the editors were delighted to get it because they didn't
carry fiction or poetry. Is that the kind of world we desire? A
humdrum homogeneous world of all brains and no heart, no
fiction, no poetry; a world of robots with human attendants
bereft of imagination, of culture? Or does North America
deserve a more exciting destiny? To become a place where
the cultures of the world crisscross. This is possible because
the United States is unique in the world: The world is here.

Checking Your Understanding

1. Reed cites Beethoven's Ninth Symphony, cubism, and surrealism as
   three examples of art that reflects the influence of multiple cultures. What examples come to mind when you think of the United
   States as "a place where the cultures of the world crisscross"?

2. Reflect on the list you made while reading. Which assumptions
   seem the most difficult to support with your own experiences and
   observations? How are your assumptions about various ethnic
   groups and cultural styles similar to or different from those of your
   classmates?

3. What are some of the groups you see yourself as a member of? What
   misconceptions and unfounded generalizations do others tend to
   make about your own ethnic, religious, or cultural group? Why do
   you think we often resort to stereotyping others rather than learning more about them?

Examining Rhetorical Strategies

1. Reread the quote that precedes Reed's essay. How does the quote serve to prepare the reader for the position Reed supports in his essay?

2. Reed does not specifically state his position until the close of the essay. How does this strategy serve Reed's purpose for writing?

EDITORIAL

As we come to the editorial, affirming discourse begins to mesh with persuasive discourse. In order to lay a foundation for change, we must at some level persuade our readers that change is necessary. President Clinton did not need to do this in his inaugural address (see Chapter Eight for this reading) because the occasion itself was evidence that many voters were already persuaded and voted accordingly.

Still, when we scan the editorial page of the newspaper we often tend to select pieces to read based on predictions of whether or not they will support our existing opinions. Just as it is pleasurable to have our ideas confirmed by others, it can raise our blood pressure to read views that are contrary to our own.

Yet reinforcement of existing beliefs is not the only reason we read editorials. Often our prior knowledge of a current event or policy debate is enhanced by the positions taken in editorials. This aspect of editorial writing foreshadows the final aim to be discussed in this book: informative writing. But by and large, we tend to have our current beliefs reinforced by the editorials we read, even when we are reading an editorial with which we take exception. In both cases, we use the information to shore up our own beliefs.

THEIR BRUTAL MIRTH

Anthony Lewis

Prereading Journal

Recall one of the most shocking actual events you have ever seen on television. What was disturbing about the event? What images stay with you to this day?

Background

Anthony Lewis is a regular columnist for *The New York Times*, where this editorial first appeared on May 20, 1991. Since that time the issue of televised executions has continued to be discussed and debated. Here he uses information from both a novelist and the U.S. Constitution to begin to persuade readers as well as to defend his opinion.

During Reading

Keep track of the references to the First Amendment.

Reading Selection

Charles Dickens was walking through London in the early morning of Nov. 13, 1849, when he came upon a crowd waiting to watch a public hanging in Horsemonger Lane. People were laughing and singing songs that mocked the condemned person, a Mrs. Manning. Later that day Dickens wrote to The Times of London: 1

"A sight so inconceivably awful as the wickedness and levity of the immense crowd . . . could be imagined by no man. . . . When the sun rose brightly, as it did, it gilded thousands upon thousands of upturned faces, so inexpressibly odious in their brutal mirth or callousness that a man had cause to feel ashamed of the shape he wore." 2

A lawsuit now pending seeks to establish, under the United States Constitution, a callousness that not even Dickens could imagine: the right of Californians to enjoy executions in the convenience of their own living rooms. Instead of standing in a cold London street, they could invite friends over for beer, pretzels and death. 3

The suit was brought by a San Francisco public television station, KQED, in Federal District Court there. It claims that the First Amendment's guarantee of press freedom entitles KQED to videotape an execution in the gas chamber at San Quentin and then to broadcast it. 4

California has not carried out a death sentence since 1967. But judicial barriers have been falling, and an execution is likely to take place before long. The state's news organizations are eager to be there. 5

The warden of San Quentin, Daniel Vasquez, first decided that 14 reporters could attend. Fourteen news organizations were chosen by what looked to be political standards. But when KQED challenged the selection process, Mr. Vasquez decided to ban all reporters rather than defend the process in court. 6

KQED, with the support of others in the press, is now challenging the complete exclusion of the press. That argu- 7 ment should have a fair chance of winning, on the basis of recent Supreme Court decisions.

Under the First Amendment, the press usually has a 8 right to publish whatever it can find out, without fear of government interference. But until lately the amendment was not read as requiring a government to give the press access to official proceedings.

Since 1980 the Supreme Court has held that the First 9 Amendment does include a limited right of access—to proceedings that historically have been open. Thus the Court upset a judge's decision to close a criminal trial to press and public.

In California, reporters have in the past been present at 10 executions, so the test of history is met. Under state law 12 citizens, not members of the press, will be chosen to attend the next execution. That gives the process a show of public accountability, but I think not enough to justify a total ban on the press.

But the hard question is television cameras. KQED's 11 lawyer, William Bennett Turner of San Francisco, makes a strong argument for letting cameras in.

"Television is indispensable," Mr. Turner says in his 12 brief, for the public to get "a sense of what the execution looked and sounded like. This is especially true when all witnesses are hand-picked by government officials and the event is so politically, emotionally, morally and religiously significant to different people in different ways."

I was present at an electrocution, many years ago in the 13 District of Columbia, and I agree that words cannot really convey what I experienced: the sight, the sound, the smell of burnt flesh.

But television will not make the business of official 14 killing real to the viewer. It will trivialize executions—reduce them to the level of entertainment, to be clicked on and off.

Some opponents of capital punishment argue that the 15 barbarity lies in executions themselves, not in televising them. Yes, it is worrying that this country alone in the Western world has executions, despite their demonstrated irrelevance to deterrence of crime.

But the issue here is television's right to be present. And 16 the First Amendment in my judgment does not require access

to scenes whose broadcast would further coarsen our society
and increase its already dangerous level of insensitivity.

We do not need to make executions just another enter-   17
tainment. We do not need to accept the banality of evil.

Checking Your Understanding

1. Do you agree or disagree with Lewis' opinion that the broadcast
   of executions "would further coarsen our society and increase its
   already dangerous level of insensitivity"? Why?
2. Do you think the event you mentioned in your prereading journal
   further coarsened our society, provided vital information for viewers, or both?
3. Reread James Alexander Thom's "The Perfect Picture" in
   Chapter Three. What side of the televised execution issue do you
   think he would be on and why?

Examining Rhetorical Strategies

1. How does Lewis' use of the Dickens' quote serve to support his
   position?
2. How does Lewis undercut Turner's argument that "television is
   indispensable" in order to support his own position on televised
   executions?

DEATH WATCH

Anna Quindlen

Prereading Journal

Reread Lewis' essay and list his main points against tele-vised executions.

Background

Anna Quindlen is a regular columnist for *The New York Times*, where this editorial first appeared on May 16, 1991. Writing about the same issue as Lewis, Quindlen also uses con-stitutional information but contrasts it with very modern images of society. She, too, demonstrates the meshing of persuasive and affirming discourse perhaps more obviously than Lewis.

During Reading

List Quindlen's main points in favor of televised executions.

Reading Selection

Before he was executed by the state of California in 1960, Caryl Chessman arranged with a reporter to communi-cate from behind the glass wall of the gas chamber. As the cyanide pellets mingled with the sulfuric acid, the convicted murderer brought his head up and down violently in a last nod. Yes, he was saying, it hurts. The reporter wrote: "Whatever medicine says, the eyes said Chessman did not die quickly, not even gracefully, after his twitching reflexes took over from a dead brain. It is probably for the best that only 60 shaken witnesses have to know exactly how it happened." 1

Three decades later, one public television station seeks 2 to enlarge the circle of shaken witnesses to include all of us at home, pale in the glow of our television sets. After the war-den at San Quentin restricted coverage of a prospective exe-cution, KQED filed suit, charging that the process for select-ing those who would cover executions was capricious and that television reporters were being denied the use of the tools of their trade by a ban on cameras.

The suit raises some interesting questions about govern- 3
ment supervision of the press, about who decides what should
be covered and how. But what this is really about is something
far less rational, something that lies deep in the gut. It is about
a vision of the future in which a few good buddies gather
round the tube with a six-pack and a pepperoni pizza for a Fry
'Em party, a future in which we will hear the pellets drop into
the pail, watch the condemned man gasp like a fish thrown
from the pond, and then cut to a commercial.

Much of the discussion has centered on television, on 4
whether the medium of the laugh track can begin to know how
to broadcast real death without cheapening the experience.

Michael Schwartz, the director of current affairs at 5
KQED, says it would not broadcast the execution live, and
that the footage would be used in a program that examined
the death penalty "in its full complexity."

That's precisely what we ourselves have failed to do. In 6
lieu of more substantive discussion of the act itself, camps have
grown up around the question of its broadcast suitability.
Some proponents of capital punishment think broadcasting
executions would be a deterrent to crime, while others think it
would turn people against the death penalty. Some opponents
also share that belief, while others think airing the brutal minutes it takes to kill by statute vaults the boundaries of decency.

There is nothing new about public participation in exe- 7
cutions. Newspapers during the 19th century describe hang-
ings at which hundreds of people gathered. Many accounts
are of crowds struck dumb by the click of the trap door and
the broken man swinging awry at the end of the rope.

"A crowd of pale and thoughtful men passed out onto the 8
street, and the mournful scene was at an end," a reporter wrote
in 1878 of the aftermath of the hanging of one John Devine.

Today we can gather in our dens to watch some of the 9
very worst life has to offer. We can turn on our televisions and
see murders, gang rapes and suicide. Simulations all, but
many of the simulations are convincing enough to make us
wince, cringe, change the channel. It's likely that those surroundings would give an execution an air of unreality, and
that is dangerous. Dangerous, too, is our usual role of voyeur
as we sit in front of the set. In this act, we are not only viewers
but participants.

There are those who say that if we are capable of looking 10
this in the eye, we have lost some of our humanity. I'm one of
those who believe that we've lost some of our humanity by allowing it in the first place, by trying to even the score with the
sociopaths by adopting some pale approximation of their tactics.
People call this kind of thing shock television, but that's 11
the old kill-the-messenger attitude. The shocking thing has
nothing to do with cameras or microphones. The shocking
thing is there whether we reporters are there or not. "It's bar-
baric," a reporter named Mary Crawford wrote after witness-
ing the Chessman execution. Having it on television makes it
no worse. It simply makes the reality inescapable, and our role
undeniable. If we want it, we should be able to look at it. If we
can't bear to look at it, maybe it's time to rethink our desires.

Checking Your Understanding

1. Both Quindlen and Lewis oppose the death penalty, yet they take
   different sides on the question of televising executions. With which
   position do you find yourself agreeing and why?
2. How did you respond to Quindlen's image: "a few good buddies
   gather round the tube with a six-pack and a pepperoni pizza for a
   Fry 'Em party"?
3. What effect do you think televised executions would have on the
   legality of the death penalty? Explain your position.

Examining Rhetorical Strategies

1. Compare and contrast the manner by which Lewis and Quindlen lay
   the foundations that support their positions.
2. How does Quindlen's position that if "we can't bear to look at [exe-
   cutions], maybe it's time to rethink our desires" serve to support her
   purpose for writing?

A SUMMARY OF AFFIRMING READING

As you can see from the range of samples in this chapter, affirming
writing is much more varied and complex than simply stating an
opinion. Some examples rely heavily on aspects of expressive discourse; others rely heavily on aspects of argumentation that fore-
shadow persuasive discourse. However, all the pieces are united by a
common purpose: *to share a thoughtfully considered opinion with others.*

We have seen, for example, that *support* for an opinion may take the form of personal experiences and observations. What we do and what we see play a vital role in the shaping of our perspectives. Life experiences shape the ideas and beliefs that we hold dear. We have also seen that information and logical support often serve the sharing of a position. What we learn from other authors, the insight we gain from those more knowledgeable than ourselves, these things, too, are valuable in supporting and reinforcing our opinions.

Along with different kinds of support comes a variety of the types of ideas, feelings, beliefs, and positions being shared. Some affirming writing reflects the author's struggle to change an assumption or abandon a once firm position. Other affirming writing tends to focus on how and why the author arrived at a certain position. Some affirming writing *seeks to reinforce the target readers' existing positions* on an issue. By strengthening readers' opinions on a topic, the author may foster in those readers a readiness to act or to respond.

How we, as readers, *respond* to affirming discourse largely depends on our prior knowledge of the topic on which a position is taken. The more expressive types of affirming writing often leave us sympathizing with an author's position, even if we disagree with that position. The more informative pieces of affirming writing often leave us appreciating the logical substantiation of an author's position, even if we are still uncertain of our own position.

Finally, the success of affirming writing depends not only on the substantiation of and rationale for the position being communicated but also on the quality of the *voice* projected by the author. In the more expressive types of affirming writing, this voice often comes across as genuine, forthright, and honest: There is no sense of a hidden agenda or masked motives. We are drawn to the personality of the author and, thus, more likely to empathize with the experiences shared and the position taken. In the more informative—sometimes argumentative—pieces of affirming discourse, this voice often comes across as knowledgeable, thoughtful, and reasonable: There is no sense of dogma or narrow-mindedness as there would be with soapbox rhetoric or propaganda.

In other words, we sense the quality in affirming writing by the genuine nature of the experiences shared and the thoughtfulness reflected in the information shared. We sense the care with which the author has considered the position taken and the importance the author places on the sharing of that position.

Chapter Seven

WRITING AFFIRMING DISCOURSE

"Share an opinion you feel strongly about," the teacher says, and at first this seems an easy step from expressive writing. After all, supporting an opinion with personal experiences and observations should be easy. You're not being asked to change your readers' views on a topic, as is the case with persuasive discourse; you just need to explain what you believe.

But sharing and supporting an opinion can often present writers with unforeseen challenges. All too often, writers of affirming discourse mistake a know-it-all or soapbox rhetoric approach for successful communication of their opinions. Sounding off about an opinion in and of itself does not make for successful affirming writing. And just because the purpose is not to change the way your target audience views the topic, does not mean "anything goes" in terms of acceptable support. You need to offer thoughtful, interesting, and even compelling support for your feelings and beliefs if your readers are to give them the serious consideration they deserve.

DETERMINING YOUR RELATIONSHIP
TO YOUR READERS

In affirming discourse, there is a very special relationship between the writer and the reader due to the assumption of a preexisting common ground. This common ground creates an important bond that we often do not feel when reading about ideas very different from our own. Whether sharing a personal opinion, supporting a position, or laying a foundation for change, we may assume that there are areas of agreement between our readers and ourselves, and that our topic already has some degree of impact on the lives of our readers.

The different kinds of affirming writing can thus be discussed in terms of how much common ground is shared and how much direct impact the topic has on the lives of our readers. The more relevant the topic is to their lives, the more motivated our readers tend to be. Thus, it is very important that before you share your opinions with others, you first decide what to focus on and why this topic is relevant to your audience.

SELECTING A FOCUS

Affirming writing presents many challenges similar to those you faced in expressive writing. You didn't arrive at your current position on a topic overnight: Numerous experiences and observations, along with a considerable amount of thought, led you to the opinion you now hold. There is a lot to choose from as you consider how best to support your opinion and develop your ideas. Sometimes you will want to share the story of how you came to see the topic the way you do. With some topics your story may be one of how you came to abandon one position in favor of another. Your support may best take the form of a single experience, shared vividly, that shaped or reinforced your opinion; in other instances it may best take the form of selectively sharing researched information that serves to undergird your opinion.

Without a good focus—the most compelling reasons for your having arrived at your opinion—your readers may be left unmoved, may be left feeling that your position is shallow rather than well considered, reactionary rather than valid. You must choose your support wisely so that your readers understand and appreciate both how you arrived at your position and why this position is important enough for you to want to write about it.

In order to write a good affirming essay, then, you will not only need to *select a topic* but also to *narrow your topic* down to one *main point* or *thesis* so as not to be overwhelmed by all the support you could share for the opinion you wish to affirm.

Selecting a Topic

The good news about affirming writing is that you do not need to persuade your readers to embrace your opinion. They do not have to agree with you or change their views for successful writing to have occurred. The bad news is that the dreaded "So what?" response is still a land mine to be avoided. As readers of affirming discourse, we approach the text expecting the author's position to be substantiated in an interesting and compelling manner. As writers of affirming discourse, then, we want the significance of our experience to grow naturally out of the focus we have selected. We want to establish our role as a thoughtful writer who has carefully considered the opinion and has compelling support for that opinion. We also want to share our opinion with readers in such a way as to help them see why it is in their interest to give thoughtful consideration to the topic in question.

The best way to select a topic for an affirming piece, then, is to make a list of your *interests* and your *beliefs*. We are all interested in numerous subjects that shape who we are and how we view the world around us. When we have strong beliefs about a subject that interests us, we are often well equipped to share those beliefs in such a manner as to capture the interest of our readers.

Narrowing Your Topic

Once you have selected a topic that interests you and about which you hold strong beliefs, you need to consider a specific aspect of the topic upon which you will *focus*. For example, one student, who had started listening to the Grateful Dead in high school, wanted to write a paper in which he took the position that this musical group was one of the most exciting and important bands of the last thirty years. When it came time to brainstorm in preparation for writing that first rough draft, however, he found himself having trouble getting started. He hadn't expected this.

He had been to several concerts, read numerous books about the band, purchased the better part of the Grateful Dead's CD catalog, and traded bootleg tapes of shows with his friends. There was so much he wanted to say about the band that didn't know where to begin. So, while he knew a lot about the band and its music, without a narrowed focus on the topic his depth of knowledge was leading to writer's block rather than the easy first draft he had expected to crank out in an hour or so.

The solution came during a small group exercise the teacher had assigned. The students broke up into groups of three and, after sharing their paper topics, began asking one another questions. When the woman to his left asked him to describe the first Grateful Dead concert he had attended, things finally started to click. Rather than trying to support his position on the band's excellence by picking and choosing from nearly thirty years of concerts and recordings, he narrowed his topic to his first Grateful Dead concert.

Once the focus of the paper had been narrowed, the topic became manageable. Soon he had a clear purpose for writing: to describe his first Grateful Dead concert in such a way as to support his position on the band's merits. This clear writing purpose led him to answer the important question, "Who needs to read this and why?" with the answer, "Those who enjoy live music but have never been to a Grateful Dead show and who wonder what all the fuss is about."

MAKING IT SIGNIFICANT FOR YOUR AUDIENCE

One aspect of affirming writing that makes it challenging is the need to juggle both personal experiences and pertinent support for your opinion. Sometimes it is easier to share impersonal facts that support your position at the expense of important personal insights. This common pitfall can result in the disappearance of your personality. The result may be logical support for an opinion that comes off as dull and lifeless, almost as if it were the voice of a computer program rather than the voice of a unique human being's experiences, observations, and insights.

As we saw in Chapter Six, there exists in affirming discourse a spectrum that moves from writing distinguished primarily by the sharing of personal experiences and observations to writing distinguished primarily by the sharing of pertinent support in order to achieve your purpose. As you consider your topic and your audience, then, you will need to consider the best way to create and sustain reader interest while sharing the kind of support that will substantiate and validate the position you embrace. To simplify these considerations, you need to decide if you want to appeal primarily to the target readers' emotions or to their desire for the reasons behind the opinion.

ORGANIZING YOUR THOUGHTS

While narrative remains a viable option for writers of affirming discourse, an additional challenge will be deciding when and how to introduce your opinion. It can be introduced at the beginning of the paper, leaving the rest of the text for development of support, or it can be saved for the close so that the experiences and ideas that led up to the opinion are suddenly infused with a compelling purpose.

Your decision about whether to focus on the evolution of an opinion, the changing of an opinion, the single event that cemented an opinion, the events or observations that reinforced an opinion, or the relevance of your opinion in light of current events, will serve to help you in choosing an *organizational strategy*. Whatever focus you decide on, however, your first draft should establish the opinion you wish to share and offer at least one reason for your belief.

As you develop the *support* for your position, you will want to consider your organizational strategies and revision goals for enhancing them. You may find that several experiences and observations need to be shared in order to create compelling support for your position or, you may find that a single experience, recounted with vivid descriptive language, is the best way to support your ideas. As you revise, don't be afraid to take some chances and try different organizational strategies.

Notes on the Opinion Essay

With this type of affirming discourse it is usually helpful to *focus* on your experiences as they relate to the opinion you are supporting. Organizing the *support* so that your opinion comes across as justified and well considered will help in achieving your *purpose* for writing. In writing the personal opinion essay, the goal is to use the descriptive and narrative skills practiced in writing expressively so as to support the opinion that grew out of, was changed by, or was reinforced by the experience being shared.

As you move from one draft to the next, you may *discover* support that you had not initially remembered. You may also begin to reevaluate or refine the opinion you are supporting. Because the writing process naturally encourages us to make discoveries as we write and revise, we are free to reconsider both our opinions and the events that served to shape them. The more you write the less unsettling these discoveries will be. It is a common misconception about writing that we must know exactly what we want to say before we ever start writing. As you become a more experienced writer you will begin to embrace writing's capacity to facilitate the discovery of new ideas, rather than fear it as a sign of poor planning.

Notes on the Position Paper

With the position paper we begin the movement away from personal experiences as the main source of support for our opinions. Thus, the sharing of a personal experience to prepare your *audience* for the position you plan to support is no longer the best way to organize your affirming discourse. Supporting a position for those who are uninformed or apathetic about your topic is a more complicated writing purpose than sharing an experience or observation to support a personal opinion. It is helpful to keep in mind that there are subtle differences between supporting a position and arguing a position. The former assumes an audience without extensive knowledge or firm opinions on the topic; the latter assumes an audience that already has some knowledge and some fairly firm opinions that differ from your own.

With this in mind, it is important to organize your position paper in such a way so as to make your position clear, your support varied. A good question to ask as you plan and draft your position paper is "What do I know about this topic, and how did I come by this knowledge?" Answers to the second part of this question may include things you've observed, read, heard, and experienced.

Notes on the Editorial

With the editorial your writing *purpose* is to lay the foundation for change. With this kind of affirming discourse you will begin to anticipate some of the techniques used in successful persuasive writing. To generalize, the purpose of editorializing is not to change the minds of the readers, but to provide, through your support the kind of food for thought that may make them ripe for persuasion later on. The audience for editorials does not necessarily disagree with the position taken by the author. In fact, we often select the editorials we read because the title suggests that our current positions will be reinforced. Nevertheless, the primary readers of most editorial writing are those who need more information before they embrace a position or those who are sitting on a fence—not yet certain which way they may come down on the topic.

THE WRITING PROCESS AT WORK

Supporting your position in a compelling fashion can be achieved in numerous ways. In this section we will examine two drafts of a student writer's paper on his interest in fishing, an interest he had not expected to develop. In "The Joys and Rewards of Fishing" you will see Edward Hardy developing his *support* in greater and greater detail as he revises from one draft to the next.

THE JOYS AND REWARDS OF FISHING

Edward Hardy

Background

Hardy was a first-year student when he wrote this essay for the third assignment in his composition class. Hardy had become interested in fishing during the summer before he started college. Later in the semester he wrote an informative paper on the art of fly casting.

First Draft

Fishing. Many thoughts come to mind when I think of that word. It can mean kicking back on a hot, lazy summer day. It can mean the thrill of the catch. It can mean just being by myself, and being one with nature. 1

Most people feel that fishing is a very boring thing to do. Some even think that it is a big waste of time. I felt that way when I first started to fish but then something happened, I had a change of heart. It was a long time ago and I was out fishing with my friend. I was bored stiff. All that I could think about was to throw my friend into the lake and go home to do something more exciting like rearranging my underwear and sock drawer. I vowed that day I would never go fishing again. But then something happened, I got a nibble, I got a strike, but he got away. I stood there for two more hours just trying to get that fish, with no avail. I had a good time after that, and I learned my first lesson through fishing, and that was not to give up on anything too easy, at least without giving it a fair chance. 2

Fishing is a stress reliever. Sometimes the hustle and bustle of life grows on me like a wart. And to burn off that wart I grab a pole, a couple of worms and try to outsmart the fish, just like people try to outsmart me. Fishing is more of a state of mind than anything. When I brain-stormed in the beginning I thought: fishing—relaxation to relieve stress; fishing—a challenge to myself to be smarter than that fish; and fishing—peace and quiet. 3

Here is one of my typical fishing stories. It's 10:00 in 4
the morning. I just woke up after a lousy night's sleep. A
thought goes through my mind: it's Saturday! A long week
of working in the factory is over, temporarily. I grasp my
Garcia reel and my Ugly Stick pole. I decide whether I
should go fishing at Venture Lake, just to be away from any
other people. I go out to my mother's garden and dig up a
few worms. Off to the peace and quiet! I find a good spot
where fish usually are, which is a big tree that was struck by
lightning, years ago, by the gods up above (probably
because they like to fish, too). I proceed to bait my hook,
the worm wiggles with pain at first but stops because it now
realizes why it existed, it realizes its higher calling. I crank
back my pole, release the reel hold, and zoom—off it goes.
The first cast of the day is always more special than any of
the rest because of its symbolic meaning which is the throwing away of my stress, worries and problems. Then the bobber bobs, it must be a fish. I carefully wait for the right second then—yank, I've got him. The fish struggles at the
other end of the line, he knows if I get him on to the shore
it's lights out. I get him to shore and something overtakes
me. A deep thought: Am I as much of a sucker for the bait
of life as this fish is for the worm? The sun strikes my eyes
like a blind man seeing the light for the very first time. I
shudder; a strange kind of compassion fills me. I let the fish
off the hook, sort of hoping that if I were a sucker for the
bait, he'd let me go.

After that experience, I pack up my gear, pull out a beer 5
and thank the heavens above for teaching me a new lesson.
That's what fishing can offer. The day has grown short and I
have learned a new lesson.

Writer's comments I chose this topic because the interest was
a recent one that was fresh in my mind. Also, in the sample opinion essay we read for class the author talked about how she had
changed her opinion on a topic. This reminded me of how I once
thought of fishing as the most boring activity imaginable. To get
started I just thought about some of the negative things I used to
think about fishing and followed these with some experiences that
changed my mind.

Teacher's comments   This is a very nice first draft. I like the way you move from your old opinion to your new found appreciation of fishing. You have generated a lot of material for a first draft, so it will be easier to think of revision strategies. Are there additional reasons you had a negative view of fishing? What are some other reasons you came to enjoy fishing? Will your readers be familiar with terms such as "Ugly Stick," "Garcia reel," and "reel hold"? Is your audience all people who do not fish? Is there a way to narrow this audience? Would it help to narrow the focus to a specific kind of fishing? I like your role development; your personality is really coming through. How might you develop the close of the paper to strengthen your support for fishing?

Analysis

Hardy does a nice job of sharing his change of opinion in a way that reveals a clear, distinct voice. His purpose of supporting his new opinion of fishing is clear, despite some problems. Hardy has generated sufficient material in his first draft to allow numerous options for revision. He has already linked his opinion of fishing to a larger issue: not giving up on or prejudging anything without giving it a fair chance. This is something that many writers have not achieved by their final draft.

The teacher's comments are aimed at making Hardy think about ways to develop his support and narrow his target audience. There is a lot going on in his first draft—much of it good, but it runs out of steam toward the close. To understand why he feels so strongly about fishing, we need more detailed description of his experiences. What exactly is it about this activity that has led Hardy to reverse his opinion?

In the second draft, Hardy was able to develop the strengths of the first draft while working out some of the problem areas. Hardy's three major revision goals for his second draft were clear: to develop the conclusion, to add more description of his experiences, and to expand on the introduction in such a way as to immediately establish solid support for his opinion. In his final draft, Hardy will share more of his knowledge on the topic to further support his position and subtly hint at persuading others to consider taking up the sport.

Final Draft

Fishing. Many thoughts come to mind when I think of 1
that word. It can mean kicking back on a hot, lazy summer
day. It can conjure up images of a smooth, crystal clear lake
with mysteries hidden beneath its surface. The unknown of
the murky depths calls me, challenges me to offer bait to the
creatures that call it home. Fishing can mean the peaceful
wait as well as thrill of bait taken and subsequent struggle. It
can ultimately mean the fish breaking the water's surface as
it is caught, or slipping the hook—escaping unseen. It can
also mean just being by myself, and with nature.

Most people feel that fishing is a very boring thing to 2
do. Some even think that it is a big waste of time. Who wants
to sit around waiting for a bobber or fly to attract a blue gill
or bass? Or, worse yet, who wants to put a slimy, protesting
worm onto a sharp hook? I found myself asking these very
questions when I first started to fish but then something happened: I had a battle with a bass. It was a long time ago and
I was out fishing with my friend, John. I was bored stiff. All
that I could think about was wanting to throw John into the
lake and go home to do something more exciting like rearranging my underwear and sock drawer. I vowed that day I
would never go fishing again. But then it happened: I got a
nibble, then a strike, but the fish got away. I had seen it for a
fleeting moment as it broke the surface as if to laugh at me
for thinking I could hook such a large bass. I stood there for
two more hours just trying to get that big, beautiful fish, to no
avail. Unlike that bass, I was hooked—on fishing. I learned an
important lesson through fishing, and that was not to give up
on anything without giving it a fair chance.

Once I gave fishing a fair chance I knew it was some- 3
thing I would enjoy and become better at with time and experience. Fishing has many qualities to recommend it. For
starters, fishing is a stress reliever. Sometimes the hustle and
bustle of life grows on me like a wart. And to burn off that
wart I grab my fishing pole, a couple of worms and try to outsmart the fish, just like people try to outsmart me in my day
to day life. For example, at work I grow weary of the constant
competitiveness and back-stabbing that go on. Everyone
seems to want to be on the boss's good side, even if it means

stepping on co-workers to get there. Fishing isn't about defeating another human; fishing is about the challenge of knowing the right bait for the right species of fish, the lay of the lake, the best time of day, even the best temperature of both water and air for the catching of fish. Being a good fisherman takes the skills of a detective: one must learn what clues are given by various aquatic plant life (are there bass beneath that bed of reeds?), by the rippling of the water's surface, and by the motion of the bobber.

Fishing is more of a state of mind than anything. It is   4
respect for living creatures, a respect that grows as many fish escape and as those caught are cleaned and cooked for a delicious supper. It is a respect for the sounds of the outdoors without boom-boxes, car horns, or exhaust fumes. It is a respect for patience and its virtues. If you feel that being alone with your thoughts on the bank of a scenic lake is boring, this may be a hint that it's time to escape the hectic pace of the city for a while—you may be very pleasantly surprised at just how much the unspoiled outdoors has to offer by way of rejuvenating the spirit.

It may be easier for those who do not fish to appreci-   5
ate the sport if I share a typical day at the lake. It's 8:00 in the morning. I just woke up after a restless night's sleep. A thought goes through my mind: it's Saturday! A long week of working in the factory is over. I grasp my Garcia reel and my Ugly Stick pole: good gear purchased at a very reasonable price. I decide to go fishing at Venture Lake, just to be away from any other people. I go out to my mother's garden and dig up a few worms. Off to the peace and quiet! As I drive to the lake I can feel the tensions and frustrations of the week slowly recede into the recesses of my mind. I find a good spot where fish usually are, which is marked by a big tree that was struck by lightning, years ago. I proceed to bait my hook. The worm wiggles and wriggles at first, but soon it is on the hook and ready to attract a hungry fish. I crank back my pole, release the reel hold, and zoom—off it goes.

The first cast of the day is always more special than any   6
of the rest because of its symbolic meaning which is the throwing away of my stress, worries, and problems. Then the bobber bobs, it must be a fish. I carefully wait for the right

second then—yank, I've got him. The fish struggles at the other end of the line, he knows if I get him on to the shore it's lights out. I get him to shore, but once I examine this marvelous specimen of bass a strange kind of compassion fills me. I let the big fish off the hook, sort of hoping that if our roles were reversed, he'd let me go. A small hawk flies overhead, reminding me that the skies are as full of life as the waters.

After that experience, I set down my gear, pull out a   7
beer (fishing can be thirsty work) and thank the heavens above for the wonderful lake and many species of fish that lurk beneath its surface. I think back to the time when I thought of fishing as boring and am glad I gave the sport a chance. For no matter how much or how little I catch, I always leave with a renewed respect for nature and for myself: nature for her beauty, myself for new patience and thoughtfulness as I wait for a fish to take my bait. Patience in life, as in fishing, often results in unexpected rewards and successes.

Analysis

The changes between Hardy's first and final drafts help him to clarify his opinion and strengthen the use of his experience for support. He shares with us a little about why he is so anxious to escape from the atmosphere of his workplace and develops further the descriptive (and informative) aspects of his support. Also, instead of accusing those who don't want to stand on the bank of a lake of not being very reflective, he blames the hectic pace of everyday life for leading his readers to forget just how much the great outdoors has to offer.

Stylistically, Hardy has greatly enhanced the quality of his paper. Take a look at how his revisions of the introductory paragraph have improved it. He introduces the topic of fishing in a way that gets our attention and prepares us for his support of his opinion. Hardy's final draft reminds us that really fine expressive writing can provide powerful affirmation of the writer's position.

We are left with, if not a desire to run out and buy a rod and reel, a keen appreciation for why Hardy feels the way he does about the sport of fishing. He has supported his position well and in a manner that reflects the descriptive skills he gained though his expressive writing.

Exercise

Imagine that you are the author of Hardy's paper on fishing. You have just received the "final" draft back with comments from the teacher. Your teacher says that this same topic might work well with the next assignment: persuasive writing. Rewrite the introduction to the final draft with the goal of persuading your readers to try their hand at fishing.

WRITING FOR READERS

Hardy put enough time and effort into his first draft so that he had a lot to work with. Generating sufficient material for a first draft is a common problem for writers. It is easy to let perfectionism and anxiety cause blocking and frustration. Looking back at Hardy's first draft, we see that it has a lot of problems but also a lot of promise. He wasn't afraid to get his initial memories and thoughts down on paper. Sometimes it helps to think of a first draft as though it were a lump of clay on the potter's wheel. If we're not afraid to have some problems in our initial draft, it becomes much easier to get the clay on the wheel so that the process of shaping and enhancing become possible. Without a sufficient first draft "blob of clay," purposeful revision becomes a most difficult task, indeed.

STRATEGIES FOR WRITING AFFIRMING DISCOURSE

The assignment   Review the *purpose* of the assignment. Remember that affirming writing requires support for the opinions being shared. You will need to select a topic that you feel strongly about, that reveals ideas and beliefs that are important to you.

Prewriting   Make a list of opinions you hold dear and circle three or four that are especially important to you. Think about how you came to embrace these opinions and why they are important beliefs. It can be very helpful to freewrite on each of these for at least five minutes. Often the best freewriting—that which flows from the pen and evokes strong feelings you wish to share with others—will indicate a good *subject* for a paper.

Drafting   While you are writing, keep the following four goals discussed in Chapter Four in mind.

1. Determine the identity of and your relationship with your readers. Ask yourself who needs to know of your position on the topic and why that need might exist. Consider what kind of *voice* you will use to express and support the position you wish to affirm. What kind of person were you when you came to embrace the position you now hold dear? What aspects of who you are will best serve to support your beliefs and opinions?

2. Select the *focus* of your subject carefully. It is much easier to support a position once you have narrowed the focus on the subject. For example, if you decided to write a paper supporting the position that _____ (fill in the blank as you see fit) is an important and innovative musical group, the subject might be unwieldy. Yet, by narrowing the focus of the paper to one specific CD by that band, the subject becomes manageable. It is much easier to support a position once you have sufficiently narrowed the focus.

3. Make the *significance* of your position clear to your readers. Why is the subject important enough to merit your readers' attention? How does your support for your position make for a unique exploration of the subject? Remember you need not state this message explicitly, but if you do not, the significance needs to be clear through the compelling and thought-provoking nature of your support.

4. *Organize* your thoughts. Most affirming pieces make the author's position clear at the outset and follow up with various kinds of support: personal experiences, observations, anecdotes, facts, and other writers' views on the subject. Remember that some affirming discourse is best supported with emotional appeals, while other affirming discourse is best supported by logical appeals. You will learn more about these appeals in Chapters Nine and Ten.

Editing   As you edit pay particular attention to the following aspects of affirming discourse:

A good, consistent voice

A clear position on a narrowly focused topic

Compelling and thought-provoking support for the position

A strong sense of the audience with whom your position is being shared

Clear significance of the position being embraced

A main point around which all of the support revolves

Chapter Eight

FURTHER AFFIRMING READINGS

The readings contained in this chapter illustrate a wide variety of affirming discourse, ranging from the expressive support found in "Blessings" and "Deep Within," to the logical support found in President Clinton's inaugural address and Sally Clark's "Multiculturalism and Education: A Question of Perspective."

PROFESSIONAL ESSAYS AND READING TECHNIQUES

BLESSINGS

Carol Spindel

Prereading Journal

In this reading, Spindel says she "believes in Something," yet she "[doesn't] want that Something defined too clearly." Think of a time when someone or some group tried to tell you what you should believe in rather than encouraging you to make your own discoveries. What was the result of this interference? How did it differ from someone offering you guidance?

Background

"Blessings" comes from the book, *In the Garden of the Sacred Grove*. Here Spindel describes her stay in Kalikaha and her response to the Moslem blessings she continually receives. These experiences lead her to the personal opinion she states at the close of this essay.

During Reading

Keep a list of the blessings Spindel mentions that you find especially significant.

Reading Selection

Before Adama became our interpreter, the constant 1
exchange of blessings made me a little uneasy. After all, the one I received most frequently was "May Allah give you children." In Berkeley, having a child was a weighty personal decision, something one pondered for years and went to therapy to resolve, not something one wished lightly on others like, "Have a good day." When the blessing was given in Senufo, the deity was Kolotyolo, and so I could translate it, "May Ancient Mother give you children." I preferred the Senufo version because I thought that Ancient Mother was more likely to understand my feelings on the matter: children were desirable, but there were better and worse times to

receive them. As far as Allah was concerned, I imagined him to be the Grand Old Patriarch with a white beard who had never actually carried a baby on his back or wiped a runny nose, and I figured that his main concern in the matter was the production of more little Moslems. If this were true, an infidel like me was probably safe from his schemes for the grand design of things. Nevertheless, the constant collective desire of sixteen hundred people to see me become pregnant as expressed through frequent fervent blessings gave me pause for thought.

Whenever I gained a few pounds or was sick to my stom- 2
ach, I could see their eyes light up hopefully. Against this strong a collective desire, I worried that my diaphragm would prove too weak. After all, it was designed to repel mere matter. Could it really stand up against something as powerful as the collective faith of an entire village who daily invoked two different deities to aid them in their desire to see me bear a child? Did a man-made scrap of rubber, an upstart human invention, have a chance against a desire that strong and that ancient? This is what I asked myself uneasily as I muttered "*amina*" to their blessings.

Whenever Adama translated the blessings, he always 3
used the French word *Dieu* for God, and this also made me feel uneasy. I wasn't sure I believed in one. Certainly I believed in vague "forces" or "powers" in the universe, but I felt more comfortable if I left my forces in an unnamed state of spiritual ambiguity. Like many people I knew, I claimed to believe in Something. I just didn't want that Something defined too clearly.

But the forces I felt in the universe were not something I 4
invoked as personally and specifically as the people of Kalikaha invoked theirs. When Sita prayed at dawn, she seemed to open her heart to Allah in a way I had never considered doing. And when my neighbors gave me blessings, they were always concrete and specific. They asked God to give me a good afternoon or a peaceful night or to help with my work that day, to give me a child, a harmonious marriage, a safe trip back from Korhogo, and a long life. At first, I tapped my forehead to help the blessing sink in and muttered "*amina*" as a matter of course. I was pleased that I was able to catch the first word, *Allah*, and that I could respond appropriately by saying "amen."

Being around Adama changed me. When we went into 5
the village to do interviews, Adama gave out blessings to
everyone. This was something Yardjuma had never done. If
someone told Adama of a death or an illness, he immediately responded with a heartfelt blessing. "*Allah ka nagoya kay.*
May God make it better. *Allah ka hinara.* May this person go
to heaven." The blessings soothed the roughness of the
moment. This did not mean that Adama did not try to help.
He did. But first, he always invoked God's aid.

"May God give your children life," Adama said fervent- 6
ly to every mother. And they all, no matter how young and
hopeful or how old and wizened, whispered intently, "*amina*"
and their eyes thanked Adama for expressing the concern
that they lived with daily in their hearts.

This giving out of blessings was more than polite utter- 7
ance. It was a way of sharing hope, for people in Kalikaha
needed hope to survive. No abstract relationship with deities
who lived far above, this was a gritty daily contact with two
deities who seemed through people's words, to be always present in the village with us. Nor were the dieties themselves
estranged in enmity. Sometimes Adama spoke in Senufo of
Ancient Mother, sometimes in Dyula of Allah; to us he spoke
in French of *Dieu.* When I questioned him about distinctions,
he said it didn't matter, that God was always the same.

Tom and I, at the end of interviews and conversations, 8
found ourselves making up our own blessings and asking
Adama to translate and deliver them for us. I didn't do this
unconsciously, the way I sometimes picked up new words.
Rather, I found myself wanting to hand out blessings and
feeling sincerely touched and, in the most appropriate word,
blessed, when I received them.

I started a page in my Dyula notebook for blessings and 9
began to learn the hundreds of different ones that applied to
particular situations. "I need a blessing to help the potters
with their work," I would say to Adama. "One that says 'May
the firing turn out well.' "

"*Allah an jayma,*" replied Adama instantly. "May Allah 10
help us in our work."

Adama regarded my new relationship to blessings with 11
obvious approval, and the page of blessings in my dog-eared
Dyula notebook was quickly filled. There was a blessing for

the young Dyula girls who wandered through the village selling bits of soap or bouillon cubes. "God help the alleyways to
please you." When someone bought a new piece of cloth in
the market, you said, "May it wear out before you do," a pragmatic blessing if ever there was one. At about three-thirty, I
could bring smiles to the stony faces of even the most proper
Dyula elders by saying as I passed them on their way to the
mosque, "May the afternoon prayers be good."

When I gave out my favorite blessing, I could never 12
keep a totally straight face—a certain irrepressible delight in
the phrase itself always came out with it. It was so idiomatic,
so absolutely, essentially Dyula in character, that villagers
crowed with delight at the absurdity of hearing it from me. I
could astonish Dyula guests in the village by casually saying as
I told them good night, "*Allah yan kelen kelen wuli.*" Literally,
it means "May everyone here wake up one at a time."

"Do you know the value of waking up one at a time?" 13
the Dyula man who taught me this blessing asked me. I had
to admit that I had no idea.

"If there is some disaster in the night," he replied, "like a 14
fire or a death or a war, someone will call out, and we will all
wake up at once. But if the night passes in peace, each of us will
wake up in the morning at our own moment, one at a time."

When someone gave a gift, everyone present showered 15
the giver with blessings. The most frequent was "*Allah i bara-
ji.*" "May God give you something even greater than what you
have given me." This blessing represents most clearly the
sense in traditional African thought of the communal good.
For it will probably not be me who will repay you. Life is not
that neat, and Africans do not pretend that it is. To assume
the responsibility for equity yourself is a form of arrogance in
Kalikaha. You receive from those more fortunate than you—
older, wiser, or wealthier. You give to those less fortunate. The
age class system is based on these precepts. Somehow, the gift
will be returned. It will not come back in the same form. Nor
will it come back from the same hand. Years may pass.

It was not only knowing the blessing which was impor- 16
tant but also saying it at the proper time, with (of utmost
importance) the proper pauses. If I blurted out a blessing at
the wrong moment, no one understood. They didn't say
"*amina,*" even though I was sure I had gotten the words right.

Not only did I need to know the right words. I needed   17
to know the appropriate situations in which blessings were
given and the appropriate moments at which to give them.
Once Tom and I had mastered that, we progressed to multiple blessings. Blessings flowed nicely when they came in
three's. "May God heal you. May God grant you happiness.
May God give you a long life." We learned to pronounce
them one after another with just the right pause between.
Then we were rewarded with a long chorus of head-tapping
and the soft sound of "*amina, amina, amina here be.*" The best
reward of all was seeing the soft look of appreciation, that
moment of *blessedness* that came over people when they
received a string of heartfelt blessings.

The sound of the three blessings reminded me of ser-   18
vices when I was a girl and how, at the end, the rabbi always
raised his arms. We were supposed to bow our heads, but I
always looked up to see his black bell-shaped sleeves stretched
out like wings as he gave three singsong blessings in Hebrew
and English, with a long pause between each one—the same
long pause they used in Kalikaha. But in Kalikaha, I didn't
need to be a rabbi and I didn't need a long black robe.

I do not feel nearly so powerful nor so rational as I did   19
before I went to Kalikaha. There, I saw my good intentions go
awry too many times. In Kalikaha, I tried to save a child, a
month-old baby. I failed. The baby died. And when Adama
said, "It is God's will. May the child go to heaven," I felt a little bit comforted. Not everything is within our will or understanding. Not everything can be harnessed by our rational
powers. In Kalikaha, I felt a spirituality that was threaded
through every small encounter. I no longer hesitate to call on
the help of other powers and to wish that help on my friends.
When I speak to myself, I call these blessings what they truly
are: prayers.

Checking Your Understanding

1. Take a look at the list of blessings you made and select the most
    important item from it. Why is this one so important to you?
2. Why do you think Spindel's experiences in Kalikaha served to rein-
    vigorate and enlarge her spiritual awareness? What aspects of our
    society do you feel tend to positively or adversely impact on your
    sense of spirituality?

Examining Rhetorical Strategies

1. How does Spindel make you feel that you are sharing her experiences in Kalikaha?

2. What assumptions can you make about the Kalikahaian culture based on the author's experiences? How does the sharing of these experiences serve to support the author's personal opinion?

TOO LATE TO SAY "I'M SORRY"

Joseph M. Queenan

Prereading Journal

Think back on a time when someone needed your forgiveness. Describe the action or deed for which that person sought forgiveness and your ability or inability to forgive her or him.

Background

Queenan's essay first appeared in *Newsweek* on August 31, 1987. Using strategies of expressive writing, he develops his personal story here with the purpose of supporting his opinion about his father.

During Reading

Note the places where Queenan underlines words or phrases. How do these underlinings enforce the ideas he is trying to communicate?

Reading Selection

Three years ago, my recovering alcoholic father called 1 me into my mother's kitchen to apologize for all the pain he inflicted on me for so many years. "One of the things I've learned through Alcoholics Anonymous is that you have to admit that you've hurt people and have to let them know how sorry you are," he explained to me. "Son, I'm sorry for anything I may have done to harm you." He then shook my hand.

"<u>May</u> have done" was the part I liked. 2

Whether or not Alcoholics Anonymous actually tells its 3 members to go out and shake hands with their victims, this apology business has an air of the perfunctory. At least three friends have told me about tearful apologies from recovering alcoholic parents. And one woman I used to work with actually got a call from a boyfriend she hadn't heard from in 10 years; he wanted to apologize for his despicable behavior while in the grips of demon alcohol. She, like me, felt that there was something decidedly ritualistic about these apologies, as if the recovering alcoholic had a list of people he had to check off in a report to his AA sponsors.

In the case of my father, that list would require a lot of 4
phone calls. A textbook alcoholic, he beat his children, terrorized his wife, wrecked the house, went through an endless series of menial jobs and humiliated his family in front of friends. Like most alcoholics, he was a compulsive liar. Like many, he was lazy; I mean he didn't even bother to concoct new, more plausible lies. And at least three times a year he would explain disappearances of large sums of money by saying that his wallet had been stolen in the men's room at the North Philadelphia train station.

He would even implicate his children. Once, when I 5
was five, my father borrowed $20 from our parish pastor; then he took me to the local taproom, where for the next three hours we would rehearse the amount of money—$15, $10, $5—I was to tell my mother the priest had given him. He was a very persuasive coach.

One of the strongest memories of him is of the last time 6
we said the rosary together as a family. As usual, I was cranking it up in the local stickball game when my older sister came to fetch me home to worship a deity none of us were all that fond of, seeing as he seemed to be on such close terms with my father. The average rosary can be said in about 10 minutes, but Dad would drag it out to 45, by having us pause to reflect on the various spiritual incidents recounted after every 10 Hail Marys: Christ's Crucifixion, the Assumption of the Blessed Mary into Heaven. And so on. There are three sets of rosary "mysteries" said on different days and at different times of the year. They are the Joyful, the Sorrowful and the Glorious. But that last time we said the rosary together my father pitched forward dead drunk and passed out in the middle of the room. We left him there, face down on the carpet, all night. We had been saying the Glorious mysteries.

Like many alcoholics, my father behaved as though a 7
thing hadn't happened if he couldn't remember it. Coming down to breakfast to find a window on the back porch broken, he would say that he was sorry, but he had no idea how it happened. About twice a year his rampages became so violent that my mother would have to call the police, and my

father would spend the night in the cooler. He wouldn't recall that in the morning, either. He couldn't remember beatings, thefts, muggings, auto accidents, lies. He would have done well in Washington.

The next-to-last time that I saw my father, he'd come to 8 New York to borrow money. What little cash he'd had when he left Philadelphia had been stolen from his wallet by a heartless bellboy while he, the unsuspecting guest, was taking a shower in a seedy New York hotel. Bellboys. Showers. Seedy hotels. I knew the story by heart. I told him I'd give him enough money to get back to Philadelphia, but when we arrived at the Port Authority Bus Terminal, I bought the ticket and I put him on the bus. The fact that pickpockets abound on the streets of New York would only provide him with another excuse.

Mitigating circumstances: That was five years ago. Two 9 years later, at the age of 58, having no real contact with his children or grandchildren, having been thrown out of the house by my mother and having lost his job and pension, my father finally decided to do what we had been urging him to do for decades and give up drinking. After a fitful start, he's managed to go almost three years without a drink. My mother, who speaks with him occasionally (though she doesn't see him), says that he seems to be doing well, that he has a little job and lives in a little room. I wish him well, but I don't want to see him, either.

I hated my father for the first 20 years of my life. I don't 10 hate him anymore—today I understand some of the roots of his behavior. That he had an alcoholic father; that he grew up during the Depression; that he was a high-school dropout; that he served an 18-month stint in an Augusta, Ga., military prison for going AWOL to his mother's funeral. And that he had four children that he couldn't support. There are enough mitigating circumstances in my father's life to make me feel sorry for him and for others like him and to applaud their efforts to salvage something of their ruined lives. But "Tout comprendre c'est tout pardonner" is one maxim I don't buy.

I understand but I won't forgive. And so a word about 11 the etiquette of contrition. To all those who want to wipe the slate clean and launch brand-new relationships with those they <u>may</u> have harmed during their binges, stupors and rages, I would urge caution. If you're trying to pull your life together at a very late date—terrific. If you're genuinely sorry for whatever you've done and whomever you've harmed, tell them so. If feeling good about yourself is the only way to stay away from the bottle, feel free to feel good about yourself. Just don't think that a belated apology makes everything even-steven.

And don't go sticking your hand out waiting for some- 12
one to shake it. Keep it to yourself.

Checking Your Understanding

1. Queenan says that he understands his father's alcoholism but will not forgive him. Do you think he really understands? What does the tone of the piece suggest to you about the author's feelings for his father? Is the tone at odds with any claims the author makes?

2. Queenan uses a general term—"a textbook alcoholic"—to describe his father. He then gives us some common traits of alcoholics before moving on to specific incidents. Which of these incidents did you find most illuminating in helping you understand what it's like to be the child of an alcoholic? Notice the proportion of general, abstract statements to specific, concrete examples. In what ways is Queenan's use of specifics and abstractions like and unlike the other opinion essays you've read?

Examining Rhetorical Strategies

1. Queenan's essay was prompted by a specific incident—his father's asking for forgiveness. How does he use that incident to give structure to his essay? In what ways does using this incident make his structure similar to Murray's essay in Chapter Six or different from other affirming essays you have read?

2. To whom is this essay addressed? What audience do you think Queenan is trying to reach (other than readers of *Newsweek*)? What in the essay leads you to your conclusion? Do you feel that he is effective in reaching that audience?

THE MALE MANIFESTO

Andrew Kimbrell

Prereading Journal

Make a list of the images and issues that come to mind when you hear the phrase "men's movement."

Background

Andrew Kimbrell is a lawyer and environmentalist who writes frequently about men's issues. "The Male Manifesto" first appeared in *The New York Times* on June 4, 1991. He begins with a reference to a popular book along with information about the politics of "masculinity" to support this position paper on the subject of the changing role of men in society.

During Reading

Keep a list of the arguments Kimbrell makes to support his position on the development of the men's movement.

Reading Selection

In recent years, many men have awakened to a crisis of their gender. These men have begun to realize that for them and their fathers' generation, the necessities of work and career and the rising divorce rate have eroded their relationship to family, community and the natural world. This frustration and alienation has led an increasing number of men to gather in an loosely organized men's movement. 1

Most commentators don't seem to know how to react to this movement. The poet Robert Bly's best-selling book, "Iron John," has encouraged thousands of men to venture into wilderness retreats to rediscover the mythic dimensions of masculinity. 2

While some have sympathized with Mr. Bly's work, many find the sight of men drumming in the woods more humorous than provocative. Others don't know whether to be chagrined or alarmed by the prospect of men's rediscovering role models. Some confess to being a bit nervous about where the movement is headed. 3

However, few realized the political potential of the 4
men's movement. Although its roots are in consciousness
raising, the movement is forming what many are calling a
new politics of masculinity.

The politicization of the movement is based on an 5
understanding that most men are increasingly victimized.
Current statistics are grim. Teen-age and adult suicide, home-
lessness, unemployment, homicide, drug and alcohol addiction, heart disease and a variety of other stress-related health
problems plague more men at far higher rates than women.

Men are also experiencing a crisis in the family. Recent 6
polls show that an overwhelming number of men are torn
between the hours needed to support their families and the
need to share time with their families.

The situation among men who are minorities is even 7
worse. For example, black men have the lowest life expectancy of any segment of the population; more black men are in
jail than in college.

In understanding the victimization of men, the move- 8
ment has not attempted to establish a hierarchy of victimization. Men are resisting the idea, espoused by some feminists,
that maleness, and not society's system of controls and production, is responsible for the victimization of women.
Finally, men can begin to understand their victimization of
others only by acknowledging their own frustrations.

More important, men are realizing that they cannot 9
resolve their problems within the current understanding of
"masculinity." Over several generations, men have fallen victim to a defective mythology of manhood—a male mystique.
This mystique, propagated during the industrial age, has sub-
stituted mechanical attributes—efficiency, autonomy, inhuman power—for such traditional masculine traits as hus-
bandry, honor, relation to community and land.

Most significant, the factory system removed men from 10
the home, leaving a vacuum that has left generations of
young men without adequate male parenting or role models.
Moreover, the romanticized wars of this century have killed
millions of sons. It is a lingering irony that what many call a
patriarchal production system significantly degraded both
fatherhood and sonship.

Rejecting both the male mystique and anti-male ideol- 11
ogy, men have begun articulating a male manifesto—a political agenda intended to re-establish ties with one another,
their families, communities and the earth.

As men mourn the loss of fathers and family, they are 12
devoting themselves to increased parental leave and work-at-
home opportunities. As men recover a healthy sense of
inner "wildness," they are calling for more environmental
protection.

As men try to recover the dignity in their work, they 13
avoid the obeisance often called for in the corporate world in
favor of small-scale businesses. As men become aware of male
drug addiction, self-destructiveness and stress, they are organizing around men's health issues. As men realize that modern techno-war mocks the inner warrior aspect of men, they
reject modern warfare.

As the politics of the men's movement develops, it, like 14
the feminist movement, could change the face of electoral
politics. Up to now, women have been more likely than men
to support environmental protection and peaceful solutions
to world problems. The new politics of men could erase this
gender gap.

For those who thought the men's movement was just 15
about drumming or "wild men," they'd better look again.

Checking Your Understanding

1. What are the politics of the men's movement according to
    Kimbrell? How do these issues differ from the ones you listed in
    your prereading journal?
2. In our society, what are some differences between the victimization
    of men in general and of men who are minorities?

Examining Rhetorical Strategies

1. Place a star by the best argument on your during reading list and
    explain why you feel it is so effective.
2. Reread Kimbrell's last paragraph. How would the effectiveness of
    his essay be altered had he used this as his introductory paragraph?

INAUGURAL ADDRESS

William Jefferson Clinton

Prereading Journal

Many Americans watched President Clinton's inaugural address as it was broadcast live on television. If you watched the speech or saw a rebroadcast of it, briefly describe some of the accompanying visuals. If you did not watch the speech, try to imagine what some of these visuals might have been, based on visuals common to political coverage.

Background

Clinton delivered his inaugural address in the nation's capital, Washington D.C., on January 20, 1993. This political pronouncement affirms his position on the United States by both stating what is to be celebrated and proposing what is to be changed. This speech does not mean to change the audience's opinions, but rather to capture its attention, stir its emotions, and sustain its interest and enthusiasm beyond the occasion of the speech.

During Reading

Keep track of the changes President Clinton feels America must make in order to endure.

Reading Selection

My fellow citizens: 1

Today, we celebrate the mystery of American renewal.   2

This ceremony is held in the depth of winter. But, by 3
the words we speak and the faces we show the world, we force
the spring.

A spring reborn in the world's oldest democracy, that 4
brings forth the vision and courage to reinvent America.

When our founders boldly declared America's inde- 5
pendence to the world and our purposes to the Almighty,
they knew that America, to endure, would have to change.

Not change for change's sake, but change to preserve 6
America's ideals—life, liberty, the pursuit of happiness.

Though we march to the music of our time, our mission is timeless.

Each generation of Americans must define what it 7 means to be an American.

On behalf of our nation, I salute my predecessor 8 President Bush for his half-century of service to America, and I thank the millions of men and women whose stead-fastness and sacrifice triumphed over depression, fascism, and communism.

Today, a generation raised in the shadows of the Cold 9 War assumes new responsibilities in a world warmed by the sunshine of freedom but threatened still by ancient hatreds and new plagues.

Raised in unrivaled prosperity, we inherit an economy 10 that is still the world's strongest, but is weakened by business failures, stagnant wages, increasing inequality, and deep divisions among our own people.

When George Washington first took the oath I have just 11 sworn to uphold, news traveled slowly across the land by horseback and across the ocean by boat. Now, the sights and sounds of this ceremony are broadcast instantaneously to billions around the world.

Communications and commerce are global; investment 12 is mobile; technology is almost magical; and ambition for a better life is now universal. We earn our livelihood in America today in peaceful competition with people all across the earth.

Profound and powerful forces are shaking and remak- 13 ing our world, and the urgent question of our time is whether we can make change our friend and not our enemy.

This new world has already enriched the lives of mil- 14 lions of Americans who are able to compete and win in it. But when most people are working harder for less, when others cannot work at all, when the cost of health care devastates families and threatens to bankrupt our enterprises, great and small, when fear of crime robs law-abiding citizens of their freedom and when millions of poor children cannot even imagine the lives we are calling them to lead—we have not made change our friend.

We know we have to face hard truths and take strong 15 steps. But we have not done so. Instead, we have drifted, and that drifting has eroded our resources, fractured our economy, and shaken our confidence.

Though our challenges are fearsome, so are our 16 strengths. Americans have ever been a restless, questing, hopeful people. And we must bring to our task today the vision and will of those who came before us.

From our revolution to the Civil War, to the Great 17 Depression to the civil rights movement, our people have always mustered the determination to construct from these crises the pillars of our history.

Thomas Jefferson believed that to preserve the very 18 foundations of our nation, we would need dramatic change from time to time. Well my fellow Americans, this is our time. Let us embrace it.

Our democracy must be not only the envy of the world but 19 the engine of our own renewal. There is nothing wrong with America that cannot be cured by what is right with America.

So today, we pledge an end to the era of deadlock and 20 drift—and a new season of American renewal has begun.

To renew America, we must be bold. 21

We must do what no generation has had to do before. 22 We must invest more in our own people, in their jobs, and in their future, and at the same time cut our massive debt. And we must do so in a world in which we must compete for every opportunity.

It will not be easy; it will require sacrifice. But it can be 23 done, and done fairly, not choosing sacrifice for its own sake, but for our own sake. We must provide for our nation the way a family provides for its children.

Our founders saw themselves in the light of posterity. 24 We can do no less. Anyone who has ever watched a child's eyes wander into sleep knows what posterity is. Posterity is the world to come—the world for whom we hold our ideals, from whom we have borrowed our planet, and to whom we bear sacred responsibility.

We must do what America does best: offer more opportunity to all and demand more responsibility from all. 25

It is time to break the bad habit of expecting something 26 for nothing, from our government or from each other. Let us all take more responsibility, not only for ourselves and our families but for our communities and our country.

To renew America, we must revitalize our democracy.   27

This beautiful capital, like every capital since the dawn   28
of civilization, is often a place of intrigue and calculation.
Powerful people maneuver for position and worry endlessly
about who is in and who is out, who is up and who is down,
forgetting those people whose toil and sweat sends us here
and pays our way.

Americans deserve better. And in this city today, there   29
are people who want to do better. So I say to all of you here,
let us resolve to reform our politics, so that power and privilege no longer shout down the voice of the people. Let us put
aside personal advantage so that we can feel the pain and see
the promise of America.

Let us resolve to make our government a place for   30
what Franklin Roosevelt called "bold, persistent exper-
imentation," a government for our tomorrows, not our
yesterdays.

Let us give this capital back to the people to whom it   31
belongs.

To renew America, we must meet challenges abroad as   32
well as at home. There is no longer clear division between
what is foreign and what is domestic—the world economy,
the world environment, the world AIDS crisis, the world arms
race—they affect us all.

Today, as an old order passes, the new world is more   33
free but less stable. Communism's collapse has called forth
old animosities and new dangers. Clearly America must continue to lead the world we did so much to make.

While America rebuilds at home, we will not shrink   34
from the challenges, nor fail to seize the opportunities, of
this new world. Together with our friends and allies, we will
work to shape change, lest it engulf us.

When our vital interests are challenged, or the will and   35
conscience of the international community is defied, we will
act—with peaceful diplomacy whenever possible, with force
when necessary. The brave Americans serving our nation
today in the Persian Gulf, in Somalia, and wherever else they
stand are testament to our resolve.

But our greatest strength is the power of our ideas,   36
which are still new in many lands. Across the world, we see
them embraced—and we rejoice. Our hopes, our hearts, our

hands, are with those on every continent who are building democracy and freedom. Their cause is America's cause.

The American people have summoned the change we celebrate today. You have raised your voices in an unmistakable chorus. You have cast your votes in historic numbers. And you have changed the face of the Congress, the presidency, and the political process itself. 37

Yes, you, my fellow Americans, have forced the spring. 38

Now, we must do the work the season demands. 39

To that work I now turn, with all the authority of my office. I ask the Congress to join with me. But no President, no Congress, no government, can undertake this mission alone. 40

My fellow Americans, you, too, must play your part in our renewal. 41

I challenge a new generation of young Americans to a season of service—to act on your idealism by helping troubled children, keeping company with those in need, reconnecting our torn communities. There is so much to be done—enough, indeed, for millions of others who are still young in spirit to give of themselves in service, too. 42

In serving, we recognize a simple but powerful truth: We need each other. And we must care for one another. 43

Today, we do more than celebrate America; we rededicate ourselves to the very idea of America: 44

—An idea born in revolution and renewed through two centuries of challenge;

—An idea tempered by the knowledge that, but for fate, we—the fortunate and the unfortunate—might have been each other;

—An idea ennobled by the faith that our nation can summon from its myriad diversities the deepest measure of unity;

—An idea infused with the conviction that America's long heroic journey must go forever upward.

And so my fellow Americans, as we stand at the edge of the 21st Century, let us begin with energy and hope, with faith and discipline, and let us work until our work is done. The scripture says, "And let us not be weary in well-doing, for in due season, we shall reap, if we faint not." 45

From this joyful mountain top of celebration, we hear a　46
call to service in the valley.

We have heard the trumpets. We have changed the　47
guard. And now—each in our own way, and with God's
help—we must answer the call.

Checking Your Understanding

1. Clinton says that "the urgent question of our time is whether we can make change our friend and not our enemy." In what ways do you feel change has been America's friend or enemy in the time since this speech was delivered?
2. Clinton says that "you, too, must play your part in our renewal." What kind of renewal is he talking about and what part are you playing?

Examining Rhetorical Strategies

1. Whom do you feel is the primary audience for this inaugural address? How does this target audience enforce the idea that this is affirming rather than persuasive writing?
2. How is the metaphor of spring used to support Clinton's message of change?

WOMEN DIVIDED: FAMILY OR CAREER?

Ellen Goodman

Prereading Journal

Look at the title of Goodman's essay and make a list of issues and concerns you anticipate she will touch on in discussing the ways by which women are often divided between their families and their careers. Next, consider how this list might change were the title of the essay, "Men Divided: Family or Career?"

Background

Ellen Goodman writes a widely syndicated column for the *Boston Globe*, and in 1980 received a Pulitzer Prize for journalism. This editorial builds on both her own experiences and the experiences of other working women in our American society. She is entering into an argument about the role of women, but her primary purpose is to affirm rather than persuade.

During Reading

Keep track of the reasons for choosing to juggle family and career and for "deciding to go home."

Reading Selection

Every few months, there is another public announce- 1
ment of retirement from the ranks of superwoman. The notice may be posted in a newspaper or in a magazine, the woman may be a disillusioned lawyer or a disillusioned MBA, but she is sure to be a high-powered professional who decided to go home.

The articles invariably contain a paragraph or two 2
explaining how "the feminists" convinced her that she should do it all: work, wife, mother. Anything less was, well, less. But there came a moment, or a second child, when she felt something had to give and so she gave up the office. Family came first.

The responses to these announcements are almost as 3
familiar by now as the notices. In letters to the editor, one

woman will surely (and perhaps angrily) remind the author that not every mother has an economic choice. Another will resent the fact that the author blames feminism for the stress. A third will bristle at the implication that the children of employed mothers suffer.

And then, in a little while, the argument that has no 4 final answer, that remains as emotional as any in our public private life, fades out of print only to recycle over and over again.

This time it has been written large onto the cover of a 5 new book, *A Mother's Work*. The author flags the dilemma this way: "Like many women I was educated to feel that my career and my family should both come first. One day I had to make a choice."

The "I" is Deborah Fallows, a woman who wrote an 6 early retirement notice that ran some years ago in the capital city of work obsession, Washington, D.C. It got notice and notoriety. Now in a more subtle mood, Fallows struggles to defend her decision to go home, without attacking mothers who are employed. Her desire to be fair, to employed mothers and even to day care, is palpable. But in an odd way, the very delicacy, the very carefulness of the book, reminded me of how difficult it is for one woman to make claims on the turf of motherhood without raising the defenses of other women.

The qualified bottom line for Fallows is this: "Whenever 7 possible, parents should care for children themselves. . . . Other conditions being equal, children are more likely to thrive when they spend most of their day with a parent. . . ."

There is nothing intrinsically hostile about such state- 8 ments. Yet it is as hard for an employed mother to read those declarations neutrally as it is for a mother at home to react impersonally when an employed friend exclaims: "All things considered, the woman who stays at home has less impact on the world. . . . On the whole, the woman in the work place feels much better about her life."

The reality is that women take these statements person- 9 ally because they are personal. The social argument that has filled two decades is not about the behavior of rats in mazes, but about how women should live their lives and treat the people they love.

We are in a particularly uneasy state of balance now.   10
There are almost equal numbers of mothers of young children in and out of the work force. It is one thing for these
women in "mixed company" to join hands and mouth support for each other's right to choose. It is quite another to
believe it. Mothers may feel judged, challenged, by nothing
more than another's decision.

Every time a woman in an office leaves for home, every   11
time a woman in a neighborhood leaves for work, there is a
ripple effect. The waves of ambivalence can swamp self-
confidence and even friendships. In such an atmosphere,
employed mothers share their anxieties most easily with each
other; mothers at home circle their own wagons. Each group
may still, more than occasionally, feel the other attacking.

This social argument goes on and on because in fact,   12
there is no certainty, no right way to live. Even Fallows' bottom
line that children do best when they are in the day care of their
own parents is a belief, not a fact. In the business of creating
our own lives, or caring for our children, we are all experts and
amateurs, opinionated and uncertain, wildly subjective.

We have only one sample of children and a limited   13
number of years and no guaranteed rewards for our behavior. Parents—mostly mothers—who have choices must make
them. Not in a vacuum but in a space inundated with worries
about our psyches and pocketbooks, our children and selves,
the present and future. We do make these choices but our
confidence may be fragile and our skin thin. The shifting
winds of the social argument, blowing pros and cons at us, all
too easily raise the hackles of our own anxieties.

For Better or For Worse®   **by Lynn Johnston**

Checking Your Understanding

1. Goodman discusses many of the conflicts involved with the difficult decisions facing women who wish to have both a family and a career. Explain the main opinion she is trying to share with us through her examination of these conflicts.

2. Compare and contrast the dilemmas facing women as described by Goodman in this essay with those facing men described in the previous essay by Andrew Kimbrell. What do these differences say about our culture's assumptions about gender?

3. In the cartoon from "For Better or Worse," our attention is focused on the emotional side of this issue—the guilt women feel if they stay at home or if they work. How does the emotional power of this issue affect the women caught up in it? Why is the issue so emotionally charged?

Examining Rhetorical Strategies

1. Why do you think Goodman has chosen to keep her focus narrowed on the dilemma between having both a career *and* a family? Why does she ignore the choice of a career and no children or children and no career? Does her failure to acknowledge this option detract from the impact of the essay?

2. Rather than disagree with Fallows' "bottom line that children do best when they are in the day care of their own parents," Goodman points out that this position is "a belief, not a fact." What strategy do you think is at work here, and how does it serve Goodman's purpose for writing?

STUDENT ESSAYS AND WRITING TECHNIQUES

DEEP WITHIN

Marliese Goehring

Background

Goehring wrote this essay about her experiences as a gymnast in response to an assignment asking her to share a meaningful experience or aspect of her life that led to or reinforced a strongly held belief. Notice how her recollections of training for gymnastics serve to support the belief she is sharing?

Reading Selection

I watched Marcy fingerpaint. The colors oozed in every 1 direction and her design formed no apparent shape. My first reaction was to tell her to stay on the paper and not get any paint on her overalls. But instead of scolding her, I watched her messy little hands with envy.

I wanted to feel the paint between my fingers, under- 2 neath my nails, and against my skin. Most of all, I wanted to share the pure joy of her accomplished masterpiece—a masterpiece composed of nothing more than imperfect shapes and a mess of rainbow-brown mixed colors. I envied both her free flow of life and her beautiful childhood imperfections.

I never had either of these privileges.   3

By the age of twelve, I had achieved the standing of 4 Massachusetts State Champion for three consecutive years in two different leagues. I was recognized as a potential nationally ranked gymnast both for my age category as well as my overall abilities. I was a Danvers Yellowjacket, dressed in black and yellow and trained for competition.

I wasn't even a teenager yet. My body was a muscle- 5 developed flexible machine built by long hours of daily training after school and intensive summer work-outs at the US gymnastics training center. I was a serious and determined four-foot eleven inch dynamo denied of my feelings and any wishes I had of being a less than perfect child.

My hands were covered with rips and bleeding sores 6
while my heels ached from tumbling and running. I was a
silent obeyer of a coach driven to perfection. I would endure
long minutes of my coach's screaming how my moves weren't
strong enough, that my run down to the vault wasn't fast
enough, and that my legs weren't straight enough. My days of
aimless doll-playing were quickly hidden away and forgotten.

Children, such as myself, who endure such strenuous 7
physical training at a young age face tremendous developmental difficulties as they reach maturity. This is a result of
messages such as these sent during childhood.

"Infant athletes" as I like to call them, become simply 8
extensions of their parents or coaches. The motivation
behind them is the driving force from deep within their families or coaches. They are too young to even understand what
motivation is. The fuel behind their fires is not even theirs.

These children learn an incredible tolerance of physi- 9
cal pain and strain. In some Olympic arenas, medication is
prescribed to stunt growth. A tall or large gymnast is not a
medal winner. The children become machines, raped of not
only their normal physical growth, but also their emotional
stability.

The message sent to these children is "do not, under 10
any circumstances, show your feelings." Tears are not tolerat-
ed in the gym. Champions do not cry; they endure.
"Moderation never produces a winner" is taught in daily
training sessions. "It is a sign of mediocrity," coaches insist.

The most devastating messages sent are the most subtle. 11
A child under such a perfection regime learns he or she is
never good enough. Even more damaging is the idea that
grows within these children that they are not lovable unless
medals hang continuously around their necks. No wonder that
little Marliese did not get a hug after she fell off the balance
beam at Nationals. A dangerous association of love and achievement is instilled. I wish someone could have loved me with my
unpointed toes, bent legs, and sometimes wobbly steps.

What becomes of many of these children seems almost 12
to be a self-fulfilling prophecy. They become adults who are
highly self-critical and terrified of expressing feelings. Lack
of self-confidence is most evident. A day of less than the best
performance at work festers those old childhood wounds of

training days. Olympic trained adults without medals are sent home as disgraces to their countries.

And long after the competitions have ended, crying 13 children are still deep within them.

Thinking About Writing

Parts of this essay focus on expressively sharing the author's memories of rigorous training at the expense of more common-place childhood activities. While many readers could look at this piece as primarily an expressive essay, what makes this paper a piece of affirming writing rather than a paper trying simply to share a personal recollection? How might you have reacted to the essay had the author opened with a blunt statement of her position: "Young athletes pushed too hard to excel become adults who are very self-critical and afraid of expressing feelings," rather than in the manner she selected?

Writing Assignment

Select a position you now hold dear about an issue that is important to you. Think back to how this position took shape and evolved as new experiences and observations became a part of how you view yourself and the world around you. It doesn't have to be a serious or controversial topic, but think about how and why your views have changed and how this change reflects other changes in yourself and your ideas. For example, one of the authors of this book takes the position that Bob Dylan is one of the most talented performing artists of this century. This opinion first began to take shape when as an adolescent the author watched the film, *A Concert for Bangladesh*. As the years passed and albums (now CDs) were purchased and concerts attended, the new experiences and additional reflections caused the author's position to evolve and gain depth.

Whatever your position, try to capture the key experiences and observations that led to its evolution.

PLEASE OPEN MY EYES

Jennifer Klinefelter

Background

Klinefelter was responding to an assignment that asked her to write about some idea or event that she was still in the process of working through and had not yet managed to resolve. She immediately thought of a very brief incident, a moment stopped at a traffic light, that had made her re-examine the way she saw and evaluated people. It made her wonder if she could see them at all.

Reading Selection

Rain ran down the side window of the van as a foggy circle appeared around my finger, trying to hold onto a drop that was on the outside. Puddles splashed up onto the window, creating new patterns, erasing the old ones that I had become accustomed to. Neon lights seemed to be endless, just lines that continued outside of the van in wet fluid strokes. The pavement was splashed with color, red, green, yellows. The darkness made the buildings we passed one-dimensional, like all that existed was the front and that maybe there was nothing behind the glow of lights in the windows. There were no people, just cars, buildings, and objects. On the street I saw no emotion, no smiles, no laughter, no embraces, nobody; just the rain and the lights that took over the darkness in the puddles. 1

The van stopped at an intersection and I traced an imaginary circle in the steam, creating a smaller window. There was a very dark building on my side of the street. Unlike all the other buildings and stores we passed, this one had few lights on and the entrance was made of etched glass so that you couldn't see inside. The blinds on the windows were all drawn as if the building had been shut down and vacated. But in some of the windows a thin line of light escaped where the blind had missed the sill. A plastic lit sign out front read, The Paul Revere Hotel. There was a hole above the "R," exposing the light bulbs inside. 2

We couldn't have been at that intersection for more 3
than five minutes, but it seems to me that I am still there
looking at those windows, at the door, hoping that one of
them would open, and let me see inside. I was certain that
large men with tattooed arms sat with beers in their hands
and prostitutes waited for their next clients, while men and
women sat in dark corners with tracks on their arms, waiting
to fly away from their darkness. I could see drunks and
thieves making temporary homes in the rooms. I pictured
the lobby of the hotel behind the etched glass, smoky, damp,
dimly lit. But the shades were drawn and the door never
opened and our van pulled away.

Weeks went by and I had placed the darkness of that 4
night in a corner of my mind where memories like that are
kept. One evening I sat watching television as I ate my dinner. I was flipping through the channels quickly catching
only glimpses of the programs. Passing one by I stopped
and went back, hearing something that had caught my
attention. The Paul Revere Hotel. I waited through the
commercial for the program to return, expecting to finally
have the building's blinds lifted, its insides exposed, the
door of the lobby opened, and its guests revealed. I expected to see the images and faces I had in my mind appear on
the screen.   5

The picture on the television showed a young mother
with four children all under the age of six. They were in a
room within the hotel, a room that was brightly lit, clean,
comfortable. The host of the program described the situation of the mother and of the many other families within the
hotel.

They were homeless, victims of situations that they 6
hadn't directly brought on themselves. They weren't prostitutes, drug addicts, thieves, or bums. They were mothers,
fathers, and children living sometimes up to a year in this
place they had to call home.

My throat felt tight. I watched children play outside in 7
the parking lot, neat, happy, well-behaved children. I
watched as a mother explained how difficult it was at first for
the children not to have their own room and not be able to
have all their toys because it was so crowded. She told how
hard it was at times because the entire family had only one

room. There was no place to get away to, no place to be alone except on the street or in the alley. The program mentioned the drawn shades in the windows of the Paul Revere Hotel. They were closed because children were napping, families were sleeping, because they didn't want people like me staring into their home.

I turned off the television and closed my eyes. I   8 pulled the memory of that night from the corner where I had placed it. I again saw the darkness, the rain, the hollow rooms that let only light escape from them. I saw the etched glass door. The images of the people inside remained the same. The shades were open, but I couldn't see children inside. The thought of people like me living within that structure was too disturbing. I couldn't bring together the two images that I had seen, the reality didn't seem to fit, it didn't make sense. My mind couldn't mesh the two together, allowing me to see that bleak threatening hotel and the faces of smiling children in one image. I don't know why. It isn't shock or disbelief, just an inability to see things beyond how they appear, or how I assume them to be. I felt as if I had judged something that I didn't know anything about, and therefore had judged things that maybe shouldn't be judged at all. I don't know how to stop it. In my mind I still see the image in a rainy dark blur, with quick flashes of sunshine and children in a parking lot far away.   9

I wonder how many other times I've let an image stand on its own, assuming things that may or may not be true. I know there have been so many people that I have placed into some category just by looking at things around them, not what's inside. I want to know why I make assumptions about things and people that aren't always true. I put places and people into stereotypes that limit them, make them less than they are or maybe more than they should be. I am afraid that I've not been really seeing. Somehow I've come to see things in patterns to keep me from seeing life as it really is. I've been taught to believe them. I want to stop. I know that ideas based on patterns are meaningless and wrong. But they are still a part of me.   10

Even when the shades are open, sometimes I still can't see inside.

Thinking About Writing

The event Klinefelter experienced that made her aware of her opinion about stereotyping is hardly an event at all—she stops at a traffic light and looks at the building in front of her. Yet this event becomes significant first as we get Klinefelter's interpretation of the life contained in the building and then later as we watch her trying to make the real lives of the people in the building (as shown on the TV program) correspond to her fabricated images. How do these two images of the building support what she says about her ability to see? What does she mean when she says, "I still see the image in a rainy dark blur, with quick flashes of sunshine and children in a parking lot far away"? Also, even though she is talking only about herself, how does she make us think about our own tendencies to stereotype?

Writing Assignment

Not all affirming writing reflects definitive positions or opinions that have ceased to evolve and develop. Because revision means "re-seeing" our ideas and making discoveries, open text that leaves gaps for readers and reflects authors' ongoing struggle with their positions can be quite effective. Think of a belief or idea you have that is still developing, still taking shape and prompting reflection. Share one such developing opinion with all of the speculation, conjecture, and struggle that is still banging around in your head. Good affirming writing does not always have to express a carved-in-stone opinion in order to be meaningful to your readers. Inviting others to share in our journey from confusion to some sort of clarity can provide a context for meaningful communication.

CULTURAL LITERACY HYPOCRISY
John W. Potter

Background

Potter shares an experience that forced him to modify his position on cultural literacy. As we noted with the "Deep Within" and "Please Open My Eyes" papers, sharing the struggle with and evolution of an opinion is a valid and useful form of affirming writing. Notice how Potter uses his past and recent experiences to explain his past and current position on the general education requirements and cultural literacy.

Reading Selection

I was having dinner with a science major last night, and our conversation turned to the subject of general education requirements. He cannot understand why, as a pre-med student, he is being forced to take courses in history, literature, philosophy, and the arts. As far as he is concerned, these subjects are irrelevant to the career and life he has chosen. Hesitantly, and as humbly as I could, I suggested that perhaps the administration feels that in order for us to be competent and well-rounded citizens we need to be somewhat familiar with the basics of disciplines outside our own area of specialization and interest. 1

Before last semester I would have jumped much more aggressively at this opportunity to extol the principles of "cultural literacy." I had read E.D. Hirsch's book of that title over semester break of my freshman year, and ever since I had been on a crusade to reform the common student attitude of "I want to learn what I need, and I don't need to learn any more." I always had plenty of people to whom I could preach. No matter what the class someone would always complain that it was boring and a waste of time, and I would then consider it my duty to enlighten that complainer on the intellectual freedom that belongs to those who are conversant in several subjects. 2

Mind you, it was not that Hirsch had so much reformed me as it was that he had called me to arms on an 3 issue in which I had already been trained. Hirsch gave a lucid voice and the formal arguments for the maxims I had been hearing from my father for as long as I could remember. Indeed, it was my father who had encouraged me to major in philosophy in order to gain a perspective on and exposure to the major world-views that pervade people's thought and communication. I suppose it was a combination of this childhood training, my excitement at the almost tangible increase in knowledge I felt after only one semester in college, and a generous sprinkling of pride that made me such a willing, perhaps presumptuous, flagman for cultural literacy.

My outspoken career was short-lived, however. It was 4 amazing how quickly my words lost their charm when I was the one disoriented and bored by a course. The course was a required combined chemistry/physics course and it turned me into a hypocrite.

I had never liked science. I had had one year of chem- 5 istry in high school, and my opinion of it was summed up when I told a friend, "Chemistry serves no purpose, but to bring down your G.P.A." Of course, with my renewed vision of the culturally literate student I had been making every effort to look forward to my required science classes. Nevertheless, my bubble burst after the first exam.

I was rapidly learning what people had meant when 6 they told me that they were not "cut out" for philosophy, or some other liberal art; I was definitely not cut out for chemistry or physics.

I began doing what I had always scorned in others. 7 Instead of working harder, I slacked off, did not do homework, and in every situation, sought only to learn what I needed to pass. A couple of times I barely studied for the tests because it was just too boring. I even stooped to the point of justifying my behavior by saying that I would "never use this stuff anyway."

I guess it is easy to support a cause that does not threat- 8 en your own *status quo*. As long as I only had to worry about being culturally literate in the humanities, it was easy for me to criticize those who found such subjects difficult. I did not have to work too hard to do well, so I was all for making everyone take the classes. I never realized what I was demanding of people until I was placed in a situation that demanded it of me.

Thinking About Writing

Potter is writing about a topic that has received a lot of attention over the past few years. What prior knowledge and preconceived notions of cultural literacy and general education requirements did you bring to the reading experience? Did this prior knowledge lead you to applaud or criticize Potter's changing view on the topic? How would your response as a reader change if Potter had used his experience in his chemistry class as the basis for a persuasive paper arguing for fewer general education requirements?

Writing Assignment

Often we tend to have rather definite ideas on topics which we have read about and discussed but that have not really touched our lives. Perhaps you thought unions were too strong until you got a summer job in a factory. Or perhaps you thought the government doled out too much money on social programs until you were laid off at a job and needed unemployment benefits in order to eat. Or maybe you were very sure of where you stood on freedom of speech until a group of neo-Nazis held a rally in your town.

Select a time when one of your definite ideas was disrupted by new experiences and knowledge and share the manner in which your views changed.

MULTICULTURALISM AND EDUCATION: A QUESTION OF PERSPECTIVE

Sally Clark

Background

Clark was asked to choose a topic she felt strongly about, select two essays on that topic, synthesize the main points of the two essays, and—using this synthesis as a basis for her discussion—establish her own position on the topic. Notice how she moves from sharing positions found in the essays she read, to sharing her own experiences with the topic, to establishing her position on the topic.

Reading Selection

Multiculturalism is on the minds of students and edu-   1
cators alike as our nation begins to celebrate rather than gloss over its ethnic and cultural diversity. Appreciation of one's ethnic heritage and identity has prompted changes in the way history is viewed and the way numerous classes are taught. While this trend is, for the most part, a very positive one, I have personally experienced the down side of multi-culturalism in education. What had sounded so promising in theory—the opening up of the literary canon in an overdue spirit of inclusion—did not work well in a drama class I recently took. While this experience has not dampened all my enthusiasm for an evolving canon, it has made me recon-sider how best this evolving canon may manifest itself in the classroom.

Two recent articles—"Multiculturalism: E Pluribus   2
Plures" by Diane Ravitch and "In Dispute on Bias, Stanford Is Likely to Alter Western Culture Program" by Richard Bernstein—serve to illuminate some aspects of the debate on many campuses across America as to the merits and dangers of reshaping course curriculum with multicultural represen-tation as the main objective.

Ravitch begins her essay by praising some of the influ-   3
ences multicultural awareness has brought to education. For example, she finds it healthy that teaching history

"demands an unflinching examination of racism and discrimination in our history" (577). Such honest "warts-and-
all" appraisals of America's past are indeed beneficial if we
are to get beyond deeply entrenched myths such as that of
the noble Frontiersmen and savage Indians which once
served as an excuse for the genocide performed on Native
Americans in this country.

Yet, despite such positive effects of multiculturalism in   4
education, Ravitch is concerned by recent developments:
"Almost any idea, carried to its extreme, can be made perni-
cious, and this is what is happening now to multiculturalism"
(578). While Ravitch notes that pluralistic multiculturalism
leads to a richer common culture (578), she is alarmed that
"[a]dvocates of particularism propose an ethnocentric curriculum to raise the self-esteem and academic achievement
of children from racial and ethnic minority backgrounds"
(578). In other words, the particularistic version of multiculturalism unabashedly promotes an excessive reverence of
one's ancestors at the expense of a more rounded, objective
sense of the past (578).

I have seen such "particularistic" educational practices   5
played out in a literature course I took last fall in a suburban
community college. I had heard very positive things about
Introduction to Drama from a few of my friends, and was
anxious to register for it. Unfortunately, the content had
been changed since my friends took the class. What was once
an overview of the acknowledged great playwrights from the
nineteenth and twentieth centuries had been reduced to an
around-the-world with drama course. While it was interesting
to read some plays by little known playwrights from Italy,
Australia, Brazil, and Kenya, I felt as though the course
description had become misleading. These writers were not
included because they were the most important or compelling; their inclusion in the course was simply a result of
pressure placed on the professor to be "politically correct."
This problem leads me to the issues touched on by Richard
Bernstein in his essay.

Bernstein examines Stanford's shift away from a   6
Western culture course in favor of a more multicultural
approach. He notes that opponents of curriculum changes
feel that "to label history's most influential works as exam-

ples of a white male culture and little else is to make a travesty of Western culture itself" (27). As a woman living in a male dominated society, I am uncomfortable defending the exclusion of most females and minorities in literature courses. But it is not their exclusion for which I argue. My position is that survey courses should include the very best writers of the period and genre in question. Many people disagree on who the best writers are, which is as it should be. Yet the debate over reading lists now seems to be not one of quality, but of diversity. I feel that diversity at the expense of quality is a disservice to the students paying tuition.

As an aspiring actress I enrolled in Introduction to 7 Drama last year with hopes of reading classic plays from Shakespeare to Ibsen to O'Neill. Instead, I was subjected to playwrights I had never heard of from places unknown to me. I do not feel that the course provided me with a foundation upon which to build my understanding of drama. If the best playwrights of the past two hundred years are mostly white males, so be it. The next century may go a long way in changing the nature of the playwright canon. Am I suggesting that unknown playwrights from little known countries are of no consequence and should not be studied? Of course not. All of the great playwrights were unknown at one time or another. But an introduction course should focus on established masters, not an eclectic group of unknowns selected to appease as many ethnic groups as possible.

Am I a white student disturbed by the inclusion of 8 minorities in a drama course? No. I am an Italian-American, proud of my heritage. Yet the issue here is who are the best playwrights, not why doesn't this list include an equal portion of all ethnic groups. The reason it doesn't may very well have to do with the privileged status men have enjoyed for too long; privilege in education, wealth, and personal freedom would seem to aid the playwright's task. Nonetheless, reading lists must be created on the basis of quality—however subjective that notion may be, rather than on the basis of ethnic heritage.

I feel that multiculturalism means we are aware of and 9 take interest in traditions and cultures different from our own. I do not feel that it means making me, for example, feel better about myself as an Italian-American because a mediocre Italian playwright was included in a course that had promised to introduce me to the best of the best in the history of staged drama. No one wins when standards are lowered in the name of diversity in the literary canon. In any area of study the first priority must be exposing students to the best and brightest. To exclude gifted thinkers and artists because of race or gender is an unacceptable and heinous form of racism, even if those who are excluded happen to be white males.

Works Cited

BERNSTEIN, RICHARD. "In Dispute on Bias, Stanford Is Likely to Alter Western Culture Program." *The Informed Reader*. Ed. Charles Bazerman. Boston: Houghton Mifflin, 1989. 25–31.
RAVITCH, DIANE. "Multiculturalism: E Pluribus Plures." *Our Times 2*. Ed. Robert Atwan. Boston: St. Martin's, 1991. 575–91.

Thinking About Writing

Clark is given a more difficult task than the earlier writers of affirming discourse cited in this chapter. Like the other authors, Clark shares her own experiences to support her opinion of what she sees as a misguided approach to multiculturalism in the classroom. Yet she is also asked to share support gathered from other writers' affirming discourse. To do this, Clark must document the sources she uses. Notice how she cites her sources in text and then in the Works Cited section. (You will find more information about documentation in the Appendix.)

In supporting her opinion of the drama course she took, Clark anticipates a few of the arguments her readers might have with her position. This tactic will serve you well in the persuasive writing you will be asked to do later in this course. Yet, despite the presence of some persuasive strategies, Clark's essay is primarily affirming rather than persuasive in nature. Why do you think this is so? What revisions would Clark need to make in her next draft to move into the realm of persuasive writing? Who might disagree with her views on the drama class she took, and why might this audience disagree?

Writing Assignment

Keeping in mind the advice on writing summaries found in Chapter 1, write a summary of Clark's essay. As you reread the essay, take notice of how Clark incorporates quotes into her article.

In addition to writing the summary, select several quotes you particularly like and explain why these quotes stand out to you. Taking note of how authors successfully incorporate outside sources into their writing is an important reading skill to practice. In later assignments—especially informative writing—you will be asked to support your ideas and inform your readers with quotes from texts you've read and people you've talked to.

After you've summarized Clark's essay and discussed her use of your favorite quotes, select an essay on a topic that you find especially interesting. Share the author's main ideas with readers who have never read the essay as a means of creating a foundation upon which to establish your own position on the topic. You don't have to agree with the author of the essay for it to be a useful jumping off point for your own beliefs and feelings. By sharing information outside of your own personal experience and anticipating some of the reasons others may see the topic differently, you will gain valuable practice with some of the skills necessary for successful persuasive and informative writing.

Part Four

PERSUASIVE DISCOURSE

When we as readers approach *persuasive discourse*, we recognize that the writer is going to do more than just share with us—the writer is going to want something from us. If the writing is successful, we will take a stand, see the movie, agree with the proposal, hire the applicant, or buy the product.

What separates persuasive discourse from affirming discourse is that the writer is not simply sharing and supporting an opinion; the writer wants us to agree with that opinion. Often the piece ends with a call to action: "This can no longer be allowed to continue" or "We must work together to achieve the goal" or "This is what I intend to do for you" or "A is more desirable than B, therefore, A must be implemented."

Persuasive writing ranges from the obvious "Buy this product" forms of advertising to the more subtle form found in proposals that offer a solution to social, political, or academic issues. The wide range of persuasive writing includes even such things as letters of application where you convince an employer to give you an interview or a job, to book and movie reviews which give information that leads you to buy "it" or ignore "it."

The relationship between the reader and the writer in the more obvious forms of persuasion is a close one as the writer takes on the voice of one who knows what the reader needs. In the subtler forms, the writer's voice may be built on a more "objective" basis, relying on logic and the accumulation of reasons to convince the audience that one action, one idea, one solution is better than the rest. Whatever the approach, persuasive writers involve their readers in the topic and build toward an imperative.

And writers ask much of us. Persuasive discourse is best exemplified by advertising. Through appeals to our emotions, as well as our reasonable needs, advertisers present their products to us as the best available choice: "Three out of five dentists recommend . . ." or "for people who love their cats. . . ."

But persuasive discourse is not always so bold; in fact it is sometimes best when it is more subtle as you will see in some of the subsequent readings.

Chapter Nine

READING PERSUASIVE DISCOURSE: THE READER/WRITER RELATIONSHIP

As readers, we approach persuasive writing with the understanding that the writer expects something from us. What the writer wants may not be clear at the beginning of the piece, but by its conclusion we are well aware that the writer is evaluating something, arguing for a position, or advocating a particular solution to a specified problem. The purpose of the writing becomes clear to us—the writer wants a response. This response is the persuasive imperative which is at the core of all persuasive writing.

The relationship between the reader and the writer is an important one. If as readers we do not accept the author's reasons or arguments, we will ignore the call to action and dismiss the topic. But if the writer has engaged us through a logical argument, through a careful delineation of the facts, through an appeal to our emotions, through a powerful story, then we are drawn to the text and more likely to respond.

There are many types of persuasive writing, but all types rely on a credible voice supported by emotional or logical appeals to the reader. The development within the essays moves the reader to response either through words and images that evoke a strong emotional response or through the more objective use of facts, reasons, and information which allow the reader to see that the stated imperative is the logical response given the established context. The following three essays will illustrate examples of the reader/ writer relationship in persuasive writing: evaluation, argument, and proposal.

EVALUATION

FREE AT LAST

Andrea R. Vaucher

The evaluation essay is a common, albeit subtle, form of persuasive discourse. Beginning with the writer's subjective response to a book, a movie, or an organization, the essay presents the criteria for the judgment that is being shared with the reader.

This means that the writer's authority is crucial. What tone is used? How does the tone give you confidence in what the writer has to say? Why do you believe that this is a knowledgeable, credible authority on this particular topic?

This establishment of the authority is also demonstrated by the criteria used to support the evaluation. As a reader it is necessary to look at the "facts" that are presented. Often this means that writers will use quotations from the book or descriptions of scenes from the movie to create an impression on the reader. That impression can be either favorable or not. Based on the writer's purpose, this support will seek to create an emotional response in the reader that will be the imperative to enjoy the same experience or to avoid it like the plague.

As with all writing that seeks a response from the reader, the organization of criteria is meaningful. The support needs to be more than a listing of details. Reasons, quotations, observations, and personal experiences must be organized and developed in such a way as to give the reader an overall impression. This may be done through highlighting the most important aspects or by building the case from lesser to stronger arguments, descriptions, and reasons.

Although we are often asked to give informal opinions on a particular subject, the evaluative essay is a formal, considered writing meant to move us to a response. After reading such writing, we make our decision to buy the album, see the movie, or read the book based on the trust we have in the writer.

Prereading Journal

If you could write about someone's life, whose would it be? What aspects of that person's life would you include? What elements of storytelling would you address? What would be your purpose in writing it?

Background

Arthur Ashe was a world-champion tennis player who died from AIDS. Although he had been ill for several years, it was not until a news tabloid threatened to print the cause of his illness that he admitted publicly to having the disease. This review of his autobiography was published in the *Boston Globe* on June 13, 1993. Vaucher establishes her authority by knowledgeably discussing Ashe's public image and using passages from the book to persuade us that this is a book worth reading.

During Reading

Note how Vaucher integrates her opinions with excerpts from the book. List each opinion and the support she gives for it. Also identify what she says about the book and what she says about the man.

Reading Selection

"The problem with you," Jesse Jackson once told Arthur Ashe during a political discussion, "is that you're not arrogant enough." 1

Jackson thought arrogance would have better served this low-key tennis great who, with his high profile and raised consciousness, was in an excellent position to further the cause of blacks around the world. "Days of Grace," Ashe's memoir, written with the help of Arnold Rampersad (a historian at Princeton and biographer of Langston Hughes), demonstrates that the qualities Ashe cultivated instead— ruthless introspection and forthright humility, for example— make for much more interesting reading. 2

Arthur Ashe, the only black American male ever to have won a Grand Slam tennis event, died of AIDS in February, at age 49. Born in Richmond when segregation was a fact of life, Ashe was a true Southern gentleman; his painstaking analysis of every facet of every situation may sometimes have been 3 mistaken for ambivalence. (After Ashe quotes Jackson on arrogance, he continues, in his inimitably diplomatic style, to modify the remark by explaining that the arrogance Jackson was calling for was one where the ego was in service to a larger idea.) But despite an overwhelming need to do the right thing and alienate no one along the way, Ashe pulls few punches in this book. Although he warns us from the first page that "I can no more easily renounce my concern with what people think of me than I can will myself to stop breathing," this memoir is proof of the power of AIDS to liberate an individual to say things that he previously had held back.

In reading Ashe's words, I recalled a statement by Cyril 4 Collard, the French filmmaker and novelist, who recently died of AIDS and whom I interviewed for a book of my own. "After the artist says he has AIDS, he can say anything," Collard confessed. Obviously, Ashe felt the same way; "Days of Grace" is fueled by freedom and urgency.

In 1980, after a heart attack and a quadruple coronary- 5 bypass operation, Ashe was forced to retire from tennis at age 38. He also, for the first time, confronted his mortality. Although by then he had won three of the four Grand Slam events and twice been the top-ranked player in the world, he now "felt a subtle but persuasive dissatisfaction with life." He equates the life of a professional athlete with that of a court jester. "I wanted to be taken seriously," he writes.

Ashe probed his dissatisfaction and, with the help of a 6 psychiatrist, traced the roots of his angst to the untimely death of his mother when he was 6. He also explored his "iciness" (he had been stuck with the epithet ever since Life magazine put him on its cover in 1968 with the headline: "The Icy Elegance of Arthur Ashe") and his discomfort expressing his feelings. Ashe examines the correlation between his disowned emotions and his unabashed love/hate relationship with John McEnroe, who played on the Davis Cup team Ashe captained from 1980 to 1985. According to Neil Amdur, who collaborated with Ashe on his earlier book, "Off the Court," the fiery McEnroe forced Ashe to "deal with the most delicate frames of his psyche." Ashe writes, "John was expressing my own rage, my own anger for me, as I could never express it; and perhaps I was even grateful for him doing so."

Ashe analyzes every twist of his life with this same brutal 7
frankness. Not only does he reveal the most intimate aspects
of his existence, he exposes the thoughts and emotions
behind every experience. Rarely has a man been so in touch
with his feelings—perhaps no professional athlete ever has.
We have courtside seats at the edge of Ashe's psyche as he
probes incidents as disparate as his first sexual experience,
the various medical options available to the AIDS patient, his
conception of God, his relationship to material wealth and
the mortal and emotional legacy he hopes to leave his daughter, Camera. This is a personal and candid biography.

In 1983, after a second bypass operation, Ashe received 8
AIDS-tainted blood that ultimately would chart his destiny.
(He didn't find this out until five years later, when he began
experiencing the symptoms of toxoplasmosis, one of the
opportunistic infections associated with AIDS.) But as Ashe
told a reporter, "AIDS isn't the heaviest burden I have had to
bear. . . . Being black is the heaviest burden I've had to bear."
From childhood, when he was forced to sit behind a white
line on the bus and often was barred from playing with white
players on public courts, segregation had left Ashe "a marked
man, forever aware of the shadow of contempt that lay across
my destiny and over my self-esteem." In the years after his
Davis Cup captaincy, Ashe threw himself into politics, often
protesting on behalf of black Americans. He also fought
against South African apartheid, supported the plight of
Haitian refugees and spoke out against what he regarded as
"the insult of affirmative action."

When Ashe discovered in 1988 that he had AIDS, he 9
and his family decided to tell only their closest friends and relatives. Then in April 1992, he was forced to reveal his illness
when USA Today was going to publish reports of it. "The truth
is I had been made to feel guilty without having committed a
sin," he writes about that experience. But what at first seemed
to some an unpardonable and abhorrent act of aggression by
the media eventually became something positive.

Marlon Riggs, the filmmaker, who is HIV-positive, said 10
to me, "When you're dealt what might be considered a bad
hand, you've got to transform it in such a way that all that is
considered a handicap becomes a virtue, a means of empow-
erment." Arthur Ashe had a similar perception. "You come to

the realization that life is short," he writes. "These are extra-ordinary conditions, and you have to step up." And step up he did, throwing his weight behind the campaign against AIDS with the same energy and visibility he applied to other political causes.

The reader of "Days of Grace" may be disoriented at   11 times by a haphazard chronology of dropped dates. When Ashe describes Nelson Mandela's 1990 Wall Street ticker-tape parade, for example, he assumes we can recall the exact year and thus put it in political and personal context. Likewise, he will occasionally make sweeping statements—"I had several stirring conversations with him, which formed the highlight of my visit," again referring to Mandela—without enlighten-ing us further as to the content. Sometimes the book seems an amalgam of financial planning guide, safe-sex manual, essay on gays and lesbians in professional tennis and open letter to his daughter. And there's one preposterous section in which Ashe equates the various types of opportunistic infections with the different ways people become infected with AIDS.

Toward the end of the book, Ashe writes, "As I settled   12 deeper into this new stage in my life, I became increasingly conscious of a certain thrill, an exhilaration even, about what I was doing. Experience as an athlete had taught me that in time of danger I had to respond with confidence, authority and grace." Despite the minor flaws, it is this grace—and rig-orous honesty—that illuminates the words and thoughts of Arthur Ashe.

Checking Your Understanding

1. The persuasive imperative is implied in this review rather than stat-ed. What does Vaucher want the readers to "do"? What evidence is there in the article that leads you to that impression?
2. How persuasive is this book review for you? Does reading this essay interest you in reading the book? Why or why not?

Examining Rhetorical Strategies

1. Look at the selections Vaucher pulls from the book itself. Why do you think she chose those excerpts? What do they tell you about the book?
2. What is Vaucher's authority? How is her authority established in the review itself?

ARGUMENT

NOT BY CONDOMS ALONE: SOCIETY AND THE AIDS EPIDEMIC

David R. Carlin, Jr.

Perhaps the most well-known writing within the spectrum of persuasive discourse is the argumentative essay. The purpose of the argumentative essay is to take a controversial issue and present a debate of the facts, with the intention of leading the audience to the "obvious" response.

The argument begins with a particular situation. But for the purpose of argumentation, the situation is a controversial one, one which invokes debate. The audience, then, tends to be those who already hold a position on the issue. And, more than not, the paper is directed to those who may actually be hostile to the view presented. The argument is meant to get the readers to change their minds, or, at the very least, to consider the viewpoint being presented.

To convince the readers to do that considering requires that information is well presented and used to provide both reason and support for the position. This does not mean that both sides of the argument have to be presented, but it does mean that at least one side of the debate is presented clearly, logically, and powerfully for the audience. For example, if the issue were handgun control it would not be necessary to present information related to both positions on the ownership of handguns. But, an argument will take one view, against handguns, and might present statistics on accidental deaths, the availability of guns to youths, and the European ban on handguns to argue against owning them.

Persuasive argument takes a stand on a broad issue and seeks to add the reader to those who support that view.

Prereading Journal

Stopping the spread of AIDS is one of the major issues facing health care today. Brainstorm a list of possible ways to bring it under control. Now go back over your list and pick one which seems the most likely to you. Explain why you selected that one over the others.

Background

When C. Everett Koop was surgeon general of the United States, he suggested that the government begin informing people about "safe sex" and the use of condoms as a means to stop the AIDS epidemic. People reacted against his ideas, suggesting that such information leads impressionable young people to become sexually active. Carlin's position on condoms and their use to stop AIDS was in *Commonweal* where he is a columnist.

During Reading

List the facts that Carlin uses to build his arguments. How might those facts also build an emotional response in readers?

Reading Selection

As I write this, in mid-February, Liberace has been dead 1 for nearly two weeks, *Time* is running a cover story titled "The Big Chill: How Heterosexuals Are Coping with AIDS," and the stock market value of companies that manufacture condoms is skyrocketing.

The AIDS epidemic, which had receded from the front 2 pages for a time, thus giving those of us who measure social crises in terms of front-page headlines a false sense of security, is back with a bang, and the bang is louder than ever. Facts, as the man said, are stubborn things. Unlike certain naughty children, inattention does little to improve them.

The present moment of the AIDS crisis might be titled: 3 "By condoms ye shall be saved." If only Americans would get in the habit of wearing condoms while engaged in sexual intercourse, especially anal intercourse; if only we could remove ridiculous taboos against TV advertising for condoms, thereby unleasing those great public health educators, the condom manufacturers; if only we could go into the high schools, junior high schools, and grade schools of America to teach our dear children the dangers of unsafe sex and the merits of condom use; if only we could do all these things, why, then, our problems would be largely solved. When the Angel of Death visits our street, he will pass over our household if we post evidence at the front door that we own a six-month supply of condoms and have successfully completed a course of instruction on how to use them.

It's not that I doubt the hygienic utility of condom use. 4 I have no doubt that the widespread use of condoms will cut down on the spread of AIDS among those having gay sex, promiscuous sex, sex with intravenous drug users, and so forth. Cultural antediluvian that I am, I confess that I have moments of weakness in which I doubt the wholesomeness of such categories of sexual activity. But these things happen. So mark me down as a condom proponent.

But if anyone really believes that sex education, TV 5 commercials, and a national enthusiasm for condom use will prove anything like sufficient to curb the spread of AIDS, I respectfully submit that individual should have his or her head examined. I suspect, however, that very few people really do believe this. It's just that in the ideological atmosphere surrounding the AIDS epidemic—an atmosphere, I think it is not too harsh to say, of intellectual cowardice and dishonesty (of this, more later)—persons who actually know better feel compelled to pretend that propaganda plus prophylactics will do the job until either a vaccine or an antidote is discovered.

U.S. Surgeon-General C. Everett Koop has compared 6 AIDS with the Black Death, the bubonic plague that killed about 30 percent of the western European population within a few years in the middle of the fourteenth century. To some, this comparison has seemed a bit hysterical; after all, there are only about 30,000 diagnosed AIDS victims in the United States today out of a total population of around 240,000,000. But bear the following in mind: between one and two million persons are carrying the virus that causes AIDS; once someone contracts the virus, it doesn't go away; and of those having the virus, 50 percent or more may eventually develop AIDS. If the present doubling rate keeps up (the number of AIDS victims doubles every eighteen months or so), millions will have the disease by the year 2000, and tens of millions will be carrying the lethal virus. So Dr. Koop is right on target when he makes his comparison with the Black Death. Unless things change drastically, a considerable fraction of the population of the United States will be killed off by AIDS in the next twenty-five years.

If this disease did not have sexual associations, especially homosexual associations, certain perfectly obvious public health steps would have been taken by now. We would have widespread and semi-compulsory blood tests to identify carriers of the AIDS virus (e.g., blood tests are prerequisites for marriage licenses, for all hospital in-patients, for all persons being treated for sexually transmitted diseases, for all drug rehab clients). We would also trace and notify parties who have had sexual contact with infected persons. 7

Yet there are certain parties who oppose such common-sense measures. 8

(1) The gay rights movement is opposed. The stated reason for this opposition is a conviction that the measures will not work and might even be counter-productive. The real reason is that such measures will disproportionately affect gays, thus undermining the social legitimacy of homosexuality, the achieving of which remains the chief goal, the truly essential goal, on the gay rights agenda. 9

(2) Sex education enthusiasts are opposed, since such steps are inconsistent with their fundamental superstition, namely, that all our sex-related problems will be solved if only we can instruct people more thoroughly in sexuality. Such enthusiasts, in fact, though shedding sincere tears for the victims of AIDS, see the present crisis as a golden moment, a teachable moment, for spreading the evangel of sex education. 10

(3) A certain kind of civil libertarian is opposed, the kind who tends to see sexual activity as the paradigmatic instance of action protected by the right of privacy. Any government snooping into our sex lives, especially snooping into the sex lives of a hitherto oppressed group like gays, imperils the entire structure of American liberty. 11

(4) Certain Christians with overdeveloped organs of compassion and underdeveloped organs of good judgment are unhappy with such measures. Their admirable and tender hearts go out to gays who are undergoing the difficult and painful experience of coming to terms with their sexuality; the last thing such Christians want to see is anything 12

that has the potential for thrusting gays back into the pariah status from which they are in the process of emerging.

And what about the rest of us—those who do not belong   13 to any of the above groups, yet have been unwilling to call for obvious public health steps? We are the intellectual cowards I mentioned above. We know what needs to be done, but we fear being called anti-gay or homophobic or intolerant or puritanical or sexually unenlightened or conservative or Falwell-ish or lacking in Christian charity. Better that millions should be infected and die than that we should suffer the anguish of having such dreadful adjectives hurled at us.

Checking Your Understanding

1. Carlin suggests that stopping the spread of AIDS through condoms is too simplistic. Why? What examples does he give? What examples can you lend to his argument?
2. What is your reaction to the issue of mandatory AIDS testing? Explain and defend your position on the subject.

Examining Rhetorical Strategies

1. Carlin lists four parties opposed to his call for mandatory testing. How does he use their opposition to support his argument? What other groups can you think of who might be opposed? Why would they oppose testing? Explain why you think Carlin might not include them in his discussion.
2. How does Carlin conclude his essay? What affect does it have on you as a reader? Are you the intended audience for this piece? Why or why not?

PROPOSAL

A PROPOSAL FOR A MULTILINGUAL AMERICA
Daniel Shanahan

One of the most pragmatic forms of writing is the proposal. In this form of persuasive discourse the author identifies a problem and then proposes a solution. The writing includes research into the problem and develops the argument needed to convince the reader that the proposal is indeed a reasonable solution. The action that the writer seeks is the acceptance of the proposal and its subsequent implementation.

Proposals are used by companies and contractors seeking to be employed for specific kinds of work, by agencies wishing to address social issues, and even by student governments to change conditions on college campuses. All the strategies of problem solving are involved in the writing of a proposal—defining the problem, brainstorming possibilities, developing the argument, and presenting support for the chosen solution. The readers can be either those who have recognized the problem and are calling for a solution or those who are not sure the problem exists.

Gathering solid information and developing it into a clear, logical argument are essential to a well-written proposal. In this way elements of informative writing become part of the persuasive purpose. So the persuasive writer is not just manipulating the reader into action but is also guiding the reader through the given information to the proposed solution.

Prereading Journal

With the emphasis on multicultural education in the schools, should there be a corresponding emphasis on multilingualism? Should American students be required to become proficient in a second language? Write about your experiences or lack of experiences with another language and where you stand on the issue of becoming a multilingual society.

Background

This proposal was first published as an editorial in 1989 in the *Chronicle of Higher Education*. It was addressed to an audience of college faculty and administration. Notice how Shanahan uses a chronological order to structure his definition of the problem.

During Reading

What is the problem as Shanahan sees it? List the details of the chronology he uses to define the problem. What are the details of his proposed solution?

Reading Selection

In 1904, at a hearing on the mistreatment of immigrant laborers, the president of the Reading Railroad told a Congressional committee: "These workers don't suffer—they don't even speak English." 1

Working conditions in the United States have come a long way since then, but the attitude in this country toward people who do not speak English hasn't changed very much. While few of us would support the contention that non-English speakers somehow have no right to equal protection under the law, it has become more acceptable in recent years to oppose such things as bilingual education and bilingual ballots that attempt to address problems faced by speakers of languages other than English. 2

The issue is a relatively simple one, but it has a complex social and historical background. Before the revival of ethnic pride in the 1960's and 70's, most immigrants who came to this country tried to "launder" much of their cultural past, and their native languages were among the first things to go. For them, learning English was an act of faith in the new land they had adopted. Although the price was steeper than many of them realized at the time, most were willing, even happy, to pay it. 3

But in the 1960's, the civil-rights movement forced a reassessment of what was "American," and many once-acceptable means of distinguishing among groups were seen as undemocratic, to be ferreted out and eliminated wherever they were found. It is unfortunate that during that period the issue of language (largely as it applied to Hispanic Americans) became fused with the issue of civil rights. 4

As a result, bilingual issues were overwhelmed by emo- 5
tional baggage, first the liberal guilt of the 60's and 70's and
then the conservative reaction of the Reagan era. Lost in the
shuffle was a much more vital issue, and one which pivots, not
on questions of deprivation of civil rights, but on America's
ability to remain a viable actor in the increasingly global environment by becoming more competent linguistically.

The "official language" propositions that have been 6
passed in 17 states in recent years—three in last fall's elec-
tions—are clear signs that the electorate does not understand
the true effect of the language issue on the national interest.
Most such propositions pass because of fear and resentment
on the part of the majority language group. While the campaign advertisements run by supporters of the proposals do
not overtly express resentment over money spent to serve
those who do not speak English, the sentiments expressed by
voters who support the initiatives often can be summed up in
some variation of the statement: "My parents had to learn
English when they came to this country. . . ."

Resentment is, of course, a more or less unacceptable 7
basis for policy analysis, so supporters' justifications of
English-only initiatives usually play on fears: of social dis-
unity, of economic hardship, of the cost of cultural plurality. Canada is most frequently cited as an example of the
way cultural plurality, maintained through linguistic plurality, can lead to social instability. Putting aside for the
moment the fact that Canada not only survived Quebec's
"quiet revolution" but also profited from it, as the economic boom in Quebec is now demonstrating, such analysis of the language issue ignores the extent to which the
entire world is rapidly becoming a stage on which the players must speak more than one language to survive and
compete economically.

The Japanese have led the way in learning second—and 8
third—languages to further their economic competitiveness.
It can be argued that the difficulty of their own language
made it unlikely that foreigners would learn it and forced
them to learn the languages of others, but it can just as easily be argued that this apparent liability simply led them to see
the handwriting on the wall more quickly than others, and it
thus became a competitive advantage.

Europeans have always been proficient in other lan- 9
guages, largely because of the high concentration of different languages in their relatively small geographic space.
Being multilingual is helping them establish an economic
union that looms as a powerful force in the already crowded
and competitive global marketplace.

Even in developing countries, where one might expect 10
lack of education to limit multilingualism, many people
speak a regional dialect at home and the language of the
dominant cultural group in the workplace; some also speak
the European language of the colonial period as well.
Against this international backdrop, the spectacle of
Americans passing laws to limit the languages used in their
country can only be seen as self-destructive.

Of course, there must be a standard language in a 11
country, if only for the purpose of efficiency, but the language is designated by practice, not by law. In the United
States, the standard language is and always has been
English. The question should not be whether we should
spend money to make it possible for immigrants to use their
native languages in official situations, nor should it be
whether we encourage others, children especially, to maintain a language other than English. Quite clearly, the question ought to be whether we should undertake a nationwide
effort to encourage, enhance, and expand multilingual proficiency among native speakers of English, as well as among
non-natives.

The answer to that question must be a resounding and 12
unequivocal Yes.

It is nothing less than criminal for a country so 13
admittedly language poor and so strapped for competitive
advantages in the international marketplace to be adopting myopic and regressive language laws that reinforce
the naive monolingual bias that threatens to isolate and
weaken it. Yet it is also understandable that Americans
want clarity and perhaps a degree of reassurance in our
increasingly volatile and shifting ethnic and linguistic
environment.

A compromise addressing both sides of the issue must 14
be found, and I believe it will not be as hard to come by as
some people might imagine.

Let Congress pass a law designating English the "stan-   15
dard" language of the United States, but let the measure also
include the appropriation of sufficient money to insure that
20 years from now, all Americans graduating from high
school will be proficient in a second language.

Let a high-school diploma and college admission be   16
denied to anyone without a sufficient level of proficiency. And
let proficiency in a second language—at the level of a native
speaker—be required for graduation from college and entry
into civil-service and private-sector white-collar employment.
In other words, let us put our money where our mouths are.
The price tag for instituting such requirements—including
the cost of training the needed teachers over five years—
would be less than the budget for the Strategic Defense
Initiative for two fiscal years. Moreover, the benefits would be
far greater. For only with such determined policies can we
hope to calm fears about language plurality and insure that
we do not become a culture of monolingual dinosaurs.

We have 20 years, nearly triple the time President   17
Kennedy allowed when he committed us to reaching the
moon. By comparison, the expenditures required to create a
linguistically proficient nation would be insignificant. The
benefits, not only in economic terms but also in terms of
enhancing our understanding of other cultures and of ourselves, would be beyond measure. The costs, should we fail to
act decisively, could eventually prove to be catastrophic.

Checking Your Understanding

1. Consider the implications of Shanahan's proposal. Is it feasible?
    Does it address the problem he defined? What implications would it
    have for his audience of faculty and administration?
2. Respond to Shanahan's proposal by writing him a letter. In that let-
    ter voice your assent or dissent and support your position by draw-
    ing on your own experiences as described in your journal.

Examining Rhetorical Strategies

1. Persuasion often appeals to the readers' emotions. In what way is
    Shanahan making an emotional appeal? What words or phrases
    does he use to make that appeal?
2. Review the organization of the proposal. How does Shanahan build
    his argument for his intended audience?

A SUMMARY OF PERSUASIVE READING

The common purpose of this wide range of persuasive writing is to *call the reader to action*. Depending on the subject and the audience, that persuasion is handled in a variety of complex ways.

First, we have seen the importance of *support* in the discourse. Virtually all aspects of persuasive writing use facts and details or images and feelings in order to appeal to the reader. But that information is filtered through the writers' opinions and beliefs. The writer's voice establishes the writer as a credible authority and that *credibility* is supported by the organization of logic and/or emotion.

Second, the *audience* plays an important part in the shape and the style of the discourse. Readers who already agree with the writer influence the discourse differently than those who are uncertain or those who are opposed to the ideas being presented. And conversely, how we as readers feel about the subject will affect the response we have to it. If we are sympathetic to the cause or moved from indecision, we will respond as the writer encourages us to do; we will read the book, make the decision, accept the proposal. Or if we are unimpressed or in opposition, we will complain to our roommate or even pick up a pen (or keyboard) and respond in kind with a persuasive discourse of our own.

Third, the primary purpose of our reading is to consider another's opinion with the *possibility of changing* our own. In this regard the persuasive essay is similar to affirming discourse, but the difference is that we know the writer will want us to take a specific action as a result of our reading.

The success of persuasive writing depends on the fact that as readers, we do something. A truly persuasive piece of discourse makes a difference in the way we think, the way we choose, and the way we believe.

Chapter Ten

WRITING PERSUASIVE DISCOURSE

Turning an opinion into a persuasive essay would not seem to be such a difficult task. We all have opinions and we all want others to agree with them. All we need to do then is lay it on thick; hit them over the head with details and examples, and tell them what to do. Any intelligent individual will agree, right? Wrong. Persuasive writing requires much more. It means having to analyze your audience to know what information readers will need in order to see the issue your way. It means having to know something about the subject beyond the simplistic "it's right" or "it's wrong." It also means creating an imperative tone that will encourage your readers to respond. Like all forms of writing, it requires your careful thought and consideration.

DETERMINING YOUR RELATIONSHIP TO YOUR READERS

As in all writing, *audience* plays an integral part in the writing situation. It is important to decide on your audience and direct your argument to your readers. For whom are you writing? Who is it that you intend to move to a response?

Perhaps more difficult than identifying the audience, is addressing the audience. As you develop the essay you will need to use examples and experiences that are relevant to those readers. You should begin by analyzing the intended audience in order to identify the support which will be most effective in moving them to change or to take action.

Analyzing Your Audience

Who is the audience? Are they your peers who are trying to decide whether or not to use the new fitness center? Are they administrators who need to be persuaded to build a campus fitness center? Are they those who will be voting for either a fitness center or a new computer lab in the library? In each case the reasons, experiences, and factual details that you use to develop your essay will be slightly different.

In your analysis you determine whether the issue is best addressed through an appeal to the readers' emotions or to their intellect. In carefully considering both the issue and the audience, you can decide if your audience will respond to feelings, to facts, or to a stronger, more authoritative voice.

SELECTING A FOCUS

The question that must be answered in expressive and affirming writing is "So what?" In persuasive essays the question that guides your writing is "So, what do you want?" Because you want to do more than share with your audience, your point has to be crystal clear. You will be leading your readers toward an imperative: asking them to change their thinking, to use your advice, to accept your proposal. That imperative cannot be part of a guessing game; it needs to be defined and clarified. It would be fatal for the audience to be left without knowing exactly what you want from them.

In order to write a good persuasive essay, then, you will need not only to *select a topic* but also to *decide on your imperative*—what do you want from your audience?

clarity

Selecting a Topic

As with any writing, the best way to begin is to brainstorm from your own experience. If the ultimate purpose is to prove your authority, you need to begin with something that you know or believe or experience. For an evaluative essay you will be sharing your feelings on a book, a movie, or an article. Be sure it is something about which you have an opinion; something that has raised strong emotions in you. An argument begins with an issue that you want to move people toward or against. It needs to be one that is controversial, one with more than one side so that the imperative will be to ask the reader to take your side. Proposals begin with a problem in need of a solution or, more specifically, a problem in need of a solution you have in mind.

Once selected, you should list your *authority* and *knowledge* on the topic. What do you know about this subject? What are your personal experiences? What are things that you have heard or read? What emotions are raised by this issue? Such brainstorming for an evaluative essay might require rereading the article or re-seeing the movie. For the evaluative essay you must become the expert on the topic. In argumentation and proposal writing you might want to do some *library research* to gather facts or *interview* others affected by the topic. The focus for this gathering of knowledge and experience is to identify the *emotional* aspects of the topic as well as the *logical* ones in order to build and support your authority.

Choosing Your Imperative

Once you have listed your opinions and gathered reasons, responses, and relevant ideas, you need to decide on your *purpose for persuasion.* If you have chosen persuasive discourse then you must consider the imperative. What do you want from your audience based on their reading of your essay? Obviously if you are writing about a movie or a book, you would like them to either flock to it or run from it. If you are raising an issue and arguing a side, you might want the readers to respond by agreeing with you or by showing their agreement in some way. If you begin with a problem the imperative is to accept the solution you will put before them.

Once your purpose is established, you need to decide which experiences or aspects lend support to the imperative you will set before the reader. As with affirming discourse, the audience must understand and appreciate your opinions, but because your purpose is to move them to action, they must also know what it is you want them to do.

MAKING IT SIGNIFICANT FOR YOUR AUDIENCE

Because you are attempting to move readers to action, you must establish yourself as someone worth listening to. This will mean establishing a credible voice. Your readers want to know what gives you the "right" to give them an evaluation, to argue a change, to propose a policy. They need to know why you are justified in rallying them to a response.

Establishing your authority may be as simple as pointing out their need for the product or as complicated as critically analyzing a difficult problem. In any case, your authority must be established with the intended audience in mind. What authority will cause parents to take your advice? Why should the nonprofit organization use your proposal to raise money? Why are you the best person for the advertised job?

Then you must decide on the best way to say what you have to say. *Consider the language* that will help the audience identify you as someone who knows. Such language changes as the audience changes. *Tone* also adds authority to a persuasive essay. Are you patronizing? Sarcastic? Detached? A sarcastic book review might be a creative way to move your peer readers to a response, but such a tone may not be what your English professor has in mind when you are asked to review a novel for class.

In persuasive writing, you begin with some common ground from which to develop your argument for your audience in order to move them toward a response. Establishing that common ground means anticipating the kinds of questions they will raise and the kinds of information they want to know.

ORGANIZING YOUR THOUGHTS

As with any writing, early drafts will be a place for you to simply get those ideas, examples, and reasons down in writing. As you brainstorm, you will want to begin sorting and weeding. What kind of support is emerging? Much of this will depend on the particular type of persuasive discourse you are developing. If this is a proposal, you may want to discuss the initial problem, present a variety of solutions, and then carefully delineate your solution for the reader. If you are reviewing a program, you need to decide on the characteristics that make it worth somebody's time. If you are arguing a position, you will need to clarify the reasons that back up your claims.

Once you have your central idea you can work on the best way to organize the support for the intended audience. You might consider *comparing* your side of an issue with the opposing position. This would allow you to analyze and critique the alternatives in *contrast* with your position.

In writing a proposal, *definition* will be important. What is the problem? What is your solution to it? For readers who want the answers to these questions, a careful definition can help guide your organization.

It is possible that the final decision on organization will come as you are writing. Even after drafting your piece with one type of organization in mind, you might decide that another is more appropriate for your audience and the topic. It is important to remember that the organization, even the supporting details, examples, and events, should be used because of the audience you have identified. The information you use to support a position on selling alcohol to underage students will vary according to the audience you are trying to reach and the response you wish to initiate. If you are developing a proposal for the city council, you may use statistics, interviews, and a survey to lend support to your solution. If you were instead calling for underage students to be more responsible, you might support your position with personal experience and medical information regarding alcohol abuse.

Persuasive discourse has often developed a negative connotation because of the way that information seems to be manipulated for the purpose. Persuasion may indeed develop from the distortion of needs and situations, but not all persuasion involves that kind of language abuse. In fact, we would argue that persuasion should not involve distorting the information at all. Rather, persuasion is about moving the readers to your position, getting them to recognize the importance of an issue, to hire you for the job, to vote for your qualified candidate; it has to do with your conviction and the best way to convince your audience to share it.

Notes on the Evaluative Essay

If you are reviewing any book, movie, program, activity, event, you need to establish your authority to write immediately. By its very nature, you are addressing the audience with the authority of someone who knows. This can be done through a recounting of a personal experience or by supporting your views with quotes and excerpts that show your familiarity with the subject. You might compare this one with others of a similar type or genre, further establishing yourself as the expert in the field.

The imperative that you are developing is one which leads the readers to a decision on the subject. Should they see it, read it, take part in it? Often this is written with a familiar tone, starting from the common ground that you are just like the reader and this is what you've come to believe about the subject. In creating your authority you will need to be as specific as possible in the details you present.

Notes on Argumentation

If you are arguing an issue, you need to start with a controversial one. Using personal experience may help you develop an emotional ground from which to present your view. Audience here is very important; an antagonistic reader requires different support than a supportive reader will. In fact, the antagonistic reader may be impossible to persuade, but what about those who already are inclined toward your way of thinking? Here, then is a common ground from which to develop your persuasive imperative.

The imperative is to have the reader agree with you, vote your way, sign the petition, hire you for the job. Your tone and support need to be built with the appropriate goal in mind.

Notes on the Proposal

If you are proposing a solution to a problem, you need to carefully define the problem, your authority, and the best solution that you see. The audience is that reader who is in a position to do something about your solution, either to implement it or fight for its implementation. Your authority comes from the way you define the problem and its significance to the reader.

Because your imperative is based on readers accepting your solution, that solution needs your attention and support. You can show the logic and reasonableness of your solution by comparing and contrasting it to other solutions, or by establishing a cause-and-effect relationship between the problem and your proposed solution.

THE WRITING PROCESS AT WORK

Although the assignment to "be persuasive" may sound simple, balancing subject, support, and audience is not an easy task. As with all types of writing, it begins with an idea which we evaluate, revise, and shape for a specific purpose. Often, we begin with one intention in mind, only to find that it will not work for the identified audience. But the process leads us to another perspective, another angle, another purpose.

In the following section we will follow a student as she works through an opinion and develops it into an essay asking students to be more aware and less quick to judge. When she began, she had a clear sense of her imperative, but as she revised she found another one emerging.

SUPPORTING COMMUNITY

Roxanne M. Carlone

Background

Carlone was a Resident Assistant (R.A.) at a state college. Before the persuasive essay was assigned, a fire broke out in one of the on-campus dormitories. No one was seriously injured, but there was extensive property damage. Although Carlone was not the R.A., she suddenly felt the weight of responsibility of that position as she realized how easily it could have happened on her floor.

First Draft

"Why do you R.A.'s always have to spoil our fun?" He 1 was standing at the sink waiting for his turn to pour out his beer as I had demanded. "So the music is a little loud and we're not 21 yet. Big deal!"

Yeah, it is a big deal, I wanted to tell him. I could have 2 called campus security to come break up the party. Or the police department could have arrived to arrest everyone for drinking underage and disturbing the peace. And he's complaining because I asked him to lower the stereo and get rid of the alcohol?

"We're not here to spoil your fun," I answered. "We're 3 here to make sure you are having fun responsibly, and that you are in no way endangering yourself or others."

I know it is a response straight from the Resident 4 Assistant Handbook, but how can I make him understand the problem he and his friends have created? I was there to respond to a noise complaint. A woman on the 2nd floor called the office saying the people above her were so loud she thought they might burst through her ceiling. When I arrived, the music was making the whole building shake and I almost broke the door down with my kicks before they realized someone was knocking. Inside I found 8 people in a 2 person room, all drinking, and neither of the residents being of legal age.

Big deal? What if a woman gets so drunk that she loses 5 the power to say no to that guy who's hitting on her all night?

What if the guy is so trashed that he doesn't care that she is saying no? What if that man who's had 5 funnels gets in a car and hits a tree on his way home? Even worse, what if he hits another car, and what if he kills someone?

In such situations it is the Resident Assistants who 6 always appear as the bad guys. We bust parties. We confiscate candles and incense. We don't allow stuffed furniture in resident rooms. We make people lower the music, and we have the power to "write you up."

However, R.A.'s don't really wear the eye mask and 7 black ten-gallon hats that some are so eager to point out. Instead we wear a sense of pride—a pride in our community. And for me, that pride is reflected through concern for my fellow students. If someone's rights to Mandatory Quiet Hours are being violated, I will work to assure those rights. If an area's safety is at risk because a resident insists on burning candles, I will interfere to guarantee that safety. The R.A.'s job is to create a safe and healthy living environment, and for the sake of my residents, I take pride in achieving that goal.

R.A.'s, however, do much more than disciplinary work. 8 We are programmers, providing food socials, recreation events, and educational programs. We are counselors, mediating such conflicts as "My roommate always borrows my clothes without asking," and advisors, answering questions like "I think I want to change majors, what should I do?" We are also building managers, "My light bulb burnt out again!" and we are role models. And, in addition to all this, we are stressed out college students, and we are sensitive human beings.

I wish the student complaining that I spoiled his fun 9 would realize all that we do. I also wish he could have seen what I did last night. It was past midnight, and I had just finished studying for an 8:00 a.m. exam. I had just crawled into bed when there was a knock on my door. It was a resident, huddled within a blanket crying. She was the unfortunate victim of the latest flu epidemic. She was sick and hurting, and her roommate had merely told her to roll over and go to sleep. So she found her way to my door, looking for comfort and looking for a friend.

I took her in. I gave her an aspirin and took her tem- 10 perature. I let her lie on my bed and hold my teddy bear. We talked, and I told her funny stories about me being sick to make her smile. We stayed up together for 2 hours, and when she was ready I walked her back to her room and tucked her in.

The next day she slipped a note under my door. She 11 said she was feeling much better, and she thanked me for being her R.A. and for helping her out.

I know all students can't be expected to look at 12 Resident Assistants as angels of mercy. But I do wish they would stop seeing us as bad guys. Those people who I made dump their alcohol will probably never thank me for a job well done. And they probably will never understand that I acted for their best interest. But if students stop blaming R.A.'s for getting in the their way, maybe they will finally come to realize that we are here just to help them.

Writer's comments   I am trying to say that R.A.'s aren't bad people! I want my audience to open their eyes and give us credit for all we do. I'm concerned about whether or not I'm just looking for sympathy.

Analysis

Carlone's purpose is clear; she is defending herself against the charges of students who accuse R.A.'s of spoiling their fun. She does this by contrasting the alcohol dumping with the flu victim. Her examples are both taken from her personal experience. But she does more than simply contrast two events in the life of an R.A. Carlone also introduces the idea of community. She raises a series of questions asking her readers to imagine what might happen to the community if certain rules were not obeyed.

That series of questions in paragraph 5 does two things for her draft. First, it serves to draw the reader into her position. In this way Carlone is establishing that common ground. She is asking the reader "What would you do? How would you feel?" The appeal is very direct and leads to her final imperative that if students, her readers, would stop blaming the R.A., they might understand the job better.

The second aspect of the questions is more important in terms of the direction Carlone will take in her next draft. She recognizes how what she does and what students do influence the community. The first draft is very personal; it is, in fact, a personal response to a specific situation. But as she explores the questions she poses, she identifies another issue: "pride in our community."

This idea of community is what guided her revisions in her second draft, beginning by influencing the structure of her sentences. A peer commenter had said that her support sounded repetitive. Carlone recognized that she tended to list her reasons and so in her revision she varied her sentence structure to avoid giving that sense. The result is that her reasons are emphasized rather than stacked one on top of the other. For example, paragraph 8 on R.A. responsibilities in draft two was revised to read:

> A healthy environment, however, requires much more than just this type of disciplinary work. R.A.'s also work as programmers—providing food socials, recreation events, and educational programs. And we act as counselors, dealing with such problems as "my roommate always borrows my clothes without asking," and "I think I want to change my major, what should I do?" We take on the responsibility of building managers, getting light bulbs replaced, toilets unclogged, and locks repaired. And, in addition to all this, we are busy, stressed out college students and sensitive human beings.

The structure is no longer "and we are role models and we are stressed . . . and we are sensitive." In the revision, she elaborates rather than lists. The entire paragraph is now used to support the idea of creating a "safe and healthy living environment" for the residents.

In her second draft, she also worked on being more descriptive. In revising her opening scene, for example, she describes the music as not just being loud, but that it "had the entire building vibrating." She also shaped this event to reinforce the responsibility that an R.A. carries. She is not spoiling his fun; she is asking him to be more responsible to those around him. And, in this responsibility, she finds the key ingredient to community. The position she is developing is now less of a defense of her actions and more an explanation of the role R.A.'s play on campus.

What has been important for Carlone in the drafting process has been the sense of discovery. Beginning with just emotion, she has tried to shape her position for a broader audience, calling them to respond to a sense of pride in their college community.

In writing her final draft, Carlone realized that her original passion had passed, that her anger had dissipated into a more logical approach to the incident: "At first I was *angry*. I wanted to let everyone know that I may be an R.A., but I'm human too. People have so many negative ideas about R.A.'s and I wanted a chance to defend myself. [But] I ended up not defending myself, but defending the idea of a community, and how to be responsible to that group." Rather than defending herself against insensitive students, Carlone found her imperative—that all of them, students and R.A.'s, needed to work together.

Final Draft

"Why do you R.A.'s always have to spoil our fun?" He 1 was standing at the sink, waiting for his turn to pour out his beer as I had demanded. "So the music is a little loud and we're not 21 yet. Big deal!"

Yes, it is a big deal, I wanted to tell him. I could have 2 called campus security to come break up the party. Or the police department might have arrived to arrest everyone for drinking underage and disturbing the peace. And he's complaining because I asked him to lower the stereo and get rid of the alcohol?

"We're not here to spoil your fun," I answered. "We're 3 here to make sure you are having fun responsibly, and that you are in no way endangering yourself or others."

I knew this was a response straight out of the Resident 4 Assistant Handbook, but how could I have possibly made him understand the problem he and his friends had created? How could I tell him he was hurting the community, the community I worked so hard to create?

As a Resident Assistant, building this sense of commu- 5 nity is my job. In the residence hall, students from varying backgrounds meet to study, to relax, to prepare for their future career, to eat, to sleep, and to *live*. It is my responsibility, as an R.A., to create a safe and healthy environment for them to enjoy. I work hard for this by presenting educational programs, organizing socials, filing maintenance request orders, providing counseling and advising, being a good listener, and by being a friend. I do my part but I can't create this community all by myself. Each resident must participate in achieving this goal, for by its very definition a community demands that all must work together to achieve a common good.

This is why it is such a "big deal" when residents violate 6 this sense of community. I was at that party scene because a resident of the floor below called me with a noise complaint. They were so loud, she said, she was afraid they were falling through her ceiling. When I arrived, the stereo volume had the entire building vibrating, and I almost broke down the door with my kicks before they even realized someone was knocking. Inside I found eight people in a two person room, all drinking, and all under the age of twenty-one.

I disbanded their party, their "fun" as the student 7 termed it, out of protection for the community. The students' lack of responsibility, their disrespect for their fellow residents, threatened the residence hall environment. Not only were they ignoring Mandatory Quiet Hours, preventing students from studying and forcing upon them their own personal choice of music, but they were also endangering the very lives of the party-going residents. Imagine a woman getting so drunk that she loses the power to say no to the man who's been hitting on her all night, or imagine that the man is so trashed that he doesn't even care that she is trying to say no. And think about the intoxicated resident who might get into his car to go out for a drive. What if he manages to crash into a tree? What if he hits another car, and what if he kills someone?

In such a situation, it should be obvious that the dis- 8 ruptive students are the ones at fault for failing to fulfill their required responsibilities. However, all too often it is the Resident Assistants who are blamed instead. We bust parties. We confiscate candles and incense. We don't allow stuffed furniture in residents' rooms. We force people to lower their music. We have the power to "write you up," and we prevent students from having their fun.

However, R.A.'s are not the bad guys. The only thing we 9 are guilty of is pride—a pride in our community and a pride we work to instill in others.

For me, this pride is revealed through concern for my 10 fellow students. Within the residence hall, all students are deserving of certain rights. When these rights are violated, it is my prerogative to interfere. Thus, if studying is prevented because of someone's blatant disregard for Quiet Hours, I will ask the volume to be turned down. If an area is continually at risk because a student insists on burning candles, I will interfere to protect the area's safety. And, as in the case of the party, if the well-being of the residents themselves is in danger, I will step in to ensure its preservation.

If others shared this pride, if residents accepted their   11
responsibility, then such disciplinary action would be unnecessary. Act responsibly and respect your community, and confiscations, reprimands, and incident reports can all be avoided. After all, the R.A.'s intent is not to spoil fun, but to encourage it, for fun is the greatest part of the residence hall experience. But, that fun must not threaten the community; it must support it.

Analysis

Carlone's position and support are very clear. She both defends Resident Assistants and defines the role they play in the college community. The support she uses is based on the common experience of living in a residence hall. As she revised, she defined the role of community in more specific terms and explored the responsibility all students share in creating that environment. In her first draft, Carlone had been reacting solely to the student who did not want her to ruin his fun; but by the final draft, that anger had been used to shape the definition of community and responsibility that she wanted her readers to accept.

The organization of her paper, then, was based on that shifting focus. She no longer needed the contrasting incident of the woman with the flu which would have kept the focus on her personal experience. Instead she used the opening scene to point out what happens when students fail to accept their responsibility within the campus environment. While the story of the flu victim is a great expression of Carlone's commitment to community, it was too personal to support the broader response she wanted from her readers. Like all good writers, she was not afraid to delete what did not work—and save it for another assignment with another purpose.

Exercise

Carlone's initial purpose was to defend herself against the accusation that R.A.'s only spoil the fun. Did you feel the anger in her description? What other emotions would you feel in such a situation? Is emotion enough to support a call to community?

In persuasive writing it may also be necessary to develop factual information and reasons. Try developing your own call for community—to your neighbors, your classmates, your campus. What emotional appeal will you make? What facts and reasons will you use to support your call to action?

WRITING FOR READERS

By the final draft, Carlone has recognized that the audience is not just those who feel as the party goers do, but all students who live on the college campus. That shift in audience played an important role in the support and organization of her essay. She claims that it "softened" her persuasion, but in establishing her authority and a common ground, she could not simply vent her frustration. Carlone's voice becomes more credible as she stops establishing herself as the authority and instead appeals to peers that "we're all in this together."

Now she can use the emotional opening to show what happens when students do not think of themselves as a community and appeal to their sense of reason. In fact, her argument becomes stronger as she decides that she does not simply want students to be more sympathetic, but that she wants them to understand their role in the campus community. It is that call to respond that establishes her persuasive purpose.

STRATEGIES FOR WRITING PERSUASIVE DISCOURSE

The assignment Review the *purpose* of the assignment. Remember that persuasive writing contains an imperative—a call to action that is supported by emotional and logical reasoning.

Prewriting Select your *subject* thoughtfully. You might begin by recounting a personal experience which has led you to feel the necessity for action. Then, you can list reasons you will use to convince your reader and emotions which will reinforce those details. Brainstorming your ideas in either list or map form may be a useful way for you to put ideas down on paper.

Drafting   While you are writing, keep in mind the following four goals discussed in this chapter.

1. Determine your relationship to your readers. How will you establish your *authority*? What *voice* will best reinforce that authority and lend credibility to your imperative? What action do you want from your readers based on this essay? What impression of you do the readers need in order to respond to your imperative?

2. Select your *focus* thoughtfully. What support can you give on this issue? What book, movie, program, or event can you recommend? Or will you dissuade your readers rather than persuade them? Consider the use of a common ground from which to begin your argument.

3. Make the *significance* clear to your readers. How would they answer the question "So, what do you want?" What is your imperative? What are the emotional, logical, and informational forms of support for that imperative? Consider how you will make your readers care as much about this subject as you do.

4. *Organize* your thoughts. Although the organization may change with the specific purpose, devise a plan which best brings your subject, purpose, and audience together. The imperative should be apparent and the reader should be able to clearly follow your support and its significance to the subject.

Editing   As you edit pay particular attention to the following aspects of persuasive writing:

An appropriate, consistent voice
A clearly defined issue or subject
Emotional, logical, and/or informational details and experiences
A purposeful arrangement of the supporting material
Personal investment and authority
An evident action for the reader to take

Chapter Eleven

FURTHER PERSUASIVE READINGS

The readings contained in this chapter illustrate a wide range of persuasive discourse. Some are overtly persuasive such as Pam Bombard as she proposes that school officials reconsider a required program; others are more subtle, such as Jeff Smith as he establishes the value of American cooking. Yet in all essays, the writer develops a persuasive imperative by appealing to emotion, reason, and logic.

PROFESSIONAL ESSAYS AND READING TECHNIQUES

THE FRUGAL GOURMET COOKS AMERICAN

Jeff Smith

Prereading Journal

Describe your favorite food. What do you know about the origins of that food? What memories do you associate with that food?

Background

Jeff Smith's introduction to his cookbook, *The Frugal Gourmet Cooks American,* is more than just a summary of what you can find in the cookbook. It is meant to persuade readers that in understanding the foods Americans eat, we also understand the American culture. And through this evaluation of foods, readers are persuaded that there is, indeed, an American cuisine.

During Reading

What does Smith suggest is the purpose for this cookbook? List the details he uses to support that purpose. What need does he suggest his book will fulfill for the reader? How does he personalize that need for you?

Reading Selection

We Americans have had a bad image of ourselves and our food for a long time, and I am done with it. I am so tired of people from the New World bowing to Europe, particularly France, when it comes to fine eating. We seem to think that if it comes from Europe it will be good, and if it comes from America it will be inferior. Enough! We really do not understand our own food history, and I think that means we do not actually understand our own culture.

Most Americans do not think of themselves as an ethnic group, but we are an ethnic body, all of us put together. The word *ethnic* comes from the Greek *ethnos,* meaning "nation." It refers not necessarily to a bloodline but to a group of persons distinguished by singular customs, characteristics, and language. While we are a nation populated for the most part by immigrants, we are nevertheless an ethnic group, a strange mixture, perhaps, but an ethnic group. We share a common language, but more importantly, we share a common memory. And there certainly is such a thing as American ethnic cooking. It is cooking that helps us remember and restore that common cultural memory.

A favorite philosopher of mine, Lin Yutang, once asked 3 this question: "What is patriotism except memories of that which we ate as a child?" This cookbook is a collection of memories that can be recalled and celebrated by everyone who calls himself/herself an American. It has nothing to do with the fact that your blood is not Native American, but it has much to do with the fact that even though you speak fluent Chinese, and learned same from your grandmother in San Francisco, you will be marked in China as an American. We are a special group with a very special memory.

All ethnic groups have foods that help them continue 4 to identify themselves. Most of us Americans are not aware of the wonderfully complex history of our own foods . . . since most of us still think that everything there came over from Europe or some other part of the world. The following is a list of food products that are ours, coming from one of the Americas, and these products were unknown in Europe prior to the discovery of the New World:

corn	cocoa
turkey	vanilla beans
peanuts	potatoes
black walnuts	sweet potatoes
tomatoes	avocados
kidney beans	pimentos
lima beans	allspice
navy beans	bell peppers
string beans	cranberries
squashes	wild rice
pumpkins	

So there! These foods belong to us, and they actually do 5 help define us. You enjoy turkey at Christmas even though your grandmother was born in Sicily. And the influence that these foods have had upon the rest of the world should never be overlooked. Italy had no tomatoes, Ireland no potatoes, and Switzerland had no vanilla or chocolate. Spain had no bell peppers or pimentos and China had no corn, peanuts, or sweet potatoes. These last three edibles kept most of China alive at the beginning of this century. American foods have influenced the diet of the world.

When thinking about who we are we must remember 6 that America was discovered by the Europeans while on a search for food. Columbus was not after property for housing developments, he was after trade routes for valuable spices! And ever since the Europeans began moving about between the New World and the Old there has been such a thing as American ethnic food, food that is ours and is foreign to the rest of the planet. You see, I am not talking about hamburgers and hot dogs, though these are the delicacies that most Americans use in answering the question about "real American food."

Our real American foods have come from our soil and 7 have been used by many groups—those who already lived here and those who have come here to live. The Native Americans already had developed an interesting cuisine using the abundant foods that were so prevalent. You will enjoy the recipes that I have found from various peoples and tribes.

The influence that the English had upon our national 8 eating habits is easy to see in the Colonial section. They were a tough lot, those English, and they ate in a tough manner. They wiped their mouths on the tablecloth, if there happened to be one, and ate until you would expect them to burst. European travelers to this country in those days were most often shocked by American eating habits, which included too much fat and too much salt and too much liquor. Not much has changed! And, the Revolutionists refused to use the fork since it marked them as Europeans. The fork was not absolutely common on the American dinner table until about the time of the Civil War, the 1860s. Those English were a tough lot.

Other immigrant groups added their own touches to 9 the preparation of our New World food products. The groups that came still have a special sense of self-identity through their ancestral heritage, but they see themselves as Americans. This special self-identity through your ancestors who came from other lands was supposed to disappear in this country. The term *melting pot* was first used in reference to America in the late 1700s, so this belief that we would all become the same has been with us for a long time. Thank goodness it has never worked. The various immigrant groups continue to add flavor to the pot, all right, but you can pick out the individual flavors very easily.

The largest ancestry group in America is the English.   10 There are more people in America who claim to have come from English blood than there are in England. But is their food English? Thanks be to God, it is not! It is American. The second largest group is the Germans, then the Irish, the Afro-Americans, the French, the Italians, the Scottish, and the Polish. The Mexican and American Indian groups are all smaller than any of the above, though they were the original cooks in this country.

Some unusually creative cooking has come about in this   11 nation because of all those persons that have come here. Out of destitution comes either creativity or starvation, and some of the solutions that the new Americans have come up with are just grand. Only in America would you find an Italian housewife sharing recipes with her neighbor from Ireland. It has always been this way. The Native Americans were gracious enough to teach the first Europeans how to cook what was here, and we have been trading favorite dishes with one another ever since.

I am talking about American food—food that has come   12 to us from the early days, using American products, and that continues to provide one of the best diets on earth. I am not talking contemporary artsy plates, nor am I talking about *nouvelle gauche.* And, I am not talking about meat loaf and lumpy mashed potatoes. Even at the time of the writing of the Declaration of Independence we were celebrating one of the most varied, and probably the best, cuisines in the world. It has not changed.

The following chapters will help you better understand   13 your roots in terms of true American cooking, from the Native American gifts to the wonderful regional dishes that we can celebrate regularly.

Pour a glass of sherry and run through these recipes and   14
stories. Think of your own childhood . . . the house and the
front room. Think of the kitchen and how it smelled, and who
was seated at the dining-room table. Lin Yutang is right: The
memories of what we ate as a child form a sort of patriotism
that lasts throughout our life. We are a special group of citizens
who eat special foods in order to recall who we are. I stand with
my young friend Alexandra, my editor's daughter, who said,
upon hearing of this book, "Mom, it's about time. Instead of
saying, 'Let's eat Northern Chinese tonight, or Thai, or
Armenian,' we can say, 'Let's eat American,' and mean it. I
think he's got something here!" Thank you, Alexandra, this
whole country has got something, and it is wonderful.

Now, call your grandmother and ask for those recipes   15
you have been meaning to get, and we can get started on eating our own history lessons, on tasting our spirit of patriotism.

I wish you well.   16

—JEFF SMITH
September 1987
On the 200th anniversary of
the Constitutional Convention of
These United States

". . . *in order to form a more perfect union* . . . "

Checking Your Understanding

1. Having read this essay, are you now interested in buying and/or
   reading the cookbook? Why or why not?
2. How does Smith's use of information work to develop interest in the
   book? What does that information suggest about the cookbook itself?
   From this introduction what do you expect the cookbook to be like?

Examining Rhetorical Strategies

1. This introduction is an evaluative essay, establishing the value of
   American cuisine. Discuss the writer's voice in this essay. What
   impression do you have of him based on this? How has he established himself as an authority?
2. Consider your favorite food. Write a letter to Smith in which you evaluate its inclusion in this cookbook. Review the stated purpose for the
   cookbook and persuade him that your food fits that purpose.
   Personalize your persuasion by drawing from your prereading journal.

TEACH DIVERSITY—WITH A SMILE

Barbara Ehrenreich

Prereading Journal

Multiculturalism has become an educational buzzword. What does it mean to you? What instances of multicultural education have you experienced?

Background

This essay first appeared in the April 8, 1991, issue of *Time* magazine. In this example of argumentation, Ehrenreich defines the issue of multiculturalism and language. She argues for a diversity that does not take itself so seriously and uses her own upbringing to establish an authority for the argument.

During Reading

Ehrenreich contrasts monoculturalism with multiculturalism. As you read, list the defining characteristics of each.

Reading Selection

Something had to replace the threat of communism, 1 and at last a workable substitute is at hand. "Multiculturalism," as the new menace is known, has been denounced in the media recently as the new McCarthyism, the new fundamentalism, even the new totalitarianism— take your choice. According to its critics, who include a flock of tenured conservative scholars, multiculturalism aims to toss out what it sees as the Eurocentric bias in education and replace Plato with Ntozake Shange and traditional math with the Yoruba number system. And that's just the beginning. The Jacobins of the multiculturalist movement, who are described derisively as P.C., or politically correct, are said to have launched a campus reign of terror against those who slip and innocently say "freshman" instead of "freshperson," "Indian" instead of "Native American" or, may the Goddess forgive them, "disabled" instead of "differently abled."

So you can see what is at stake here: freedom of speech, 2
freedom of thought, Western civilization and a great many
professorial egos. But before we get carried away by the
mounting backlash against multiculturalism, we ought to
reflect for a moment on the system that the P.C. people aim
to replace. I know all about it; in fact it's just about all I *do*
know, since I—along with so many educated white people of
my generation—was a victim of monoculturalism.

American history, as it was taught to us, began with 3
Columbus' "discovery" of an apparently unnamed, unpeo-
pled America, and moved on to the Pilgrims serving pump-
kin pie to a handful of grateful red-skinned folks. College
expanded our horizons with courses called Humanities or
sometimes Civ, which introduced us to a line of thought that
started with Homer, worked its way through Rabelais and
reached a poignant climax in the pensées of Matthew
Arnold. Graduate students wrote dissertations on what long-
dead men had thought of Chaucer's verse or Shakespeare's
dramas; foreign languages meant French or German. If there
had been high technology in ancient China, kingdoms in
black Africa or women anywhere, at any time, doing anything
worth noticing, we did not know it, nor did anyone think to
tell us.

Our families and neighborhoods reinforced the dogma 4
of monoculturalism. In our heads, most of us '50s teenagers
carried around a social map that was about as useful as the
chart that guided Columbus to the "Indies." There were
"Negroes," "whites" and "Orientals," the latter meaning
Chinese and "Japs." Of religions, only three were known—
Protestant, Catholic and Jewish—and not much was known
about the last two types. The only remaining human categories were husbands and wives, and that was all the diversity
the monocultural world could handle. Gays, lesbians,
Buddhists, Muslims, Malaysians, Mormons, etc. were simply
off the map.

So I applaud—with one hand, anyway—the multicul- 5
turalist goal of preparing us all for a wider world. The other
hand is tapping its fingers impatiently, because the critics are
right about one thing: when advocates of multiculturalism
adopt the haughty stance of political correctness, they quickly descend to silliness or worse. It's obnoxious, for example,

to rely on university administrations to enforce P.C. standards of verbal inoffensiveness. Racist, sexist and homophobic thoughts cannot, alas, be abolished by fiat but only by the time-honored methods of persuasion, education and exposure to the other guy's—or, excuse me, woman's—point of view.

And it's silly to mistake verbal purification for genuine 6 social reform. Even after all women are "Ms." and all people are "he or she," women will still earn only 65¢ for every dollar earned by men. Minorities by any other name, such as "people of color," will still bear a hugely disproportionate burden of poverty and discrimination. Disabilities are not just "different abilities" when there are not enough ramps for wheelchairs, signers for the deaf or special classes for the "specially" endowed. With all due respect for the new politesse, actions still speak louder than fashionable phrases.

But the worst thing about the P.C. people is that they 7 are such poor advocates for the multicultural cause. No one was ever won over to a broader, more inclusive view of life by being bullied or relentlessly "corrected." Tell a 19-year-old white male that he can't say "girl" when he means "teen-age woman," and he will most likely snicker. This may be the reason why, despite the conservative alarms, P.C.-ness remains a relatively tiny trend. Most campuses have more serious and ancient problems: faculties still top-heavy with white males of the monocultural persuasion; fraternities that harass minorities and women; date rape; alcohol abuse; and tuition that excludes all but the upper fringe of the middle class.

So both sides would be well advised to lighten up. The 8 conservatives ought to realize that criticisms of the great books approach to learning do not amount to totalitarianism. And the advocates of multiculturalism need to regain the sense of humor that enabled their predecessors in the struggle to coin the term P.C. years ago—not in arrogance but in self-mockery.

Beyond that, both sides should realize that the benefi- 9 ciaries of multiculturalism are not only the "oppressed peoples" on the standard P.C. list (minorities, gays, etc.). The "unenlightened"—the victims of monoculturalism—are oppressed too, or at least deprived. Our educations, whether at Yale or at State U, were narrow and parochial and left us ill-equipped to navigate a society that truly is multicultural and is becomming more so every day. The culture that we studied was, in fact, *one* culture and, from a world perspective, all too limited and ingrown. Diversity is challenging, but those of us who have seen the alternative know it is also richer, livelier and ultimately more fun.

Checking Your Understanding

1. Explain the proposal that Ehrenreich is making in regard to multiculturalism. What is she arguing for and against?
2. Although Ehrenreich deals with multi- and monoculturalism, her title refers to diversity. How would you define "diversity"? How is it related to the point that she wishes to make?

Examining Rhetorical Strategies

1. Much of what Ehrenreich says has to do with the use of language. How does language influence the way you think or feel? How does it detract from "genuine social reform"?
2. Answer Ehrenreich's challenge to teach diversity with a smile. Develop a situation which might broaden a monocultural viewpoint without making the point too seriously.

COLLEGE LECTURES: IS ANYBODY LISTENING?

David Daniels

Prereading Journal

Design your ideal learning situation. How much time is spent in lectures? In reading? In interacting with peers and faculty? Now, how much of your actual college time is spent in those ways?

Background

In this selection originally published in the November 1987 issue of *Trend*, Daniels is arguing for a change in the way college courses are taught. His argument draws on anecdotal, historical, and hypothetical information to support his position that a shift away from lectures should be at the center of educational reform.

During Reading

Daniels develops his position by describing both the problems with lectures and the reasons he believes they are preferred. List these two lines of thinking and the details he uses to support them.

Reading Selection

Intro

A former teacher of mine, Robert A. Fowkes of New 1 York University, likes to tell the story of a class he took in Old Welsh while studying in Germany during the 1930s. On the first day the professor strode up to the podium, shuffled his notes, coughed, and began, "*Guten Tag, Meine Damen und Herren*" ("Good day, ladies and gentlemen"). Fowkes glanced around uneasily. He was the only student in the course.

Toward the middle of the semester, Fowkes fell ill and 2 missed a class. When he returned, the professor nodded vaguely and to Fowkes's astonishment, began to deliver not the next lecture in the sequence but the one after. Had he, in fact, lectured to an empty hall in the absence of his solitary student? Fowkes thought it perfectly possible.

Today, American colleges and universities (originally 3
modeled on German ones) are under strong attack from
many quarters. Teachers, it is charged, are not doing a good
job of teaching, and students are not doing a good job of
learning. American businesses and industries suffer from
unenterprising, uncreative executives educated not to think
for themselves but to mouth outdated truisms the rest of the
world has long discarded. College graduates lack both basic
skills and general culture. Studies are conducted and reports
are issued on the status of higher education, but any changes
that result either are largely cosmetic or make a bad situation
worse.

One aspect of American education too seldom chal- 4
lenged is the lecture system. Professors continue to lecture
and students to take notes much as they did in the thirteenth
century, when books were so scarce and expensive that few
students could own them. The time is long overdue for us to
abandon the lecture system and turn to methods that really
work.

To understand the inadequacy of the present system, it 5
is enough to follow a single imaginary first-year student—let's
call her Mary—through a term of lectures on, say, introductory psychology (although any other subject would do as
well). She arrives on the first day and looks around the huge
lecture hall, taken a little aback to see how large the class is.
Once the hundred or more students enrolled in the course
discover that the professor never takes attendance (how can
he?—calling the role would take far too much time), the class
shrinks to a less imposing size.

Some days Mary sits in the front row, from where she 6
can watch the professor read from a stack of yellowed notes
that seem nearly as old as he is. She is bored by the lectures,
and so are most of the other students, to judge by the way
they are nodding off or doodling in their notebooks.
Gradually she realizes the professor is as bored as his audience. At the end of each lecture he asks, "Are there any questions?" in a tone of voice that makes it plain he would much
rather there weren't. He needn't worry—the students are as
relieved as he is that the class is over.

Mary knows very well she should read an assignment 7
before every lecture. However, as the professor gives no

quizzes and asks no questions, she soon realizes she needn't prepare. At the end of the term she catches up by skimming her notes and memorizing a list of facts and dates. After the final exam, she promptly forgets much of what she has memorized. Some of her fellow students, disappointed at the impersonality of it all, drop out of college altogether. Others, like Mary, stick it out, grow resigned to the system and await better days when, as juniors and seniors, they will attend smaller classes and at last get the kind of personal attention real learning requires.

I admit this picture is overdrawn—most universities 8 supplement lecture courses with discussion groups, usually led by graduate students, and some classes, such as first-year English, are always relatively small. Nevertheless, far too many courses rely principally or entirely on lectures, an arrangement much loved by faculty and administrators but scarcely designed to benefit the students.

One problem with lectures is that listening intelligently 9 is hard work. Reading the same material in a textbook is a more efficient way to learn because students can proceed as slowly as they need to until the subject matter becomes clear to them. Even simply paying attention is very difficult; people can listen at a rate of four hundred to six hundred words a minute, while the most impassioned professor talks at scarcely a third of that speed. This time lag between speech and comprehension leads to daydreaming. Many students believe years of watching television have sabotaged their attention span, but their real problem is that listening attentively is much harder than they think.

Worse still, attending lectures is passive learning, at 10 least for inexperienced listeners. Active learning, in which students write essays or perform experiments and then have their work evaluated by an instructor, is far more beneficial for those who have not yet fully learned how to learn. While it's true that techniques of active listening, such as trying to anticipate the speaker's next point or taking notes selectively, can enhance the value of a lecture, few students possess such skills at the beginning of their college careers. More commonly, students try to write everything down and even bring tape recorders to class in a clumsy effort to capture every word.

Students need to question their professors and to have   11
their ideas taken seriously. Only then will they develop the
analytical skills required to think intelligently and creatively.
Most students learn best by engaging in frequent and even
heated debate, not by scribbling down a professor's often
unsatisfactory summary of complicated issues. They need
small discussion classes that demand the common labors of
teacher and students rather than classes in which one person, however learned, propounds his or her own ideas.

The lecture system ultimately harms professors as well.   12
It reduces feedback to a minimum, so that the lecturer can
neither judge how well students understand the material nor
benefit from their questions or comments. Questions that
require the speaker to clarify obscure points and comments
that challenge sloppily constructed arguments are indispensable to scholarship. Without them, the liveliest mind can
atrophy. Undergraduates may not be able to make telling
contributions very often, but lecturing insulates a professor
even from the beginner's naive question that could have trig-
gered a fruitful line of thought.

If lectures make so little sense, why have they been   13
allowed to continue? Administrators love them, of course.
They can cram far more students into a lecture hall than into
a discussion class, and for many administrators that is almost
the end of the story. But the truth is that faculty members,
and even students, conspire with them to keep the lecture
system alive and well. Lectures are easier on everyone than
debates. Professors can pretend to teach by lecturing just as
students can pretend to learn by attending lectures, with no
one the wiser, including the participants. Moreover, if lectures afford some students an opportunity to sit back and let
the professor run the show, they offer some professors an
irresistible forum for showing off. In a classroom where
everyone contributes, students are less able to hide and professors less tempted to engage in intellectual exhibitionism.

Smaller classes in which students are required to   14
involve themselves in discussion put an end to students' pas-
sivity. Students become actively involved when forced to
question their own ideas as well as their instructor's. Their
listening skills improve dramatically in the excitement of
intellectual give and take with their instructors and fellow

students. Such interchanges help professors do their job better because they allow them to discover who knows what—
before final exams, not after. When exams are given in this
type of course, they can require analysis and synthesis from
the students, not empty memorization. Classes like this
require energy, imagination, and commitment from professors, all of which can be exhausting. But they compel students to share responsibility for their own intellectual
growth.

Lectures will never entirely disappear from the universi- 15
ty scene both because they seem to be economically necessary
and because they spring from a long tradition in a setting that
rightly values tradition for its own sake. But the lectures too
frequently come at the wrong end of the students' educational careers—during the first two years, when they most need
close, even individual, instruction. If lecture classes were
restricted to junior and senior undergraduates and to graduate students, who are less in need of scholarly nurturing and
more able to prepare work on their own, they would be far
less destructive of students' interests and enthusiasms than
the present system. After all, students must learn to listen
before they can listen to learn.

Conclusions

Checking Your Understanding

1. Make a visual representation of Daniels' argument. Illustrate in
    words, symbols, or pictures the point that Daniels is making.
2. Compare your first year experience with Mary's (Daniels' hypothet-
    ical student). How do they compare? Would your experience sup-
    port Daniels' position?

Examining Rhetorical Strategies

1. Write a response as a letter to Daniels. You may either concur and
    add support to his views or you may defend the use of lectures based
    on your own experiences.
2. Reread Daniels' argument. How does he reinforce the points he is
    making? How is his argument organized? Discuss his use of the
    hypothetical situation. What effect does that have on you as the
    reader?

TWO TEACHERS OF LETTERS
Margaret Metzger and Clare Fox

Prereading Journal

Has anyone ever given you advice in making a decision? What information was presented to you? How was it used to favor one choice over another? Were you persuaded to respond in a particular way? How did the advice influence the decision you made?

Background

Clare Fox was a college graduate in 1984 who wrote to her former high school teacher seeking advice about the teaching profession. Using the letter format, Margaret Metzger presents an argument for the teaching profession. These letters were first published in *Harvard Review* and later used by *Teacher* magazine as part of an article about convincing "a doubting beginner to remain in the classroom."

During Reading

The first letter from Fox details the choice facing her. As you read Metzger's response, list details and experiences she uses to address Fox's concerns. How does Metzger develop her authority to speak for the teaching profession?

Reading Selection

Spring 1984

Dear Mrs. Metzger,

I am writing to you as a former student who has just 1 graduated from Brown University and who is considering teaching English next year. I remember you as a compelling and demanding teacher who seemed to enjoy her job. At the moment, you are the only person I know who would support my career choice. Almost everyone else is disparaging about teaching in public schools.

I am told that I didn't have to go to Brown University to 2 become a teacher. I am told that teaching is a "wonderful thing to do until you decide what you really want to do with your life." I am told that it's "nice" that I'm going to be a teacher. Why does it seem that the decision to teach in our society is analogous with the decision to stunt one's growth, to opt out intellectually in favor of long summers off?

But teaching matters. I know that. You mattered to me, 3 and other teachers have mattered to me. I enjoyed student teaching and I look forward to next year. I have imaginary dialogues with the students in my mind. I hear myself articulating my policy on borderline grades, explaining why I keep switching the chairs from circles to rows as I flounder in my efforts to decide what's best, or laughing with the students as I struggle to overcome saying "okay" too often when I lecture. But I wonder how much of teaching is actually an ego trip, a ploy to be liked, accepted, and respected by a group of people who have limited say in the matter. I also know the humiliation of a student's glare. I know there will be problems. Yet I cannot deny the tremendous sense of worth I felt as a student teacher when students offered me their respect and when students worked hard and were proud of their effort.

I wonder where I would get this sense of worthwhile- 4 ness if I were to work in a New York advertising firm or as an engineer at Bell Labs. And yet, going to work for a big corporation—whether an advertising firm, a bank, or a publishing house—impresses me. It would seem "real," "grown-up," as teaching never will. Nobody would tell me that being an engineer is "nice" or a wonderful way to figure out what I "really want to do."

For graduation, my mother and sister gave me a beau- 5 tiful, sleek attaché case. My reaction was twofold. First, I realized that it would never be large enough to carry the load of an English teacher, and second, I realized that, should I ever decide to leave teaching, it would be perfect for the real world of professional writers and young executives.

My mother doesn't want me to go into teaching. She is 6 afraid I will get "stuck," that my efforts will not be appreciated or rewarded, and that I will not meet men. When I called home from Minneapolis after a long, productive, and exhilarating day interviewing at schools, my mother congratulated me and suggested that I spend the evening putting together a second resumé—a writing resumé—before I forgot everything else I know how to do. She suggested I spend the following day visiting television studios scouting for writing jobs, "just in case."

And my mother has been in public education for 7 almost twenty years! Granted, when she entered Boston College in 1952, she had to choose between teaching and nursing. I, however, have chosen to teach from among many options available to me as a Brown graduate with a strong liberal arts degree.

I write to you, Mrs. Metzger, because you were the first 8 person to excite me about the processes of writing and because your integrity in the classroom has long been an influence on me—and on my decision to teach. You mattered. I am turning to you because you are a professional; and you continue to choose teaching after eighteen years. I welcome any advice, comments, or solace you could offer me.

Sincerely,

Clare Fox

Spring 1984

Dear Clare,

I admire your courage to consider teaching. Your 9 friends and relatives are not alone in their negative opinions about teaching. I'm sure you read the claim in the President's Commission on Education that education is a national disgrace. *Newsweek's* September 1984 cover showed a teacher in a dunce cap with the headline, "Why Teachers Fail—How to Make Them Better." NBC ran a three-hour special on education—an exposé of inadequate schools. At least four blue-ribbon studies have concluded that teacher education is inadequate, that the pay is the lowest of all professions, that schools have deplorable management, and that the job is full of meaningless paperwork.

I know that much of the criticism is valid. However, the 10 reports sensationalize and do not tell the whole truth. I appreciate your letter because you are giving me a chance to defend a profession I love.

Clare, I look forward to teaching. By mid-August I 11
start planning lessons and dreaming about classrooms. I
also wonder whether I'll have the energy to start again with
new classes. Yet after September gets under way, I wake up
in the morning expecting to have fun at work. I know that
teaching well is a worthwhile use of my life. I know my work
is significant.

I am almost forty years old, and I'm happier in my job 12
than anyone I know. That's saying a lot. My husband, who
enjoys his work, has routine days when he comes home and
says, "Nothing much happened today—just meetings." I
never have routine days. When I am in the classroom, I usually am having a wonderful time.

I also hate this job. In March I wanted to quit because 13
of the relentlessness of dealing with one-hundred antsy adolescents day after day. I lose patience with adolescent issues: I
think I'll screech if I have to listen to one more adolescent
self-obsession. I'm physically exhausted every Friday. The
filth in our school is an aesthetic insult. The unending petty
politics drain me. Often I feel undermined on small issues by
a school system that supports me well on academic freedom.

Like all jobs, teaching has inherent stresses. As you 14
know from student teaching, you must know how to discipline a roomful of adolescents; you need to have a sense of
purpose about what you are teaching; you need to cope with
the exhaustion; and as an English teacher you must get the
paper grading under control. I am always saddened by the
number of excellent teachers who leave teaching because
they think these difficult problems are unsolvable.

A curious irony exists. I am never bored at work, yet my 15
days are shockingly routine. I can tell you exactly what I have
done every school day for the past eighteen years at 10:15 in
the morning (homeroom attendance), and I suspect I will do
the same for the next twenty years. The structure of the
school day has changed little since education moved out of
the one-room schoolhouse. All teachers get tired of the
monotonous routine of bookkeeping, make-up assignments,
twenty-minute lunches, and study hall duties. I identify with
J. Alfred Prufrock when he says, "I have measured out my life
with coffee spoons." My own life has been measured out in
student papers. At a conservative estimate I've graded over

30,000—a mind-boggling statistic which makes me feel like a very dull person indeed.

The monotony of my schedule is mirrored in the 16 monotony of my paycheck. No matter how well or poorly I teach, I will be paid the same amount. There is absolutely no monetary reward for good job performance, or any recognition of professional growth or acquired expertise. My pay depends on how long I've taught and my level of education. I work in a school district in which I cannot afford to live. I am alternatively sad and angry about my pay. To the outside world it seems that I am doing exactly the same job I did in 1966—same title, same working conditions, same pay scale (except that my buying power is 8 percent less than it was when I earned $5,400 on my first job). To most people I am "just a teacher."

But this is the outside reality. The interior world of the 17 teacher is quite different. Although you have to come to some terms with the outward flatness of the career, I want to assure you that teachers change and grow. So little research has been done on stage development of teachers that the literature recognizes only three categories—intern, novice, and veteran. This is laughably over-simplified. There is life after student teaching; there is growth after the first year. You will some day solve many of the problems that seem insurmountable during your exhilarating student teaching and your debilitating first year.

Sometimes I am aware of my growth as a teacher, 18 and I realize that finally, after all these years, I am confident in the classroom. On the very, very best days, when classes sing, I am able to operate on many levels during a single class: I integrate logistics, pedagogy, curriculum, group dynamics, individual needs, and my own philosophy. I feel generous and good-natured towards my students, and I am challenged by classroom issues. But on bad days, I feel like a total failure. Students attack my most vulnerable points. I feel overwhelmed by paperwork. I ache from exhaustion. I dream about going to Aruba, but I go to the next class.

I keep going because I'm intellectually stimulated. I 19 enjoy literature, and I assign books I love and books I want to read. I expect class discussions and student papers to give me new insights into literature. As you may remember, I tell students that in exchange for my hard work, they should keep me interested and they should teach me. They do.

To me, teaching poses questions worthy of a lifetime of 20 thought. I want to think about what the great writers are saying. I want to think about how people learn. I want to think about the values we are passing on to the next generation. I am particularly interested in teaching thinking. I love to teach writing. I am working now on teaching writing as a tool for thinking. Questions about teaching are like puzzles to me; I can spend hours theorizing and then use my classroom as a laboratory.

I am also intellectually challenged by pedagogical 21 problems. I have learned to follow the bizarre questions or the "wrong answers." Some questions reveal chasms of ignorance. For example, "Where is Jesus' body?" or "Before movies were in color, wasn't the world dull just being in black and white?" Sometimes students make shocking statements which demand careful responses: "All athletic girls are lesbians" or "Sexually abused toddlers probably really enjoy the sex." And every year, new students require new teaching skills—Cambodian boat children who have never been in school and are illiterate even in their own language, or handicapped children such as a deaf Israeli girl who is trying to learn English without being able to hear it.

And then there are all the difficult, "normal" situations: 22 students and parents who are "entitled," hostile, emotionally needy, or indifferent; students who live in chaotic homes, who are academically pressured, who have serious drug and alcohol problems. The list goes on and on. No school of education prepared me for the "Hill Street Blues" intensity and chaos of public schools. I received my combat training from other teachers, from myself, and mostly from the students. You will too.

Sometimes I think I can't do it all. I don't want to be bit- 23 ter or a martyr, so I am careful to take care of myself. I put flowers on my desk to offset the dreariness of an old school building. I leave school several times a week to run errands or to take walks in order to feel less trapped. Other teachers take courses at local colleges, join committees of adults, talk in the teacher's lounge, or play with computers. In order to give to others, teachers must nurture themselves.

Ultimately, teaching is nurturing. The teacher enters a 24 giving relationship with strangers, and then the teacher's needs must give way to students' needs. I want to work on my own writing; instead I work on students' writing. My days are spent encouraging young people's growth. I watch my students move beyond me, thinking and writing better than I have ever done. I send them to colleges I could never afford. And I must strive to be proud, not jealous, of them. I must learn generosity of heart.

I am a more compassionate person because I have 25 known teachers and students. I think differently about handicaps because I worked with Guy, who is quadriplegic from a rugby accident. Refugee problems have a human face because I've heard Nazmul tell stories about refugee camps in Bangladesh, and I've heard Merhdad tell about escaping from Iran, hidden in a camel's baggage. I have seen the school social worker give suicidal students his home phone number, telling them to call anytime. I have seen administrators bend all the rules to help individual students through personal crises. Every day I hear stories of courage and generosity. I admire other teachers.

Facing every new class is an act of courage and opti- 26 mism. Years ago, the courage required was fairly primitive. I needed courage to discipline my classes, to get them into line, to motivate them to work. But now I need a deeper courage. I look at each new class and know that I must let each of these young people into my life in some significant way. The issue is one of heart. Can I open my heart to two hundred more adolescent strangers each year? Put bluntly, can I be that loving?

I hope to love my students so well that it doesn't even 27 matter whether they like me. I want to love them in the way I love my own son—full of respect and awe for who they are, full of wanting their growth, full of wonder at what it means to lead and to follow the next generation.

Clare, when you consider a life's work, consider not 28 just what you will take to the task, but what it will give to you. Which job will give self-respect and challenge? Which job will give you a world of ideas? Which job will be intel-

lectually challenging? Which job will enlarge you and give
you life in abundance? Which job will teach you lessons of
the heart?

With deep respect,

Margaret Metzger

Spring 1986

Dear Mrs. Metzger,

After two years of teaching, I still derive strength and   29
vigor from the letter you wrote me so long ago. Your letter
makes me remember all of the best parts of teaching—the
self-evaluations written by students who liked their work and
the silliness of the class that plotted ways to walk out on me,
knowing I would catch up with them and we'd resume class
wherever we were—the library, another classroom, the basketball court. I remember lots of laughing. I laugh a lot in the
classroom, more than I do in my private life.

And I think a lot, too. There is no better way to learn a   30
book than to teach it, no better way to think through a writing problem than to wrestle through the drafts of a paper,
guiding the writer beyond frustration to resolution. I am at
my brightest, some moments, in the classroom.

And yet I have decided to leave teaching.   31

I am feeling too selfish to teach, too possessive of my   32
time and my future. I have decided to work full-time at the
publishing company where I have worked afternoons this
year, where I work on my own writing with others coaching
me, and where my writing is printed, a thousandfold and over.
I will earn almost $5,000 less than I would if I taught full-time
next year, and I will work all summer with few vacations.

After a strong, satisfying year I left my first teaching job   33
in June because I was afraid of the cycle that had already
been established. I taught six classes a day—five writing and
one advanced reading—to seventh graders. I taught at an
exceptionally demanding, academically rigorous junior high.
By February I was exhausted, and by June I had made two
friends outside of teaching. Too much of my time outside of
school had been spent on papers, or in the library looking

for good reasons to teach *Alice in Wonderland*. I spent a lot of time with other teachers from the school—a smart, professional, and fun group of people. But still we talked about school—and our shared exhaustion.

After living for Memorial Day weekend, I found myself 34 with no plans. I realized how completely I'd been absorbed by my job. I also saw myself years from now, a good teacher— better than I am now—but still without plans for a holiday weekend. And each year the kids would move on.

Yet for all my martyrdom, I have never once felt caught 35 up. I have never passed back a set of papers without wondering whom I had disappointed, who had counted on my intuitions and my goodness and not just my editorial skills. And I am only teaching part-time this year—juniors in high school. There is no room for complacency in the classroom; we are forever judged and measured. No matter how achingly we want to do it right, there is always something that could be done better. I could know more about Fitzgerald before I introduce *The Great Gatsby*; I could be more responsive to student needs if I gave up my lunch hour every day. And yet I could struggle for hours over the perfect comment for a student's paper, or the best approach to a piece of literature, and still not know which sentence the student would walk away with.

I hope to teach again some day, when I have more in my 36 life and other investments to balance with teaching. I would like to combine my teaching skills with my own writing, perhaps by coordinating a writing program or working with other teachers to promote writing across the curriculum.

In my heart I think I'll be back. And I think I'll be a bet- 37 ter teacher for having stepped out and indulged my selfishness.

Thank you for your support. You have been very impor- 38 tant to me.

Sincerely,

Clare Fox

Checking Your Understanding

1. How did Metzger's letter affect the way you have thought about the teaching profession? What have you learned about teaching by reading this exchange?

2. Based on Fox's letter, how do you think she responded to Metzger's advice? Explain why she has decided to leave teaching.

Examining Rhetorical Strategies

1. Discuss the aspects of expressive writing used by Metzger in her attempt to persuade Fox. How does Metzger use her experiences to build a persuasive argument? What do you think about her use of questions at the conclusion of her discourse?
2. Discuss the audience of the piece. How does Metzger use what she knows about Fox to create a persuasive tone? Although this is a letter directed to Fox, why might it be found in a teachers' magazine for a more general audience?

ENDICOTT COLLEGE: DISCOVER THE EXPERIENCE

College Viewbook

Prereading Journal

Discuss the reasons you have chosen the college you are attending. Did the facilities impress you? Did you visit classes or talk to students before deciding? What programs or activities caught your attention? Did you read any of the college's promotional materials before enrolling?

Background

Most colleges and universities send out promotional booklets with applications to prospective students. These advertisements contain both written material and graphic representations of the campus and student body. The introductory passages of this viewbook use persuasive strategies of evaluation, argument, and proposal to present the audience with information about the school. Endicott College is a private coeducational college near Boston, Massachusetts.

During Reading

As you read notice the style and tone of the material. How can you determine the audience? What information is given to support the persuasion?

Reading Selection

DISCOVER A VERY SPECIAL PLACE

Discover the comfort you will feel in small classes led by caring professors who know not just your name but your nuances, the traits that set you apart, the things that make you you. 1

Discover the freedom and flexibility you will enjoy at a College offering multiple options for both two-year and four-year degrees and a welcoming environment for both traditional students and adult learners. 2

Discover the career edge you will gain through internships, spending time each and every year at real jobs—in 3

Boston, in the United States, or, in some cases, around the world.

Discover the reflections you will see while looking into 4 life's mirror along with over 800 men and women from 25 states and 43 countries.

Discover Boston, the world's most exciting college town. 5

Discover the growth that comes from fulfilling the 6 promise of your own potential as a woman. Experience increased self-confidence and greater self-awareness.

Discover, most of all, the most important person you 7 will come to know during your years at Endicott College. Discover yourself!

DISCOVER YOURSELF

What makes you tick? How do you want to spend your 8 time, focus your energy, live your life? Which career might best fit who you are? Are you willing to take the necessary risks to tap your inner strengths and latent talents? These are just a few of the questions you'll address at Endicott College. You'll be challenged to reach farther and higher than ever before—in classes, in internships, during informal conversations with your professors or your peers. The warmly supportive environment on this picturesque 150-acre oceanfront campus creates the ideal conditions for answering good questions and meeting great challenges. Along the way, you'll develop a greater sense of confidence, a stronger sense of self. You'll discover what you can do and can be. You'll discover yourself!

ACADEMICS
DISCOVER TOMORROW'S
SUCCESS TODAY

Have you already decided to pursue a career in, say, 9 advertising—or business or education or interior design or nursing or social service or hotel management or another field in which Endicott offers a degree? Fine. Your focused preparation for future success will begin early: Day One.

Perhaps you're somewhat undecided or have no idea? 10 That's fine, too. At Endicott, you can test the fit of several career paths by taking courses or talking with professors in different areas. It may take a while, even a year, to connect. But connect, in time, you will.

In either case, you will benefit from the distinctive fea- 11
tures that, in combination, will give you a decided edge in the
highly competitive marketplace. By studying a core curriculum in the liberal arts, you will enhance your abilities to think
and to analyze, to speak and to write. You will have easy access
to contemporary equipment and facilities ranging from personal computers and television cameras to state-of-the-art
medical technology and an on-campus Children's Center.
You will receive professional skills training right from the
beginning of your first year. Finally, you will gain practical
and marketable work experience through internships.

If you're a top student, for example, you may welcome 12
the additional challenges of the Honors Program or Phi
Theta Kappa and Alpha Chi national scholastic honor societies. If you need extra help with any course or any academic skill, turn to the professionals in the Academic Support
Center. They're there to serve you.

If you're studying Hotel, Restaurant and Travel 13
Administration, spend a year in Switzerland as part of our
affiliation with the prestigious Les Roches Swiss Hotel
School. Interested in Japan? Spend time in Sapporo at the
Hokkaido College, our newest global partner.

The message is clear: At Endicott you don't have to wait 14
until graduation to start charting your career course and
sharpening your professional skills for the future. The
process begins at the beginning: the start of your first year.

Checking Your Understanding

1. Besides the factual information about the college itself, what other
    kinds of reasons are used to persuade the reader? What is the gen-
    eral impression of the college that you have after reading this?
2. Would you now be interested in visiting the school or writing for
    more information? Why or why not? What does your reaction say
    about the audience for this?

Examining Rhetorical Strategies

1. Discuss the use of repetition in this material. How does it work to
    emphasize the reasons for attending such a college? How does it
    emphasize an emotional appeal to the reader?
2. The tone of the piece is built on a form of direct address. Why is
    such a tone used in college viewbooks? Try taking a passage and writ-

ing it in a more formal, objective tone. What happens to the persuasive imperative?

3. College viewbooks use visual graphics as well as the written word. What graphics might be used with this to support the material? How might this material be laid out on the page to make it more visually appealing? How are such visual details part of the persuasive technique of advertising?

STUDENT ESSAYS AND WRITING TECHNIQUES

OPTIFAST

Gwen Rumburg

Background

Rumburg's experiences in this diet program led her to review the program in this essay. She draws on her experiences as the information to support her opinion but, as with all reviews, the purpose is more than just to express an opinion. As a review of the program, it includes a persuasive imperative. Through writing this review she came to realize "that despite the tendency to think we are alone in our experiences, we have the capability of touching a vast, intelligent audience."

Reading Selection

Americans today are obsessed with achieving thinness. 1 Thin people are portrayed in media and advertising as being healthy, happy, well-loved superbeings with no problems or fears—in short, thin people are perfect people. A result of this craze is an explosion of diet programs, some offering safe, long-term methods of losing weight and others, commonly known as starvation diets, promising quick and easy pound reduction for those more severely overweight. Becoming one of those thin, superior human beings is the irresistible lure of all the programs, and three years ago I made the attempt by joining a program called Optifast.

Oprah Winfrey is perhaps the best known participant of 2 Optifast, and watching her plug the diet on television convinced me to explore the option locally. I discovered that a local clinic offered Optifast and that an orientation was being presented the following month. I signed up and anxiously anticipated the night when I would find out if becoming thin before the year was out, a dream come true, was within my realm of possibilities.

Walking into orientation on the awaited night, my fears 3 of being the heaviest person in the room were immediately put to rest. I was relieved to find that the majority of the audience appeared at least as heavy as I, and some had so much extra weight they barely fit on the chairs provided. Before long, a registered dietitian and a psychiatrist stepped to the front of the room and began the orientation.

The Optifast program, they explained, is a twenty-six 4 week course consisting of three months undergoing a supervised fast and three months gradually eating food again, this time in a healthy manner. Various side effects and health risks were discussed, and it was emphasized that fasting is not a solution for everyone. Education and daily living exercises were discussed, as well as the importance of physical exercise, all of which would be focused on during the extent of the program. The presentation was fact-filled and thorough, but the reality of literally not eating for three months was easily overlooked as tale after tale of success stories lent powerful testimony to Optifast and what it would do for us. I thrilled to imagine actually achieving the perfect life as a thin woman, which was a vision I fantasized about constantly.

As the evening drew to a close I noticed an obvious 5 change in the audience. Walking in we had been united by sharing the same difficult experience, members of an exclusive, overweight club. Walking out, however, we saw each other as competitors; it had been revealed that only twenty-five slots were available for the next group, and winning candidates would need to pass a psychological exam, possess a serious health disorder directly caused by excess weight, and have their physician's permission to participate.

I left orientation with a feeling of euphoria—surely this 6 was the program for me! The opportunity to lose all my excess weight in a matter of weeks seemed a miracle, and I determinedly set about the process of making it come true. I secured a bank loan for the three thousand dollars it would take to see me through the program, telling myself it was a small price to pay for happiness. I convinced my physician, despite his doubts about the validity of the program, to write a note admitting that my blood pressure was too high and weight loss was necessary to lower it. Finally, I underwent a psychological test to determine whether I could handle undergoing a fast, although in hindsight the test seemed more of a way to pad the program psychologist's pockets than a justified diet tool. I had done everything required to be considered for the program, and all that was left to do was wait. Three long weeks later I got my answer . . . I was in!

The Optifast classes were held in the clinic, and the first   7
night was basically an introduction to our fellow fasters and preparation for what lay ahead. I spent the following week frantically shoving all manner of enticing foods into my mouth, convinced I would never again experience the pleasure of my favorite pastime, reading and pigging out simultaneously. During weigh-in at the second class I discovered I had gained four more pounds in my spree, but since we were starting the fast the following day, I didn't even care.

The morning after that second class I made the dismal   8
discovery of what my life would consist of for the next three months. Five times a day, every day, I forced myself to drink the thick, indescribably awful brown substance called "chocolate-flavored Optifast." That, diet soda, and two quarts of water every twenty-four hours were the only things that entered my mouth for ninety-two days. To my credit, not one morsel of food went past my lips, although one particular loaf of garlic bread underwent serious torture and mutilation in my attempt to render it inedible beyond the point of temptation. One man in my group (who ended up dropping out), told of drinking the juice left in a can of peas after his wife had strained them and left the kitchen. Another person broke at the county fair and wolfed down several hot dogs, resulting in severe abdominal distress after subsisting on four hundred calories several days in a row. (We had been warned that once we were deeply into the fast, eating a substantial amount of any food could land us in the emergency room.)

As if not eating for three months wasn't enough, we were   9
cautioned what to expect in terms of side effects: urinating frequently, feeling sluggish, feeling dizzy, feeling cold, getting bad breath, becoming constipated, experiencing food cravings and fantasies, suffering dry skin and skin rashes, and finally, believe it or not, temporary hair loss. We were also forbidden from the following activities: hot baths, whirlpools, scuba diving, swimming alone, diving off diving boards, piloting a plane, horseback riding, motorcycle riding, and hang gliding. Apparently four hundred calories isn't enough to keep your body reacting properly, and as I look back it must have also

affected my brain, because who in their right mind would subject themselves to such ridiculous and dangerous conditions? Despite such obvious red flags I continued with and completed the fast. Within the three months I lost seventy-five pounds, dropped five sizes, and became the object of much scrutiny and gossip at work. One afternoon, in front of a student I worked with, a co-worker approached me and actually asked if I had AIDS. For the most part, though, I was on top of the world as people congratulated my new look, and guys who had never given me a second glance began asking me out on dates. My boyfriend, friends and family expressed their pride, and I went into the last three months of Optifast, called the "refeeding," positive I was thin for life.
10

Eating food again was not new or different in any way, and I was disheartened to discover that although I had shed weight, I had not gotten rid of the tendencies and habits that made me fat in the first place. Fasting had been a temporary break in the daily struggle to eat healthy and properly sized meals, and my junk food cravings were, if anything, stronger than before. By the time the entire Optifast program ended I had all the knowledge needed to lead the proper nutritional lifestyle, but my weekly support abruptly disappeared. We were all encouraged to enroll in the maintenance program called Encore, but that required additional expenses that I could not handle. Not only that, my boyfriend and I had made the decision to move to Maine, an act that severed my Optifast ties completely.
11

Over the course of the next ten months my entire life changed. Jobs were few and far between in Maine, I sustained an injury that left me bed-ridden for two months, and my boyfriend's ex-girlfriend, unbeknownst to me, traveled up for a secret visit and never did leave. As all aspects of my life deteriorated rapidly, I did the only thing I knew how to comfort myself: I ate. And ate and ate. By the time I regained my senses enough to move back to New Hampshire on my own, I was thirteen pounds heavier than I had been before I started Optifast.
12

Today I am still struggling with my weight, but I have some perspective on the diet programs that are so prevalent in our society. I firmly believe that they prey on our fantasies and dreams, snatching the dieter's hard-earned money with no concern for the dieter or their progress after the weight is
13

off. I recently read in a reputable magazine that ninety-five percent of dieters regain their lost weight, seeming to prove that quick losses and fad programs are just a waste of consumers' time and money. I regret my participation in Optifast; I now realize that the program throws a fantasy-filled smokescreen in front of the dieter, encouraging disregard of the physical dangers of fasting and requiring an astronomically high fee that cannot be met for both the initial phase and maintenance combined. I take full responsibility for regaining my weight, but I feel betrayed knowing that the leaders of my group were aware that it was almost statistically impossible for me to stay thin after I left their care, yet they took my money anyway. I encourage any overweight person to fully investigate a weight loss program before joining, and keep in mind what my experience with Optifast taught me: no amount of money can guarantee lasting thinness, and being thin doesn't guarantee happiness. Developing your mind and enriching your life is a surer path to joy, and after that everything else, including how much you weigh, doesn't really matter any more.

Thinking About Writing

How does Rumburg develop her review of the Optifast program? What facts does she include? Does she include both positives and negatives of the program? Do you feel that reviews need to include both aspects? After reading this review do you have a better understanding of the program and what it will and will not do for its patrons? What is Rumburg's persuasive imperative here? Has that imperative been apparent throughout the piece?

Writing Assignment

Although we often associate reviews with books, movies, plays, and other such forms of entertainment, virtually anything is subject to review—weight loss programs, health clubs, new automobiles, stereos, cereals. As informed people we rely on the analysis and reviews of others who have tried the product, taken part in the program, or seen the performance. What have you tried, done, or seen recently which might be of interest to others? Write a review which not only informs the reader but also either implies or states your imperative. Keep in mind the audience who will be most interested in your review and who is basically asking you: "Should I?"

SUPPORT THE CHILDREN

Sara Carter

Background

Carter has had a personal stake in the issue of "dead beat dads"—divorced fathers who fail to pay child support. The experience that she had was traumatic and her imperative is that all members of society are in a position to work toward a solution. Carter develops her argument by drawing on her experience, her information on the issue, and then appeals to the reader to work toward legislation that would prosecute those who purposely neglect their responsibility.

Reading Selection

I timidly approached the courtroom, walking very slow- 1 ly behind my mother, who was following our attorney. As I entered the tiny room, my palms began to sweat, my mouth went dry, and I froze in my tracks: he was already there. My father looked up from his place at the defendant's table, and I quickly averted my gaze, but I was not quick enough. The anger in his eyes was unmistakable, and it was directed at me. I hurried to the other side of the room, where my mother was taking her place at the plaintiff's table. She directed her attention to our court-appointed lawyer, in an effort to avoid the hateful glances my father was sending in our direction. I took a seat on a bench against the wall, a few feet away from my mother. I kept my eyes riveted on the floor, intensely studying the pattern on the worn out carpet.

"ALL RISE!" The bailiff's sudden exclamation startled 2 me, and I practically jumped to my feet. I was vaguely aware of a trembling in my legs, but I was so busy trying to avoid my father's gaze that I paid little attention to it. As the judge entered the room and told us all to be seated, I relaxed a little and silently thanked God. Out of the corner of my eye, I watched my father's usually smug expression turn to one of total dismay: the judge was a woman. My father was a male chauvinist and the thought of a female judge deciding his fate did not sit well with him.

The proceedings got under way and I couldn't help but   3
notice that my father's growing dislike for the judge was
matched only by her growing impatience with him. His arrogant manner was not going over well with the judge, and the
bailiff looked as if he'd like to throw my father right out of
the room. The bailiff, a kindly looking gentleman in his 50's,
threw sympathetic glances in my direction every now and
then and I was grateful for his presence.

"Mr. Carter," the judge said, clearly gritting her teeth,   4
trying to keep control. "Are you aware that you are behind in
your child support payments by five months?"

"Yes, I am," he replied in a manner that suggested he   5
couldn't care less if he was behind five months or five years.
He wasn't going to pay it.

The judge looked at him evenly, reminded him that   6
he was going to have to pay it, and asked what he had done
with the money that was rightfully mine. I felt my stomach
turn over. My father loved his money more than anything
or anyone else in the world, and he did not like to think
that $100.00 of it every month belonged to me. I glanced
apprehensively in my father's direction, and waited for his
response.

With a look of pure resentment, directed at me, he said,   7
"I had more important things to pay for. Car payments, rent,
food. I need to live, you know."

I winced, as if I had been slapped, and I tried, unsuc-   8
cessfully, to hold back the tears. I was suddenly less important
than his car. I, his own flesh and blood, took second place to
a Dodge Spirit. I didn't even take second place, I was probably not even on his list of life's important things. I felt cheated and inferior. I felt worthless and unloved. I wasn't after his
money, I only wanted to be acknowledged. If I hadn't needed the money at all, I would have walked out right then. The
sad part about the whole mess was that I did need the money.
My mom worked two jobs to support the two of us. It wasn't
easy and that extra $100.00 a month really helped, especially
since I was saving for college. But suddenly none of that mattered. My mom and I could survive without his money, I
thought angrily. After all it was only a hundred dollars a
month. I would have given it all up in a second if only he
would acknowledge me and love me. I knew deep down that

if he did love me, he wouldn't mind paying the hundred dollars. He would want to help me. He certainly wasn't having financial difficulty, he just didn't want to part with any of his precious money. I couldn't understand how any father could turn his back on his child, but that's exactly what my father was doing to me.

The judge, thoroughly disgusted with my father, 9 ordered him to begin making payments immediately. The total amount he would owe me by my eighteenth birthday was $804.00. Case dismissed.

My father left the courthouse that day, furious that he 10 would have to part with a few hundred dollars. He didn't realize what the whole ordeal had really cost him. It had cost him my respect. It had cost him his relationship with me. These things are priceless and can never be retrieved . . .

That is my story, or part of it anyway. Millions of chil- 11 dren of all ages are going through similar experiences, but it doesn't have to be that way.

Currently, the state of our nation in regard to child sup- 12 port enforcement is disgraceful, to say the least. Two-thirds of all single-parent, female-headed households received no child support in 1990. Half of all those who were supposed to receive child support got less than the full amount or none at all (Children's Defense Fund 79). This is despicable.

Right now, Vermont is ranked number one in the 13 nation for collection of child support. In Vermont, 32.6% of all child support cases result in collection. This may sound pretty good when compared with other states, such as Arizona, which ranks fifty-first, with only a 5.6% collection rate, but in reality, it is still not admirable by any means (Children's Defense Fund 82). What about the other 67.4% of children in Vermont, or the 94.4% of Arizona's children who are not provided for? What about all the other children across the country and throughout the world who are in need of child support? Who will provide for them?

One important factor to keep in mind while consider- 14 ing this issue is that it is not just about numbers and statistics, percentages and graphs. Each statistic represents a broken family. Each percentage symbolizes a child: a human being with feelings and emotions. A child with a story similar to mine. These are not just "somebody else's kids." These are the children of America and they are crying out for help. Don't turn your back on them.

Federal as well as state governments are starting to   15 crack down on child support violators, but their efforts alone are not enough. To make a major change in the state of the nation's child support enforcement program, it will take effort from everyone concerned. This includes all the fathers out there who are responsible for paying child support; however, it is not totally up to them to remedy the problem. If it were, unfortunately nothing would ever get accomplished. Although there are men out there who responsibly fulfill their obligations by paying their child support, there are many others who don't. It is for this reason that everyone needs to get involved. If these men refuse to willingly take responsibility for the welfare of their children, then they should be forced to. There are children out there who need to be provided for, and if their own parents are unwilling to do so, then the burden falls to the rest of us. Anyone with a conscience, or a heart of compassion will not fail to be touched by the plight of these poor children. Many people think that, unless they are directly involved in a situation, that the situation doesn't concern them. I'm here to tell you that this situation concerns everyone. It concerns the well-being of the children of this nation. These children need more people fighting for their rights. You don't need to be the parent of one of these children in order to get involved. The more people who get involved, the better chance these kids have for a bright future. Take some time out of your busy schedule to write to your senator or representative. Contact your state representative and find out what your state laws are concerning child support enforcement. Find out what you can do to get involved. You will be crusading on behalf of children who can't fight for themselves. Get involved and give these children a fighting chance. After all, the children of today are the future of tomorrow. Invest some time and enengy into securing a bright future for America.

Work Cited

Children's Defense Fund. *The State of America's Children Yearbook 1992*. Washington: Children's Defense Fund, 1992.

Thinking About the Writing

Reread Carter's personal experience. How does she develop the expressive aspects of her argument here? What words does she use to establish the emotional context for her argument? How effective is this as a way to appeal to her readers? Many arguments begin with a personal experience. How important is the telling of that experience to the purpose of persuasion? Why does she not move from the personal into the imperative? What is the effect of the factual information on her argument? How does she argue for your involvement? Are you persuaded? Why or why not?

Writing Assignment

"Support the Children" draws on a significant personal experience and uses it to support an argument for societal input into the issue of deadbeat dads. She moves the essay from the experience, through the facts, and to the imperative. Brainstorm experiences from your own life. Now write a persuasive essay using your experience to support an argument for a broader societal issue. Perhaps an experience with asthma might lead you to advocate legislation for smoke-free environments. Or perhaps your volunteer work at a senior center might lead you to solicit funds for the center and its work. Remember that although your purpose is to persuade, you are also drawing on expressive and affirming discourses in convincing your reader to respond.

MINORITY UNDERREPRESENTATION AMONG POLICE IS DANGEROUS

Lonnie Martin

Background

Martin was asked to present an argument using research to support his ideas. Affirmative action directives had been introduced into, but later removed from, a recent local police contract. Martin saw himself as a concerned citizen who felt that progress toward racial harmony and equal opportunity in the city should be reflected in the police department's hiring policies.

Reading Selection

The recent conviction of Los Angeles police officers 1 Stacey Koon and Lawrence Powell is an example of a problem many communities face. The officers, both white, were convicted in federal court of violating the civil rights of Rodney King, an African-American. Last year in Chicago, police Commander Jon Burge and two other officers, all white, were dismissed from duty for torturing two murder suspects, both African-American. Both are examples of the abuse which occurs when one group, in this case white males, holds a dominant power over other groups. It is dangerous to allow the opportunity for these types of abuses to continue. That is why the Chicago Police Department must adopt affirmative action guidelines regarding the hiring and promotion of its officers.

Racial crimes are unfortunate, yet have happened 2 across the country for years and across western civilization for centuries. When any group maintains a majority of power and influence over others, history shows that they often use it to their advantage. Many times, with power and influence comes advanced technology and a vast supply of resources. Examples of such abuses include: the Spanish massacres of Central and South American Indians, the Anglo-European slaughters of American Indians, the enslavement of Africans in the Americas and apartheid in South Africa.

Los Angeles police officers Stacey Koon and Lawrence 3 Powell were part of a group of police officers who beat *ex* motorist Rodney King after a traffic stop. There was a state *clus* trial which resulted in acquittals for four officers on all serious charges. However, the same four were tried on federal charges. Koon and Powell were the only two convicted because it was judged that they intentionally used excessive force during the melee. There were between six and twelve officers on the scene at various times—all of them were white (Tomlin 1:1). - *Citation*

There is no way of knowing whether or not having 4 black or Hispanic officers on the scene would have prevented the incident. However, had the officer in charge been an ethnic minority, instead of Sgt. Koon, perhaps the beating would not have been so severe or even occurred at all.

Unfortunately, police brutality and abuses have been 5 found within our city's police force. Chicago Police Commander Jon Burge was found guilty, by a Chicago Police Department Office of Professional Standards (O.P.S.) review board, of torturing two African-Americans during interrogations regarding the murder of two Chicago police officers in 1982. This was not an isolated incident for Mr. Burge or officers under his command. Burge had been under investigation for abusing suspects at least seven times since 1973. During the seven months of testimony and deliberations before the O.P.S. review board, three individuals testified that they were tortured by Burge in an attempt to get them to sign confessions. Two of them were African-American, one was Hispanic and one was a native of Pakistan. According to Chicago Police Department Media Information liaison Billy Davis, "a large majority of the abuse complaints filed against Mr. Burge were by [ethnic] minorities." Additionally, an internal police department report released by a federal court judge during the hearings charges that "systematic torture" was perpetrated by at least seven officers at the South Side station from 1973 to 1986. Also, that supervisors, including then Lt. Jon Burge, knew about, condoned and participated in the abuse.

Today, you can look back at the long, troubled history   6
which the Chicago Police Department has had, citywide, with
a disproportionate number of white male officers. The most
recent statistics available show that in 1991, 2,828 complaints
of excessive force were filed with the Chicago Police
Department Office of Professional Standards. After investigating each of those, only 548 of the complaints were
deemed as "unfounded." There is no racial breakdown of the
information available; however, in 1991 almost seventy percent of police department personnel were white (Davis).

In a city where there are the same number of blacks as   7
whites, 38 percent, and one-fifth of the population is
Hispanic, the police department continues to contain a dis-
turbingly disproportionate number of white males. Of the
over 25,000 officers, only 34 percent of them are minorities
(Davis).

Racial tensions in Chicago, such as the West side race   8
riots of the late sixties, are far from being a thing of the past.
Even with all the gains made towards racial harmony, there
are areas within the city that remain ticking timebombs.
These areas could explode with only a spark, one which former Commander Burge and the beating of Rodney King
nearly provided. I believe, that an increased presence of
minority officers would ease many of these tensions. Perhaps
the nationwide race rioting of the late sixties, the King incident, and Mr. Burge's torturing tactics might not have
occurred if there were minority officers on the scene.

As negotiations for the most recent police contract   9
dragged on this past winter, Mayor Daley insisted that affirmative action clauses be included. Not only was Mr. Daley
doing the right thing, he had the numbers to back him up.
Most people don't understand the inter-related reasons
which allow this disgrace to continue. The overwhelming
majority of top officers, responsible for hiring and promo-
tions, are white males. All police officers are members of the
police union, which is also controlled, even more disproportionately, by white males. Finally, the city negotiates the
police contract with the police union. This is not to say that
white males in general are evil. They are, however, the group
which dominates the police department ranks and seems to
perpetuate this vicious cycle. The police union refuses

mandatory hiring standards so white males can continue to dominate the ranks. This lets them dominate the police union, which refuses mandatory hiring standards, and goes on and on. We can not wait to mount a stronger fight the next time around. We must fight back now so these outright unfair and prejudiced practices are not allowed to continue.

We, the voters, must raise our political voices and write, 10 phone or fax our alderman. Tell them the city has been divided for too long. The time has come to demand a city ordinance requiring the city's departments to employ proportionate to the city's demographics. All city departments and services should practice fair hiring and provide equal employment and promotion opportunity. The time to act is now!

Works Cited

Davis, Billy. Telephone Interview. 15 April and 5 May 1993.

Stein, Sherman. "Burge-Case Panel Hears of Torture." *Chicago Tribune* 11 Feb. 1992, sec. 2C:1.

———. "Second convict tells of torture by Burge." *Chicago Tribune* 20 Feb. 1992, sec. 2C:2.

———. "3rd Witness Calls Burge a Torturer." *Chicago Tribune* 21 Feb. 1992, sec. 2C:3.

———. "Burge Dismissed for Torture." *Chicago Tribune* 27 Aug. 1992, sec. 2C:1.

Tomlin, Michael. "Guilty in L.A." *Chicago Sun Times* 18 March 1993, sec. 1:1.

Thinking About Writing

Notice how Martin used sources in his essay. He conducted an interview and used various newspaper articles to gain information. Rather than referring to each of the *Chicago Tribune* articles separately in his essay, Martin summarized them to give a sense of the complete story but still listed them individually in his Works Cited.

What is your response to Martin? Are you part of his intended audience? Did you feel that Martin was talking to you? When sharing researched information rather than personal experience, it is easy to lose your voice and disappear inside the information. Do you get a feel for Martin's personality despite the prominent use of sources to support his position? How does Martin's position

relate to your own feelings and knowledge of cases of alleged brutality? Although Martin is talking about race relations within the
police force, consider representation of other ethnic minorities as
well as women. Could his argument apply equally to them? How
would this have been a different essay if he had included them all?

Writing Assignment

Research an issue that you have an opinion about. You might
consider an issue related to politics, to education, or to a problem
on your campus. The research may be from other written material, but may also include interviews, surveys, or polls. After compil-
ing your research, use it in shaping and arguing for your position.
Remember to keep your voice apparent in your argument—
despite the use of sources this is still *your* argument. Use proper
documentation of the sources and do not forget to include the
persuasive imperative.

DEAR ACADEMIC COMMITTEE

Pam Bombard

Background

Bombard was required to take an Outward Bound type of course as part of a general education requirement. It proved to be a terrifying experience for her, one which seemed at odds with the reasons the college gave for requiring such a class. Rather than simply complain to classmates, Bombard decided to write to the Academic Committee to make them aware of the situation and to reconsider the mandatory requirement.

Reading Selection

Dear Academic Committee:

1 I feel the need to write to you and ask you to reconsider the general education requirement PE100, Discovery Bound. The student handbook describes this class as, "a six week outdoor activity especially designed to develop trust, responsibility, and self confidence. . . ." This may be what is intended, but is this truly the case? I ask you to consider each student as an individual, each with unique personality, fears, and confidence. This type of class may not be good for everyone of these very different students. I can attest to this through personal experience, for I was one of those students for whom Discovery Bound was traumatic.

2 The incident occurred on the Saturday rock climbing trip with my discovery group. Fear of heights was one thing I never had to worry about. I could stand on the top floor of the John Hancock building, look out over the city and not feel one ounce of fear. This was not the case as I stood at the top of a one hundred foot rock, ready to rappel off the side of it. I was terrified and felt sick to my stomach every time I went near the edge. I was faced with threats and ridicule, "You won't pass the class if you don't do it. Don't be so chicken, everyone else did it. Face your fears." Feeling overcome by all the pressure put on me, I stepped off the edge of the rock. The next few minutes were filled with intense anxiety

and fear. I thought I was going to fall to my death. I kept
going down and down. The rope burned as it slid through
my hands. It seemed like an eternity before I made it to the
ground alive, scared, but alive. The others came up to me
and taunted me saying, "See, that wasn't so bad, even my
grandma could have done it."

Ever since that day, I have been unable to go beyond 3
an elevation of fifty feet without experiencing these same
emotions.

I strongly disagree with the concept of always facing 4
your fears and being pressured into doing something that
you are afraid of. Is not peer pressure one of the very things
we are taught to overcome?

This experience has also left me with negative feelings 5
towards my instructor and the other students in my group. I
ask you, is this developing trust?

Another area of Discovery Bound which I feel needs 6
some attention is the process by which the six week period is
concluded. Each student was required to construct a list of five
or more good qualities and five or more bad qualities for each
member of the group. Not only was this a difficult assignment
because there was not enough time to get to know seventeen
people very well, but some had more bad said about them than
good. It became a time of criticizing each other rather than
lifting them up. Does this develop self confidence?

Will you please take the time to reconsider the format 7
and structure of this class, or provide an alternative PE credit for those students who would prefer another way of developing trust, self-confidence, and responsibility?

Sincerely,
Pam Bombard

Thinking About Writing

Bombard has chosen the letter format in presenting her position to the college committee. She explains the problem based on
her experiences in the class and uses the catalogue description of
the course as contrast. Bombard might have developed a more formal position paper identifying the problem and presenting a solution. Do you think she chose the appropriate format for her audience? How would this have been different as a formal proposal?

Writing Assignment

Consider an issue on your college campus that you would like to see changed. What governing body would be your audience? What authority do you have to raise the concern or propose a change? What experiences have you had that would support your argument? What other support do you have? Once you have identified an issue and the appropriate audience, write a persuasive piece which seeks to remedy the situation or call for change. Consider whether you should use a formal proposal format, a memo to the appropriate office, or the more personal letter depending on the audience and the action you want them to take.

Part Five

INFORMATIVE DISCOURSE

Informative discourse is an integral part of our everyday lives. Stores are stocked with a wide variety of newspapers. There are magazines covering every possible recreational activity. In addition, every office has shelves of pamphlets and every bookstore has sections entirely devoted to do-it-yourself manuals—on how to travel; on how to fix, make, and do things; on how to live; and even on how to die. Ours has been called the information age, and while much of this information is now processed electronically, we still produce reams of information in print.

In informative writing, the purpose is obviously to give information, to share knowledge, and readers go to this kind of writing because they want to find out about the topic. We go to a dictionary to find out how to spell a word or what it means. We go to a movie encyclopedia to find out who won an Academy Award for Best Actress in a particular year. We go to a map to find out how to get somewhere. We read a brochure from the town we live in to find out what items are accepted for recycling.

In all of these instances, we are going to authorities on the subject. But exactly what constitutes "authority" and exactly what kind of authority we as readers are looking for varies considerably. Sometimes we want what might be considered "absolute authority" as when we consult a good dictionary for a definition or when we read an encyclopedia for the basic facts about a particular event like the French Revolution.

But other times, the authority we are looking for is not so absolute. For example, we may learn that we are suffering from a certain illness from an authority like a doctor, but the kind of information we want is not about the technical aspects of the disease. Instead we want to know what the illness is really like to live with day by day, what treatments are like, and the physical and psychological toll these may take. And we want that information, not from an objective specialist, but from someone who has lived through it; hence the current popularity of support groups for cancer and AIDS patients.

In addition to the authority of the writer varying, the stance of the readers also changes according to their own position on the expert to amateur scale. For example, an automobile mechanic discussing the latest developments in engine design with other mechanics would adjust that information to be understood by the ordinary automobile owner whose car engine is acting up.

In informative writing, then, the relationship between the reader and writer depends on the level of expertise of both. Are they equals, with one sharing a bit of knowledge or experience the other may not have, or is one the clear authority adjusting the level of expertise for a general reader?

In the next three chapters, you will read informative essays that fall within a wide range of "authority." What unites them is the writers' desire to share something they know with others.

Chapter Twelve

READING INFORMATIVE DISCOURSE: THE READER/WRITER RELATIONSHIP

As readers, we approach an informative text expecting to receive accurate information from the writer. In that sense we generally approach it with an attitude of trust. We don't expect newspapers to report on events that didn't actually happen, phone books to give us wrong numbers, maps to lead us to dead ends, or pamphlets on recycling to show us instead how to harm the environment.

On the other hand, we need to be aware that all writing, even the most objective-seeming, is written by someone, and that someone has certain biases that inevitably come through. Perhaps the biases are due to the limited data available or to certain social constraints or simply to change as when a road closes between the time the map readings were taken and the map was printed. But whatever the reason, no piece of writing can claim to be completely objective or factual. So, while we generally trust informative discourse to provide accurate information, it's helpful to add a healthy dose of skepticism to our reading or to at least be prepared to deal with possible errors and even contradictions among expert sources.

Sometimes readers forget to be skeptical because the information is presented in such a way that it does not seem possible for it to be untrue. The piece appears to cover "just the facts" and so seems impossible to dispute. One way in which writing achieves this seeming objectivity is by hiding one crucial fact—that someone wrote the piece, that there is a real person behind the prose. This fact can be especially difficult to remember when the writer is in no way acknowledged—there is no "I" and perhaps not even an author listed, as often happens in newspaper writing. It is as if the events just magically put themselves into words which then appeared on the page.

This *objective stance* is used deliberately in many situations because it is deemed appropriate by convention. For example, scholarly and academic writing often lacks an "I" or a personal voice because these are considered inappropriate for the rational thought process such writing is supposed to reflect. This stance is also taken so as to highlight the information itself rather than the source. Accident reports are often written in this objective way so as to de-emphasize the witnesses' biases or the reporter's limited point of view.

There is nothing inherently wrong with this objective stance, as long as we remember that the scholarly article is still some specific person's analysis of the data and that the report is still a compilation of all those biased witnesses' observations. We must be especially watchful for times when that detached voice is being used deliberately to camouflage a personal bias and to deceive us into thinking the piece is more objective than it is. An obvious example of this is the use of carefully selected statistics to support a particular cause.

At the other end of the spectrum, informative writing can be very personal, making no claim at objectivity. In this case, the writers provide *information from their own experience or observations.* This personal touch can be very valuable. For example, one of the authors of this book is a diabetic. When a friend's child was suddenly diagnosed with this illness, the doctor clearly explained what had happened and what to do and provided pamphlets and books for the mother to read. But when the woman returned home with her child in her arms, it was her friend she turned to for the information she really wanted—would her boy be all right? The reassuring "yes" from her friend was worth far more to her than all the information from the experts.

Informative writing, then, can range from the very personal sharing of information from experience to the most objective reports. The following essays will illustrate this range through three examples of the reader/writer relationship in informative writing: the explanation, the observation essay, and the critical analysis.

EXPLANATION

DON'T JUST STAND THERE
Diane Cole

One of the most common types of informative writing is that which explains something to us: *what* the meaning of communism is, *how* the Japanese show respect, *why* American car manufacturing is on the upswing. Some of these explanations are very straightforward like the ones that come in boxes marked "some assembly required." But the best explanations are the ones that take the reader into account in a more direct way than "Insert flap B into slot A." While we all need instructions like this at times, they do not make for very interesting reading and can even be frustrating as when flap B won't fit into slot A and the instructions provide no further help.

Well-written explanations often go beyond the basics to provide a context for the topic and to anticipate difficulties. In other words, the writer often demonstrates an interest in the readers' success in understanding the explanation and provides tips and advice to facilitate that understanding. The writer is concerned not only with the accuracy of the explanation but with getting the reader to accept the explanation as valid. Readers then must be convinced of the authority of the writer and the quality of the explanation.

This concern with quality is why we seek out experts to advise us on how to maintain our cars or cook or take care of our finances. We don't want our cars to just manage to keep going or our food to just be edible or our money to just keep us from having to declare bankruptcy. We hope that our expert mechanic, cook, or adviser will help us to drive, eat, and invest well—with quality.

The writers' concern with quality and vested interest in the subject often give a persuasive dimension to this kind of informative writing. We are not just being told that we must insert flap B into slot A, but being urged to do so in the right way so that our entire project does not fall apart. In addition, the writers often care that our project is successful because it corresponds to some agenda of their own.

The writers' concern tends to come through in the way the subject is written about—with genuine understanding, with enjoyment, with a sense of urgency, with complete confidence and competence, and with a reader in mind. The writers want to do more than just explain; they want us to feel the importance of what they are describing and a kinship with others who are interested in it, too. For example, if you wanted to learn the fine art of quilting, it would be easy enough to learn the stitches, but that would in no way help you to understand the meaning of the traditional patterns that have been passed down for generations or the atmosphere of a quilting bee or to know the stories behind the scraps of material that are being used. In other words, in good explanatory writing we can sense that the subject has some special meaning for the writer that is being passed on to us in the explanation. The writer's enthusiasm for the project and stake in it are evident whether the topic is a hobby like stamp collecting or a serious social concern like the one addressed in the essay below. Good explanatory writing is accurate information communicated well—with quality.

Prereading Journal

Imagine that you and a friend have gone to a party, and while chatting with a group of other guests, you hear one of them tell a joke that you know is offensive to your friend because of its racist or sexist or homophobic nature. How would you inform the speaker of how you felt? Would it matter if your friend could hear the joke or not? What if the joke were aimed at you?

Background

Writer, feminist, humanist Cole wrote this essay in 1989 for "A World of Difference," a special supplement to *The New York Times,* which addressed various ways of handling and ending prejudice. Cole addresses the situation posed in the prereading journal and other situations in which we are faced with bigotry. Cole explains how to handle such situations.

During Reading

Keep a list of the specific strategies Cole suggests using in responding to people who have expressed prejudiced beliefs.

Reading Selection

It was my office farewell party, and colleagues at the job 1
I was about to leave were wishing me well. My mood was one of ebullience tinged with regret, and it was in this spirit that I spoke to the office neighbor to whom I had waved hello every morning for the past two years. He smiled broadly as he launched into a long, rambling story, pausing only after he delivered the punch line. It was a very long pause because, although he laughed, I did not: This joke was unmistakably anti-Semitic.

I froze. Everyone in the office knew I was Jewish; what 2
could he have possibly meant? Shaken and hurt, not knowing what else to do, I turned in stunned silence to the next well-wisher. Later, still angry, I wondered, what else should I—could I—have done?

Prejudice can make its presence felt in any setting, but 3
hearing its nasty voice in this way can be particularly unnerving. We do not know what to do and often we feel another form of paralysis as well: We think, "Nothing I say or do will change this person's attitude, so why bother?"

But left unchecked, racial slurs and offensive ethnic 4
jokes "can poison the atmosphere," says Michael McQuillan, adviser for racial/ethnic affairs for the Brooklyn borough president's office. "Hearing these remarks conditions us to accept them; and if we accept these, we can become accepting of other acts."

Speaking up may not magically change a biased atti- 5
tude, but it can change a person's behavior by putting a strong message across. And the more messages there are, the more likely a person is to change that behavior, says Arnold Kahn, professor of psychology at James Madison University, Harrisonburg, Va., who makes this analogy: "You can't keep people from smoking in *their* house, but you can ask them not to smoke in *your* house."

At the same time, "Even if the other party ignores or 6
discounts what you say, people always reflect on how others

perceive them. Speaking up always counts," says LeNorman Strong, director of campus life at George Washington University, Washington, D.C.

Finally, learning to respond effectively also helps peo- 7
ple feel better about themselves, asserts Cherie Brown, executive director of the National Coalition Building Institute, a Boston-based training organization. "We've found that, when people felt they could at least in this small way make a difference, that made them more eager to take on other activities on a larger scale," she says. Although there is no "cookbook approach" to confronting such remarks—every situation is different, experts stress—these are some effective strategies.

When the "joke" turns on who you are—as a member of an ethnic or 8
religious group, a person of color, a woman, a gay or lesbian, an elder-
ly person, or someone with a physical handicap—shocked paralysis is
often the first response. Then, wounded and vulnerable, on some level
you want to strike back.

Lashing out or responding in kind is seldom the most 9
effective response, however. "That can give you momentary satisfaction, but you also feel as if you've lowered yourself to that other person's level," Mr. McQuillan explains. Such a response may further label you in the speaker's mind as thin-skinned, someone not to be taken seriously. Or it may up the ante, making the speaker, and then you, reach for new insults—or physical blows.

"If you don't laugh at the joke, or fight, or respond in 10
kind to the slur," says Mr. McQuillan, "that will take the person by surprise, and that can give you more control over the situation." Therefore, in situations like the one in which I found myself—a private conversation in which I knew the person making the remark—he suggests voicing your anger calmly but pointedly: "I don't know if you realize what that sounded like to me. If that's what you meant, it really hurt me."

State how *you* feel, rather than making an abstract state- 11
ment like, "Not everyone who hears that joke might find it funny." Counsels Mr. Strong: "Personalize the sense of 'this is how I feel when you say this.' That makes it very concrete"—and harder to dismiss.

Make sure you heard the words and their intent cor- 12
rectly by repeating or rephrasing the statement: "This is what

I heard you say. Is that what you meant?" It's important to give the other person the benefit of the doubt because, in fact, he may not have realized that the comment was offensive and, if you had not spoken up, would have had no idea of its impact on you.

For instance, Professor Kahn relates that he used to 13 include in his exams multiple-choice questions that occasionally contained "incorrect funny answers." After one exam, a student came up to him in private and said, "I don't think you intended this, but I found a number of those jokes offensive to me as a woman." She explained why. "What she said made immediate sense to me," he says. "I apologized at the next class, and I never did it again."

But what if the speaker dismisses your objection, saying, 14 "Oh, you're just being sensitive. Can't you take a joke?" In that case, you might say, "I'm not so sure about that, let's talk about that a little more." The key, Mr. Strong says, is to continue the dialogue, hear the other person's concerns, and point out your own. "There are times when you're just going to have to admit defeat and end it," he adds, "but I have to feel that I did the best I could."

When the offending remark is made in the presence of 15 others—at a staff meeting, for example—it can be even more distressing than an insult made privately.

"You have two options," says William Newlin, director of 16 field services for the Community Relations division of the New York City Commission on Human Rights. "You can respond immediately at the meeting, or you can delay your response until afterward in private. But a response has to come."

Some remarks or actions may be so outrageous that they 17 cannot go unnoted at the moment, regardless of the speaker or the setting. But in general, psychologists say, shaming a person in public may have the opposite effect of the one you want: The speaker will deny his offense all the more strongly in order to save face. Further, few people enjoy being put on the spot, and if the remark really was not intended to be offensive, publicly embarrassing the person who made it may cause an unnecessary rift or further misunderstanding. Finally, most people just don't react as well or thoughtfully under a public spotlight as they would in private.

Keeping that in mind, an excellent alternative is to take 18
the offender aside afterward: "Could we talk for a minute in
private?" Then use the strategies suggested above for calmly
stating how you feel, giving the speaker the benefit of the
doubt, and proceeding from there.

At a large meeting or public talk, you might consider 19
passing the speaker a note, says David Wertheimer, executive
director of the New York City Gay and Lesbian Anti-Violence
Project: You could write, "You may not realize it, but your
remarks were offensive because. . . ."

"Think of your role as that of an educator," suggests 20
James M. Jones, Ph.D., executive director for public interest
at the American Psychological Association. "You have to be
controlled."

Regardless of the setting or situation, speaking up 21
always raises the risk of rocking the boat. If the person who
made the offending remark is your boss, there may be an
even bigger risk to consider: How will this affect my job?
Several things can help minimize the risk, however. First,
know what other resources you may have at work, suggests
Caryl Stern, director of the A World of Difference—New
York City campaign: Does your personnel office handle discrimination complaints? Are other grievance procedures in
place?

You won't necessarily need to use any of these proce- 22
dures, Ms. Stern stresses. In fact, she advises, "It's usually better to try a one-on-one approach first." But simply knowing a
formal system exists can make you feel secure enough to set
up that meeting.

You can also raise the issue with other colleagues who 23
heard the remark: Did they feel the same way you did? The
more support you have, the less alone you will feel. Your
point will also carry more validity and be more difficult to
shrug off. Finally, give your boss credit—and the benefit of
the doubt: "I know you've worked hard for the company's
affirmative action programs, so I'm sure you didn't realize
what those remarks sounded like to me as well as the others
at the meeting last week. . . ."

If, even after this discussion, the problem persists, go 24
back for another meeting, Ms. Stern advises. And if that, too,
fails, you'll know what other options are available to you.

It's a spirited dinner party, and everyone's having a good time, until   25
one guest starts reciting a racist joke. Everyone at the table is white,
including you. The others are still laughing, as you wonder what to
say or do.

No one likes being seen as a party-pooper, but before   26
deciding that you'd prefer not to take on this role, you might
remember that the person who told the offensive joke has
already ruined your good time.

If it's a group that you feel comfortable in—a family   27
gathering, for instance—you will feel freer to speak up. Still,
shaming the person by shouting "You're wrong!" or "That's
not funny!" probably won't get your point across as effectively as other strategies. "If you interrupt people to condemn
them, it just makes it harder," says Cherie Brown. She suggests trying instead to get at the resentments that lie beneath
the joke by asking open-ended questions: "Grandpa, I know
you always treat everyone with such respect. Why do people
in our family talk that way about black people?" The key, Ms.
Brown says, "is to listen to them first, so they will be more likely to listen to you."

If you don't know your fellow guests well, before speaking   28
up you could turn discreetly to your neighbors (or excuse yourself to help the host or hostess in the kitchen) to get a reading
on how they felt, and whether or not you'll find support for
speaking up. The less alone you feel, the more comfortable
you'll be speaking up: "I know you probably didn't mean anything by that joke, Jim, but it really offended me. . . ." It's important to say that *you* were offended—not state how the group
that is the butt of the joke would feel. "Otherwise," LeNorman
Strong says, "you risk coming off as a goody two-shoes."

If you yourself are the host, you can exercise more con-   29
trol; you are, after all, the one who sets the rules and the tone
of behavior in your home. Once, when Professor Kahn's party
guests began singing offensive, racist songs, for instance, he
kicked them all out, saying, "You don't sing songs like that in
my house!" And, he adds, "they never did again."

Checking Your Understanding

1.   Explain why Cole so often suggests confronting the offender alone.
     Why does she feel this is more effective? Also, why does she suggest
     saying how you *personally* feel?

2. Consider again the imagined scenario in your prewriting or a simi-
    lar situation you have actually experienced. Using dialogue and
    illustrating one of Cole's strategies, show how you might respond to
    a situation in which prejudice is openly expressed.

3. Try to put yourself in the place of the person who made the offen-
    sive remark. Why might someone say such a thing? Keeping these
    reasons in mind, devise a strategy of your own for approaching this
    person.

Examining Rhetorical Strategies

1. While Cole's purpose is to provide us with instructions in how to
    handle offensive remarks, there are also elements of expressive,
    affirming, and persuasive writing in this piece. How do these ele-
    ments increase the quality of her instructions? How does she show
    her personal understanding of this issue, her opinion on this sub-
    ject, and her sincere desire for you to take her up on some of her
    suggestions?

2. Cole begins her essay with an anecdote and then provides two addi-
    tional scenarios in italics. Why do you think she inserts these exam-
    ples? What effect does her personal authority in the opening para-
    graphs have on you as a reader?

OBSERVATION

NO NEWS FROM AUSCHWITZ
A. M. Rosenthal

Another common form of informative writing seeks to draw our attention to the writer's *observations* of certain events or people. Newspapers and news magazines are good examples of this kind of writing. Journalists are sent to key places around the world to observe and record firsthand the events that are happening on a particular day. Many writers, who are specialists in a particular field, spend their lives writing about subjects from their particular point of view to show, for example, how biologists or environmentalists or physicians see the world. Other times people, who are just very good observers of life, use their skill to draw our attention to things around us that we might otherwise miss.

These writers give us a report on the world and help us focus on the significance of one part of that world. As readers, we come to this type of writing wanting to understand something better—what is happening on the other side of the globe, how other people live and think, how environmentalists view the state of our planet. While often based on one person's observations, this writing is not personal in the sense that we do not read it to learn about the writer. The writer may even be unidentified. And if the writer does use "I" it tends to be in the context of a particular *role*—"I" as physician, "I" as biologist, "I" as anthropologist. This helps us to focus on the subject being discussed rather than on the writer.

But while the writer may seem more detached, we as readers may be very moved by the scene the writer has chosen to describe. A news story about starving children in a war-torn country may have a strong emotional impact on us even if written in a very *objective style*. In fact, the objective style may make the heartbreaking event seem even more cruel and callous. The human significance of the piece may produce a very personal response in us even when the writing style is detached, as in the following "news" story from *The New York Times*.

Prereading Journal

Before you read this selection, make a list of all the things you know about the Nazi concentration camps. What facts, images, or emotions come to you when you hear the word "Holocaust"?

Background

Rosenthal is a Pulitzer Prize–winning international journalist who began his career with *The New York Times* in 1944. In 1958 he visited Auschwitz and felt compelled to report his observations even though the death camps, having been closed for fourteen years, were no longer considered "news."

During Reading

While you read, note how Rosenthal uses contrasts to highlight what he sees; for example, the children playing versus the piles of baby shoes.

Reading Selection

BRZEZINKA, POLAND—The most terrible thing of all, 1 somehow, was that at Brzezinka the sun was bright and warm, the rows of graceful poplars were lovely to look upon and on the grass near the gates children played.

It all seemed frighteningly wrong, as in a nightmare, that 2 at Brzezinka the sun should ever shine or that there should be light and greenness and the sound of young laughter. It would be fitting if at Brzezinka the sun never shone and the grass withered, because this is a place of unutterable terror.

And yet, every day, from all over the world, people 3 come to Brzezinka, quite possibly the most grisly tourist center on earth. They come for a variety of reasons—to see if it could really have been true, to remind themselves not to forget, to pay homage to the dead by the simple act of looking upon their place of suffering.

Brzezinka is a couple of miles from the better-known 4 southern Polish town of Oswiecim. Oswiecim has about 12,000 inhabitants, is situated about 171 miles from Warsaw and lies in a damp, marshy area at the eastern end of the pass called the Moravian Gate. Brzezinka and Oswiecim together formed part of that minutely organized factory of torture and death that the Nazis called Konzentrationslager Auschwitz.

By now, fourteen years after the last batch of prisoners 5
was herded naked into the gas chambers by dogs and guards,
the story of Auschwitz has been told a great many times.
Some of the inmates have written of those memories of
which sane men cannot conceive. Rudolf Franz Ferdinand
Hoess, the superintendent of the camp, before he was executed wrote his detailed memoirs of mass exterminations and
the experiments on living bodies. Four million people died
here, the Poles say.

And so there is no news to report about Auschwitz. 6
There is merely the compulsion to write something about it,
a compulsion that grows out of a restless feeling that to have
visited Auschwitz and then turned away without having said
or written anything would somehow be a most grievous act of
discourtesy to those who died here.

Brezezinka and Oswiecim are very quiet places now; the 7
screams can no longer be heard. The tourist walks silently,
quickly at first to get it over with and then, as his mind peoples the barracks and the chambers and the dungeons and
flogging posts, he walks draggingly. The guide does not say
much either, because there is nothing much for him to say
after he has pointed.

For every visitor, there is one particular bit of horror that 8
he knows he will never forget. For some it is seeing the rebuilt
gas chamber at Oswiecim and being told that this is the "small
one." For others it is the fact that at Brzezinka, in the ruins of
the gas chambers and the crematoria the Germans blew up
when they retreated, there are daisies growing.

There are visitors who gaze blankly at the gas chambers 9
and the furnaces because their minds simply cannot encom-
pass them, but stand shivering before the great mounds of
human hair behind the plate-glass window or the piles of
babies' shoes or the brick cells where men sentenced to
death by suffocation were walled up.

One visitor opened his mouth in a silent scream simply 10
at the sight of boxes—great stretches of three-tiered wooden
boxes in the women's barracks. They were about six feet
wide, about three feet high, and into them from five to ten
prisoners were shoved for the night. The guide walks quickly
through the barracks. Nothing more to see here.

A brick building where sterilization experiments were 11
carried out on women prisoners. The guide tries the door—

it's locked. The visitor is grateful that he does not have to go in, and then flushes with shame.

A long corridor where rows of faces stare from the walls. 12 Thousands of pictures, the photographs of prisoners. They are all dead now, the men and women who stood before the cameras, and they all knew they were to die.

They all stare blank-faced, but one picture, in the mid- 13 dle of a row, seizes the eye and wrenches the mind. A girl, 22 years old, plumply pretty, blond. She is smiling gently, as at a sweet, treasured thought. What was the thought that passed through her young mind and is now her memorial on the wall of the dead at Auschwitz?

Into the suffocation dungeons the visitor is taken for a 14 moment and feels himself strangling. Another visitor goes in, stumbles out and crosses herself. There is no place to pray at Auschwitz.

The visitors look pleadingly at each other and say to the 15 guide, "Enough."

There is nothing new to report about Auschwitz. It was 16 a sunny day and the trees were green and at the gates the children played.

Checking Your Understanding

1. If there is no news to report at the death camp, why does Rosenthal feel "the compulsion to write something about it"? What information about Auschwitz does he want to communicate?
2. Which of the details Rosenthal highlights about the camp are the most powerful? Why? How do they compare with the prior knowledge you recorded in your prereading?

Examining Rhetorical Strategies

1. What effect do the opening and closing paragraphs have on the information Rosenthal reports? What kind of frame do these paragraphs provide for the scene at the camp?
2. In paragraph 13, Rosenthal draws our attention to the face of a young woman, "smiling gently, as at a sweet, treasured thought." What purpose does this focused observation serve? Why did Rosenthal include that detail of the photograph? Speculate on what that young woman's thought might have been and then briefly record what you imagine was passing through her mind at that moment.

CRITICAL ANALYSIS

IMAGES OF RELATIONSHIP
Carol Gilligan

More than any other kind of writing, *analysis* is associated with *academic* and professional communication. Beginning in middle school and sometimes even earlier, schoolchildren are taught to gather together sources of information and assemble them into an informative essay. By high school, this essay has grown into the research paper complete with note cards, outlines, and bibliographies. In college, the critical analysis takes many different forms. In some disciplines, it is similar to the high school research paper; students select a topic they know nothing or little about, read the designated number of sources, and compile a paper synthesizing the information they have gathered.

But as students learn to be scholars and critical thinkers, and especially as they come to be part of a discipline, they learn to *use sources to support their own thoughts and observations.* They read and study within an interest area and then write papers to make a contribution to or observation about the research being done in that area. Students learn to defend a thesis and to prove or disprove a hypothesis of their own and to use their own and others' research to support their claims.

In becoming part of a field of study, then, writers learn to think and write as a member of their disciplines both while they are students and later as professionals. Biologists learn to record their lab results in a way that allows others to verify their findings; journalists learn to do investigative reporting; historians learn how to research, record, and interpret past events; anthropologists learn how to observe other cultures and record their findings; social workers learn to write case studies; teachers to do lesson plans; business majors to do marketing and efficiency reports; lawyers to do legal briefs; environmentalists to record field observations.

This writing done by experts is usually written to fellow experts. Readers who are not in this field may venture into these writings to find out what the experts have to say, but most non-experts find this pretty heady stuff! Fortunately, there are experts who write about the same topics but for non-expert readers. Thus, *National Geographic* brings the anthropologist's world to us and *Scientific American* fills us in on the latest scientific developments.

How we as readers, then, approach this writing, depends on our own level of interest and expertise. If we are involved in the field, we will not be daunted by the essays in scholarly journals. If we are just interested but not experts, we may seek out an interpreter who can provide the information in a way we can understand.

The critical analysis also tends to be *the most objective kind of writing in terms of style.* Seldom are the personal pronouns "I" or "you" used. The focus is completely on the information and on laying out that information in a logical, organized way. However, while the writer is simply conforming to the conventions of scholarly style, the reader should keep in mind that the essay will still reflect the point of view and thinking of the writer.

Prereading Journal

Look at the picture below and write a brief story explaining what is happening in the scene that you see.

Background

Gilligan is a professor of education at Harvard University. Her book *In a Different Voice: Psychological Theory and Women's Development* records the findings of Gilligan's study of male and female college students' associations with achievement and intimacy (affiliation). The study invited the students to do what you were just asked to do for the pre-reading journal—respond to a picture by writing a story about it. Gilligan found that the ways in which women and men responded to the pictures were markedly different.

During Reading

Note the differences between women's and men's responses to the pictures. Keep track of how these respons-es change as the images in the pictures show more or less affiliation.

Reading Selection

Four of the six pictures that comprised the test (Pollak   1 and Gilligan, 1982) were chosen for the purposes of this analysis since they provided clear illustrations of achievement and affiliation situations. Two of the pictures show a man and a woman in close personal affiliation—the couple on the bench in the river scene, and two trapeze artists grasping each other's wrists, the man hanging by his knees from the trapeze and the woman in mid-air. Two pictures show people at work in impersonal achievement situations—a man sitting alone at his desk in a high-rise office building, and two women, dressed in white coats, working in a laboratory, the woman in the background watching while the woman in the foreground handles the test tubes. The study centered on a comparison between the stories written about these two sets of pictures.

The men in the class, considered as a group, projected   2 more violence into situations of personal affiliation than they did into impersonal situations of achievement. Twenty-five percent of the men wrote violent stories only to the pictures of affiliation, 19 percent to pictures of both affiliation and achievement, and 7 percent only to pictures of achievement. In contrast, the women saw more violence in impersonal sit-uations of achievement than in situations of affiliation; 16

percent of the women wrote violent stories to the achievement pictures and 6 percent to the pictures of affiliation.

As the story about Nick, written by a man, illustrates the 3 association of danger with intimacy,[1] so the story about Miss Hegstead, written by a woman, exemplifies the projection of violence into situations of achievement and the association of danger with competitive success:

> Another boring day in the lab and that mean bitchy Miss Hegstead always breathing down the students' backs. Miss Hegstead has been at Needham Country High School for 40 years and every chemistry class is the same. She is watching Jane Smith, the model student in the class. She always goes over to Jane and comments to the other students that Jane is always doing the experiment right and Jane is the only student who really works hard, etc. Little does Miss Hegstead know that Jane is making some arsenic to put in her afternoon coffee.

If aggression is conceived as a response to the percep- 4 tion of danger, the findings of the images of violence study suggest that men and women may perceive danger in different social situations and construe danger in different ways— men seeing danger more often in close personal affiliation than in achievement and construing danger to arise from intimacy, women perceiving danger in impersonal achievement situations and construing danger to result from competitive success. The danger men describe in their stories of intimacy is a danger of entrapment or betrayal, being caught in a smothering relationship or humiliated by rejection and deceit. In contrast, the danger women portray in their tales of achievement is a danger of isolation, a fear that in standing out or being set apart by success, they will be left alone. In the story of Miss Hegstead, the only apparent cause of the

---

[1]Nick saw his life pass before his eyes. He could feel the cold penetrating ever deeper into his body. How long had it been since he had fallen through the ice—thirty seconds, a minute? It wouldn't take long for him to succumb to the chilling grip of the mid-February Charles River. What a fool he had been to accept the challenge of his roommate Sam to cross the frozen river. He knew all along that Sam hated him. Hated him for being rich and especially hated him for being engaged to Mary, Sam's childhood sweetheart. But Nick never realized until now that Mary also hated him and really loved Sam. Yet there they were, the two of them, calmly sitting on a bench in the riverbend, watching Nick drown. They'd probably soon be married, and they'd probably finance it with the life insurance policy for which Mary was the beneficiary.

violence is Jane's being singled out as the best student and thus set apart from her classmates. She retaliates by making arsenic to put in the teacher's afternoon coffee, yet all Miss Hegstead did was to praise Jane for her good work.

As people are brought closer together in the pictures, 5 the images of violence in the men's stories increase, while as people are set further apart, the violence in the women's stories increases. The women in the class projected violence most frequently into the picture of the man at his desk (the only picture portraying a person alone), while the men in the class most often saw violence in the scene of the acrobats on the trapeze (the only picture in which people touched). Thus, it appears that men and women may experience attachment and separation in different ways and that each sex perceives a danger which the other does not see—men in connection, women in separation.

But since the women's perception of danger departs 6 from the usual mode of expectation, the acrobats seeming to be in far greater danger than the man at his desk, their perception calls into question the usual mode of interpretation. Sex differences in aggression are usually interpreted by taking the male response as the norm, so that the absence of aggression in women is identified as the problem to be explained. However, the disparate location of violence in the stories written by women and men raises the question as to why women see the acrobats as safe.

The answer comes from the analysis of the stories about 7 the trapeze. Although the picture of acrobats shows them performing high in the air without a net, 22 percent of the women in the study added nets in the stories they wrote. In contrast, only 6 percent of the men imagined the presence of a net, while 40 percent either explicitly mentioned the absence of a net or implied its absence by describing one or both acrobats as plummeting to their deaths. Thus, the women saw the scene on the trapeze as safe because, by providing nets, they had made it safe, protecting the lives of the acrobats in the event of a fall. Yet failing to imagine the presence of nets in the scene on the trapeze, men, interpreting women's responses, readily attribute the absence of violence in women's stories to a denial of danger or to a repression of aggression (May, 1980) rather than to the activities of care through which the women make the acrobats safe. As women imagine the activities through which relationships are woven and connection sustained, the world of intimacy—which appears so mysterious and dangerous to men—comes instead to appear increasingly coherent and safe.

If aggression is tied, as women perceive, to the fracture 8 of human connection, then the activities of care, as their fantasies suggest, are the activities that make the social world safe, by avoiding isolation and preventing aggression rather than by seeking rules to limit its extent. In this light, aggression appears no longer as an unruly impulse that must be contained but rather as a signal of a fracture of connection, the sign of a failure of relationship. From this perspective, the prevalence of violence in men's fantasies, denoting a world where danger is everywhere seen, signifies a problem in making connection, causing relationships to erupt and turning separation into a dangerous isolation. Reversing the usual mode of interpretation, in which the absence of aggression in women is tied to a problem with separation, makes it possible to see the prevalence of violence in men's stories, its odd location in the context of intimate relationships, and its association with betrayal and deceit as indicative of a problem with connection that leads relationships to become dangerous and safety to appear in separation. The rule-bound competitive achievement situations, which for women threaten the web of connection, for men provide a mode of connection that establishes clear boundaries and limits aggression, and thus appears comparatively safe.

A story written by one of the women about the acrobats 9 on the trapeze illustrates these themes, calling into question the usual opposition of achievement and affiliation by portraying the continuation of the relationship as the predicate for success:

> These are two Flying Gypsies, and they are auditioning for the big job with the Ringling Brothers Circus. They are the last team to try out for the job, and they are doing very well. They have grace and style, but they use a safety net which some teams do not use. The owners say that they'll hire them if they forfeit the net, but the Gypsies decide that they would rather live longer and turn down the job than take risks like that. They know the act will be ruined if either got hurt and see no sense in taking the risk.

For the Gypsies in the story, it is not the big job with the circus that is of paramont importance but rather the well-being of the two people involved. Anticipating negative consequences from a success attained at the risk of their lives, they forfeit the job rather than the net, protecting their lives but also their act which "would be ruined if either got hurt."

While women thus try to change the rules in order to   10
preserve relationships, men, in abiding by these rules, depict relationships as easily replaced. Projecting most violence into this scene, they write stories about infidelity and betrayal that end with the male acrobat dropping the woman, presumably replacing the relationship and going on with the act:

> The woman trapeze artist is married to the best friend of the
> male who has just discovered (before the show) that she has
> been unfaithful to his friend (her husband). He confronted
> her with this knowledge and told her to tell her husband but
> she refused. Not having the courage to confront him himself,
> the trapeze artist creates an accident while 100 feet above
> ground, letting the woman slip out of his grasp in mid-flight.
> She is killed in the incident but he feels no guilt, believing
> that he has rectified the situation.

The prevalence of violence in male fantasy . . . is con-   11
sonant with the view of aggression as endemic in human relationships. But these male fantasies and images also reveal a world where connection is fragmented and communication fails, where betrayal threatens because there seems to be no way of knowing the truth. . . .

Thus, although aggression has been construed as instinc-   12
tual and separation has been thought necessary for its constraint, the violence in male fantasy seems rather to arise from a problem in communication and an absence of knowledge about human relationships. But as . . . women in their fantasies create nets of safety where men depict annihilation, the voices of women comment on the problem of aggression that both sexes face, locating the problem in the isolation of self and in the hierarchical construction of human relationships.

. . . The images of hierarchy and web, drawn from the   13
texts of men's and women's fantasies and thoughts, convey different ways of structuring relationships and are associated with different views of morality and self. But these images create a problem in understanding because each

distorts the other's representation. As the top of the hierarchy becomes the edge of the web and as the center of a network of connection becomes the middle of a hierarchical progression, each image marks as dangerous the place which the other defines as safe. Thus the images of hierarchy and web inform different modes of assertion and response: the wish to be alone at the top and the consequent fear that others will get too close; the wish to be at the center of connection and the consequent fear of being too far out on the edge. These disparate fears of being stranded and being caught give rise to different portrayals of achievement and affiliation, leading to different modes of action and different ways of assessing the consequences of choice.

The reinterpretation of women's experience in terms 14 of their own imagery of relationships thus clarifies that experience and also provides a nonhierarchical vision of human connection. Since relationships, when cast in the image of hierarchy, appear inherently unstable and morally problematic, their transposition into the image of web changes an order of inequality into a structure of interconnection. But the power of the images of hierarchy and web, their evocation of feelings and their recurrence in thought, signifies the embeddedness of both of these images in the cycle of human life. The experiences of inequality and interconnection, inherent in the relation of parent and child, then give rise to the ethics of justice and care, the ideals of human relationship—the vision that self and other will be treated as of equal worth, that despite differences in power, things will be fair; the vision that everyone will be responded to and included, that no one will be left alone or hurt. These disparate visions in their tension reflect the paradoxical truths of human experience—that we know ourselves as separate only insofar as we live in connection with others, and that we experience relationship only insofar as we differentiate other from self.

Works Cited

May, Robert. *Sex and Fantasy: Patterns of Male and Female Development.* New York: W. W. Norton, 1980.

Pollak, Susan, and Gilligan, Carol. "Images of Violence in Thematic Apperception Test Stories." *Journal of Personality and Social Psychology* 42, 1 (1982): 159–167.

Checking Your Understanding

1. Summarize Gilligan's findings. Then write a brief response to those findings indicating whether you agree or disagree with her conclusions based on the way you responded to the picture in your prereading. Did your response support or dispute her claims?

2. Women: In what way do you think society trains you to create "activities of care" through which people will be made safe? Have any women in your life created a safety net for you or showed you how to create one for others?

   Men: In what way do you think society trains you to see danger everywhere especially in intimate relationships? Have any men warned you about life's land mines? Have they ever indicated that women might be one of those land mines?

   Now, women, from your point of view, answer the men's question. How do you feel society trains men? And men, answer the women's question on how you think society trains women. Discuss your answers with the class. Do you agree or disagree on the way that society trains women and men?

Examining Rhetorical Strategies

1. Identify the elements in this essay that make it conform to formal academic style. What effect does this style have on you as a reader?

2. Cite places in this essay where you feel Gilligan's background, biases, or experiences come through in spite of the objective, academic style.

A SUMMARY OF INFORMATIVE READING

As you can see from the range of samples in this chapter, informative writing is complex and varies considerably. However, all the pieces are united by a common *purpose: to share knowledge with others.* How the writers choose to do this depends on the level of *objectivity* and *expertise* they want to show.

We have seen, for example, that there are varying *levels of authority*, from Diane Cole's personal experience with prejudice to the researched data of Gilligan. Which kind of authority readers want depends on the kind of information they are looking for. If what they really want is personal assurance, all the specialists in the world will not prove satisfying. If on the other hand, they are tired of listening to anecdotes and want some straightforward facts about the matter, the specialists will be the place to go.

Along with a range of authority comes a *range of objectivity*. Some informative writing openly reflects the writer's biases and experiences while other kinds of informative writing such as scholarly articles try to keep the personal intrusion to a minimum.

How we, as readers, respond to these varying types largely depends on *our own level of expertise*. The scholarly articles in an unfamiliar field may not provide us with the kind of information we can really understand, and we may seek out the scholars who write in a more accessible manner. On the other hand, if we are reading in our own field, that level of scholarship may be just the kind of information we are looking for.

Finally, the success of informative writing depends not just on the *accuracy of the information* but also on the *quality* with which the writer communicates that information. In the personal kind of informative writing, this quality is shown in the way the writer uses experiences to illustrate the idea. When the writer is trying to make observations about the world, readers sense this quality in terms of what the writer has selected to focus on—its human significance—and how well the writer draws our attention to that slice of life presented. And in the scholarly piece we are drawn to the quality of the research, the competence of the analysis, and the professionalism of the presentation.

In other words, we sense the quality in informative writing by the care, consideration, and respect shown by the writer for both the topic and the reader.

Chapter Thirteen

WRITING INFORMATIVE DISCOURSE

"We're only in the city for two days. What should we do?" some new acquaintances ask, and while you know the city well, your mind is suddenly flooded with so many things to say, you are left speechless. You don't know where to start and realize that most of the things you could say are probably irrelevant. You need more information yourself before you can be helpful to them. You need to know, for example, what kinds of things they are interested in. It would not help to give them detailed instructions for getting to the baseball park, the best golf links, and the nearest tennis courts if they have absolutely no interest in sports. It would also not be necessary to provide a list of typical tourist attractions if they had lived in the city for years and were coming back for a visit; they want to know what's happening in the city those two days, not the usual haunts of high school field trips.

Before you offer to share your expertise with others, then, you first need to decide what to focus on and how much your audience already knows about the topic.

DETERMINING YOUR RELATIONSHIP TO YOUR READERS

When you are writing an informative paper, you will need to be clear about both your and your audience's placement on the authority scale. Is this an expert to expert paper or an expert to novice paper? If you are very knowledgeable about your topic and writing to other experts, there will be a good deal of basic information you will not need to include; you can assume your readers possess a large body of background knowledge and get right to your point. You will also be able to use all of the technical vocabulary associated with your topic without explaining those terms.

On the other hand, if you are an expert writing to a novice, then your relationship to your readers is really like that of a teacher. You will need to be patient and start at square one in your explanation as well as define terms and be sensitive to how much information they will be able to process about this new topic before going on overload.

SELECTING A FOCUS

At precisely the point when you know enough about a topic to speak about it with some authority, you will often find it difficult to speak about it at all. You know so much that it's hard to decide where to begin. There are so many aspects of each topic that could be covered, it's hard to separate basic information from the complexity of detail you have come to see as basic to your own understanding.

In order to write a good informative essay, then, you will need not only to *select a topic* but also to *narrow your topic* down to one *main point* or *thesis* so as not to be overwhelmed by all the information the paper could contain.

Selecting a Topic

The best way to select a topic for an informative piece is to make a list of your knowledge areas and your interest areas. *Knowledge areas* are subjects about which you know a good deal and can speak of with some authority. This authority often comes from your *experience*—a job, a hobby, traveling, a talent. All of the hours you have spent learning about this subject now provide you with a stockpile of information from which you can draw.

Interest areas are those subjects which you do not know much about but are interested in enough to be motivated to *research*. For example, while you may not have done much traveling, you may be very interested in visiting a particular country and want to find out as much as you can about it. Or a complicated political situation may intrigue you and you wish to put your reasoning powers to work trying to understand it.

The research you conduct may be *library work* in which you read about places, people, or events. If you were interested in nutrition you might be motivated to read more about the food pyramid, eating disorders, or diet fads, and this information can be gleaned from various forms of reading material.

On the other hand, research may consist of *original data collection* in which you create and analyze your own research. Again, if you were interested in nutrition, you might have noticed that students rarely eat the most nutritional foods being served in the college dining room but instead often select foods with high fat and sugar contents. To research this topic, you might position yourself within the dining hall and *observe* the food selection of a random sampling of students. You might also distribute *surveys* or conduct *interviews* asking students what they eat and why. This original research might lead to an observation essay on students' food choice, an explanation on how to eat well in the dining hall, or an analysis of motivational factors influencing eating patterns.

Narrowing Your Topic

If you choose a topic from one of your knowledge areas, a technique that can help you narrow your topic is to temporarily block out a good deal of what you know and to think only about one small part of the subject. Then you can *focus* on covering this one part well and leave the rest for another paper. For example, one student, who had skied all his life and was now an instructor, was trying to write a paper about skiing. He was completely blocked because, as he rightly noted, he could write a book on the subject to add to the many skiing books he already had on his shelves. So, while he had plenty of information at his disposal, he felt that he could never fit it all into one paper and that even if he could, it had all been said before.

The solution came during a conference with his teacher when he began to talk about his specific job as a ski instructor of children, particularly stories about a reluctant child who refused to listen to his instructions. He told how he turned the child's interest in food into lesson plans—making wedges big pieces of chocolate cake and his poles into candy canes that he was sticking into the icing on gingerbread houses. The paper then evolved into a guide for new ski instructors about clever ways to handle incorrigible children who had been dumped on the instructors for lessons while their parents were off skiing the slopes. By taking this approach, the student was able to focus just on the information he had about this one small aspect of skiing.

If your knowledge of the topic does not come from personal experience but from library research, you will need to read as much on your topic as time allows and then formulate a *thesis statement* about the topic that can be supported by the reading. To do this, consider what one *research question* or concern you had before you started reading that has been answered by the research you did, and use your paper to explain your newfound understanding to others. If the ski instructor above had not only wanted to give helpful suggestions but also to explain why his ideas worked, he might have done some research into child psychology and explained his methods as well as the reasons for their success.

MAKING IT SIGNIFICANT FOR YOUR AUDIENCE

In addition to selecting and narrowing your topic, you will also need to answer the question: *Who cares about this information?* Deciding on an audience is crucial for knowing what kind of information you need to include. In fact, *selecting an audience often goes hand in hand with narrowing your topic.* For example, once that ski instructor had narrowed his topic to handling incorrigible children, it was easy for him to identify his *audience*—new ski instructors who would soon face this type of child and need to know what to do. Immediately, all his knowledge about clothing, equipment, techniques for skiing in different ways on different slopes, ski areas, and even a good deal of his knowledge about ski instruction that wasn't related to children could be set aside. His audience would know about those things already. Instead, he could focus on this one area in which they needed and were looking for information.

In the same way, computer manuals aimed at the new PC owner are very different from the technical articles written for programmers. And this book, written for students of writing, is very different from the articles we write for scholarly journals in rhetorical theory.

ORGANIZING YOUR THOUGHTS

Even after completing the process of narrowing your topic and selecting your audience, you still need to decide how to *organize* your information. Since you are trying to write an informative paper, your strategy for organizing needs to highlight the information in the way in which it will be most helpful for your audience to receive it. In determining your organization, try following a step-by-step process:

Step One: Write your main point or research question at the top of the page.

Step Two: List all the major discoveries you have made about your topic either through your reading or experience.

Step Three: Look for items on your list that are related to each other in some way and therefore should be covered together in the paper. The ways in which these topics relate may vary:

They may be *similar* or related ideas that need to be compared;

They may be *different* or contradictory ideas that need to be contrasted;

They may be *steps* in a process that must be completed in a specific order; or

They may be the *reasons* why certain things have occurred, the *causes* of certain events.

Step Four: Reconstruct your list so that it reflects the logical order in which your ideas need to be covered. This final step then becomes your guide for writing your first draft.

There may be times when it is not possible or desirable to narrow your topic very much. For example, if those imaginary visiting friends are really not at all sure what they want to see during their two days in the city, but instead want a bunch of options and have a wide variety of interests, then you are left with giving them an *overview* of the whole place. In that case, it is wise to think of your topic in terms of *categories of information*. You might, for example, divide the city up into its main geographical areas and then talk about the sightseeing or special events in each area.

Dividing your subject into *subtopics* and even using *subheadings*, as this book does, can be very helpful in organizing your information and very helpful for readers in first getting an overview of the topic and then finding the specific information that interests them.

Notes on the Explanation Essay

You can help yourself organize your explanation essay if you keep asking yourself: What am I trying to explain and to whom? If you are explaining a *procedure or process* to beginners, you need to imagine what that process was like for you the first time you did it. Try to put yourself in the shoes of those who are clueless about how to do this activity and carefully guide them through it. Listing the steps of the procedure and then asking someone who has never done it to follow them is the best way to insure accuracy.

If your readers are not beginners, you will need to decide what specific piece of expert knowledge you want to share with them (as the ski instructor did) and again remember how it was to learn it the first time yourself.

If you are explaining a variety of ways in which to do something, giving advice on options, you need to make a *priority list.* What suggestions are most effective or most important? These should be discussed first and in the greatest detail. Others may come later and may even take a different form such as a list.

Notes on the Observation Essay

Gathering and organizing data for an observation essay demands a combination of knowing what you are looking for and being open to whatever you may discover. In other words, you need to be both certain and uncertain about your work. On the one hand, observation essays demand that you position yourself somewhere and carefully observe what goes on around you, but this observation process must have a *purpose.* You should have selected this place deliberately because you expect to be able to learn something specific about what happens here; you need to know what you're looking for.

On the other hand, you also need to observe with an open mind trying to *discover* what you can learn here. While you need to be certain about what activity you have come to watch, you need to be open about what you will learn from observing it.

For example, the nutrition researcher who suspects that students do not eat well might go to the dining hall specifically to observe the trays of students as they leave the serving line, looking for foods with high fat or sugar content. However, the observer must be open to discovering that students, in fact, are nutrition conscious and to finding that each tray is loaded with vegetables. In other words, you must come to your activity as a *seeker* not with your answers already determined. The point is not to confirm the suspicion that students eat bad food but to *answer the research question of whether that is true*.

The same blend of certainty and openmindedness is needed if your observations are of a person or a place rather than an activity. You will have chosen this person or place for some specific reason— the person is a fascinating celebrity in your town or the place has historical significance. But you will still need to determine during the process of observing what specific *angle* you will want to take on this subject. You will, therefore, need to gather enough data to formulate an *overall impression*—what makes the celebrity fascinating or why this historical place survived when other buildings of its time were destroyed—that you want to communicate to others. You can then organize your observations so that they support this impression.

Notes on the Analysis Essay

The general organizational pattern for the analysis essay is: (1) an explanation of the thesis or research question; (2) an explanation of the reading or original research that was done; (3) an analysis of the research; and (4) conclusions about what the research means. In the Gilligan essay in the previous chapter, for example, we saw how she established the research question of the relation of achievement and affiliation to students' interpretations of pictures. She then went on to describe what she did, what the results were, and her interpretation of the findings.

THE WRITING PROCESS AT WORK

In the section below we will watch a student as he works his way through these decisions of selecting a *relationship to his readers*, a *focus*, an *audience*, and a way to *organize* his explanation essay.

RESIDENT ASSISTANT: A COMPREHENSIVE JOB DESCRIPTION

Scott E. Bergeron

Background

Bergeron had been a Resident Assistant in his dorm for a year and was now in the process of interviewing prospective R.A.'s for the next year. In conducting these interviews and answering questions about what the job entailed, he began to realize what a huge responsibility the job was and how much time it took. He decided to tap into this *knowledge area* and try to put in writing all that he did and therefore all that his successors would have to do.

Prewriting

Step One for Bergeron was articulating his main point which was to answer the question: What are all the duties and responsibilities of an R.A.?

In Step Two, Bergeron made a list of all the things he had to do as part of his job:

Room inspection
Floor meetings
Hall maintenance (MRO's)
Discipline
Night duty
Programming
In-hall responsibilities
Committees
R.A. interviews
Social and information sessions
Uphold college policies
Educational resource
Counselor
Role model
One-on-one meetings
Staff meetings
Dealing with crises

In-services
Arranging lectures
Maintaining a 2.25 gpa
Learning about room draw
Judicial hearings
Fall training
Spring training
Bulletin boards
Name tags
Confrontations

Step Three, then, meant examining this rather cumbersome list and reorganizing it into related categories; he came up with seven areas he wanted to talk about:

Training
Major general responsibilities
In-hall responsibilities
Programming
Night duty
Discipline
Meetings

These categories made the task seem more manageable, but as Bergeron tried to turn his list into prose he found that he still didn't have a clear purpose or audience and so wasn't sure how to explain this information in a helpful way.

First Draft

Many people each year apply to become Resident 1
Assistants without having significant knowledge as to what the job entails. Many people would be discouraged from applying had these individuals been properly informed.

Responsibilities for those selected to become R.A.'s 2
begin two full weeks before students arrive for the fall semester. It is during this training period that new R.A.'s get a hint of what they're in for. Training begins each day at 8:30 a.m. and on average ends at about eleven o'clock at night. During those two weeks just a brief discussion of future responsibilities takes place. There are constant programs presented every day with an hour break for lunch and dinner.

First there are very basic principles that R.A.'s must use 3
as guidelines. This means upholding all college policies
whether agreeing or not with those policies. R.A.'s are
expected to be resources both emotionally and educational-
ly. Thus these individuals typically act as counselors for the
thirty to ninety-three residents under their supervision.

The next level that R.A. responsibilities are most appar- 4
ent are at the in-hall level. Each R.A. is responsible for a total
of eight programs a semester. Four need to be educational,
three need to be social and one needs to be recreational. The
educational programs must follow the specific focus area designated by the R.A.'s director. The R.A. must also have a floor
meeting once a month and a room inspection as well. Each
R.A. is also responsible for bulletin boards on his or her floor
or area as well as nametags on every student's door at the
beginning of the semester. Furthermore, this person is
responsible for the paperwork necessary to file maintenance
problems that residents might have.

Duty nights are another major responsibility for R.A.'s. 5
These are basically office hours from 7:00 p.m. to 11:00 p.m.
Sunday–Wednesday, Thursday is 7:00–12:00 and Saturday
and Sunday until 1:00 a.m. Confrontation plays a major part
in these responsibilities. Approaching people violating college policy is probably one of the toughest jobs an R.A. has.
Incident reports need to be filed and attendance at a disciplinary hearing from R.A.'s may be required. Many times
the Duty R.A. will need to confront crises. This may include
anything from a false fire alarm to a possible sexual assault
victim.

When not on duty, these people are expected to serve 6
on a variety of committees and attend numerous lectures.
These things are made mandatory. In order to keep
informed of these things and to be completely informed,
attendance at weekly staff meetings which last anywhere
from two to three hours is required. Also a one-on-one meeting with the area director is held weekly or bi-weekly for an
hour.

This isn't to mention the expectation placed on present 7
R.A.'s to participate in the Room Draw process as well as the
R.A. selection process by holding group and individual inter-
views and attending information and social sessions. Above

all this, an R.A. is expected to maintain a cumulative gpa of
2.25 or higher.
Now what does a would be applicant think?   8

Writer's comments   I'm trying to inform R.A. applicants what
responsibilities these individuals might have if they are selected for
the job. I don't expect them to have too much understanding
except for what they have seen in their own R.A.'s. I picked this
topic because I wished I had had more of this information before
I took the job so that I could have had a clue as to what I was getting myself into. I want this to be a comprehensive job description
including all the things that are expected of R.A.'s.

Teacher's comments   This is a good topic for you because you
know exactly what this job entails. But you need to think more
about who needs this information. In your comment you identify
an audience, but that reader is not coming through clearly yet.
Can you speak directly to someone who has just applied for the
position or who is considering applying? How would they get this
information? You also have lots of duties here. Can you make this
easier to read and follow? It also seems pretty general. Is that OK
or can you give some examples?

Peer's comments   The current perspective of the paper seems
to be trying to *discourage* people from applying. Are you trying to?
If not, then get rid of all of the things that sound like warnings. If
you want to just be informative, write it in categories, explaining
when necessary. Hard part—intro paragraph—make sure not to
get across any kind of negative opinion.

Analysis

Bergeron's comments clearly indicate his purpose: to inform
R.A. applicants about the job. This statement also gives him a clear
audience, as his teacher points out: applicants who don't know
very much about the job except what they've gleaned from watching their own R.A.'s. He has also indicated that he does not want
to focus on one aspect of the job but to give a comprehensive
overview.

While all this is clear to Bergeron, it is not all coming
through clearly in his draft. First, although he knows his *audience*,
he does not address them. The applicants are referred to as "many

people," "these individuals," and finally "a would be applicant" rather than the person who has already applied. In other words, he has a defined group to whom he is speaking—a list of applicants— but he does not have them clearly in mind as he writes.

Second, his *purpose* of informing, as his peer commenter indicated, is not clear. It seems as if he is not informing but discouraging applicants from wanting this job. He emphasizes the hardships of the position and his last question to them is almost a sarcastic challenge.

Finally, the piece is hard to read in the sense that we are given a lot of information to sort through but very little guidance in doing that. Bergeron's *organization* needs to be stronger. If you look at Bergeron's brainstorming list of categories, you will see that he has turned the list into paragraph form. So, after his introduction, "training" becomes paragraph 2, "major general responsibilities" becomes paragraph 3, and so on. But without that list to follow and those categories identified, the information seems haphazard.

Bergeron tried various ways to work through these problems. In a second draft, he tried a different approach. Here is how he started:

First Paragraph, Draft Two

If you are interested in becoming an R.A., here is some information that you might want to know about but which no one told you. The responsibilities of an R.A. tend to be overwhelming but here they are broken into distinct categories with a brief explanation and some examples.

Training: Training takes on many different forms . . . .

While this is not a very compelling opening and his discouraging attitude is still showing, Bergeron has actually solved two problems: (1) He has addressed his audience directly, and (2) he has used *subheadings* to solve the difficulty readers would have following all his information. In draft three, he went a step further.

First Paragraph, Draft Three

If you are interested in applying to become a Resident Assistant, it is in your best interest to gain some information as to what is expected from the people who hold this job. The list can get to be overwhelming and somewhat confusing so a breakdown of responsibilities into categories is provided below. With each responsibility there is a brief description and an example where appropriate. . . .

In this draft, Bergeron is trying to tone down the negative voice. He says knowing this information is in the "best interest" of the applicants rather than saying that these are things no one else will tell them. He also is trying to sound encouraging in saying that the duties can be confusing so he is here to help with his categories.

While these were all steps in the right direction, Bergeron realized at this stage that there was something else interfering with his writing this paper—his decision about *audience*. He really wanted to explain the duties of the job, but he was trying to explain them to people who weren't really committed to the job yet and who really didn't need all this information just to decide whether to apply. He realized that the level of information he wanted to give his audience was much more appropriate for someone whose application had been accepted and who now *needed* to know the specific duties involved.

He also realized that writing to readers who were already "on board" would help him eliminate his negative, warning tone; as long as he was dealing with people who had not made up their minds yet, he kept falling into persuasion because he felt obliged to help them make their decision. By selecting an audience already committed, he could now assume a welcoming attitude and treat this exactly as he had wanted to all along—as a straight informative piece written to someone who needed his expert knowledge.

With this new audience and with his relation to them clear, with a focus on welcoming people to a new job and explaining their duties, and with his subheadings and categories to help him with organization, Bergeron tried again.

Final Draft

March 22, 1993

TO: Judy Smith
FROM: Scott Bergeron, Residential Life Staff
RE: Comprehensive job description for R.A. position

Welcome to the Residential Life Staff. Your participa-   1
tion in the application process has proven that you have a
reasonable understanding of what an R.A. does. But to fur-

ther your understanding we are providing this list and brief description of our expectations and your duties.

Training: There are many areas of training for R.A.'s. 2 Fall training is by far the longest and most intense. It takes place for two weeks before the start of the semester so you will need to plan to get here two weeks early. Beginning at 8:30 a.m. each day (including both weekend days), a series of programs, lectures and activities is presented. These sessions continue until 11:00 p.m.

Another training period of this format occurs for two 3 days before the start of the spring semester. New R.A.'s must also take an R.A. class once a week for an hour, which lasts four to eight weeks. All R.A.'s are required to attend three in-services per semester which are hour long educational programs presented by Residence Directors. An additional four hours of training for the room draw process is also required.

Meetings: Each week you must attend area staff meet- 4 ings. These meetings are to develop staff relationships as well as to increase communication among R.A.'s. They also keep you updated and on track.

An hour long, one-on-one meeting will be held 5 between you and your Residence Director usually once every two weeks. This meeting provides the R.D. with a chance to discuss in private problems or concerns you have with the position or your personal life.

General Responsibilities: R.A.'s are responsible for being 6 role models, counselors, and resource aids. As a role model, you will be expected to observe all college policies and uphold them personally. You should exemplify a model student.

You will also often act as a counselor as residents many 7 times will approach you with personal problems. For instance, the student whose grandparent dies or the student who has just ended a long term relationship may need someone to talk to and the R.A. is expected to be that person if needed.

As a resource aide, you are expected to be knowledge- 8 able about organizations and services on campus. If a student has a particular question about academic help or is bored and looking for something to do, you should be able to refer that student to the appropriate place or social organization.

Programming: You will be responsible for planning and 9 promoting four social and four educational programs a

semester. Social programs provide an opportunity for interaction among residents and help to develop community. One
of these "socials" must be recreational which means it must
require some form of physical activity. A dance or hiking
would count as a social recreational program.

The four educational programs must fall under a spe-   10
cific focus area designated by the Residence Director. The six
focus areas are spiritual, cultural, political, emotional, sexual, and life planning. A workshop or presentation dealing
with self-esteem, for instance, would be an example of an
emotional educational program.

Duty Nights and Discipline: Several times a month you   11
must be "on duty" which means you must be in the designated R.A. office with a security radio. Hourly rounds must be
made followed by recording an account of the round in a log
book. Duty begins at 7:00 p.m. and ends at 11:00 p.m. Sunday
through Wednesday, 12:00 a.m. on Thursday and 1:00 a.m.
on the weekend. The R.A.'s on duty on Friday and Saturday
are still "on duty" until 7:00 p.m. the next day. You do not
need to be in the office but must be in the building at all
times.

While on rounds, you are responsible for confronting   12
individuals breaking college rules. This could include a wide
array of incidents such as a failure to observe quiet hours, hall
sports, or party situations. You will need to file the necessary
incident reports, and individuals involved must report to the
Residence Director within two days. Incident reports are
detailed accounts of the entire incident as observed by the
R.A. If the incident was a second offense the issue may be
brought to a judicial hearing, at which time the R.A. who filed
the report must be present. Hearings can last anywhere from
fifteen minutes to seven hours depending on the incident.

In-Hall Responsibilities: Name tags for all residents' doors   13
must be made and put up before the beginning of school.
You must keep bulletin boards up-to-date on your floor.
MRO's or Maintenance Request Orders are to be filed by you
for your residents. Floor meetings are to be held monthly as
well as safety inspections of rooms. There are also tasks designated for each R.A. by the area director such as common
area bulletin boards, the monthly newsletter, staff development, or payroll.

Miscellaneous Expectations: You are expected to attend 14
many different lectures on campus relevant to residential
life. You are also expected to participate in banquets for residential life staff, as well as interviews for the R.A. selection
process. Finally, you are required to maintain a cumulative
G.P.A. of at least a 2.25.

This information will all be discussed again in more 15
depth during that fall training session in August. If you have
any questions or concerns, we will be able to address them
fully at that time. It does seem like a lot for the financial
stipend that you will receive, but the leadership experience is
more than you could attain almost anywhere else at this point
in your career. We look forward to seeing you, and once
again, Judy, welcome to the Residential Life Staff.

Analysis

Bergeron has done a good job of clearing up the problems he had in his earlier drafts. He now has a *focus:* he is running down the basic job description including all the major
duties Judy will have when she joins the staff. He has also
cleared up his *audience* problem by writing a form memo to be
sent to all new R.A.'s who are in a position to need this information. While they may still find it overwhelming, he is able to
be encouraging, assuring them of the benefits of the job and
that all the questions spurred on by this memo will be
answered at the training sessions. Also, while the duties may
still sound harsh, new R.A.'s need to know them; this is no time
for sugarcoating the responsibilities because these are now
their responsibilities.

In terms of *organization,* Bergeron stuck with his original
idea of wanting to give an overview instead of focusing on one
duty. He, thus, uses subheads to guide our reading and processing
of all this information. While many of these categories remain the
same as in his original brainstorming list, they are now organized
to focus on (1) the different kinds of training, both one-time and
on going, (2) responsibilities from general to specific, and (3)
miscellaneous expectations. While this organization does not hide
the time commitment R.A.'s are making, it does emphasize, by
putting training and meetings first, that help in the form of information sessions, social meetings, and one-on-one support will be
there all year long.

Exercise

Bergeron's first paragraph went through many revisions as he struggled to make the piece informative. Assume he decided to change his purpose to persuasive and to make the audience prospective R.A.'s. Rewrite his first paragraph for this audience to warn them about how difficult the job is. You may decide to actually discourage people from applying, or you may want to be realistic about the amount of work involved but try to convince them it's worth it.

WRITING FOR READERS

By his last draft, Bergeron was thinking about his reader as he wrote, recognizing Judy Smith's need for an overview of the job, some reassurance that it can be done and that she will get support, and some guidance in working her way through all of this information. He no longer seems overwhelmed by how much he needs to tell his audience and therefore does not overwhelm the reader with the information.

STRATEGIES FOR WRITING INFORMATIVE DISCOURSE

The assignment Review the *purpose* of the assignment. Remember that informative writing focuses on communicating about the subject, not on your personal feelings or opinions about it. Make sure you can speak about this subject without feeling the need to editorialize too much.

Prewriting Review both your *knowledge areas* and your *interest areas* to find a good topic. Once you have selected a good topic, follow the steps discussed in this chapter:

Step One: Write down your main point or research question.
Step Two: List all the main ideas you want to cover about this topic that you have learned from experience, from data collection, or from library research.

Step Three: Categorize your list looking for commonalities, contrasts, or other logical connections.

Step Four: Reconstruct your list and let it guide your draft.

Drafting While you are writing, keep the following four goals discussed in this chapter in mind:

1. Determine your relationship to your readers. Consider how much of an expert you are and they are. Are you writing to equals who do not need background or terms defined or to people who are beginners and need extra guidance from you?
2. Select the focus of your subject so that all of your information is manageable.
3. Select your audience and remember that narrowing your topic will often be easier if you decide on an audience.
4. Organize your thoughts according to the kind of paper you are writing.

For the explanation essay, record the procedure or process you are describing either in the order the steps need to be completed or according to your priorities with the most important aspect of the process being given the most attention.

For the observation essay, record the overall impression you have gathered from your observations and then use your specific findings for support.

For the critical analysis, explain your thesis, your research, your analysis of the research, and your conclusions about its significance.

Editing As you edit pay particular attention to the following aspects of informative writing:

An authoritative voice that demonstrates your firm grasp of the subject.

A clear thesis statement, adequately supported by your experience, observations, or research.

A logical organizational pattern that corresponds to the kind of paper you are writing.

A clear sense of audience, of who cares about this information.

Chapter Fourteen

FURTHER INFORMATIVE READINGS

The readings contained in this chapter illustrate a wide range of authority levels, from personal knowledge sharing in the student essay, "Diabetes: What They Might Not Have Told You" to the scholarly voice of the professional essay "To the Other Side of Silence" from the book *Women's Ways of Knowing: The Development of Self, Voice, and Mind.*

PROFESSIONAL ESSAYS AND READING TECHNIQUES

THE PSYCHOPHARMACOLOGY OF CHOCOLATE

Diane Ackerman

Prereading Journal

Cravings, especially for certain foods, seem to strike all of us at some time. Perhaps the craving developed from being deprived of a certain food in childhood. Or perhaps it gives you a tremendous sense of happiness and well-being. Write about a time when you had to satisfy a food craving.

Background

Ackerman's field of study is English and she has received awards for her poetry. But her most famous work is as a researcher of the natural world. In *The Natural History of the Senses* Ackerman devotes one section of the book to each of the five senses, recording interesting facts about each of them. The essay below comes from the section on "Taste." In this essay Ackerman *explains* where that good feeling we often get when we eat chocolate may come from.

During Reading

Keep a list of all the possible reasons why people crave chocolate. Which of these do you find true for yourself?

Reading Selection

What food do you crave? Ask the question with enough 1 smoldering emphasis on the last word, and the answer is bound to be chocolate. It was first used by the Indians of Central and South America. The Aztecs called it *xocoatl* ("chocolate"), declared it a gift from their white-bearded god of wisdom and knowledge, Quetzalcoatl, and served it as a drink to members of the court—only rulers and soldiers could be trusted with the power it conveyed. The Toltecs honored the divine drink by staging rituals in which they sacrificed chocolate-colored dogs. Itzá human-sacrifice victims were sometimes given a mug of chocolate to sanctify their journey. What Hernán Cortés found surrounding Montezuma was a society of chocolate worshipers who liked to perk up their drink with chili peppers, pimiento, vanilla beans, or spices, and serve it frothing and honey-thick in gold cups. To cure dysentery, they added the ground-up bones of their ancestors. Montezuma's court drank two thousand pitchers of chocolate each day, and he himself enjoyed a chocolate ice made by pouring the drink over snow brought to him by runners from the mountains. Impressed by the opulence and restorative powers of chocolate, Cortés introduced it to Spain in the sixteenth century. It hit the consciousness of Europe like a drug cult. Charles V decided to mix it with sugar, and those who could afford it drank it thick and cold; they, too, occasionally added orange, vanilla, or various spices. Brillat-Savarin reports that "The Spanish ladies of the New World are madly addicted to chocolate, to such a point that, not content to drink it several times each day, they even have it served to them in church." Today, chocolate-zombies haunt the streets of every city, dreaming all day of that small plunge of chocolate waiting for them on the way home from work. In Vienna, the richest chocolate cakes are decorated with edible gold leaf. More than once, I've been seriously tempted to fly to Paris for the afternoon, just to go to Angelina, a restaurant on the rue de Rivoli where they melt a whole chocolate bar into each cup of hot chocolate. How many candy bars *don't* contain chocolate? Chocolate, which began as an upper-class drink, has become déclassé, trendy, cloaked in a tackiness it doesn't deserve. For example, an ad in *Chocolatier Magazine* offers a one-quarter-pound chocolate "replica of a 5 ¼-inch floppy disk." In fact, the company can provide an entire "computer work-station comprised of a chocolate terminal, chocolate computer keyboard, chocolate chip and chocolate byte." Their slogan is "Boots up into your mouth, not in your disk drive." One September weekend in 1984, the Fontainebleau Hotel in Miami offered a Chocolate Festival Weekend, with special rates, menus, and events. People could fingerpaint in chocolate syrup, attend lectures on chocolate, sample chocolates from an array of companies, learn cooking techniques, or watch a TV actor be dunked in six hundred gallons of chocolate syrup. Five thousand people attended. Chocolate festivals rage in cities all across America, and there are highly

popular chocolate tours of Europe. In Manhattan last month
I heard one woman, borrowing the jargon of junkies, say to
another, "Want to do some chocolate?"

Because chocolate is such an emotional food, one we eat   2
when we're blue, jilted, premenstrual, or generally in need of
TLC, scientists have been studying its chemistry. In 1982, two
psychopharmacologists, Dr. Michael Liebowitz and Dr.
Donald Klein, proposed an explanation for why lovesick people pig out on chocolate. In the course of their work with
intense, thrill-seeking women who go into post-thrill depres-
sions, they discovered that they all had something remarkable
in common—in their depressed phase, virtually all of them
ate large amounts of chocolate. They speculated that the phenomenon might well be related to the brain chemical
phenylethylamine (PEA), which makes us feel the roller
coaster of passion we associate with falling in love, an amphet-
aminelike rush. But when the rush of love ends, and the brain
stops producing PEA, we continue to crave its natural high, its
emotional speed. Where can one find lots of this luscious,
love-arousing PEA? In chocolate. So it's possible that some
people eat chocolate because it reproduces the sense of well-
being we enjoy when we're in love. A sly beau once arrived at
my apartment with three Droste chocolate apples, and every
wedge I ate over the next two weeks, melting lusciously in my
mouth, filled me with amorous thoughts of him.

Not everyone agrees with the PEA hypothesis. The   3
Chocolate Manufacturer's Association argues that:

> the PEA content of chocolate is extremely small, especially in
> comparison with that of some other commonly consumed
> foods. The standard serving size of three and a half ounces of
> smoked salami contains 6.7 mg of phenylethylamine; the
> same size serving of cheddar cheese contains 5.8 mg of
> phenylethylamine. The standard 1.5-ounce serving of choco-
> late (the size of the average chocolate bar) contains much less
> than 1 mg (.21 mg). Obviously, if Dr. Liebowitz's theory were
> true, people would be eating salami and cheese in far greater
> amounts than they are today.

And Dr. Liebowitz himself, in *The Chemistry of Love*, later
asked of chocolate craving:

> Could this be an attempt to raise their PEA levels? The prob-
> lem is that PEA present in food is normally quickly broken

down by our bodies, so that it doesn't even reach the blood, let alone the brain. To test the effect of ingesting PEA, researchers at the National Institute of Mental Health ate pounds of chocolate, and then measured the PEA levels in their urine for the next few days; the PEA levels didn't budge.

As a thoroughgoing chocoholic, I should say that I do 4 indeed eat a lot of cheese. Smoked salami is too unhealthy for me even to consider; the Cancer Society has suggested that people should not eat foods that are smoked or contain nitrites. So, it's entirely possible that cheese fills some of my PEA need. What else do chocoholics eat? In other words, what is the total consumption of PEA from all sources? Chocolate may be a more appealing, even if smaller, source of PEA because of its other associations with luxury and reward. The NIMH study tested average people, but suppose people who crave chocolate aren't average? Isn't that the idea? Liebowitz now says that PEA may break down too fast to affect the brain. We still know very little about the arcane ways in which some drugs do this, not enough to completely dismiss chocolate's link with PEA.

Wurtman and others argue that we crave chocolate 5 because it's a carbohydrate, which, like other carbohydrates, prompts the pancreas to make insulin, which ultimately leads to an increase in that neurotransmitter of calm, serotonin. If this were true, a plate of pasta, or potatoes, or bread would be equally satisfying. Chocolate also contains theobromine ("food of the gods"), a mild, caffeinelike substance, so, for the sake of argument, let's say it's just the serotonin and the relative of caffeine we crave, a calm stimulation, a culinary oxymoron few foods provide.* It might even explain why some women crave chocolate when they're due to menstruate, since women who suffer PMS have been found to have lower levels of serotonin, and premenstrual women in general eat 30 percent more carbohydrates than they do at other times of the month. But if it were as simple as that, a doughnut and a cup of coffee would do the trick. Furthermore,

---

*In a one-and-a-half-ounce milk-chocolate bar, there are about nine milligrams of caffeine (which the plant may use as an insecticide); a five-ounce cup of brewed coffee has about 115 milligrams; a twelve-ounce cola drink between thirty-two and sixty-five.

there's a world of difference between people who enjoy chocolate, women who crave chocolate only at certain times of the month, and serious chocoholics. Chocoholics don't crave potato chips and pasta; they crave chocolate. Substitutes in any combination won't do. Only the chocoholic in a household fresh out of chocolate, on a snowy night when the roads are impassable, knows how specific that craving can be. I'm not sure why some people crave chocolate, but I am convinced that it's a specific need, and therefore the key to solving a specific chemical mystery to which we'll one day find the solution.

The Four Seasons restaurant in Manhattan serves a 6 chocolate bombe that's the explosive epitome of chocolate desserts, two slices of which (the standard serving) few people are able to finish because it's so piquantly rich. On the waterfront in St. Louis I once had a mousse called "Chocolate Suicide," which was drug-level chocolate. I felt as if my brain had been hung up in a smokehouse. I can still remember the first time I had Godiva chocolates at a friend's house; they were Godivas from the original factory in Brussels, with a perfect sheen, a twirling aroma, heady but not jarring, and a way of delicately melting on the tongue. One of the reasons why chocolates are superb in Belgium, Vienna, Paris, and some of our American cities is that chocolate candy is in considerable part a dairy product. The chocolate flavor may come from the plant, but the silken, melting delight comes from the milk, cream, and butter, which must be fresh. The people who create designer chocolates have learned that their confections must provide just the right melting sensation, and feel quintessentially creamy and luscious, with no grittiness or aftertaste, for people to be thoroughly wowed by them. In George Orwell's *1984*, sex is forbidden and chocolate is "dull-brown crumbly stuff that tasted . . . like the smoke of a rubbish fire." Just before Julia and Winston risk making love, they eat real, full-bodied "dark and shiny" chocolate. Their amorous feast had its precedents. Montezuma drank an extra cup of chocolate before he went to visit his women's quarters. Glamorous movie stars like Jean Harlow used to be shown eating boxes of chocolates. M. F. K. Fisher, the diva of gastronomy, once confided that her mother's doctor prescribed chocolate as a cure for debilitating lovesickness. On the other hand, Aztec women were forbidden chocolate; what secret terror was it thought to unleash in them?

Further Readings

Brillat-Savarin, Anthelme, trans. and annotated by H. F. R. Fisher. *The Physiology of Taste.* San Francisco, California: North Point Press, 1986.
Liebowitz, Michael. *The Chemistry of Love.* New York: Berkeley Books, 1984.

Checking Your Understanding

1. The scientific theories Ackerman cites on PEA, serotonin, and theobromine all fall short of explaining why people crave chocolate. Explain what these scientific theories seem to miss. What is your personal theory on why a plate of pasta won't do as a substitute for a Hershey bar?

2. From the point of view of a chocoholic, describe what would happen if you found yourself "in a household fresh out of chocolate, on a snowy night when the roads are impassable."

Examining Rhetorical Strategies

1. Ackerman begins her essay on chocolate with a question. In what ways does this single question serve as an effective introduction? How does it draw you into the piece and spark your interest?

2. Ackerman also ends this essay with a question. Does it serve as an effective conclusion? Does it also spark further interest in the subject?

3. The first part of the essay explains the history of chocolate. Why do you think Ackerman included this information? How does it add to her credibility as a writer? How does it add to the legitimacy of your chocolate addiction?

ON SOCIETY AS ORGANISMS

Lewis Thomas

Prereading Journal

In what ways do you feel connected, attached, in tune with the people around you? Has there ever been a group you belonged to—a sports team, a family unit, a group of friends, a club—in which the members became so close that at some moments they could think and act almost as one? Describe a time when you felt connected to someone else, a real sense of community with at least one other person.

Background

Thomas was a distinguished physician, researcher, teacher, and administrator. Yet in the midst of his other responsibilities, he also found time to write a monthly column for the *New England Journal of Medicine*. Twenty-nine of these essays ranging from Thomas' analysis of organelles to his observations on language were collected into the book *The Lives of a Cell* from which this essay is taken. Thomas called his column "Notes of a Biology-Watcher" and in this essay, Thomas shows both his power of *observation* and his knowledge of biology.

During Reading

While you read, note the kinds of information other organisms are able to communicate with one another.

Reading Selection

Viewed from a suitable height, the aggregating clusters 1 of medical scientists in the bright sunlight of the boardwalk at Atlantic City, swarmed there from everywhere for the annual meetings, have the look of assemblages of social insects. There is the same vibrating, ionic movement, interrupted by the darting back and forth of jerky individuals to touch antennae and exchange small bits of information; periodically, the mass casts out, like a trout-line, a long single file unerringly toward Childs's. If the boards were not fastened down, it would not be a surprise to see them put together a nest of sorts.

It is permissible to say this sort of thing about humans. 2
They do resemble, in their most compulsively social behavior,
ants at a distance. It is, however, quite bad form in biological
circles to put it the other way round, to imply that the operation of insect societies has any relation at all to human
affairs. The writers of books on insect behavior generally take
pains, in their prefaces, to caution that insects are like creatures from another planet, that their behavior is absolutely
foreign, totally unhuman, unearthly, almost unbiological.
They are more like perfectly tooled but crazy little machines,
and we violate science when we try to read human meanings
in their arrangements.

It is hard for a bystander not to do so. Ants are so much 3
like human beings as to be an embarrassment. They farm
fungi, raise aphids as livestock, launch armies into wars, use
chemical sprays to alarm and confuse enemies, capture
slaves. The families of weaver ants engage in child labor,
holding their larvae like shuttles to spin out the thread that
sews the leaves together for their fungus gardens. They
exchange information ceaselessly. They do everything but
watch television.

What makes us most uncomfortable is that they, and the 4
bees and termites and social wasps, seem to live two kinds of
lives: they are individuals, going about the day's business
without much evidence of thought for tomorrow, and they
are at the same time component parts, cellular elements, in
the huge, writhing, ruminating organism of the Hill, the
nest, the hive. It is because of this aspect, I think, that we
most wish for them to be something foreign. We do not like
the notion that there can be collective societies with the
capacity to behave like organisms. If such things exist, they
can have nothing to do with us.

Still, there it is. A solitary ant, afield, cannot be consid- 5
ered to have much of anything on his mind; indeed, with
only a few neurons strung together by fibers, he can't be
imagined to have a mind at all, much less a thought. He is
more like a ganglion on legs. Four ants together, or ten,
encircling a dead moth on a path, begin to look more like an
idea. They fumble and shove, gradually moving the food
toward the Hill, but as though by blind chance. It is only
when you watch the dense mass of thousands of ants, crowd-

ed together around the Hill, blackening the ground, that you begin to see the whole beast, and now you observe it thinking, planning, calculating. It is an intelligence, a kind of live computer, with crawling bits for its wits.

At a stage in the construction, twigs of a certain size are 6 needed, and all the members forage obsessively for twigs of just this size. Later, when outer walls are to be finished, thatched, the size must change, and as though given new orders by telephone, all the workers shift the search to the new twigs. If you disturb the arrangement of a part of the Hill, hundreds of ants will set it vibrating, shifting, until it is put right again. Distant sources of food are somehow sensed, and long lines, like tentacles, reach out over the ground, up over walls, behind boulders, to fetch it in.

Termites are even more extraordinary in the way they 7 seem to accumulate intelligence as they gather together. Two or three termites in a chamber will begin to pick up pellets and move them from place to place, but nothing comes of it; nothing is built. As more join in, they seem to reach a critical mass, a quorum, and the thinking begins. They place pellets atop pellets, then throw up columns and beautiful, curving, symmetrical arches, and the crystalline architecture of vaulted chambers is created. It is not known how they communicate with each other, how the chains of termites building one column know when to turn toward the crew on the adjacent column, or how, when the time comes, they manage the flawless joining of the arches. The stimuli that set them off at the outset, building collectively instead of shifting things about, may be pheromones released when they reach committee size. They react as if alarmed. They become agitated, excited, and then they begin working, like artists.

Bees live lives of organisms, tissues, cells, organelles, all 8 at the same time. The single bee, out of the hive retrieving sugar (instructed by the dancer: "south-southeast for seven hundred meters, clover—mind you make corrections for the sundrift") is still as much a part of the hive as if attached by a filament. Building the hive, the workers have the look of embryonic cells organizing a developing tissue; from a distance they are like the viruses inside a cell, running off row after row of symmetrical polygons as though laying down crystals. When the time for swarming comes, and the old queen prepares to leave with her part of the population, it is as though the hive were involved in mitosis. There is an agitated moving of bees back and forth, like granules in cell sap. They distribute themselves in almost precisely equal parts, half to the departing queen, half to the new one. Thus, like an egg, the great, hairy, black and golden creature splits in two, each with an equal share of the family genome.

The phenomenon of separate animals joining up to 9 form an organism is not unique in insects. Slimemold cells do it all the time, of course, in each life cycle. At first they are single amebocytes swimming around, eating bacteria, aloof from each other, untouching, voting straight Republican. Then, a bell sounds, and acrasin is released by special cells toward which the others converge in stellate ranks, touch, fuse together, and construct the slug, solid as a trout. A splendid stalk is raised, with a fruiting body on top, and out of this comes the next generation of amebocytes, ready to swim across the same moist ground, solitary and ambitious.

Herring and other fish in schools are at times so close- 10 ly integrated, their actions so coordinated, that they seem to be functionally a great multi-fish organism. Flocking birds, especially the seabirds nesting on the slopes of offshore islands in Newfoundland, are similarly attached, connected, synchronized.

Although we are by all odds the most social of all social 11 animals—more interdependent, more attached to each other, more inseparable in our behavior than bees—we do not often feel our conjoined intelligence. Perhaps, however, we are linked in circuits for the storage, processing, and retrieval of information, since this appears to be the most basic and universal of all human enterprises. It may be our biological function to build a certain kind of Hill. We have access to all the information of the biosphere, arriving as elementary units in the stream of solar photons. When we have learned how these are rearranged against randomness, to make, say, springtails, quantum mechanics, and the late quartets, we may have a clearer notion how to proceed. The circuitry seems to be there, even if the current is not always on.

The system of communications used in science should 12 provide a neat, workable model for studying mechanisms of information-building in human society. Ziman, in a recent

Nature essay, points out, "the invention of a mechanism for the systematic publication of *fragments* of scientific work may well have been the key event in the history of modern science." He continues:

> A regular journal carries from one research worker to another the various . . . observations which are of common interest. . . . A typical scientific paper has never pretended to be more than another little piece in a larger jigsaw—not significant in itself but as an element in a grander scheme. *This technique, of soliciting many modest contributions to the store of human knowledge, has been the secret of Western science since the seventeenth century, for it achieves a corporate, collective power that is far greater than one individual can exert* [italics mine]. 13

With some alternation of terms, some toning down, the passage could describe the building of a termite nest. 14

It is fascinating that the word "explore" does not apply to the searching aspect of the activity, but has its origins in the sounds we make while engaged in it. We like to think of exploring in science as a lonely, meditative business, and so it is in the first stages, but always, sooner or later, before the enterprise reaches completion, as we explore, we call to each other, communicate, publish, send letters to the editor, present papers, cry out on finding. 15

Reference Notes

Ziman J. M. "Information, Communication, Knowledge," *Nature*, 224: 318–24, 1969.

Checking Your Understanding

1. After citing all the amazing examples of communication among various creatures, Thomas must admit that as people we "do not often feel our conjoined intelligence." What does Thomas mean by this? How might this ability benefit the human race?

2. Why do scientists (and others) in spite of the lack of conjoined intelligence still "call to each other"?

3. Observe a group of organisms working together—an ant hill, a tank of fish, a group of neighborhood children, a dorm floor, a basketball team, an A.A. meeting, a family unit, a group of office workers. Take notes on what you see happening—how they communicate and interact, how they find support in each other or compete with each other, how they work together or fight with each other—and then record and interpret your findings about this social group.

Examining Rhetorical Strategies

1. Thomas is famous for his masterful use of language, his vivid descriptions of his observations of the natural world. In this essay he personifies various creatures: ants, slimemold cells, bees, termites. Why does he choose to describe them this way when he admits this personification makes people, especially biologists, "uncomfortable"?

2. Thomas begins and ends his essay speaking about humans. Why does he frame his discussion of non-human life forms in this way? How does it strengthen the comparisons he is making?

BODY RITUAL AMONG THE NACIREMA

Horace Miner

Prereading Journal

Our days are filled with ritual-like behavior, things we do habitually, in the same way every day. Describe one of your daily habits and recall, if you can, how you learned to perform this ritual.

Background

Miner is an anthropologist particularly interested in North American groups. This essay appeared first in 1956 in *American Anthropologists*, Volume 58, Number 3, pages 503–507. In it Miner *observes* and records some of the values, behaviors, and customs of a particular tribe.

During Reading

Notice Miner's use of the objective, scholarly stance in this piece. How does this stance make you respond to his findings?

Reading Selection

The anthropologist has become so familiar with the 1 diversity of ways in which different peoples behave in similar situations that he is not apt to be surprised by even the most exotic customs. In fact, if all of the logically possible combinations of behavior have not been found somewhere in the world, he is apt to suspect that they must be present in some yet undescribed tribe. This point has, in fact, been expressed with respect to clan organization by Murdock. In this light, the magical beliefs and practices of the Nacirema present such unusual aspects that it seems desirable to describe them as an example of the extremes to which human behavior can go.

Professor Linton first brought the ritual of the 2 Nacirema to the attention of anthropologists twenty years ago, but the culture of this people is still very poorly understood. They are a North American group living in the territory between the Canadian Cree, the Yaqui and Tarahumare of Mexico, and the Carib and Arawak of the Antilles. Little is known of their origin, although tradition states that they came from the east. . . .

Nacirema culture is characterized by a highly devel- 3 oped market economy which has evolved in a rich natural habitat. While much of the people's time is devoted to economic pursuits, a large part of the fruits of these labors and a considerable portion of the day are spent in ritual activity. The focus of this activity is the human body, the appearance and health of which loom as a dominant concern in the ethos of the people. While such a concern is certainly not unusual, its ceremonial aspects and associated philosophy are unique.

The fundamental belief underlying the whole system 4 appears to be that the human body is ugly and that its natural tendency is to debility and disease. Incarcerated in such a body, man's only hope is to avert these characteristics through the use of the powerful influences of ritual and ceremony. Every household has one or more shrines devoted to this purpose. The more powerful individuals in the society have several shrines in their houses and, in fact, the opulence of a house is often referred to in terms of the number of such ritual centers it possesses. Most houses are of wattle and daub construction, but the shrine rooms of the more wealthy are walled with stone. Poorer families imitate the rich by applying pottery plaques to their shrine walls.

While each family has at least one such shrine, the ritu- 5 als associated with it are not family ceremonies but are private and secret. The rites are normally only discussed with children, and then only during the period when they are being initiated into these mysteries. I was able, however, to establish sufficient rapport with the natives to examine these shrines and to have the rituals described to me.

The focal point of the shrine is a box or chest which is 6 built into the wall. In this chest are kept the many charms and magical potions without which no native believes he could live. These preparations are secured from a variety of specialized practitioners. The most powerful of these are the medicine men, whose assistance must be rewarded with substantial gifts. However, the medicine men do not provide the curative potions for their clients, but decide what the ingredients should be and then write them down in an ancient and secret language. This writing is understood only by the medicine men and by the herbalists who, for another gift, provide the required charm.

The charm is not disposed of after it has served its pur- 7 pose, but is placed in the charm-box of the household shrine. As these magical materials are specific for certain ills, and the real or imagined maladies of the people are many, the charm-box is usually full to overflowing. The magical packets are so numerous that people forget what their purposes were and fear to use them again. While the natives are very vague on this point, we can only assume that the idea in retaining all the old magical materials is that their presence in the charm-box, before which the body rituals are conducted, will in some way protect the worshipper.

Beneath the charm-box is a small font. Each day every 8 member of the family, in succession, enters the shrine room, bows his head before the charm-box, mingles different sorts of holy water in the font, and proceeds with a brief rite of ablution. The holy waters are secured from the Water Temple of the community, where the priests conduct elaborate ceremonies to make the liquid ritually pure.

In the hierarchy of magical practitioners, and below the 9 medicine men in prestige, are specialists whose designation is best translated "holy-mouth-men." The Nacirema have an almost pathological horror of and fascination with the mouth, the condition of which is believed to have a supernatural influence on all social relationships. Were it not for the rituals of the mouth, they believe that their teeth would fall out, their gums bleed, their jaws shrink, their friends desert them, and their lovers reject them. They also believe that a strong relationship exists between oral and moral characteristics. For example, there is a ritual ablution of the mouth for children which is supposed to improve their moral fiber.

The daily body ritual performed by everyone includes a 10 mouth-rite. Despite the fact that these people are so punctilious about care of the mouth, this rite involves a practice which strikes the uninitiated stranger as revolting. It was reported to me that the ritual consists of inserting a small bundle of hog hairs into the mouth, along with certain magical powders, and then moving the bundle in a highly formalized series of gestures.

In addition to the private mouth-rite, the people seek 11 out a holy-mouth-man once or twice a year. These practitioners have an impressive set of paraphernalia, consisting of a variety of augers, awls, probes, and prods. The use of these objects in the exorcism of the evils of the mouth involves almost unbelievable ritual torture of the client. The holy-mouth-man opens the client's mouth and, using the above mentioned tools, enlarges any holes which decay may have created in the teeth. Magical materials are put into these holes. If there are no naturally occurring holes in the teeth, large sections of one or more teeth are gouged out so that the supernatural substance can be applied. In the client's view, the purpose of these ministrations is to arrest decay and to draw friends. The extremely sacred and traditional character of the rite is evident in the fact that the natives return to the holy-mouth-men year after year, despite the fact that their teeth continue to decay.

It is to be hoped that, when a thorough study of the 12 Nacirema is made, there will be careful inquiry into the personality structure of these people. One has but to watch the gleam in the eye of a holy-mouth-man, as he jabs an awl into an exposed nerve, to suspect that a certain amount of sadism is involved. If this can be established, a very interesting pattern emerges, for most of the population shows definite masochistic tendencies. It was to these that Professor Linton referred in discussing a distinctive part of the daily body ritual which is performed only by men. This part of the rite involves scraping and lacerating the surface of the face with a sharp instrument. Special women's rites are performed only four times during each lunar month, but what they lack in frequency is made up in barbarity. As part of this ceremony, women bake their heads in small ovens for about an hour. The theoretically interesting point is that what seems to be a preponderantly masochistic people have developed sadistic specialists.

The medicine men have an imposing temple, or *latipso*, 13 in every community of any size. The more elaborate ceremonies required to treat very sick patients can only be performed at this temple. These ceremonies involve not only the thaumaturge but a permanent group of vestal maidens who move sedately about the temple chambers in distinctive costume and headdress.

The *latipso* ceremonies are so harsh that it is phenome- 14 nal that a fair proportion of the really sick natives who enter the temple ever recover. Small children whose indoctrination is still incomplete have been known to resist attempts to take them to the temple because "that is where you go to die." Despite this fact, sick adults are not only willing but eager to undergo the protracted ritual purification, if they can afford to do so. No matter how ill the supplicant or how grave the emergency, the guardians of many temples will not admit a client if he cannot give a rich gift to the custodian. Even after one has gained admission and survived the ceremonies, the guardians will not permit the neophyte to leave until he makes still another gift.

The supplicant entering the temple is first stripped of 15 all his or her clothes. In everyday life the Nacirema avoids exposure of his body and its natural functions. Bathing and excretory acts are performed only in the secrecy of the household shrine, where they are ritualized as part of the body-rites. Psychological shock results from the fact that body secrecy is suddenly lost upon entry into the *latipso*. A man, whose own wife has never seen him in an excretory act, suddenly finds himself naked and assisted by a vestal maiden while he performs his natural functions into a sacred vessel. This sort of ceremonial treatment is necessitated by the fact that the excreta are used by a diviner to ascertain the course and nature of the client's sickness. Female clients, on the other hand, find their naked bodies are subjected to the scrutiny, manipulation and prodding of the medicine men.

Few supplicants in the temple are well enough to do 16 anything but lie on their hard beds. The daily ceremonies, like the rites of the holy-mouth-men, involve discomfort and torture. With ritual precision, the vestals awaken their miserable charges each dawn and roll them about on their beds of pain while performing ablutions, in the formal movements of which the maidens are highly trained. At other times they insert magic wands in the supplicant's mouth or force him to eat substances which are supposed to be healing. From time to time the medicine men come to their clients and jab magically treated needles into their flesh. The fact that these temple ceremonies may not cure, and may even kill the neophyte, in no way decreases the people's faith in the medicine men.

There remains one other kind of practitioner, known as 17
a "listener." This witchdoctor has the power to exorcise the devils that lodge in the heads of people who have been bewitched. The Nacirema believe that parents bewitch their own children. Mothers are particularly suspected of putting a curse on children while teaching them the secret body rituals. The counter-magic of the witchdoctor is unusual in its lack of ritual. The patient simply tells the "listener" all his troubles and fears, beginning with the earliest difficulties he can remember. The memory displayed by the Nacirema in these exorcism sessions is truly remarkable. It is not uncommon for the patient to bemoan the rejection he felt upon being weaned as a babe, and a few individuals even see their troubles going back to the traumatic effects of their own birth.

In conclusion, mention must be made of certain prac- 18
tices which have their base in native esthetics but which depend upon the pervasive aversion to the natural body and its functions. There are ritual fasts to make fat people thin and ceremonial feasts to make thin people fat. Still other rites are used to make women's breasts larger if they are small, and smaller if they are large. General dissatisfaction with breast shape is symbolized in the fact that the ideal form is virtually outside the range of human variation. A few women afflicted with almost inhuman hypermammary development are so idolized that they make a handsome living by simply going from village to village and permitting the natives to stare at them for a fee.

Reference has already been made to the fact that excre- 19
tory functions are ritualized, routinized, and relegated to secrecy. Natural reproductive functions are similarly distorted. Intercourse is taboo as a topic and scheduled as an act. Efforts are made to avoid pregnancy by the use of magical materials or by limiting intercourse to certain phases of the moon. Conception is actually very infrequent. When pregnant, women dress so as to hide their condition. Parturition

given to modes of learning, knowing, and valuing that may be specific to, or at least common in, women. It is likely that the commonly accepted stereotype of women's thinking as emotional, intuitive, and personalized has contributed to the devaluation of women's minds and contributions, particularly in Western technologically oriented cultures, which value rationalism and objectivity (Sampson 1978). It is generally assumed that intuitive knowledge is more primitive, therefore less valuable, than so-called objective modes of knowing. Thus, it appeared likely to us that traditional educational curricula and pedagogical standards have probably not escaped this bias. Indeed, recent feminist writers have convincingly argued that there is a masculine bias at the very heart of most academic disciplines, methodologies, and theories (Bernard 1973; Gilligan 1979, 1982; Harding and Hintikka 1983; Keller 1978, 1985; Janssen-Jurreit 1980; Langland and Gove 1981; Sherman and Beck 1979). Feminists are beginning to articulate the values of the female world and to reshape the disciplines to include the woman's voice, while continuing to press for the right of women to participate as equals in the male world.

Explain the difference between the two modes of thinking discussed here.

THE ABSENCE OF WOMEN IN PSYCHOLOGY

Explain how research about human nature has traditionally excluded women.

Until recently women have played only a 5 minor role as theorists in the social sciences. The authors of the major theories of human development have been men. As Carol Gilligan (1979) has pointed out, women have been missing even as research subjects at the formative stages of our psychological theories. The potential for bias on the part of male investigators is heightened by the recurring tendency to select exclusively or predominantly male samples for research. This omission of women from scientific studies is almost universally ignored when scientists draw conclusions from their findings and generalize what they have learned from the study of men to lives of women. If and when scientists turn to the study of women, they typically look for ways in which women conform to or diverge from patterns found in the study of men. With the Western tradition of dividing human nature into dual but parallel streams, attributes traditionally associated with the masculine are valued, studied, and articulated, while those associated with the feminine tend to be ignored. Thus, we have learned a great deal about the development of autonomy and independence, abstract critical thought, and the unfolding of a morality of rights and justice in both men and women. We have learned less about the development of interdependence, intimacy, nurturance, and contextual thought (Bakan 1966; Chodorow 1978; Gilligan 1977, 1979, 1982; McMillan 1982). Developmental theory has established men's experience and competence as a baseline against which both men's and women's development is then judged, often to the detriment or misreading of women.

Nowhere is the pattern of using male experience to define the human experience seen more clearly than in models of intellectual development. The mental processes that are involved in considering the abstract and the impersonal have been labeled "thinking" and are attributed primarily to men, while those that deal with the personal and interpersonal fall under the rubric of "emotions" and are largely relegated to women. As dichotomous "either/or thinking" is so common in our culture and as we tend to view human beings as closed systems, the expenditure of energy in one part of the system has been seen inevitably to lead to depletion elsewhere. Historically, it has been assumed that the development of women's intellectual potential would inhibit the development of their emotional capacities and that the development of men's emotion- 6

Why were men discouraged from developing their emotional side?

al range would impair intellectual functioning. Although it seems ludicrous to us now, just a century ago the belief that women who engaged in intellectual pursuits would find their reproductive organs atrophying was widely held and used to justify the continued exclusion of women from the academic community (Rosenberg 1982).

From the moment women gained a foot in 7 the academic world, they sought to examine and dispel beliefs suggesting sexual polarities in intelligence and personality characteristics. However, research studies and critical essays on the topic have focused on the demonstration of women's intellectual competence, minimizing any differences that were found between the sexes (Maccoby and Jacklin 1974; Rosenberg 1982). The focus has been on studying the intellectual capacities most often cultivated by men rather than on identifying aspects of intelligence and modes of thought that might be more common and highly developed women.

Why is demonstrating women's intellectual competence in ways cultivated by men not enough?

WOMAN'S VOICE IN DEVELOPMENTAL THEORY: THE WORK OF CAROL GILLIGAN

See Chapter Twelve for a review of Gilligan's research.

When the woman's voice is included in the 8 study of human development, women's lives and qualities are revealed and we can observe the unfolding of these qualities in the lives of men as well. The power of the woman's voice in expanding our conceptions of human development is amply illustrated in the work of Carol Gilligan (1982).

By listening to girls and women resolve seri- 9 ous moral dilemmas in their lives, Gilligan has traced the development of a morality organized around notions of responsibility and care. This conception of morality contrasts sharply with the morality of rights described by Piaget (1965) and Kohlberg (1981, 1984), which is based on the

What is "rights morality"?

study of the evolution of moral reasoning in boys and men. People operating within a rights morality—more commonly men—evoke the metaphor of "blind justice" and rely on abstract laws and universal principles to adjudicate disputes and conflicts between conflicting claims impersonally, impartially, and fairly. Those operating within a morality of responsibility and care—primarily women—reject the strategy of blindness and impartiality. Instead, they argue for an understanding of the context for moral choice, claiming that the needs of individuals cannot always be deduced from general rules and principles and that moral choice must also be determined inductively from the particular experiences each participant brings to the situation. They believe that dialogue and exchange of views allow each individual to be understood in his or her own terms. They believe that mutual understanding is most likely to lead to a creative consensus about how everyone's needs may be met in resolving disputes. It is the rejection of blind impartiality in the application of universal abstract rules and principles that has, in the eyes of many, marked women as deficient in moral reasoning.

In recent work Gilligan and her colleague, 10 Nona Lyons (1983), have extended their study of gender-related differences in moral perspectives to the area of identity development. They have shown how the responsibility orientation is more central to those whose conceptions of self are rooted in a sense of connection and relatedness to others, whereas the rights orientation is more common to those who define themselves in terms of separation and autonomy. Although these differences in self-definition do not necessarily divide along gender lines, it is clear that many more women than men define themselves in terms of their relationships and connections to others, a point which has also been made by

What is the "morality of responsibility and care"?

How does identity relate to morality?

Nancy Chodorow (1978) and Jean Baker Miller (1976). When men define themselves in terms of connection, they also frame their moral judgments in terms of responsibility rather than rights (Lyons 1983).

Such insights are transforming our understanding and study of psychology and human development, paralleling transformations that are occurring in all of the intellectual disciplines that have begun to include the woman's voice. When scientific findings, scientific theory, and even the basic assumptions of academic disciplines are reexamined through the lens of women's perspectives and values, new conclusions can be drawn and new directions forged that have implications for the lives of both men and women.

11

References

Aries, E. (1976). Interaction patterns and themes of male, female, and mixed groups. *Small Group Behavior, 7,* 7–14.

Bakan, D. (1966). *The duality of human existence.* Boston: Beacon Press.

Bernard, J. (1973). My four revolutions: An autobiographical history of the American Sociological Society. *American Journal of Sociology, 78,* 773–791.

Chodorow, N. (1978). *The reproduction of mothering.* Berkeley: University of California Press.

Clance, P. R., & Imes, S. A. (1978). The imposter phenomenon in high achieving women: Dynamics and therapeutic intervention. *Psychotherapy: Theory, Research, and Practice, 15,* 241–247.

Cross, P. (1968). College women: A research description. *Journal of the National Association of Women Deans and Counselors, 32,* 12–21.

Eakins, B., & Eakins, G. (1976). Verbal turn-taking and exchanges in faculty dialogue. In B. L. Dubois & I. Crouch (Eds.), *The sociology of the language of American women* (pp. 53–62). San Antonio, TX: Trinity University.

Gallese, L. R. (1985). *Women like us.* New York: William Morrow.

Gilligan, C. (1977). In a different voice: Women's conceptions of self and of morality. *Harvard Educational Review, 47,* 481–517.

Gilligan, C. (1979). Woman's place in man's life cycle. *Harvard Educational Review, 49,* 431–446.

Gilligan, C. (1982). *In a different voice: Psychological theory and women's development.* Cambridge, MA: Harvard University Press.

Hagen, R. I., & Kahn, A. (1975). Discrimination against competent women. *Journal of Applied Social Psychology, 5,* 362–376.

Hall, R., & Sandler, B. R. (1982). *The classroom climate: A chilly one for women?* Washington, DC: Project on the Status and Education of Women, Association of American Colleges.

Harding, S., & Hintikka, M. B. (Eds.). (1983). *Discovering reality: Feminist perspectives on epistemology, metaphysics, methodology, and philosophy of science.* Dordrecht, Holland: Reidel.

Howe, F., & Lauter, P. (1980 February). The impact of women's studies on the campus and the disciplines. *Women's Studies Monograph Series.* Washington, DC: Department of Health, Education & Welfare, National Institute of Education.

Janssen-Jurreit, M. (1980). *Sexism: The male monopoly on history and thought.* New York: Farrar, Straus, & Giroux.

Kanter, R. M. (1977). *Men and women of the corporation.* New York: Basic Books.

Keller, E. F. (1978). Gender and science. *Psychoanalysis and Contemporary Thought, 1,* 409–433.

Keller, E. F. (1985). *Reflections on gender and science.* New Haven, CT: Yale University Press.

Kohlberg, L. (1981). *The philosophy of moral development.* New York: Harper & Row.

Kohlberg, L. (1984). *The psychology of moral development.* New York: Harper & Row.

Langland, E., & Gove, W. (Eds.). (1981). *A feminist perspective in the academy.* Chicago: University of Chicago Press.

Lyons, N. (1983). Two perspectives on self, relationships and morality. *Harvard Educational Review, 53,* 125–145.

Maccoby, E., & Jacklin, C. (1974). *The psychology of sex differences.* Stanford, CA: Stanford University Press.

McMillan, C. (1982). *Women, reason, and nature.* Princeton, NJ: Princeton University Press.

Miller, J. B. (1976). *Towards a new psychology of women.* Boston: Beacon Press.

Piaget, J. (1965). *The moral judgment of the child.* New York: Free Press. (Originally published 1932.)

Piliavin, J. A. (1976). On feminine self-presentation in groups. In J. I. Roberts (Ed.), *Beyond intellectual sexism* (pp. 138–159). New York: McKay.

Rosenberg, R. (1982). *Beyond separate spheres: Intellectual roots of modern feminism.* New Haven, CT: Yale University Press.

Ruddick, S., & Daniels, P. (Eds.). (1977). *Working it out.* New York: Pantheon Books.

Sadker, M. P., & Sadker, D. M. (1982). *Sex equity handbook for schools.* New York: Longman.

Sadker, M. P., & Sadker, D. M. (1985, March). Sexism in the schoolroom of the 80's. *Psychology Today,* pp. 54–57.

Sampson, E. E. (1978). Scientific paradigm and social value: Wanted—a scientific revolution. *Journal of Personality and Social Psychology, 36,* 1332–1343.

Sassen, G. (1980). Success anxiety in women: A constructivist interpretation of its source and its significance. *Harvard Education Review, 50,* 13–24.

Serbin, L. A., O'Leary, K. D., Kent, R. N., & Tonick, I. J. (1973). A comparison of teacher response to pre-academic and problem behavior of boys and girls. *Child Development, 44,* 796–804.

Sherman, J., & Beck, E. (Eds.). (1979). *The prism of sex.* Madison, WI: University of Wisconsin Press.

Swaker, M. (1976). Women's verbal behavior at learned and professional conferences. In B. L. Dubois & I. Crouch (Eds.), *The sociology of the languages of American women* (pp. 155–160). San Antonio, TX: Trinity University.

Thorne, B. (1979 September). *Claiming verbal space: Women, speech, and language in college classrooms.* Paper presented at the Research Conference on Educational Environments and the Undergraduate Woman, Wellesley College, Wellesley, MA.

Treichler, P., & Kramarae, C. (1983). Women's talk in the ivory tower. *Communication Quarterly, 31,* 118–132.

West, C., & Zimmerman, D. H. (1983). Small insults: A study of interruptions in cross-sex conversations between unacquainted persons. In B. Thorne, C. Kramarae, & N. Henley, (Eds.), *Language, gender, and society* (pp. 103–118). Rowley, MA: Newbury House.

Checking Your Understanding

1. Consider the many ways in which you learn that you listed in your prereading. How many of these ways of knowing are being used in your college classes? What is the most common way of learning used in academic settings? How does this support the authors' point about women feeling alienated in academic settings?
2. Why do you think that the complex mental processes involved in managing personal and interpersonal relationships successfully have never achieved the same status as abstract and impersonal thought processes?

Examining Rhetorical Strategies

1. While this is an academic piece of writing, recording both original and secondary research, the authors still use the personal pronoun "we" and openly state the feminist perspective from which the book was written. Why do you think they did not use a more objective voice?
2. Compare this essay to that of Gilligan in Chapter Twelve. In what ways are the essays similar and different in terms of purpose, voice, audience, content, and style? What do you think accounts for these similarities and differences?

THE HUNGER FOR THE KING IN A TIME WITH NO FATHER

Robert Bly

Prereading Journal

Think about the adult men you knew when you were growing up. What kind of life did you imagine or know them to lead? Were they the traditional three-piece-suit office type? Were they laborers? How much time did they spend with their families? What kinds of family activities did they participate in? Describe one man you knew when you were young. In what ways did he fit the pattern of men you saw around you and how was he different?

Background

Robert Bly is a poet who has also become one of the leaders in the current men's movement. He has been leading men's retreats for fifteen years and helping men come to terms with their own maleness in light of the changing roles of women and men in society. This essay, taken from his book *Iron John, critically analyzes* the consequences of the absence of fathers in the lives of their sons.

During Reading

Note the differences between father/son relationships in tribal versus industrial cultures.

Reading Selection

Disturbances in Sonhood

As I've participated in men's gatherings since the early 1980s, I've heard one statement over and over from American males, which has been phrased in a hundred different ways: "There is not enough father." The sentence implies that father is a substance like salt, which in earlier times was occasionally in short supply, or like groundwater, which in some areas now has simply disappeared.

Geoffrey Gorer remarked in his book *The American People* that for a boy to become a man in the United States in

1940 only one thing was required: namely, that he reject his father. He noticed, moreover, that American fathers expect to be rejected. Young men in Europe, by contrast, have traditionally imagined the father to be a demonic being whom they must wrestle with (and the son in Kafka's "The Judgment" does wrestle his father to the death and loses). Many sons in the United States, however, visualize the father as a simple object of ridicule to be made fun of, as, in fact, he is so often in comic strips and television commercials. One young man summed it up: "A father is a person who rustles newspapers in the living room."

Clearly, "father water" in the home has sunk below the 3 reach of most wells.

TOO LITTLE FATHER

When the father-table, the groundwater, drops, so to 4 speak, and there is too little father, instead of too much father, the sons find themselves in a new situation. What do they do: drill for new father water, ration the father water, hoard it, distill mother water into father water?

Traditional cultures still in existence seem to have plen- 5 ty of father. In so-called traditional cultures, many substitute fathers work with the young man. Uncles loosen the son up, or tell him about women. Grandfathers give him stories. Warrior types teach weaponry and discipline, old men teach ritual and soul—all of them honorary fathers.

Bruno Bettelheim noticed, too, that in most traditional 6 cultures Freud's version of father-son hatred doesn't hold. The wordless tension between fathers and sons in Vienna, which he assumed to be universal and based on sexual jealousy, was, in Bettelheim's opinion, true mostly in Vienna in the late nineteenth century.

Fathers and sons in most tribal cultures live in an 7 amused tolerance of each other. The son has a lot to learn, and so the father and son spend hours trying and failing together to make arrowheads or to repair a spear or track a clever animal. When a father and son do spend long hours together, which some fathers and sons still do, we could say that a substance almost like food passes from the older body to the younger.

The contemporary mind might want to describe the 8
exchange between father and son as a likening of attitude, a
miming, but I think a physical exchange takes place, as if
some substance was passing directly to the cells. The son's
body—not his mind—receives and the father gives this food
at a level far below consciousness. The son does not receive a
hands-on healing, but a body-on healing. His cells receive
some knowledge of what an adult masculine body is. The
younger body learns at what frequency the masculine body
vibrates. It begins to grasp the song that adult male cells sing,
and how the charming, elegant, lonely, courageous, half-
shamed male molecules dance.

During the long months the son spent in the mother's 9
body, his body got well tuned to female frequencies: it
learned how a woman's cells broadcast, who bows to whom in
that resonant field, what animals run across the grassy clearing, what the body listens for at night, what the upper and
lower fears are. How firmly the son's body becomes, before
birth and after, a good receiver for the upper and lower frequencies of the mother's voice! The son either tunes to that
frequency or he dies.

Now, standing next to the father, as they repair arrow- 10
heads, or repair plows, or wash pistons in gasoline, or care for
birthing animals, the son's body has the chance to retune.
Slowly, over months or years, that son's body-strings begin to
resonate to the harsh, sometimes demanding, testily humorous, irreverent, impatient, opinionated, forward-driving,
silence-loving older masculine body. Both male and female
cells carry marvelous music, but the son needs to resonate to
the masculine frequency as well as to the female frequency.

Sons who have not received this retuning will have 11
father-hunger all their lives. I think calling the longing
"hunger" is accurate: the young man's body lacks salt, water,
or protein, just as a starving person's body and lower digestive tract lack protein. If it finds none, the stomach will eventually eat up the muscles themselves. Such hungry sons hang
around older men like the homeless do around a soup
kitchen. Like the homeless, they feel shame over their condition, and it is nameless, bitter, unexpungeable shame.

Women cannot, no matter how much they sympathize 12
with their starving sons, replace that particular missing sub-

stance. The son later may try to get it from a woman his own age, but that doesn't work either.

DISTRUST OF OLDER MEN

Only one hundred and forty years have passed since 13 factory work began in earnest in the West, and we see in each generation poorer bonding between father and son, with catastrophic results. A close study of the Enclosure Act of England shows that the English government, toward the end of that long legislative process, denied the landless father access to free pasture and common land with the precise aim of forcing him, with or without his family, to travel to the factory. The South Africans still do that to black fathers today.

By the middle of the twentieth century in Europe and 14 North America a massive change had taken place: the father was working, but the son could not see him working.

Throughout the ancient hunter societies, which appar- 15 ently lasted thousands of years—perhaps hundreds of thousands—and throughout the hunter-gatherer societies that followed them, and the subsequent agricultural and craft societies, fathers and sons worked and lived together. As late as 1900 in the United States about ninety percent of fathers were engaged in agriculture. In all these societies the son characteristically saw his father working at all times of the day and all seasons of the year. . . .

TEMPERAMENT WITHOUT TEACHING

When a father, absent during the day, returns home at 16 six, his children receive only his temperament, and not his teaching. If the father is working for a corporation, what is there to teach? He is reluctant to tell his son what is really going on. The fragmentation of decision making in corporate life, the massive effort that produces the corporate willingness to destroy the environment for the sake of profit, the prudence, even cowardice, that one learns in bureaucracy—who wants to teach that?

We know of rare cases in which the father takes sons or 17 daughters into his factory, judge's chambers, used-car lot, or insurance building, and those efforts at teaching do reap some of the rewards of teaching in craft cultures. But in most families today, the sons and daughters receive, when the father returns home at six, only his disposition, or his temperament, which is usually irritable and remote.

What the father brings home today is usually a touchy   18
mood, springing from powerlessness and despair mingled
with longstanding shame and the numbness peculiar to those
who hate their jobs. Fathers in earlier times could often
break through their own humanly inadequate temperaments
by teaching rope-making, fishing, posthole digging, grain
cutting, drumming, harness making, animal care, even
singing and storytelling. That teaching sweetened the effect
of the temperament. . . .

In our time, when the father shows up as an object of   19
ridicule (as he does, as we've noted, on television), or a fit
field for suspicion (as he does in *Star Wars*), or a bad-tempered fool (when he comes home from the office with no
teaching), or a weak puddle of indecision (as he stops inheriting kingly radiance), the son has a problem. How does he
imagine his own life as a man?

Works Cited

Bettelheim, Bruno. *Symbolic Wounds*. Glencoe: Free Press, 1954.
Gorer, Geoffrey. *The American People*. New York: W. W. Norton, 1964.

Checking Your Understanding

1. How do the patterns of male behavior you noted in your prereading
    compare with those that Bly discusses? Did the men you knew take
    their sons to where they worked? Did they bring home a "touchy
    mood"?
2. Why does Bly feel that teaching is so important to the development
    of the father–son relationship?
3. Defend or dispute Bly's idea that sons are well tuned to "female frequencies" because of time spent in the womb.

Examining Rhetorical Strategies

1. Compare the idea of hungering for a father in Bly with that of
    Wright in "Conquering the Streets of Memphis" (Chapter Three).
    What is it that the two writers are actually hungering for?
2. Notice Bly's use of metaphor in relation to fathers ("father water,"
    "father is a substance like salt," "'father is a person who rustles newspapers in the living room'"). How do these ways of expressing
    fatherhood contribute to Bly's point about there not being enough
    father?

STUDENT ESSAYS AND WRITING TECHNIQUES

WARMING THE WINTER HOLLOW

Brian Ladewig

Background

Cozy indoor winter scenes always include a fire burning in the hearth. But like many other small household chores, creating the picture-perfect fire takes a skilled hand. Through lots of practice and not a few mistakes, Ladewig had developed that skill and wanted to share it with others. He wrote this piece envisioning it in a "Holiday Tips" section of a local newspaper. Notice how he uses narrative and descriptive elements to frame his list of instructions.

Reading Selection

Picture this . . . 1

It's the afternoon of Thanksgiving. A light snow has covered the ground and continues to fall outside among the snowy pines. The house is filled with smells of holiday cooking and the anticipation of the guests' arrival. In his best holiday dress, he sets out to make the evening truly memorable by building a warm and cozy fire. He envisions glowing embers and crackling wood as the comfortable guests enjoy the company and the holiday feast. 2

Unfortunately, it doesn't go quite right. The logs are a little wet and he fails to use enough kindling. The few pieces of paper he has put under the grate burn quickly with a fiery blaze, leaving the logs barely touched. After repeated attempts he decides to dismantle his dismal failure, hoping to salvage the mess he's made. Instead, he transfers the mess to himself, becoming covered with soot and dirt. More frustrated than before, he gives up on the fire, leaving the disarray of logs and paper in the fireplace, hoping no one will notice. He hastily runs upstairs to change his clothes before the company arrives. 3

How many times has this scene been repeated in your house? Most people take a good fire for granted. If they can't 4 build one they would just as soon go without, or let someone else "go to the bother." It's not unusual for people to fear failing at such a simple task. Humans have been harnessing the benefits of fire for thousands of years. Admitting that you can't build a fire in the twentieth century acknowledges that you're a little behind the times, as well as domestically unaccomplished. But when you've used a whole book of matches and the whole Sunday paper and you still can't get it going, it's hard not to be discouraged.

But it doesn't have to be this way. By remembering a few 5 pointers you can escape the fear of failure and bask in the glow of a job well done:

1.   Select your logs carefully. Make sure your wood has aged for at least two seasons. The logs that you start the fire with should be thin wedges of a dry soft wood. I recommend pine or cedar. Never try to use whole logs or wood that is even slightly "green." Larger logs will burn well once the fire has started and established a bed of embers.

2.   Once you have selected your logs and brought them inside, remove the screen in front of the fireplace and smooth out the ashes underneath the grate, between the andirons. If you don't have a grate, lay two large logs next to each other, about a foot apart. You can build your fire on these quite easily. Note: Most fireplaces have an accompanying set of tools that stand precariously upright in their own stand. They may look obtrusive and difficult to use, but with practice, they can be your fire maintenance friends.

3.   Take several sections of old newspaper and begin tightly twisting *individual* pieces of paper into tight bundles. Never attempt to twist more than one piece of paper for it may unravel and be difficult to light. Pack these tightly twisted pieces under the grate. Pack enough to be tight fitting, but not so tight that they can't "breathe." Place as many twisted pieces of paper above the grate as you did below the grate. Note: The number of pieces that you use will depend on the size of the grate as well as your patience. Be thorough. Your work will pay off later.

4. In a crisscross pattern, lay your kindling sticks on top of your twisted paper. Kindling can be bought in pre-arranged bundles from stores like L. L. Bean or, for the industrious fire builder, felled sticks can be gathered early in the spring and dried out for the following season. Whatever your resources, be ample. You can't over kindle.

5. Place two of the thin wedge logs you selected earlier on top of the kindling. Be sure to lay the logs parallel to each other, lengthwise on the kindling. Place a third wedge log on top, across the two already in place. The idea is to build a sort of pyramid with the logs so that the flames can circulate among the wood. A common mistake of novice fire builders is adding too many pieces of wood at this stage. Stick with three for now. You can add more later, but having to take any out will result in a messy chore.

6. Now you're ready to light your masterpiece. Be calm and strike a match (wooden preferably). Light the corners and edges of the paper above and below the grate. Move quickly to utilize the duration of the match, but not so quickly that you put the match out. Be sure the four corners are lit before you retire the match. Note: To light a fire that lasts for hours with a single match is a skill that will undoubtedly impress your family and friends as well as instill in you a sense of real pride and accomplishment.

7. Let the fire burn for at least 10 minutes before you add any other logs. Replace the screen to prevent an embarrassing as well as potentially dangerous accident, which may result from "popping" dry wood. Sit back and admire your creation. Take the compliments from those who appreciate your work with a quiet satisfaction. Know that you've accomplished a simple but essential task.

So, as the snow sifts through the darkening sky this Thanksgiving and the house becomes rich with the aromas of seasonal joy, remember these few simple tips. A cozy fire this holiday season can warm the hearts of your family and 6 friends and add joy and comfort to an already happy and exciting time of year.

Thinking About Writing

Ladewig provides accurate, easy-to-follow information on how to build a fire in seven steps. But Ladewig also provides a picture of a man (himself, really) bungling the job completely in the beginning and ruining that picture-perfect Thanksgiving hearth image. Think about why he begins with that scene and how that contrasts with his last paragraph. How does this scene and the way he describes the process show his concern not just with information but with quality?

Writing Assignment

Select a task that you do very well, and provide a set of easy step-by-step instructions to follow for completing it: cooking an omelet, studying for an exam, taking notes in lectures, pumping your own gas, sewing on a button, programming a VCR, arranging a dorm room. Explain the process as clearly as you can to someone who really does not know how to do this. In fact, it will be helpful if you let such a person read your first draft so you know how explicit these instructions need to be. Also make sure you show the reader your own enthusiasm about the topic.

DIABETES: WHAT THEY MIGHT NOT HAVE TOLD YOU

Heidi Pfau

Background

Pfau was diagnosed with diabetes when she was only nine. At that young age, as she said, "I couldn't grasp the concept." Then at thirteen, she was hospitalized again. And at that age she "first realized how diabetes affected my life." She still vividly remembers all the fears this sudden realization caused and how drastically she thought her life would change. In this essay, Pfau wants to talk to people in the same situation she was—diabetic teenagers who are worried about what life will be like for them. She wants to tell them about all they *can* do at a time when they are hearing about limitations from everyone else. While you read, notice what information Pfau seems to be aiming at that teen audience.

Reading Selection

You have just been hospitalized for diabetes, and 1 whether you were newly diagnosed with this disease or your blood sugars need a little adjustment, this can be an extremely frightening event. Everyone tells you all of the drastic ways in which your life will have to be altered. Yes, these are important, but they are not the only truths about being diabetic. Your whole life does not need to change just because you have this disease.

For example, if you play sports, stay on the team. 2 Diabetes will not exclude you from athletic events. Diabetics compete in sports at all levels ranging from grade school and high school to professional. Jonathan Hayes is a member of the Kansas City Chiefs, and Bill Carlson is an Iron Man Triathlete. Both are diabetic. Although it is important that you keep your blood sugars under control while you exercise, diabetes in no way stops you from being physically active and competitive.

The current trend toward eating healthy and exercising 3 makes following a meal plan easier for you, too. Not only will there be a larger variety of foods on restaurant menus that fit your diet needs, but also no one will have a second thought about the fact that you don't order dessert. Furthermore, many foods in the supermarket contain artificial sweeteners and are lower in fat and cholesterol. These foods are healthier for everyone. If you select a variety of different foods, eating "right" doesn't need to feel like dieting.

Having diabetes doesn't prevent you from attending 4 social events either. When you go out, however, you should remember to carry some form of sugar with you in case you have a reaction. Because people cannot tell diabetics from non-diabetics simply by looking at them, carrying identification, like a medic alert, to inform others of your diabetes in case of an emergency is important as well. Traveling has also been made easier for you. A magazine published by the American Diabetes Association, *Diabetes Forecast,* sells carrying cases for medical supplies that are designed for insulin, syringes, and blood glucose monitors as well as insulin coolers for longer trips. Don't pass up an opportunity for a trip, especially an overnight one, because you think diabetes will get in the way. Prepare yourself and have fun!

Alcohol can be consumed in moderation as long as 5 your diabetes is properly regulated. If you drink, there are some things you should be aware of. First, never consume alcohol without eating food; this helps with absorption of the alcohol and controls variations in blood sugar levels. Also, alcohol is not considered a "free" food item and must be calculated into your total caloric intake. It is important for you to realize that some drinks, such as schnapps and rum, contain large amounts of sugar, and these should be avoided.

Perhaps the most crucial thing you must know about 6 having diabetes is that it doesn't stop you from having friends. Although you may not feel comfortable telling others of your condition, most people you are close to not only care but are a source of both friendship and support. Similarly, your parents, who are feeling confused, sad and guilty about your disease just like you, are one of the best sources of support you can have. It is important to share your feelings and problems with them and encourage them to learn about diabetes with you. Although at times this disease is difficult to deal with, the understanding of others can be helpful.

While at first this disease may make you feel both 7 scared and lonely, you are not alone. Millions of others share this disease with you, and even people without this disease care about you. I played basketball in high school, and although it wasn't always easy for me, the help of my family, coach, and team was tremendous. Sometimes during games I would have to eat Three Musketeer Bars and drink Mountain Dew on the bench to prevent reactions. My teammates couldn't understand how I could eat junk food and then play basketball, but they knew it was something I had to do. Eventually, it ended up as sort of a team joke. By the end of the season, my teammates were bringing me chocolate bars and soda before games, instead of my mother! No one else on the team had diabetes, but they were caring and supportive of me.

So, while everything people are telling you now may be 8 overwhelming, try not to get discouraged. Diabetes does not stop you from setting goals and following your dreams.

Thinking About Writing

Pfau is dealing with an audience of nervous, perhaps even frightened readers. While she is not a doctor, not a specialist in this area, she has been there and that experience gives her not only the authority she needs but also the inside knowledge about what her readers need and want to hear. In what ways does she provide comfort to them? How does she keep this comfort from sounding patronizing? Why might they listen to her at a time when they just don't want to hear anymore about this illness? How does she make this information inviting?

Writing Assignment

We have all become knowledgeable about some things through experience. Life has made us experts in handling difficult siblings or divorced parents, in knowing how to win and lose, in helping friends through tragedies, in coping with the pressures of school or a job. For this paper, share your hard-earned knowledge with someone just facing one of these challenges for the first time. Try to give the reader the information needed to handle this experience.

BUYING THE RIGHT BICYCLE HELMET

Louis Carparelli

Background

As a bicycle rider and parent, Carparelli had become concerned with the issue of safety in riding. It made him angry to see people riding without helmets when that one small safety measure could save people's lives. Carparelli felt that many people think an accident won't happen to them, but too often they are wrong. To help people take this step toward safety, Carparelli wrote some guidelines for helmet buyers to use in selecting the correct helmet for them and their safety. He explained why he chose this topic this way: "I felt it was something I knew something about, and yet when I started to research it I realized how much the technology had changed. I wanted to inform people of that because the helmet they have they may think is safe and it's not."

Reading Selection

By now you've been to three bike shops, two retail out- 1
lets, and looked through numerous mail order catalogs—all in search of a bicycle helmet. It's not that they're hard to find; it's the infinite selection that's available which makes choosing the correct one so difficult. There are several basic styles and numerous materials used in their construction which you need to consider before purchasing. All these choices can be confusing.

Let me first emphasize that style should be the last con- 2
sideration in the selection of a bicycle helmet. Some of the most visually appealing helmets, although beautiful to look at, may offer the least amount of protection. So having said that, let us begin our quest by discussing helmet construction and the safety standards all helmets should meet.

Helmet construction falls into three basic categories. 3
The first and oldest is the leather over foam hair net style which was popular among professional bicycle racers for over a century. This type offers little or no protection and meets none of the modern day safety standards by which today's

helmets are tested. And for this reason, this type shouldn't even be considered in your selection process. Second is the hard shell variety which utilizes a hard plastic or fiberglass shell over an expanded polystyrene inner liner. This type of helmet is the most popular and would seem to offer the most protection, and for the last ten to fifteen years was the best available. This is no longer the case for it has been found that in an accident this type of helmet may transmit too much of the impact energy to the head. As Richard L. Stainaker, an Ohio State University Automotive Safety Engineer explains:

> The purpose of the helmet is to absorb the energy of impact, but when it is too stiff it transmits most of the impact to the head. It's the padding next to the head that absorbs the impact. However, an outer shell with some stiffness is needed to protect against piercing and against tearing of the padding. ("Better Bicycle" 6)

This leads us to the third and newest variety which addresses the above mentioned problems. This type of helmet is constructed of a polystyrene foam which acts as the energy absorption material and a fabric covering which is often lycra. This helmet addresses the energy transfer problem by replacing the stiff outer shell with the flexible lycra covering. The lycra covering prevents the polystyrene foam from separating or tearing in the event of an impact. It's also much lighter. A helmet constructed of polystyrene and lycra weighs approximately half as much as a helmet constructed of polystyrene and fiberglass. This is a desirable feature in a helmet in that it reduces fatigue of the neck, back and shoulder muscles, all of which were problems encountered with some of the fiberglass and plastic helmets. Also, in a recent comparison of bicycle helmets conducted by *Consumer Reports*, it was found that the helmets that rated the highest were the "no shell models," or lycra over polystyrene ("Bike Helmets" 332).

Now that you have familiarized yourself with the types of construction and materials available, the question remains how you, the consumer, will know that the helmet you purchase will protect you in the event of an accident. Although there are no government regulations or safety criteria, there are now three organizations which test and rate bicycle helmets. The two oldest organizations are the American National Standards Institute (ANSI) and The Snell Memorial Foundation (Snell) which test helmets for impact resistance and buckle and strap integrity. The third and newest organization is the American Society for Testing and Materials (ASTM). They are currently working on tougher requirements especially in the new issue of helmet retention. As Fred Zahradnik, technical editor for *Bicycling Magazine*, states:

> Present certification doesn't address how well a helmet stays on the head during impact, other than a simple strap pull to make sure the buckle won't fail. The new test tilts the headform forward and attaches a weighted strap to the back of the helmet. When the weight is dropped, the helmet must stay on the headform or it fails. (120)

This test would insure that the helmet would stay properly positioned on the head during an impact.

Any helmets that have been tested by these safety orga- 5 nizations will be clearly labeled and marked. I strongly recommend purchasing a helmet that meets the safety criteria of at least one of these organizations. I should also mention that the safety standards are constantly being revised and updated. When purchasing a helmet, you should carefully check the date on the safety sticker; in this way you will assure yourself of the benefits of the latest technologies and safety standards.

Finally, you will need to consider fit, and this will prob- 6 ably be the deciding factor in most helmet purchases. Bicycling helmets come in only three standard sizes which you then adjust through the use of some form of variable padding. You should find a helmet that fits you with the least amount of additional padding to insure that in the event of an accident the helmet will not shift leaving the head vulnerable to injury. Your next concern are the straps and buckles. Do they provide adequate adjustment? You can check this by placing the helmet on your head, adjusting the straps so the helmet is level front to back and side to side, then grasping the helmet and trying to rotate it off your head. The helmet shouldn't move enough to allow any space to be created between it and your head. If it does, add more padding. If this fails to correct the situation, either select a smaller size or try a different helmet. Even the slightest difference between manufacturers' sizing systems might just give you that perfect fit.

I hope that this information has clarified some of the 7 questions that you might have had, and enabled you to purchase a helmet with confidence and peace of mind.

Works Cited

"Better Bicycle Helmets Needed." *USA Today* April 1991: 6.
"Bike Helmets." *Consumer Reports* 56 (1991): 331-4.
Zahradnik, Fred. "A Better Biff Bucket." *Bicycling* September/October 1993: 120.

Thinking About Writing

Notice how Carparelli organizes his information: definition of helmet types, safety concerns, and fit. Within each general category of information, he also offers specific descriptions and advice so that someone going to a store to buy a helmet will know exactly what to look for. He also uses sources to support his information. Why are the specific sources he has chosen particularly effective in terms of making his readers believe the information he is telling them?

Writing Assignment

Write a consumer report either on a product that you know a good deal about and probably use, as Carparelli did, or conduct some experiments on a product whose advertising claim you have always wondered about and report on your findings. Remember that you are not trying to persuade anyone to buy a particular product—this is not an advertising campaign—but to report on various options as well as features or findings they should take into account.

ENVIRONMENTALISM MATTERS

John Shepardson

Background

As an environmental studies student, John was well aware of the way our environment is being destroyed. He felt this would not happen so much if we could all recognize our dependence on other life forms remaining healthy. In this paper he tried to explain this interconnectedness and to show a way in which we might feel this more as our ancestors did. While you read, notice how he challenges us to examine our disconnectedness and then tries to show how unrealistic this point of view is.

Reading Selection

About a half-million years ago (Dott & Batten, 1988, p. 610), conditions in the ecosystem permitted humans to establish themselves as a species. There was a niche we could exploit and we did. Unfortunately for much of earth's life, as our numbers grew, so did our arrogance. Our unique communication skills allowed the sharing of knowledge in a synergistic process that expanded the ability to exploit our niche into the ability to exploit the entire ecosystem. 1

Early humans, the hunter-gatherers and the first agrarian societies, were intimately connected to the earth's natural processes. They understood on a gut level the importance of sun and rain, for example. Without them, these people died of thirst and starvation. For them, the link was clear and immediate. We have, in the last few thousand years, progressed to the point where this link to nature is totally invisible to much of our population. Water comes from faucets, food from stores. 2

This disconnection from our ecosystem is reinforced for many people by their belief, learned early in life, that "man" is the supreme life form and that everything else was put on earth for our use. This fits well with another belief that humans are at the top of the food chain, that we have no natural enemies. Once there were predators that humans 3 feared. They were the big carnivores—tigers, lions, and bears. We overcame them with our brains which enabled us to invent weapons. Now, we are supreme. Or are we? What about the tiniest creatures, the viruses and bacteria that kill us every day? We are not really supreme. We are part of the system of life on this planet and we must live within the constraints of that system if we are to survive.

We have much to learn about these constraints, but we 4 already know some important things. One is that species of plants and animals appear and disappear over geologic time, depending on how well suited to the existing environmental conditions they are. When conditions change and a species cannot tolerate the new ones, it becomes extinct. Many species are threatened with extinction now. Many have already been lost. Some of this would happen naturally, but the large number of threatened species appears to be caused mostly by human activity. Habitat destruction is one of our activities that kills a species. Like us, if they have no shelter or food, they perish.

Many humans, especially in Western society, do not 5 have much understanding of the interdependence of life on this planet. This is a root cause of the continuing assault on the environment. If people understood that their own survival is connected to the species we are driving into extinction, the behavior that is doing the damage would start to change. In a greatly simplified overview, let me list some of the things other forms of life do that allow us to survive.

First, breathing. We take oxygen from the air to fuel our 6 bodily processes. It is in the air because plants release it as a byproduct of their metabolism. If we lose too many plants, we will not have enough oxygen. Plants need soil with nutrients and water to grow. The nutrients are recycled by microorganisms that break down dead organic matter (Nebel, 1990, p. 165). Many of the chemicals we release into the environment kill the microorganisms. We cannot ordinarily see these creatures, but they are essential to our survival.

Our next most critical need is water. We take it for 7 granted, but most of what we consume is polluted to some degree, and it is getting worse in most places. There are natural processes that clean the water, one of which is the filtration that happens when rainwater slowly works its way through a forest floor and down into the aquifer. On the other end, rivers flow into tidal flats where the water is slowly filtered through plants before going back into the ocean. These both depend on healthy plants to work.

Then there is our food, all of which comes from plants, either directly or indirectly. The bottom line is this, there is no supreme species. All are interdependent. Except perhaps us. Try to think of any species that would miss humans if they were to become extinct besides those we have trained to be dependent on us. We may be the only species the world would be better off without. If we are to thrive, we must understand that bacteria decomposing dead organic matter into nutrients for plants are just as important as we are. The famous Pogo quote, "We have met the enemy, and he is us," sums up the problem. 8

The damage humans are doing to the environment is a serious problem, made worse because many people do not understand how their actions hurt other life. The lack of understanding is largely due to our disconnection from nature, but this goes back to the line about water comes from faucets and food comes from stores. 9

There are many ways to eliminate this disconnection, but one that is often suggested is to put a box of dirt in the sun and to grow some of our own food rather than letting large corporations do it for us (Cunningham & Saigo, 1992, p. 214). This food both nourishes us and teaches us about how the environment works. We can learn early on that a praying mantis is not an ugly bug to be stepped on but rather a friend who can keep the vegetarian bugs from eating the entire crop. We can enjoy food that is not sprayed with chemical poisons. We can gain a whole new appreciation for rainy days, and the idea of acid rain may not seem so remote. In short, we can re-establish connections to the environment that our ancestors knew well. They depended on that environment for survival. We do, too. 10

References

Cunningham, W. P., & Saigo, B. W. (1992). *Environmental science: A global concern.* Dubuque, IA: William C. Brown.

Dott, R. H., Jr., & Batten, R. L. (1988). *Evolution of the earth.* New York: Macmillan.

Nebel, B. J. (1990). *Environmental science: The way the world works.* Englewood Cliffs, NJ: Prentice Hall.

Thinking About Writing

Notice how Shepardson organizes his essay. In the first section he sets up the fact that interdependence used to exist. He then goes on to say how we have come to feel disconnected from our environment. But then he tries to prove that we are just as interdependent even if we no longer think about where our water and food come from. Finally, he suggests a way to make this connectedness feel more real to us by growing a little of our own food. In the end he brings us back to his idea of our ancestors to remind us that things really weren't so different for them if we would only realize our interdependence. Shepardson is informing us about this issue and a way to begin to understand it better. In what way does this organization reflect his main point about connectedness?

Writing Assignment

Select a rather complex social issue and explain it to an audience that needs to understand it. Make sure we see the complexity of the issue by explaining its history or its various aspects or its implications for our lives. You might also, as Shepardson does, suggest ways to help us understand the issue better.

Part Six
READERS AND WRITERS ON READING AND WRITING

"... a woman must have money and a room of her own if she is to write ..."

Virginia Woolf

Virginia Woolf

some will strut and some will fret
see this an hour on the stage
others will not but they'll sweat
in their hopelessness in their rage
we're all the same the men of anger and the women of the page

they published your diary
and that's how i got to know you
key to the room of your own and a mind without end
here's a young girl on a kind of a telephone line through time
the voice at the other end comes like a long-lost friend
so i know i'm alright
my life will come my life will go
still i feel it's alright

i just got a letter to my soul
when my whole life is on the tip of my tongue
empty pages for the no longer young
the apathy of time laughs in my face
you say each life has its place

the hatches were battened
thunderclouds rolled and the critics stormed
battles surrounded the white flag of your youth
but if you need to know that you weathered the storm of cruel
    mortality
a hundred years later i'm sitting here living proof
so you know it's alright
your life will come your life will go
still you'll feel it's alright
someone will get a letter to your soul
when your whole life was on the tip of your tongue
empty pages for the no longer young
the apathy of time laughed in your face
did you hear me say each life has its place

the place where you hold me is dark in a pocket of truth
the moon has swallowed the sun and the light of the earth
and so it was for you when the river eclipsed your life
but sent your soul like a message in a bottle to me and it was my
    rebirth
so we know it's alright
life will come and life will go
still we know it's alright
someone will get a message to your soul
then you know it's alright
and you feel it's alright . . .

Indigo Girls

These lyrics express a feeling that many people have about reading—that it can have a profound and lasting influence on our lives. The Indigo Girls paint a vivid portrait of a young girl reading Woolf's diary, and though separated by a hundred years, the writer still reaches out ("a kind of a telephone line through time") to the reader. Through Woolf's act of writing and the girl's act of reading something profound happens between them.

We began this book with the idea that reading and writing change us. We are influenced by the ideas we take in and by the act of shaping our ideas so they can be understood by others. In this section of the book, we will listen to writers discuss how reading or writing has influenced them—how writers reach out, uninhibited by the barriers of time, and send messages in bottles to us to touch our lives with their words.

Chapter Fifteen

WRITINGS ABOUT READING FROM OUR PROFESSIONAL WRITERS

Reading matters. It is a simple yet profound thought for a writer to keep in mind. Reading influences the way we experience events, the way we formulate our opinions, the way we respond to others' ideas, and the way we gain knowledge. It then also influences our ability to articulate our own experiences, opinions, ideas, and knowledge in our writing.

College students are asked to read all the time. Usually, students do informative reading of a textbook in order to pass a test. But as we have seen, reading goes beyond this practical consideration. The reading experience is one of understanding someone else's words in a way that fills us with worlds and ideas we might never encounter on our own. As writers we can learn how to express ourselves, support our ideas, persuade, or inform by paying attention to how others do this. Reading is the foundation on which all writers build.

In this chapter we have returned to four professional writers you have encountered in previous chapters to hear what they say about reading: Annie Dillard ("Mother," Chapter Five), Richard Wright ("Conquering the Streets of Memphis," Chapter Three), Lewis Thomas ("On Society as Organisms," Chapter Fourteen), and Donald Murray ("Haunted by the Inglorious Terrors of War," Chapter Six).

READING IS SUBVERSIVE

Annie Dillard

Prereading Journal

What was your first experience with books? Were you read to? Were you encouraged to read on your own? How often did you read? Explain what reading meant to you as a child.

Background

In this selection from *An American Childhood,* Dillard writes about her experience with books. She draws on her personal reflection to explain to the reader why she read and the difference reading made in her life.

During Reading

Make a list of the types of books Dillard is reading. Keep track of what she is seeking from these books.

Reading Selection

It was clear that adults, including our parents, approved 1 of children who read books, but it was not at all clear why this was so. Our reading was subversive, and we knew it. Did they think we read to improve our vocabularies? Did they want us to read and not pay the least bit of heed to what we read, as they wanted us to go to Sunday school and ignore what we heard?

I was now believing books more than I believed what I 2 saw and heard. I was reading books about the actual, histori-cal, moral world—in which somehow I felt I was not living.

The French and Indian War had been, for me, a pure- 3 ly literary event. Skilled men in books could survive it. Those who died, an arrow through the heart, thrilled me by their last words. This recent war's survivors, some still shaking, some still in mourning, taught in our classrooms. *"Wir waren ausgebommt,"* one dear old white-haired Polish lady related in German class, her family was "bombed out," and we laughed, we smart girls, because this was our slang for "drunk." Those who died in this war's books died whether they were skilled or not. Bombs fell on their cities or ships, or they starved in the camps or were gassed or shot, or they stepped on land mines and died surprised, trying to push their intestines back in their abdomens with their fingers and thumbs.

What I sought in books was imagination. It was depth, 4 depth of thought and feeling; some sort of extreme of subject matter; some nearness to death; some call to courage. I myself was getting wild; I wanted wildness, originality, genius, rapture, hope. I wanted strength, not tea parties. What I sought in books was a world whose surfaces, whose people and events and days lived, actually matched the exaltation of the interior life. There you could live.

Those of us who read carried around with us like mar- 5 tyrs a secret knowledge, a secret joy, and a secret hope: There is a life worth living where history is still taking place; there are ideas worth dying for, and circumstances where courage is still prized. This life could be found and joined, like the Resistance. I kept this exhilarating faith alive in myself, concealed under my uniform shirt like an oblate's ribbon; I would not be parted from it.

We who had grown up in the Warsaw ghetto, who had 6 seen all our families gassed in the death chambers, who had shipped before the mast, and hunted sperm whale in Antarctic seas; we who had marched from Moscow to Poland and lost our legs to the cold; we who knew by heart every snag and sandbar on the Mississippi River south of Cairo, and knew by heart Morse code, forty parables and psalms, and lots of Shakespeare; we who had battled Hitler and Hirohito in the North Atlantic, in North Africa, in New Guinea and Burma and Guam, in the air over London, in the Greek and Italian hills; we who had learned to man minesweepers before we learned to walk in high heels—were we going to marry Holden Caulfield's roommate, and buy a house in Point Breeze, and send our children to dancing school?

After Reading: An Expressive Response

Select one of your most significant reading experiences and describe it for us so that we can feel what it meant to you and why—what it taught you about yourself, about life, or about the world.

DISCOVERING BOOKS

Richard Wright

Prereading Journal

Have you ever been denied the right to read a book? This might have been because your parents considered you too young or because the book was "banned." How did that make you feel? What reasons might people have for keeping certain books from certain readers? Is this a good or necessary restriction?

Background

In this selection, Wright tells of how he got to use the public library as an African-American in Mississippi in the 1920s, and how once he was able to borrow books, his life was never quite the same. He writes about the experience and the dramatic influence it had on his desire to write.

During Reading

Draw a timeline to represent the changes that reading brought to Wright's everyday life.

Reading Selection

One morning I arrived early at work and went into the bank lobby where the Negro porter was mopping. I stood at a counter and picked up the Memphis *Commercial Appeal* and began my free reading of the press. I came finally to the editorial page and saw an article dealing with one H. L. Mencken. I knew by hearsay that he was the editor of the *American Mercury*, but aside from that I knew nothing about him. The article was a furious denunciation of Mencken, concluding with one, hot, short sentence: Mencken is a fool.

I wondered what on earth this Mencken had done to call down upon him the scorn of the South. The only people I had ever heard denounced in the South were Negroes, and this man was not a Negro. Then what ideas did Mencken hold that made a newspaper like the *Commercial Appeal* castigate him publicly? Undoubtedly he must be advocating ideas that the South did not like. Were there, then, people other than Negroes who criticized the South? I knew that during the Civil War the South had hated northern whites, but I had not encountered such hate during my life. Knowing no more of Mencken than I did at that moment, I felt a vague sympathy for him. Had not the South, which had assigned me the role of a nonman, cast at him its hardest words?

Now, how could I find out about this Mencken? There 3 was a huge library near the riverfront, but I knew that Negroes were not allowed to patronize its shelves any more than they were the parks and playgrounds of the city. I had gone into the library several times to get books for the white men on the job. Which of them would now help me to get books? And how could I read them without causing concern to the white men with whom I worked? I had so far been successful in hiding my thoughts and feelings from them, but I knew that I would create hostility if I went about this business of reading in a clumsy way.

I weighed the personalities of the men on the job. 4 There was Don, a Jew; but I distrusted him. His position was not much better than mine and I knew that he was uneasy and insecure; he had always treated me in an offhand, bantering way that barely concealed his contempt. I was afraid to ask him to help me to get books; his frantic desire to demonstrate a racial solidarity with the whites against Negroes might make him betray me.

Then how about the boss? No, he was a Baptist and I 5 had the suspicion that he would not be quite able to comprehend why a black boy would want to read Mencken. There were other white men on the job whose attitudes showed clearly that they were Kluxers or sympathizers, and they were out of the question.

There remained only one man whose attitude did not 6 fit into an anti-Negro category, for I had heard the white men refer to him as a "Pope lover." He was an Irish Catholic and was hated by the white Southerners. I knew that he read books, because I had got him volumes from the library several times. Since he, too, was an object of hatred, I felt that he might refuse me but would hardly betray me. I hesitated, weighing and balancing the imponderable realities.

One morning I paused before the Catholic fellow's 7
desk.

"I want to ask you a favor," I whispered to him.   8

"What is it?"   9

"I want to read. I can't get books from the library. I won- 10
der if you'd let me use your card?"

He looked at me suspiciously.   11

"My card is full most of the time," he said.   12

"I see," I said and waited, posing my question silently. 13

"You're not trying to get me into trouble, are you, boy?" 14
he asked, staring at me.

"Oh, no, sir."   15

"What book do you want?"   16

"A book by H. L. Mencken."   17

"Which one?"   18

"I don't know. Has he written more than one?"   19

"He has written several."   20

"I didn't know that."   21

"What makes you want to read Mencken?"   22

"Oh, I just saw his name in the newspaper," I said.   23

"It's good of you to want to read," he said. "But you 24
ought to read the right things."

I said nothing. Would he want to supervise my reading? 25

"Let me think," he said. "I'll figure out something."   26

I turned from him and he called me back. He stared at 27
me quizzically.

"Richard, don't mention this to the other white men," 28
he said.

"I understand," I said. "I won't say a word."   29

A few days later he called me to him.   30

"I've got a card in my wife's name," he said. "Here's 31
mine."

"Thank you, sir."   32

"Do you think you can manage it?"   33

"I'll manage fine," I said.   34

"If they suspect you, you'll get in trouble," he said. 35

"I'll write the same kind of notes to the library that you 36
wrote when you sent me for books," I told him. "I'll sign your
name."

He laughed.   37

"Go ahead. Let me see what you get," he said.   38

That afternoon I addressed myself to forging a note. 39
Now, what were the names of books written by H. L.
Mencken? I did not know any of them. I finally wrote what I
thought would be a foolproof note: *Dear Madam: Will you
please let this nigger boy*—I used the word "nigger" to make the
librarian feel that I could not possibly be the author of the
note—*have some books by H. L. Mencken?* I forged the white
man's name.

I entered the library as I had always done when on 40
errands for whites, but I felt that I would somehow slip up
and betray myself. I doffed my hat, stood a respectful distance from the desk, looked as unbookish as possible, and
waited for the white patrons to be taken care of. When the
desk was clear of people, I still waited. The white librarian
looked at me.

"What do you want, boy?"   41

As though I did not possess the power of speech, I 42
stepped forward and simply handed her the forged note, not
parting my lips.

"What books by Mencken does he want?" she asked.   43

"I don't know, ma'am," I said, avoiding her eyes.   44

"Who gave you this card?"   45

"Mr. Falk," I said.   46

"Where is he?"   47

"He's at work, at the M———— Optical Company," I said. 48
"I've been in here for him before."

"I remember," the woman said. "But he never wrote 49
notes like this."

Oh, God, she's suspicious. Perhaps she would not let 50
me have the books? If she had turned her back at that
moment, I would have ducked out the door and never gone
back. Then I thought of a bold idea.

"You can call him up, ma'am," I said, my heart pounding. 51

"You're not using these books, are you?" she asked 52
pointedly.

"Oh, no, ma'am. I can't read."   53

"I don't know what he wants by Mencken," she said 54
under her breath.

I knew now that I had won; she was thinking of other 55
things and the race question had gone out of her mind. She
went to the shelves. Once or twice she looked over her shoul-

der at me, as though she was still doubtful. Finally she came forward with two books in her hand.

"I'm sending him two books," she said. "But tell Mr. 56 Falk to come in next time, or send me the names of the books he wants. I don't know what he wants to read."

I said nothing. She stamped the card and handed me 57 the books. Not daring to glance at them, I went out of the library, fearing that the woman would call me back for further questioning. A block away from the library I opened one of the books and read a title: *A Book of Prefaces.* I was nearing my nineteenth birthday and I did not know how to pronounce the word *preface.* I thumbed the pages and saw strange words and strange names. I shook my head, disappointed. I looked at the other book; it was called *Prejudices.* I knew what that word meant; I had heard it all my life. And right off I was on guard against Mencken's books. Why would a man want to call a book *Prejudices?* The word was so stained with all my memories of racial hate that I could not conceive of anybody using it for a title. Perhaps I had made a mistake about Mencken? A man who had prejudices must be wrong.

When I showed the books to Mr. Falk, he looked at me 58 and frowned.

"That librarian might telephone you," I warned him. 59

"That's all right," he said. "But when you're through 60 reading those books, I want you to tell me what you get out of them."

That night in my rented room, while letting the hot 61 water run over my can of pork and beans in the sink, I opened *A Book of Prefaces* and began to read. I was jarred and shocked by the style, the clear, clean, sweeping sentences. Why did he write like that? And how did one write like that? I pictured the man as a raging demon, slashing with his pen, consumed with hate, denouncing everything American, extolling everything European or German, laughing at the weaknesses of people, mocking God, authority. What was this? I stood up, trying to realize what reality lay behind the meaning of the words. . . . Yes, this man was fighting, fighting with words. He was using words as a weapon, using them as one would use a club. Could words be weapons? Well, yes, for here they were. Then, maybe, perhaps, I could use them as a weapon? No. It frightened me. I read on and what amazed me was not what he said, but how on earth anybody had the courage to say it.

Occasionally I glanced up to reassure myself that I was   62 alone in the room. Who were these men about whom Mencken was talking so passionately? Who was Anatole France? Joseph Conrad? Sinclair Lewis, Sherwood Anderson, Dostoevski, George Moore, Gustave Flaubert, Maupassant, Tolstoy, Frank Harris, Mark Twain, Thomas Hardy, Arnold Bennett, Stephen Crane, Zola, Norris, Gorky, Bergson, Ibsen, Balzac, Bernard Shaw, Dumas, Poe, Thomas Mann, O. Henry, Dreiser, H. G. Wells, Gogol, T. S. Eliot, Gide, Baudelaire, Edgar Lee Masters, Stendhal, Turgenev, Huneker, Nietzsche, and scores of others? Were these men real? Did they exist or had they existed? And how did one pronounce their names?

I ran across many words whose meanings I did not   63 know, and I either looked them up in a dictionary or, before I had a chance to do that, encountered the word in a context that made its meaning clear. But what strange world was this? I concluded the book with the conviction that I had some-how overlooked something terribly important in life. I had once tried to write, had once reveled in feeling, had let my crude imagination roam, but the impulse to dream had been slowly beaten out of me by experience. Now it surged up again and I hungered for books, new ways of looking and see-ing. It was not a matter of believing or disbelieving what I read, but of feeling something new, or being affected by something that made the look of the world different.

After Reading: An Affirming Response

Write about a time when reading introduced you to a differ-ent way of thinking. For example, perhaps in reading *The Adventures of Huckleberry Finn* you first realized that not all children are raised by two concerned parents. Or perhaps reading *Lord of the Flies* made you wonder about whether human nature is basically good or evil. Explain both your initial point of view and the point of view you experienced through the book.

NOTES ON PUNCTUATION
Lewis Thomas
Prereading Journal

Have you ever found something difficult to read because of the way it was written? Perhaps the sentences were very long and filled with difficult words. Perhaps the writer's tone was very dry and that made the piece boring. Perhaps the use of ellipses, italics, or dialogue made it difficult to figure out what was going on. Write about the influence that style can have on your ability to understand a piece of writing.

Background

In this humorous selection from Thomas' collection, *The Medusa and the Snail,* Thomas discusses the influence punctuation can have on our reading: how it tells us when and how to read, how it tries to manipulate our feelings, and even how it can be dangerous.

During Reading

Note places where Thomas not only discusses the punctuation mark but also illustrates what he is saying about it.

Reading Selection

There are no precise rules about punctuation (Fowler 1 lays out some general advice (as best he can under the complex circumstances of English prose (he points out, for example, that we possess only four stops (the comma, the semicolon, the colon and the period (the question mark and exclamation point are not, strictly speaking, stops; they are indicators of tone (oddly enough, the Greeks employed the semicolon for their question mark (it produces a strange sensation to read a Greek sentence which is a straightforward question: Why weepest thou; (instead of Why weepest thou? (and, of course, there are parentheses (which are surely a kind of punctuation making this whole matter much more complicated by having to count up the left-handed parentheses in order to be sure of closing with the right number (but if the parentheses were left out, with nothing to work with but the stops, we would have considerably more flexibility in the deploying of layers of meaning than if we tried to separate all the clauses by physical barriers (and in the latter case, while we might have more precision and exactitude for our meaning, we would lose the essential flavor of language, which is its wonderful ambiguity)))))))))))).

The commas are the most useful and usable of all the 2 stops. It is highly important to put them in place as you go along. If you try to come back after doing a paragraph and stick them in the various spots that tempt you you will discover that they tend to swarm like minnows into all sorts of crevices whose existence you hadn't realized and before you know it the whole long sentence becomes immobilized and lashed up squirming in commas. Better to use them sparingly, and with affection, precisely when the need for each one arises, nicely, by itself.

I have grown fond of semicolons in recent years. The 3 semicolon tells you that there is still some question about the preceding full sentence; something needs to be added; it reminds you sometimes of the Greek usage. It is almost always a greater pleasure to come across a semicolon than a period. The period tells you that that is that; if you didn't get all the meaning you wanted or expected, anyway you got all the writer intended to parcel out and now you have to move along. But with a semicolon there you get a pleasant little feeling of expectancy; there is more to come; read on; it will get clearer.

Colons are a lot less attractive, for several reasons: first- 4 ly, they give you the feeling of being rather ordered around, or at least having your nose pointed in a direction you might not be inclined to take if left to yourself, and, secondly, you suspect you're in for one of those sentences that will be labeling the points to be made: firstly, secondly and so forth, with the implication that you haven't sense enough to keep track of a sequence of notions without having them numbered. Also, many writers use this system loosely and incompletely, starting out with number one and number two as though counting off on their fingers but then going on and on without the succession of labels you've been led to expect, leaving you floundering about searching for the ninethly or seventeenthly that ought to be there but isn't.

Exclamation points are the most irritating of all. Look! they say, look at what I just said! How amazing is my thought! It is like being forced to watch someone else's small child jumping up and down crazily in the center of the living room shouting to attract attention. If a sentence really has something of importance to say, something quite remarkable, it doesn't need a mark to point it out. And if it is really, after all, a banal sentence needing more zing, the exclamation point simply emphasizes its banality! 5

Quotation marks should be used honestly and sparingly, when there is a genuine quotation at hand, and it is necessary to be very rigorous about the words enclosed by the marks. If something is to be quoted, the *exact* words must be used. If part of it must be left out because of space limitations, it is good manners to insert three dots to indicate the omission, but it is unethical to do this if it means connecting two thoughts which the original author did not intend to have tied together. Above all, quotation marks should not be used for ideas that you'd like to disown, things in the air so to speak. Nor should they be put in place around clichés; if you want to use a cliché you must take full responsibility for it yourself and not try to fob it off on anon., or on society. The most objectionable misuse of quotation marks, but one which illustrates the dangers of misuse in ordinary prose, is seen in advertising, especially in advertisement for small restaurants, for example "just around the corner," or "a good place to eat." No single, identifiable, citable person ever really said, for the record, "just around the corner," much less "a good place to eat," least likely of all for restaurants of the type that use this type of prose. 6

The dash is a handy device, informal and essentially playful, telling you that you're about to take off on a different tack but still in some way connected with the present course—only you have to remember that the dash is there, and either put a second dash at the end of the notion to let the reader know that he's back on course, or else end the sentence, as here, with a period. 7

The greatest danger in punctuation is for poetry. Here it is necessary to be as economical and parsimonious with commas and periods as with the words themselves, and any marks that seem to carry their own subtle meanings, like 8 dashes and little rows of periods, even semicolons and questions marks, should be left out altogether rather than inserted to clog up the thing with ambiguity. A single exclamation point in a poem, no matter what else the poem has to say, is enough to destroy the whole work.

The things I like best in T. S. Eliot's poetry, especially in   9 the *Four Quartets,* are the semicolons. You cannot hear them, but they are there, laying out the connections between the images and the ideas. Sometimes you get a glimpse of a semicolon coming, a few lines farther on, and it is like climbing a steep path through woods and seeing a wooden bench just at a bend in the road ahead, a place where you can expect to sit for a moment, catching your breath.

Commas can't do this sort of thing; they can only tell 10 you how the different parts of a complicated thought are to be fitted together, but you can't sit, not even take a breath, just because of a comma,

After Reading: A Persuasive Response

Select one of the opinions about punctuation Thomas expressed that you disagree with, and write him a letter trying to convince him that he's wrong about this matter of periods or commas or dashes. Or select one of the other writers you have read in this book whose style you found difficult. Write that person a letter trying to convince her or him to change and explaining why a different style would be more effective.

READING AS A READER

Donald M. Murray

Prereading Journal

Throughout this textbook you have been given much information about reading and how to read. Imagine you were asked to give other students some helpful hints for improving reading. List as many strategies as you can to share with them.

Background

Murray is interested in reading and writing and the connection between these two skills. In this excerpt from *Read to Write,* he gives the audience information about reading and includes practical suggestions for reading for a particular purpose. For him, as for the other authors profiled here, it is the reading process that contributes to good writing.

During Reading

List the ways Murray connects reading and writing. How is reading an essential part of the writing process?

Reading Selection

READING FOR INFORMATION

When we read for information we experience the text 1 in a different way. Depending on the information we seek, we may not want to enter into the story, and we do not much care how the writing is written, as long as the writing does not get in the way of the information we need. Our newspapers know we want information on stocks and football standings, and so they give us this information in the form of tables and listings. That writing is hardly "written" at all. Other times we need information that is hidden in a normal text of sentences and paragraphs. In that case we have to mine the text and extract the information we need. In this kind of reading we may choose to stand apart from the text, not to be involved in but simply to make use of what is said.

Scanning

To extract information from a text we need to scan, 2
swooping over the text, looking for any clues that may help
us find where the information is. We may turn first to an
index or table of contents to see if it will tell us where the
information we need is placed. In the case of an academic
article we may read the abstract, a summary paragraph usually printed in small type at the beginning of the article to
serve information gatherers and save them time.

Watching for Road Signs

If we think the text has the information we need, we 3
should run through it, paying attention to chapter headings,
crossheads (such as the one above, "Watching for Road
Signs"), illustrations, diagrams, or other signals designed to
help us get to the information we need. When we confront
the text itself we should look for key words that will tell us
that the information may be nearby. For example, if we are
looking for information on the low salaries of women office
workers, we may look for such words as "secretaries," "file
clerks," "typists," "receptionists," "salaries," "wages," "com-
pensation," "sexism," "prejudice," "women," "girls," "office
workers," and so on. We can run through many pages of type
easily, stopping only when we see something that tells us the
information may be nearby.

Making Notes

In reading for information we usually have a notebook 4
or note cards handy so that we can put down the information
we find. If the information is to be quoted directly, we should
put quotation marks around it so that we know when we
come to use it that the note is precisely as the author presented it. If we are to put the information in our own words
it's helpful to do that immediately. It's also important to note
the context in which the information was presented. The
context for the information on office workers might be a
feminist political statement, a report by a male scholar, a
study by a union that wants to organize office workers, a statement by a corporation, or a survey by a government agency.
It is most important that the note include the precise reference so that it can be included in the text and so that you and

your reader can go back and find the information. This means the title of the publication, the author, and all of the details about the publication itself.

After Reading: An Informative Response

Both Murray and this textbook have given you much information about reading and the importance of reading in the writing process. Now share that information with next year's class of writing students. Develop an essay in which you explain to students coming into this course how to read in order to be a good writer. Inform them of the strategies that are necessary to become a reading writer.

Chapter Sixteen

A READING ABOUT WRITING FROM ONE OF OUR STUDENT WRITERS

Writing, like reading, can be very influential in our lives. The act of articulating our thoughts, feelings, and opinions on paper helps us to understand them better, and struggling to articulate our ideas may help us to see that we don't really understand them very well at all yet.

Most students encounter writing for the first time as adults in their college composition classes. For some, this is a chance to discover or rediscover a talent, to see writing as reaching beyond just course requirements into the realm of communication, to interact with others and learn how to give and accept criticism, and to develop an understanding of their own writing processes. For a few students this even becomes the beginning of a commitment to a career in writing.

But for other students, this first encounter with writing in college can be difficult. It can be the first time that their work is really scrutinized carefully, the first time they are expected to discover their own topics, to genuinely revise, to take responsibility for their own writing process. Sometimes these new expectations come with less support and guidance than students may need, and then writing, like many other college experiences, becomes intimidating and even frightening.

Whether the experience is positive or negative, college composition courses are often memorable and influential. For one of the student writers you have already met earlier in this book, the course was so significant that he wrote about it and used the writing experience to reflect on his current feelings about writing in his life. Below is an essay by Todd Craig, whose piece, "Fall," you read in Chapter Five.

LIGHTNING STRIKES
Todd Craig

Background

Craig was one of those students who discovered the joy of writing in his first college composition class. He was so taken with the desire "to get things down and a strong love of words" that he signed up for every writing class he could take, did independent studies in writing, kept his own daily journal, and finally became editor of his school's student literary magazine. For Craig, discovering writing was like discovering the power of lightning.

Ninth (Or-So) Draft

I'm not at all sure how it happened. It just did. Bang. For   1
the first writing assignment we had to write a narrative essay. I just sat down and did it. I wrote a brief narrative essay about when my dog was born. I never thought about it while I was writing it or revising it, but after it was completed I was surprised to find myself excited at having created something. Not only was it a finished piece with a beginning and an ending but it had meaning, both to others and to me. It told people about how my dog was born and revealed how important the experience was. When I held the essay in my hands I had a concrete account of the event. I no longer had to think about it to remember. I only had to read what I had written. There it was. I had said something, something important to me.

The next assignment found me sitting in my professor's   2
office wondering if I had made a wrong move. I had handed in a rough draft of an essay that didn't meet the actual assignment and it was very personal. I began to regret it.

She looked at me and smiled. She handed me my essay.   3
No red pen marks. I read through her comments and saw she was happy that I wrote it. She told me that it wasn't what the rest of the class was doing but that was okay; what was important to her at the time was that I was saying something. Like the story of the birth of my dog, it was something I wanted to get down for good.

I was fortunate to learn early on that writing is about 4
telling and sharing, about getting things out. For the rest of
the semester I did just that: I wrote about things that were
important to me. I put down the strings of words that said
what I wanted to say—not what I thought my professor wanted to hear.

In high school I had handed in term papers and essays 5
that had nothing to do with me. I handed in pages and pages
of what I was supposed to say. I never thought writing could
really be about who I was and exactly what I thought. But that
is what my professor wanted. She wanted the truth about me.
When I had to write a persuasive essay, I had to convince
everyone else that my way was the right way. My thoughts
were important. I was important. And this writing business
had everything to do with me.

A writer doesn't simply sit at a desk and line up mean- 6
ingful words together, making sense of what is obscure. A
writer frees his or her mind of what is crammed up there.
About anything. Writing is like an electrical storm. Lightning
strikes when the thoughts that roam our minds fall into a sentence that gets punctuated on the page. And when the sentences and the paragraphs are read, then there is thunder.
Currents shoot back and forth. It strikes. You think the paper
will catch on fire. When the thunder resounds you know you
have created something concrete: evidence of your existence. There's a pile of cinder blocks on your desk.

When the semester was over I had a handful of essays 7
that I had written. Some were good, some were pretty shoddy. But they were accurate about me. I started to show them
to family and friends. Usually what was on the page better
explained what was in my head. But it wasn't over. There were
more things I wanted to write down. There were other experiences, other thoughts and feelings that were authentic. I
wanted to get everything down and say to everyone that this
is who I am and this is what matters to me.

Your mind is like a dark road. A thought comes along 8
like a car, the headlights are dim and they get brighter as the
car gets closer. You can hear the purr of the engine and faster
and faster the car comes and the headlights are full in your
face. You can't see a thing. Then the car passes. This happens
all the time to us. It is when the car stops right in front of us

that we know we have to write. When you hear the engine of
a thought idling in your mind then you know you have to do
something.

Lightning strikes.   9

Four years later I am still writing. I am still telling sto- 10
ries about things I have done and been through, and I always
have an opinion. When I first wrote that essay about the birth
of my dog I didn't quite know what I was doing or that this
was going to be the start of something so tremendous: being
crazy over words.

Now it is a combination of wanting to get things down 11
and a strong love of words. When I started writing I was just
retelling and explaining. I would sit down at the typewriter
and let fly whatever was on my mind. But now I muse. I ponder. I think not only about what I want to say, but also how I
want to say it and how I think it will be read—how the thunder will sound to others.

And you find yourself being wrapped up in words, 12
each sentence being a necklace, every word a bead that has
significance. How the words sound, how they jumble
together becomes important. You want the thunder to crack
and peal. Sometimes you want the sentences to just rumble,
even whisper.

Once I was taking a train back from Boston to where I 13
was living. The track led through woods and through towns
and cut up backyards. In the afternoon sun, kids were playing.
I remember one little girl with a mop of brown stringy hair
that went crazy as she chased a boy around a small fenced in
yard. She had a headless doll in her hand and she was screaming something. I couldn't hear her in the train, but her mouth
was like a canyon and her face was all contorted in what
looked like a cross between sheer anger and absolute joy. I
cannot remember the little boy's face, but if that girl was ever
chasing me I know I would have a look of horror.

Watching these kids romp after school and before din- 14
ner reminded me of my own childhood. I thought about all
the crazy things we did. I was never chased by a headless doll,
but I lived a real kid's life. In my mind there was a traffic jam.
Too many cars were idling—there were so many stories to tell
and share. I couldn't write right there but I did ask a woman
for a pen and I used part of a shopping bag to write down

notes—the license plates of all the cars—so later I could sit down to create a string of sketches about growing up.

As the train kept going I saw the sun sinking more 15 and more, the day becoming less and less. The leaves were off all the trees, exposing all the nooks where children gather on breezy fall afternoons to play all their dastardly games. I didn't just want to talk about my memories, I wanted to bring people there. I wanted people to experience my childhood, if only in their head while their eyes swim through the sentences I have laid out end to end.

I wanted them to hear the thunder and then remember 16 it.

Analysis

The joy and urgency that Craig feels about writing is coming through clearly in this draft. His thoughts are reflecting the electrical storm of writing. But the piece still needs more quiet reflection time of musing and pondering to make all the power flow in one direction.

For example, Craig has two guiding metaphors working in this piece: the thunderstorm and the traffic jam. Both work, but for a brief paper two controlling images is one too many. So, Craig needed to decide which of the two would actually be used to guide the paper.

Secondly, he recognized a problem with structure. The first part of the paper is telling the story of how he got started writing. He then talks about the present, what is happening four years later. He is essentially drawing conclusions about what the last four years have taught him. But the ending on the train goes back to some previous time and provides another specific past example of how he learned that writing was important to him. He therefore needs to reconsider his structure so he tells the history of his development as it occurred and then draws conclusions from all of those previous experiences.

Craig also knew he needed to work more on wording, clarity, and eliminating repetitious phrases. This detail work, as you will see, is evident in his final draft.

Final Draft

I'm not at all sure how it happened. It just did. Bang. 1 For the first writing assignment we had to write a narrative essay. I just sat down and did it. I wrote a sketch about when my dog was born. I didn't spend much time or effort writing or revising it, but after it was completed I was surprised to find myself excited at having created something. Not only was it a finished piece with a beginning and an ending but it had meaning. Both to others and to me. It told people about how my dog was born and revealed how important the experience was. When I held the essay in my hands I had a concrete account of the event. There it was. I had said something, something important to me.

The next assignment found me sitting in my professor's 2 office wondering if I had made a wrong move. I had handed in a rough draft of an essay that didn't meet the requirements of the assignment, and it was very personal. I was regretting ever having written it.

She looked at me and smiled. She handed me my essay. 3 No red pen marks. Only comments that told me she was happy that I had written it. She told me that it wasn't what the rest of the class was doing but that was okay; what was important to her at the time was that I was saying something. Like the story of the birth of my dog, this topic was something I wanted to get down on paper for good. And that was what mattered to her.

I was fortunate to learn early on that writing is about 4 telling and sharing, about getting things out. For the rest of the semester I did just that: I wrote about things that were important to me. I put down the strings of words that said what I wanted to say—not what I thought my professor wanted to hear. And as it turned out, what I wanted to say was what she wanted to hear.

In high school I had handed in term papers and essays 5 that had nothing to do with me. I had handed in pages and pages of what I was supposed to say. I never thought writing could really be about who I was and exactly what I thought. Now I knew it could. When I had to write a persuasive essay, I had to convince everyone else that my way was the right way. My thoughts were important. I was important. And this writing business had everything to do with me.

Writing is like an electrical storm. Lightning strikes 6 when the thoughts that roam our minds fall into a sentence that gets punctuated on the page. And when the sentences and the paragraphs are read, then there is thunder. Currents shoot back and forth. Lightning strikes. You think the paper will catch on fire. When the thunder resounds you know you have created something concrete: evidence of your existence. There's a pile of cinder blocks on your desk.

When the semester was over I had a handful of essays 7 that I had written. Some were good, some were pretty shoddy. But they were truthful about who I was, capturing fragments of my personality. I started to show them to family and friends. Usually what was on the page clearly explained what was in my head. But it wasn't over. There were more things I wanted to write down. There were other experiences, other thoughts and feelings that were authentic. I wanted to get everything on paper and say to everyone, "This is who I am and this is what matters to me." And I did.

Lightning strikes. 8

When I first wrote that essay about the birth of my dog 9 I didn't quite know what I was doing. I would sit down at the typewriter and let fly whatever was on my mind. But then I started to muse. To ponder. To think not only about what I wanted to say, but also how I wanted to say it and how I thought it would be read—how the thunder would sound to others.

Once I was on a train creeping through the suburbs of 10 Boston. The track led through woods and through towns and it cut up backyards. Kids were playing. I remember one little girl with a mop of brown stringy hair who went crazy as she chased a boy around a small fenced in yard. She had a headless doll in her hand and she was screaming something. I couldn't hear her in the train, but her mouth was like a canyon and her face was all contorted in what looked like a cross between sheer anger and absolute joy. I cannot remember the little boy's face, but if that girl were ever chasing me I know my face would have a look of horror.

Watching these kids romp after school and before din- 11 ner reminded me of my own childhood. I thought about all the crazy things we did. I had never been chased by a headless doll, but I had my own unique experiences—my own childhood stories I wanted to tell and share. I asked a woman for a pen and I used part of a shopping bag to take down the beginnings of sketches and ramblings, everything I could remember about growing up.

As the train moved on I saw the sun sinking more and 12
more, the day becoming less and less. The leaves were off the
trees, exposing all the nooks where children gather on
breezy fall afternoons to play their dastardly games. I didn't
just want to talk about my memories, I wanted to bring people to them. I wanted people to experience my childhood, if
only in their heads while their eyes swam through the sentences I had laid out end to end.

Four years later I am still writing. I am still telling sto- 13
ries about things I have done and been through, and I always
have an opinion.

And I find myself wrapped up in words, each sentence 14
being a necklace, every word a bead that has significance.
How the words sound, how they jumble together is important. Sometimes I want the thunder to crack and peal.
Sometimes I want the sentences to just rumble, even whisper.

But I always want others to hear the thunder and 15
remember it.

Analysis

Craig has created a much tighter piece by cutting and reorganizing. He now provides the story of his development as a writer, moving from his first assignment to his second, more risky one, through
the first semester to the train incident, and finally to the present. He
also has settled on one metaphor, the storm, to carry us through the
piece and to express his idea of what writing is about. This is not to
say that the car metaphor was not successful; he could just as easily
have chosen to work with that one. But one had to be sacrificed,
which only means that one can be saved for a future paper.

He also interweaves his ideas about writing into the story so
that after he begins to understand what writing can mean for him,
he also explains how this attitude differs from the one he had in
high school. Later, after explaining how he began to be aware of
audience, he provides the train incident when he first wanted to
make people experience his childhood with him.

He has also done the minor revisions at the word and sentence level that make the whole piece read more smoothly and better reflect his thoughts. He is illustrating through his revision the
commitment to writing and to each bead on the necklace that he
speaks about in the piece. In other words, he practices what he
preaches.

Exercise

In addition to the controlling metaphor of the lightning, there are other images in this piece that help to make it vivid. Select one of these images (cinder blocks or beads on a necklace, for example) and expand it into a paragraph that explains what the writing experience is like.

Chapter Seventeen

FURTHER READINGS ON READING AND WRITING

The readings contained in this chapter illustrate a wide variety of experiences with and views on reading and writing by professional and student writers, from Malcolm X's self-empowerment through his rigorous studies while in prison, to Tisa Wettach's growing awareness of the liberating nature of seeing reading as an opportunity for discovery.

**PROFESSIONAL ESSAYS ABOUT READING
AND WRITING**

COMING TO AN AWARENESS OF LANGUAGE
Malcolm X
Prereading Journal

Sometimes, when there is something very important on our minds that we need to share with someone, we find that the words we need to express ourselves escape our grasp. Think of a time when you were in such a situation. Why was it so hard to communicate what was on your mind? How did it make you feel, this inability to articulate your thoughts and feelings? Did it motivate you to improve your language skills? Describe the circumstances surrounding the dilemma that made communication so difficult.

Background

Malcolm X, one of the most articulate and outspoken spokespersons for African-Americans in the 1960s, was assassinated at the age of thirty-nine on February 21, 1965. In the following chapter from *The Autobiography of Malcolm X,* he shares his frustration at being unable to articulate his ideas and beliefs.

During Reading

Note the goals that motivate Malcolm X to learn to express himself in an articulate and powerful manner.

Reading Selection

I've never been one for inaction. Everything I've ever 1
felt strongly about, I've done something about. I guess that's why, unable to do anything else, I soon began writing to people I had known in the hustling world, such as Sammy the Pimp, John Hughes, the gambling house owner, the thief Jumpsteady, and several dope peddlers. I wrote them all about Allah and Islam and Mr. Elijah Muhammad. I had no idea

where most of them lived. I addressed their letters in care of the Harlem or Roxbury bars and clubs where I'd known them.

I never got a single reply. The average hustler and crim-   2
inal was too uneducated to write a letter. I have known many slick, sharp-looking hustlers, who would have you think they had an interest in Wall Street; privately, they would get someone else to read a letter if they received one. Besides, neither would I have replied to anyone writing me something as wild as "the white man is the devil."

What certainly went on the Harlem and Roxbury wires   3
was that Detroit Red was going crazy in stir, or else he was trying some hype to shake up the warden's office.

During the years that I stayed in the Norfolk Prison   4
Colony, never did any official directly say anything to me about those letters, although, of course, they all passed through the prison censorship. I'm sure, however, they monitored what I wrote to add to the files which every state and federal prison keeps on the conversion of Negro inmates by the teachings of Mr. Elijah Muhammad.

But at that time, I felt that the real reason was that the   5
white man knew that he was the devil.

Later on, I even wrote to the Mayor of Boston, to the   6
Governor of Massachusetts, and to Harry S. Truman. They never answered; they probably never even saw my letters. I handscratched to them how the white man's society was responsible for the black man's condition in this wilderness of North America.

It was because of my letters that I happened to stum-   7
ble upon starting to acquire some kind of a homemade education.

I became increasingly frustrated at not being able to   8
express what I wanted to convey in letters that I wrote, especially those to Mr. Elijah Muhammad. In the street, I had been the most articulate hustler out there—I had commanded attention when I said something. But now, trying to write simple English, I not only wasn't articulate, I wasn't even functional. How would I sound writing in slang, the way I would *say* it, something such as, "Look daddy, let me pull your coat about a cat. Elijah Muhammad—"

Many who today hear me somewhere in person, or on   9
television, or those who read something I've said, will think I

went to school far beyond the eighth grade. This impression is due entirely to my prison studies.

It had really begun back in the Charlestown Prison, 10 when Bimbi first made me feel envy of his stock of knowledge. Bimbi had always taken charge of any conversation he was in, and I had tried to emulate him. But every book I picked up had few sentences which didn't contain anywhere from one to nearly all of the words that might as well have been in Chinese. When I just skipped those words, of course, I really ended up with little idea of what the book said. So I had come to the Norfolk Prison Colony still going through only book-reading motions. Pretty soon, I would have quit even these motions, unless I had received the motivation that I did.

I saw that the best thing I could do was get hold of a dic- 11 tionary—to study, to learn some words. I was lucky enough to reason also that I should try to improve my penmanship. It was sad. I couldn't even write in a straight line. It was both ideas together that moved me to request a dictionary along with some tablets and pencils from the Norfolk Prison Colony school.

I spent two days just riffling uncertainly through the 12 dictionary's pages. I'd never realized so many words existed! I didn't know *which* words I needed to learn. Finally, just to start some kind of action, I began copying.

In my slow, painstaking, ragged handwriting, I copied 13 into my tablet everything printed on that first page, down to the punctuation marks.

I believe it took me a day. Then, aloud, I read back, to 14 myself, everything I'd written on the tablet. Over and over, aloud, to myself, I read my own handwriting.

I woke up the next morning, thinking about those 15 words—immensely proud to realize that not only had I written so much at one time, but I'd written words that I never knew were in the world. Moreover, with a little effort, I also could remember what many of these words meant. I reviewed the words whose meanings I didn't remember. Funny thing, from the dictionary first page right now, that "aardvark" springs to my mind. The dictionary had a picture of it, a long-tailed, long-eared, burrowing African mammal, which lives off termites caught by sticking out its tongue as an anteater does for ants.

I was so fascinated that I went on—I copied the dictio-   16
nary's next page. And the same experience came when I
studied that. With every succeeding page, I also learned of
people and places and events from history. Actually the dictionary is like a miniature encyclopedia. Finally the dictionary's A section had filled a whole tablet—and I went on into
the B's. That was the way I started copying what eventually
became the entire dictionary. It went a lot faster after so
much practice helped me to pick up handwriting speed.
Between what I wrote in my tablet, and writing letters, during
the rest of my time in prison I would guess I wrote a million
words.

I suppose it was inevitable that as my word-base broad-   17
ened, I could for the first time pick up a book and read and
now begin to understand what the book was saying. Anyone
who has read a great deal can imagine the new world that
opened. Let me tell you something: from then until I left that
prison, in every free moment I had, if I was not reading in the
library, I was reading on my bunk. You couldn't have gotten
me out of books with a wedge. Between Mr. Muhammad's
teachings, my correspondence, my vistors . . . and my reading
of books, months passed without my even thinking about
being imprisoned. In fact, up to then, I never had been so
truly free in my life.

Checking Your Understanding

1. What are Malcolm X's reasons for wishing to become educated? Are
   these the same reasons that you have chosen to go to college or are
   your motivations different? What are some factors that might
   account for these differences or similarities?
2. Define "free" as Malcolm X uses it in his final sentence.

Examining Rhetorical Strategies

1. Malcolm X makes a distinction between being "articulate" and
   being "functional." How does he explain this distinction? How does
   it relate to the main point of the essay?
2. Explain Malcolm X's position in this essay. How does he use his
   experience to support this position? Is his position stated explicitly
   or is it implied?

DESPERATION WRITING

Peter Elbow

Prereading Journal

Think about a time when you suffered from writer's block or anxiety over an assignment. Describe how you felt as you struggled to get your ideas on paper. How did you overcome the blockage?

Background

Elbow is the author of numerous articles and books on writing, teaching, and learning. Among these are *Writing Without Teachers* (1973), *Writing with Power* (1981), and *Embracing Contraries* (1986). In this essay Elbow confronts the "panic" many people feel about writing and offers some suggestions for how to overcome the fear and "just write."

During Reading

Keep track of the strategies Elbow employs to overcome his fear that he won't be able to "produce coherent speech or thought."

Reading Selection

I know I am not alone in my recurring twinges of panic 1 that I won't be able to write something when I need to, I won't be able to produce coherent speech or thought. And that lingering doubt is a great hindrance to writing. It's a constant fog or static that clouds the mind. I never got out of its clutches till I discovered that it was possible to write something—not something great or pleasing but at least something usable, workable—when my mind is out of commission. The trick is that you have to do all your cooking out on the table: Your mind is incapable of doing any inside. It means using symbols and pieces of paper not as a crutch but as a wheelchair.

The first thing is to admit your condition: Because of 2 some mood or event or whatever, your mind is incapable of anything that could be called thought. It can put out a babbling kind of speech utterance, it can put a simple feeling, perception, or sort-of-thought into understandable (though terrible) words. But it is incapable of considering anything in relation to anything else. The moment you try to hold that thought or feeling up against some other to see the relationship, you simply lose the picture—you get nothing but buzzing lines or waving colors.

So admit this. Avoid anything more than one feeling, 3 perception, or thought. Simply write as much as possible. Try simply to steer your mind in the direction or general vicinity of the thing you are trying to write about and start writing and keep writing.

Just write and keep writing. (Probably best to write on 4 only one side of the paper in case you should want to cut parts out with scissors—but you probably won't.) Just write and keep writing. It will probably come in waves. After a flurry, stop and take a brief rest. But don't stop too long. Don't think about what you are writing or what you have written or else you will overload the circuit again. Keep writing as though you are drugged or drunk. Keep doing this till you feel you have a lot of material that might be useful; or, if necessary, till you can't stand it any more—even if you doubt that there's anything useful there.

Then take a pad of little pieces of paper—or perhaps 5 3×5 cards—and simply start at the beginning of what you were writing, and as you read over what you wrote, every time you come to any thought, feeling, perception, or image that could be gathered up into one sentence or one assertion, do so and write it by itself on a little sheet of paper. In short, you are trying to turn, say, ten or twenty pages of wandering mush into twenty or thirty hard little crab apples. Sometimes there won't be many on a page. But if it seems to you that there are none on a page, you are making a serious error—the same serious error that put you in this comatose state to start with. You are mistaking lousy, stupid, second-rate, wrong, childish, foolish, worthless ideas for no ideas at all. Your job is not to pick out *good* ideas but to pick out ideas. As long as you were conscious, your words will be full of things that could be called feelings, utterances, ideas—things that can be squeezed into one simple sentence. This is your job. Don't ask for too much.

After you have done this, take those little slips or cards, 6
read through them a number of times—not struggling with
them, simply wandering and mulling through them; perhaps
shifting them around and looking through them in various
sequences. In a sense these are cards you are playing solitaire
with, and the rules of this particular game permit shuffling
the unused pile.

The goal of this procedure with the cards is to get them 7
to distribute themselves in two or three or ten or fifteen different piles on your desk. You can get them to do this almost
by themselves if you simply keep reading through them in
different orders; certain cards will begin to feel like they go
with other cards. I emphasize this passive, thoughtless mode
because I want to talk about desperation writing in its pure
state. In practice, almost invariably at some point in the procedure, your sanity begins to return. It is often at this point.
You actually are moved to have thoughts or—and the difference between active and passive is crucial here—to *exert*
thought, to hold two cards together and *build* or *assert* a relationship. It is a matter of bringing energy to bear.

So you may start to be able to do something active with 8
these cards, and begin actually to think. But if not, just allow
the cards to find their own piles with each other by feel, by
drift, by intuition, by mindlessness.

You have now engaged in the two main activities that 9
will permit you to get something cooked out on the table
rather than in your brain: writing out into messy words, sum-
ming up into single assertions, and even sensing relationships between assertions. You can simply continue to deploy
these two activities.

If, for example, after that first round of writing, asser- 10
tion-making, and pile-making, your piles feel as though they
are useful and satisfactory for what you are writing—paragraphs or sections or trains of thought—then you can carry
on from there. See if you can gather each pile up into a single assertion. When you can, then put the subsidiary assertions of that pile into their best order to fit with that single
unifying one. If you *can't* get the pile into one assertion, then
take the pile as the basis for doing some more writing out into
words. In the course of this writing, you may produce for yourself the single unifying assertion you were looking for; or you

may have to go through the cycle of turning the writing into assertions and piles and so forth. Perhaps more than once. The pile may turn out to want to be two or more piles itself; or it may want to become part of a pile you already have. This is natural. This kind of meshing into one configuration, then coming apart, then coming together and meshing into a different configuration—this is growing and cooking. It makes a terrible mess, but if you can't do it in your head, you have to put up with a cluttered desk and a lot of confusion.

If, on the other hand, all that writing *didn't* have useful 11 material in it, it means that your writing wasn't loose, drifting, quirky, jerky, associative enough. This time try especially to let things simply remind you of things that are seemingly crazy or unrelated. Follow these odd associations. Make as many metaphors as you can—be as nutty as possible—and explore the metaphors themselves—open them out. You may have all your energy tied up in some area of your experience that you are leaving out. Don't refrain from writing about whatever else is on your mind: how you feel at the moment, what you are losing your mind over, randomness that intrudes itself on your consciousness, the pattern on the wallpaper, what those people you see out the window have on their minds—though keep coming back to the whateveritis you are supposed to be writing about. Treat it, in short, like ten-minute writing exercises. Your best perceptions and thoughts are always going to be tied up in whatever is really occupying you, and that is also where your energy is. You may end up writing a love poem— or a hate poem—in one of those little piles while the other piles will finally turn into a lab report on data processing or whatever you have to write about. But you couldn't, in your present state of having your head shot off, have written that report without also writing the poem. And the report will have some of the juice of the poem in it and vice versa.

Checking Your Understanding

1. Describe the role played by the unconscious mind in the writing strategies Elbow discusses. Where in his process does the conscious mind come into play?

2. What is the root of writer's block for Elbow? Is this what usually causes your own writer's block? Which of his suggestions do you think you might try the next time you get stuck? Why would these help you the most?

Examining Rhetorical Strategies

1. Look at Elbow's introductory paragraph. Why is this personal confession an effective way to begin this piece?

2. Elbow uses a number of images to describe writing: cooking, being in a fog, being drugged or drunk, playing solitaire. How do these images work to reflect the message he is trying to get across about what the writing process is really like?

THE HUMAN USE OF LANGUAGE

Lawrence L. Langer

Prereading Journal

Think of a time when you received discouraging or harsh feedback on something you had worked on very hard. Describe how this feedback made you feel and the impact it had on your motivation to pursue that work further.

Background

Lawrence L. Langer is professor of English, emeritus at Simmons College in Boston and has published extensively on literature related to the atrocities committed during World War II. Among his books are *The Holocaust and the Literary Imagination* (1975) and, most recently, *Holocaust Testimonies: The Ruins of Memory* (1991), which won the National Book Critics Circle Award for criticism. The following essay first appeared in *The Chronicle of Higher Education* in 1977 and concerns the need to use language meaningfully and honestly and how seldom this happens.

During Reading

Note the examples of inhuman language that Langer mentions in his essay.

Reading Selection

A friend of mine recently turned in a paper to a course 1 on behavior modification. She had tried to express in simple English some of her reservations about this increasingly popular approach to education. She received it back with the comment: "Please rewrite this in behavioral terms."

It is little wonder that human beings have so much trou- 2 ble saying what they feel, when they are told that there is a specialized vocabulary for saying what they think. The language of simplicity and spontaneity is forced to retreat behind the barricades of an official prose developed by a few experts who believe that jargon is the most precise means of communication. The results would be comic, if they were not so poisonous; unfortunately, there is an attitude toward the use of language that is impervious to human need and drives some people back into silence when they realize the folly of risking human words on insensitive ears.

The comedy is easy to come by. Glancing through my 3 friend's textbook on behavior modification, I happened on a chapter beginning with the following challenging statement: "Many of the problems encountered by teachers in the daily management of their classes could be resolved if. . . ." Although I was a little wary of the phrase "daily management," I was encouraged to plunge ahead, because as an educator I have always been interested in ideas for improving learning. So I plunged. The entire sentence reads: "Many of the problems encountered by teachers in the daily management of their classes could be resolved if the emission of desirable student behaviors was increased."

Emission? At first I thought it was a misprint for "omis- 4 sion," but the omission of desirable student behaviors (note the plural) hardly seemed an appropriate goal for educators. Then I considered the possibility of metaphor, both erotic and automotive, but these didn't seem to fit, either. A foot-note clarified the matter: "'Emission' is a technical term used in behavioral analysis. The verb, 'to emit,' is used specifically with a certain category of behavior called 'operant behavior.' Operant behaviors are modified by their consequences. Operant behaviors correspond closely to the behavior collo-quially referred to as voluntary." Voluntary? Is jargon then an attack on freedom of the will?

Of course, this kind of abuse of language goes on all the 5 time—within the academic world, one regrets to say, as well as outside it. Why couldn't the author of this text simply say that we need to motivate students to learn willingly? The more I read such non-human prose, and try to avoid writing it myself, the more I am convinced that we must be in touch with ourselves before we can use words to touch others.

Using language meaningfully requires risk; the sen- 6 tence I have just quoted takes no risks at all. Much of the dis-course that poses as communication in our society is really a decoy to divert our audience (and often ourselves) from that shadowy plateau where our real life hovers on the precipice of expression. How many people, for example, have the courage to walk up to someone they like and actually *say* to them: "I'm very fond of you, you know"?

Such honesty reflects the use of language as revelation, and that sort of revelation, brimming with human possibilities, is risky precisely because it invites judgment and rebuff. Perhaps this is one reason why, especially in academe, we are confronted daily with so much neutral prose: Our students are not yet in touch with themselves; not especially encouraged by us, their instructors, to move in that direction; they are encouraged indeed to expect judgment and hence perhaps rebuff, too, in our evaluation of them. Thus they instinctively retreat behind the anonymity of abstract diction and technical jargon to protect themselves against us—but also, as I have suggested, against themselves.

This problem was crystallized for me recently by an encounter only peripherally related to the issue. As part of my current research, I have been interviewing children of concentration-camp survivors. One girl I have been meeting with says that her mother does not like to talk about the experience, *except with other survivors.* Risk is diminished when we know in advance that our audience shares with us a sympathy for our theme. The nakedness of pain *and* the nakedness of love require gentle responses. So this survivor is reticent, except with fellow victims.

But one day a situation arose which tempted her to the human use of language although she could not be sure, in advance, of the reception her words would receive. We all recognize it. This particular woman, at the age of 40, decided to return to school to get a college degree. Her first assignment in freshman composition was to write a paper on something that was of great importance to her personally. The challenge was immense, the risk was even greater. For the first time in 20 years, she resolved to confront a silence in her life that she obviously needed to rouse to speech.

She was 14 when the Germans invaded Poland. When the roundup of the Jews began a year later, some Christian friends sent their young daughter to "call for her" one day, so that they might hide her. A half hour later, the friends went themselves to pick up her parents, but during that interval, a truck had arrived, loaded aboard the Jewish mother and father—and the daughter never saw them or heard from them again. Their fate we can imagine. The girl herself was eventually arrested, survived several camps, and after the war came to America. She married, had children of her own, and except for occasional reminiscences with fellow survivors, managed to live adequately without diving into her buried personal past. Until one day her instructor in English composition touched a well-insulated nerve, and it began to throb with a painful impulse to express. I present verbatim the result of that impulse, a paper called "People I Have Forgotten":

"Can you forget your own Father and Mother? If so—how or 11 why?

"I thought I did. To mention their names, for me is a great 12 emotional struggle. The brutal force of this reality shakes my whole body and mind, wrecking me into ugly splinters; each crying to be mended anew. So the silence I maintain about their memory is only physical and valid as such but not true. I could never forget my parents, nor do I want to do it. True, I seldom talk about them with my husband or my children. How they looked, who they were, why they perished during the war. The love and sacrifices they have made for me during their lifetime, never get told.

"The cultural heritage to which each generation is entitled 13 to have access seems to be nonexistent [*sic*], since I dare not talk about anything relating to my past, my parents.

"This awful, awesome power of non-remembering, this 14 heart-breaking sensation of the conspiracy of silence is my dilemma.

"Often, I have tried to break through my imprisoning wall 15 of irrational silence, but failed: now I hope to be able to do it.

"Until now, I was not able to face up to the loss of my par- 16 ents, much less talk about them. The smallest reminder of them would set off a chain reaction of results that I could anticipate but never direct. The destructive force of sadness, horror, fright would then become my master. And it was this subconscious knowledge that kept me paralyzed with silence, not a conscious desire to forget my parents.

"My silent wall, my locked shell existed only of real necessi- 17 ty; I needed time.

"I needed time to forget the tragic loss of my loved 18 ones, time to heal my emotional wound so that there shall come a time when I can again remember the people I have forgotten."

The essay is not a confrontation, only a prelude, yet it 19 reveals qualities which are necessary for the human use of language: In trying to reach her audience, the author must touch the deepest part of herself. She risks self-exposure—when we see the instructor's comment, we will realize how great was her risk—and she is prepared for judgment and perhaps even rebuff, although I doubt whether she was prepared for the form they took. This kind of prose, for all its hesitant phraseology, throws down a gauntlet to the reader, a challenge asking him to understand that life is pain as well as plenty, chaos as well as form. Its imagery of locked shells and imprisoning walls hints at a silent world of horror and sadness far less enchanting than the more familiar landscape of love where most of us dwell. Language is a two-edged tool, to pierce the wall which hides that world, or build high abstract barriers to protect us from its threats.

The instructor who graded the paper I have just read 20 preferred walls to honest words. At the bottom of the last page she scrawled a large "D-minus," emphatically surrounded by a circle. Her only comment was: "Your theme is not clear—you should have developed your 1st paragraph. You talk around your subject." At this moment, two realms collide: a universe of unarticulated feeling seeking expression (and the courage and encouragement to express) and a nature made so immune to feeling by heaven-knows-what that she hides behind the tired, tired language of the professional theme-corrector.

Suddenly we realize that reading as well as writing 21 requires risks, and that the metaphor of insulation, so central to the efforts of the Polish woman survivor to re-establish contact with her past, is a metaphor governing the response of readers, too. Some writing, like "the emission of desirable student behaviors," thickens the insulation that already separates the reader from the words that throw darts at his armor of indifference. But even when language unashamedly reveals the feeling that is hidden behind the words, it must contend with a different kind of barrier, the one behind which our instructor lies concealed, unwilling or unable to hear a human voice and return a human echo of her own.

Ironically, the victor in this melancholy failure at com- 22 munication is the villain of the piece, behavior modification. For the Polish survivor wrote her next theme on an innocuous topic, received a satisfactory grade, and never returned to the subject of her parents. The instructor, who had encountered a problem in the daily management of her class in the form of an essay which she could not respond to in a human way, altered the attitude of her student by responding in a non-human way, thus resolving her problem by increasing the emission of desirable student behavior. The student now knows how vital it is to develop her first paragraph, and how futile it is to reveal her first grief.

Even more, she has learned the danger of talking 23 around her subject: She not only refuses to talk *around* it now, she refuses to talk *about* it. Thus the human use of language leads back to silence—where perhaps it should have remained in the first place.

Checking Your Understanding

1. Why does Langer feel that reading as well as writing requires risks?
2. How does the discouragement you wrote about in your prereading journal compare with the example Langer discusses? How do you feel about assignments that ask you to share highly personal experiences? By what standards would you say Langer thinks such writing should be evaluated? Do you agree with him?

Evaluating Rhetorical Strategies

1. How do the examples that Langer uses support his main point? Why does he include the entire paper his friend wrote?
2. Note the repetition of the phrase "the emission of desirable student behaviors." What is the meaning and significance of this phrase for Langer? How does it relate to his ideas about writing and reading?

QUALITY

Robert Pirsig

Prereading Journal

Select an item from your pocket or from the room in which you are sitting and write about it for twenty minutes.

Background

Pirsig taught composition and rhetoric from 1959 until 1962 and worked as a technical writer from 1963 until 1973. In 1974 his novel *Zen and the Art of Motorcycle Maintenance* was published, and Pirsig became a full-time professional writer. In this essay, he describes the experience of a writing teacher, called "Phaedrus," and his efforts to get his students to understand what "quality" in writing is all about.

During Reading

Note the places in this excerpt where Pirsig describes a classroom situation that you can relate to your own experiences as a student.

Reading Selection

Today now I want to take up the first phase of his journey into Quality, the nonmetaphysical phase, and this will be pleasant. It's nice to start journeys pleasantly, even when you know they won't end that way. Using his class notes as reference material I want to reconstruct the way in which Quality became a working concept for him in the teaching of rhetoric. His second phase, the metaphysical one, was tenuous and speculative, but this first phase, in which he simply taught rhetoric, was by all accounts solid and pragmatic and probably deserves to be judged on its own merits, independently of the second phase. 1

He'd been innovating extensively. He'd been having trouble with students who had nothing to say. At first he thought it was laziness but later it became apparent that it wasn't. They just couldn't think of anything to say. 2

One of them, a girl with strong-lensed glasses, wanted 3 to write a five-hundred-word essay about the United States. He was used to the sinking feeling that comes from statements like this, and suggested without disparagement that she narrow it down to just Bozeman.

When the paper came due she didn't have it and was 4 quite upset. She had tried and tried but she just couldn't think of anything to say.

He had already discussed her with her previous instruc- 5 tors and they'd confirmed his impressions of her. She was very serious, disciplined and hardworking, but extremely dull. Not a spark of creativity in her anywhere. Her eyes, behind the thick-lensed glasses, were the eyes of a drudge. She wasn't bluffing him, she really couldn't think of anything to say, and was upset by her inability to do as she was told.

It just stumped him. Now *he* couldn't think of anything 6 to say. A silence occurred, and then a peculiar answer: "Narrow it down to the *mainstreet* of Bozeman." It was a stroke of insight.

She nodded dutifully and went out. But just before her 7 next class she came back in *real* distress, tears this time, distress that had obviously been there for a long time. She still couldn't think of anything to say, and couldn't understand why, if she couldn't think of anything about *all* of Bozeman, she should be able to think of something about just one street.

He was furious. "You're not *looking*!" he said. A memory 8 came back of his own dismissal from the University for having *too* much to say. For every fact there is an *infinity* of hypotheses. The more you *look* the more you *see*. She really wasn't looking and yet somehow didn't understand this.

He told her angrily, "Narrow it down to the *front* of *one* 9 building on the main street of Bozeman. The Opera House. Start with the upper left-hand brick."

Her eyes, behind the thick-lensed glasses, opened wide. 10

She came in the next class with a puzzled look and 11 handed him a five-thousand-word essay on the front of the Opera House on the main street of Bozeman, Montana. "I sat in the hamburger stand across the street," she said, "and started writing about the first brick, and the second brick, and then by the third brick it all started to come and I couldn't stop. They thought I was crazy, and they kept kidding me, but here it all is. I don't understand it."

Neither did he, but on long walks through the streets of town he thought about it and concluded she was evidently stopped with the same kind of blockage that had paralyzed him on his first day of teaching. She was blocked because she was trying to repeat, in her writing, things she had already heard, just as on the first day he had tried to repeat things he had already decided to say. She couldn't think of anything to write about Bozeman because she couldn't recall anything she had heard worth repeating. She was strangely unaware that she could look and see freshly for herself, as she wrote, without primary regard for what had been said before. The narrowing down to one brick destroyed the blockage because it was so obvious she *had* to do some original and direct seeing. 12

He experimented further. In one class he had everyone write all hour about the back of his thumb. Everyone gave him funny looks at the beginning of the hour, but everyone did it, and there wasn't a single complaint about "nothing to say." 13

In another class he changed the subject from the thumb to a coin, and got a full hour's writing from every student. In other classes it was the same. Some asked, "Do you have to write about both sides?" Once they got into the idea of seeing directly for themselves there was no limit to the amount they could say. It was a confidence-building assignment too, because what they wrote, even though seemingly trivial, was nevertheless their own thing, not a mimicking of someone else's. Classes where he used that coin exercise were always less balky and more interested. 14

As a result of his experiments he concluded that imitation was a real evil that had to be broken before real rhetoric teaching could begin. This imitation seemed to be an external compulsion. Little children didn't have it. It seemed to come later on, possibly as a result of school itself. . . . 15

There's a large fragment concerning Phaedrus' first class after he gave that assignment on "What is quality in thought and statement?" The atmosphere was explosive. Almost everyone seemed as frustrated and angered as he had been by the question. 16

"How are *we* supposed to know what quality is?" they said. "You're supposed to tell *us*!" 17

Then he told them he couldn't figure it out either and 18
really wanted to know. He had assigned it in the hope that
somebody would come up with a good answer.

That ignited it. A roar of indignation shook the room. 19
Before the commotion had settled down another teacher
had stuck his head in the door to see what the trouble was.

"It's all right," Phaedrus said. "We just accidentally 20
stumbled over a genuine question, and the shock is hard to
recover from." Some students looked curious at this, and the
noise simmered down.

He then used the occasion for a short return to his 21
theme of "Corruption and Decay in the Church of Reason."
It was a measure of this corruption, he said, that students
should be outraged by someone trying to *use* them to seek
truth. You were supposed to *fake* this search for the truth, to
imitate it. To actually *search* for it was a damned imposition.

The truth was, he said, that he genuinely did want to 22
know what they thought, not so that he could put a grade on
it, but because he really wanted to know.

They looked puzzled. 23

"I sat there all night long," one said. 24

"I was ready to cry, I was so mad," a girl next to the win- 25
dow said.

"You should warn us," a third said. 26

"How could I warn you," he said, "when I had no idea 27
how you'd react?"

Some of the puzzled ones looked at him with a first 28
dawning. He wasn't playing games. He really wanted to know.

A most peculiar person. 29

Then someone said, "What do *you* think?" 30

"I don't *know*," he answered. 31

"But what do you *think*?" 32

He paused for a long time. "I think there is such a thing 33
as Quality, but that as soon as you try to define it, something
goes haywire. You can't do it."

Murmurs of agreement. 34

He continued, "Why this is, I don't know. I thought 35
maybe I'd get some ideas from your papers. I just don't know."

This time the class was silent. 36

In subsequent classes that day there was some of the 37
same commotion, but a number of students in each class vol-

unteered friendly answers that told him the first class had
been discussed during lunch.

A few days later he worked up a definition of his own 38
and put it on the blackboard to be copied for posterity. The
definition was: "Quality is a characteristic of thought and
statement that is recognized by a non-thinking process.
Because definitions are a product of rigid, formal thinking,
quality cannot be defined."

The fact that this "definition" was actually a refusal to 39
define did not draw comment. The students had no formal
training that would have told them his statement was, in a
formal way, irrational. If you can't define something you have
no formal rational way of knowing that it exists. Neither can
you *really* tell anyone else what it is. There is, in fact, no formal difference between inability to define and stupidity.
When I say, "Quality cannot be defined," I'm really saying for-
mally, "I'm stupid about Quality."

Fortunately the students didn't know this. If they'd 40
come up with these objections he wouldn't have been able to
answer them at the time.

But then, below the definition on the blackboard, he 41
wrote, "But even though Quality cannot be defined, *you know
what Quality is!*" and the storm started all over again.

"Oh, no, we don't!" 42

"Oh, yes, you do." 43

"Oh, *no*, we *don't!*" 44

"Oh, yes, you *do!*" he said and he had some material 45
ready to demonstrate it to them.

He had selected two examples of student composition. 46
The first was a rambling, disconnected thing with interesting
ideas that never built into anything. The second was a mag-
nificent piece by a student who was mystified himself about
why it had come out so well. Phaedrus read both, then asked
for a show of hands on who thought the first was best. Two
hands went up. He asked how many liked the second better.
Twenty-eight hands went up.

"Whatever it is," he said, "that caused the overwhelming 47
majority to raise their hands for the second one is what I
mean by Quality. So *you* know what it is."

There was a long reflective silence after this, and he just 48
let it last.

This was just intellectually outrageous, and he knew it. He wasn't teaching anymore, he was indoctrinating. He had erected an imaginary entity, defined it as incapable of definition, told the students over their own protests that they knew what it was, and demonstrated this by a technique that was as confusing logically as the term itself. He was able to get away with this because logical refutation required more talent than any of the students had. In subsequent days he continually invited their refutations, but none came. He improvised further. 49

To reinforce the idea that they already knew what Quality was he developed a routine in which he read four student papers in class and had everyone rank them in estimated order of Quality on a slip of paper. He did the same himself. He collected the slips, tallied them on the blackboard and averaged the rankings for an overall class opinion. Then he would reveal his own rankings, and this would almost always be close to, if not identical with the class average. Where there were differences it was usually because two papers were close in quality. 50

At first the classes were excited by this exercise, but as time went on they became bored. What he meant by Quality was obvious. They obviously knew what it was too, and so they lost interest in listening. Their question now was "All right, we know what Quality is. How do we get it?" 51

Now, at last, the standard rhetoric texts came into their own. The principles expounded in them were no longer rules to rebel against, not ultimates in themselves, but just techniques, gimmicks, for producing what really counted and stood independently of the techniques—Quality. What had started out as a heresy from traditional rhetoric turned into a beautiful introduction to it. 52

He singled out aspects of Quality such as unity, vividness, authority, economy, sensitivity, clarity, emphasis, flow, suspense, brilliance, precision, proportion, depth and so on; kept each of these as poorly defined as Quality itself, but demonstrated them by the same class reading techniques. He showed how the aspect of Quality called unity, the hanging-togetherness of a story, could be improved with a technique called an outline. The authority of an argument could be jacked up with a technique called footnotes, which gives authoritative reference. Outlines and footnotes are standard 53 things taught in all freshman composition classes, but now as devices for improving Quality they had a purpose. And if a student turned in a bunch of dumb references or a sloppy outline that showed he was just fulfilling an assignment by rote, he could be told that while his paper may have fulfilled the letter of the assignment it obviously didn't fulfill the goal of Quality, and was therefore worthless.

Now, in answer to that eternal student question, "How 54 do I *do* this?" that had frustrated him to the point of resignation, he could reply, "It doesn't make a bit of difference *how* you do it! Just so it's good." The reluctant student might ask in class, "But how do we know what's good?" but almost before the question was out of his mouth he would realize the answer had already been supplied. Some other student would usually tell him, "You just *see* it." If he said, "No, I don't," he'd be told, "Yes, you do. He proved it." The student was finally and completely trapped into making quality judgments for himself. And it was just exactly this and nothing else that taught him to write.

Up to now Phaedrus had been compelled by the acad- 55 emic system to say what he wanted, even though he knew that this forced students to conform to artificial forms that destroyed their own creativity. Students who went along with his rules were then condemned for their inability to be creative or produce a piece of work that reflected their own personal standards of what is good.

Now that was over with. By reversing a basic rule that 56 all things which are to be taught must first be defined, he had found a way out of all this. He was pointing to no principle, no rule of good writing, no theory—but he was pointing to something, nevertheless, that was very real, whose reality they couldn't deny. . . . Students, astonished, came by his office and said, "I used to just *hate* English. Now I spend more time on it than anything else." Not just one or two. Many. The whole Quality concept was beautiful. It worked. It was that mysterious, individual, internal goal of each creative person, on the blackboard at last.

Checking Your Understanding

1. Describe the process the teacher takes his students through to help them understand what quality is. Why does this process work?

2. Compare your classroom experience with that described in the essay. Have you taken classes in which learning was "faked"? How are they different from ones in which genuine learning took place? Which classes have fostered your creativity and which have hindered it? Has the grading system fostered or hindered your learning and creativity?

Examining Rhetorical Strategies

1. Persig is describing the learning process of a classroom of students. How does he make us experience this learning process with them?
2. Both Persig's and Elbow's essays suggest strategies for overcoming writer's block. Contrast the two writers in terms of the way in which they have chosen to share this advice with us. Also, how are Persig's and Elbow's suggestions similar and different?

STUDENT ESSAYS ABOUT READING AND WRITING

WITCHCRAFT AND VERMIN
Heather Quarles

Background

Whenever the topic of essay tests would come up, Quarles would always laugh as she remembered her *Macbeth* essay. Finally, she decided that she should write the story down because of the positive reception it always received whenever the story was told. It serves as both a reminder to teachers to be careful about the kinds of questions they ask on tests and to students to remember the value of the five paragraph theme.

Reading Selection

The teacher lifted her hand and made an ominous chopping motion in the air. It was the signal to begin the exam. Within seconds, the only sound in the classroom was the hum of the electric clock and the furious scratching of pencils. I had exactly 43 minutes in which to "craft a well thought out essay explaining Shakespeare's symbolic use of light and dark imagery in the play *Macbeth,* using specific examples from the text." And it had to be good because it would determine my entire grade for eleventh grade honors English. 1

I sat at my desk trying not to panic. I had not read *Macbeth* . . . not even the prologue. Not even the cliff notes. Still, I did have several things going for me: 2

1) The test was open book.

2) I had once seen a cartoon called "Macbeth the Mouse" or something like that, about 3 witch-mice standing around a cauldron saying magic words and conjuring up a cat. Because the paperback cover of my play also featured a sketch of three witches around a cauldron, I assumed that the main character, Macbeth, was a witch—presumably, the head witch—and that *mice* had something to do with the story as well. That, at least, was a start.

3) I knew exactly the kind of essay that teachers loved to read—the 5 paragraph theme. It was practically infallible.

If you wanted an "A," you just had to squeeze whatever you wanted to say into five parts—an intro, 3 supporting paragraphs, and a conclusion which said the same thing as the intro. If you did that, and made sure your handwriting was pretty neat, it didn't really matter what you put *in* the paragraphs. Teachers ate it up.

I mustered up my courage and began with a bold and 3 eloquent topic sentence. "In his famous work, *Macbeth,* Shakespeare has once again succeeded in brilliantly manipulating light and dark imagery into his text, thus helping us as readers view the topics of witchcraft and vermin in . . ."—I checked the back of the book for a date—"the eleventh century in an entirely unique Shakespearian fashion." That sounded good. With growing confidence, I continued, "Shakespeare does this in several places, of which the following three are examples. . ."

Thirty-five minutes later, I had crafted a complete essay, 4 sticking carefully to 5 paragraph form, and putting in as many long words as I could. My three supporting paragraphs were centered around two isolated uses of the word "light" and one of the word "dark" which I had found by skimming through the play several times, scanning quickly up and down each page for those particular words.

Only two things were still bothering me. I hadn't 5 noticed any mention of mice anywhere. And also, the name "Macbeth" seemed to be frequently followed by the pronoun "he." If Macbeth was a "he" and Macbeth was a witch, wouldn't that make Macbeth a warlock? I skimmed a couple of pages, searching for a clue that might help me with Macbeth's true identity. They only mentioned him being a "Thane." That could mean anything . . . but it sounded political.

Finally, I nudged the student next to me. "Brett," I 6
hissed. "Was Macbeth a witch or a king?"

"What?" 7

I wrote on the desktop between us: 8

Macbeth—a witch or a king? 9

He looked irritated, but circled the word "King." 10

Only five minutes left. Hastily, I went through the paper 11
erasing the words "Witchcraft" and "Vermin" and substituting the words "Royalty" and "Political Stature." Then, shaking

the eraser dust from the page, I walked to the front of the class and handed it in.

I got an A on the paper and an A in honors English. I   12
never did read *Macbeth*.

Thinking About Writing

Quarles shares a common experience of unprepared students: faking knowledge. In Quarles' story she is rewarded with an "A" for her desperate attempt to write about a complex play that she has never read. What does the high mark she received suggest about the author? How do you feel about her triumph over the teacher and the test? How does she create this response in you?

Writing Assignment

Essay tests are a particular kind of writing and take a special skill. And while Quarles' example brought out the humorous aspect of the formulaic way in which essay writing can be done, her thinking is not altogether wrong when it comes to taking exams.

To successfully complete an essay test you should (1) read the question carefully to determine what is being asked of you; (2) organize (list) the main points you want to cover; (3) write a good introduction that includes a list of these points; (4) cover each point in a paragraph of its own; and (5) write a brief conclusion that pulls the significance of these ideas together. While it may not be an exciting, creative way to write (and while your essay should not be so generic that "Witchcraft" could substitute for "Royalty"), this form will clearly communicate to your teachers that you understand the question and the material and it will be easy to read and follow, something which can be crucial when a teacher has a great number of essays to read quickly.

Create an essay question you are likely to face on an upcoming exam and construct a well-written, well-organized answer to it that thoroughly covers the material and is easy for someone else to read and follow. Take as much time as you need to prepare to write, but do the writing under the time constraints you will actually face during the exam.

READING

Tisa Wettach

Background

Wettach had gone through high school, as many students do, without realizing the value of the literature her teachers were trying to share with her. Reading was boring and life was filled with better ways to spend time. And then one day, in the library, she learned on her own what her teachers had been trying to tell her—that books can grab the soul.

Reading Selection

When I was in high school I never cared to read. I, like other high school students, preferred to do other things. I would watch television or talk on the telephone, anything except read. When I looked at magazines like *Newsweek, National Geographic,* or *Life,* I was only looking at the pictures. I preferred spending time thinking about my life instead of reading valuable history about someone else's. 1

One day I was forced to wait in the public library until I could get my ride home. I had a two hour wait in a place I had no interest in being. I remember sitting there opening up my school textbook to read an assignment from one of my classes. I did not want to do this particular assignment because reading was involved, and it was a lengthy reading. I knew I had two hours to waste. My attention lasted one minute. 2

I started watching people around me in the library. There were so many people in there, and yet it was so quiet. What was making these people so content? I watched people draw books in and out of the shelves, delicately. 3

I was amused at the way their eyes would squint side by side while reading the back of the book. I watched their eyebrows shuffle around. They looked funny to me. I was picturing them as boring little aliens. But, the more I studied them, the more I saw that their faces were full of so much expression and these expressions did not look bored. Their face muscles 4 transformed them into sad, happy, worried, compelled, and fascinating people. They were involved. These people, young people, like me, were focused on those thick, thin, or dusty books that they were holding. They were oblivious to their surroundings and noises around them. I watched people read as their legs were carrying them out the door.

I realized they were in the library because they wanted 5 to be. They were choosing these books, and looking at them, by choice. They did not want to leave. No one was bored. OK, I thought, what is pulling them inside these pages? What is drawing their minds in? It was time for me to find out for myself.

I approached a shelf. A few people were around. 6 Figuring this had to be one of the better sections of books, I randomly drew a book off the shelf. It was a book of poetry by e. e. cummings. There were no titles to any of the poems so I opened up a page in the center of the book. It was a love poem. I read it about three times before I could understand what this poem was saying. Once I did, goose bumps popped out on my skin, and I started blushing. I read the next poem, the next, and the next. Poem after poem. Page after page. Some gave me no reaction at all. Others made me feel sad, lonely, happy, and loved. It was the most intense feeling. I realized I had just discovered two wonderful things—poetry and reading. I realized I was addicted when I found myself sitting on the floor next to this gigantic shelf, surrounded by books.

I ended up spending the rest of my two hours looking 7 through a variety of books. I wrote down the titles of many that looked interesting. I saw that shelves were packed tightly with row after row of interesting, exciting looking books. Every subject, idea, or thought was covered by a title. It was endless.

I now realize that reading is the best way to learn. Just 8 by simply reading I am learning about words and how to express myself and write. There is a book for every interest I can possibly have.

Reading is like stepping out of my life and into some- 9 one else's world. The world I enter will be my choice: an escape that feels good. And once I started reading that book that grabbed my soul, I had only one regret—what took me so long?

Thinking About Writing

Wettach is describing a discovery process in this piece; she moves from hating reading and books to understanding their purpose and power. Notice how the changes in her physical activities and settings correspond to her changing attitude. When she is the most negative about reading, she is trying to do her homework and failing. She is also sitting at a table but wishing she were somewhere else. We then see her become an observer of others, then a tentative participant, and finally wholly absorbed in the activity of reading. In the same way she moves from her isolated table to being surrounded by books. How does the close correspondence of attitude, setting, and action increase the effectiveness of the piece?

Writing Assignment

Most of us have read something in our lives that made an impression on us. It may have been something as profound as the Bible and Shakespeare or something as seemingly insignificant as an advertisement on the back of a baseball card. Perhaps we were moved by a note left for us by a friend or a special card sent to us with love. Or perhaps reading a pamphlet explaining some issue made us get involved in a cause or reading a review of a particular movie made us go to see it. Recall some time when reading made a difference in your life. Try to capture the context for the reading and the process you went through as the reading affected you.

AN AMALGAM OF TEDDY BEARS DANCING ON MY HEAD

Brian Van Brunt

Background

Van Brunt was a psychology major who was also very interested in creative writing. This essay began as a response to a free journal for an expository writing class. Van Brunt decided to explore the question: Why do people write? His creative bent made him do that exploration in a very unusual and entertaining way.

Reading Selection

The blue glow of the computer screen cast a soft velvet 1 shadow on the enveloping darkness. Faint outlines of a chair, a bed . . . perhaps a table are all visible if one squints hard enough into the blue-blackness of the room. Gargoyles and unlit candles line the desk next to the old computer—ever watchful eyes lurking near the long extinguished sources of light. Music from previous ages fills the chamber, bringing with it the passion and fervor of centuries past.

A lone figure sits in the darkness—his fingers dancing 2 on the keyboard resting in his lap. They create wonderful things . . .

"Intertwining rose petals of confusion hum against the 3 midnight sky . . . sliding . . . skittering . . . falling now . . . do I dare . . . will I ever . . . stop?" stop.

This is how I write. 4

I sit in my room leafing through papers, essays, poems, 5 short stories . . . an entire myriad of work, a plethora of manuscripts . . . collected and cherished, crumpled and discarded.

I sit in my room, amongst my scribblings, thinking 6 about the ancient question. What better topic to write about? Without a writing about writing what are all my writings except for miscellaneous writings which merely consist of paper . . . perhaps a staple, a grade from an illustrious teacher, a specific audience, an authoritative voice, a definite style, a purpose . . . yet what is it all for?

Why do we write?   7

Dear Sir or Madam,   8

I am writing you concerning the answer to the question: Why do we write? I have reason to believe you may have the answer to my dilemma. Please send me any information you may have on this topic. Thank you for your time and consideration.

> Sincerely,
> A Concerned Student

Dear Concerned Student,   9

We do have the information you require in regards to: Why we write? Please send a check or money order to our address in the amount of $19.95 plus postage and handling and we will rush you a copy of our answer.

> Sincerely,
> Sir and Madame

Perhaps we write to impress the scholar who may per- 10
chance peruse our papyrus and thus behold the expertise and competence in which we manipulate and command a tremendous vocabulary. Blind everyone with our impressive, amazing, prominent, penetrating, tremendous use of a thesaurus?

Hereafter the party of the first part shall be known as 11
the party who wishes to file a petition to understand "Why we write." The party of the second and third parts shall be related to the party of the first part, the undersigned, here-to-for without firm benefit to any of the parties. All judgment concerning "Why we write" will be left to an elusive fourth party who knows about the first party and understands the previous stipulations about the second and third.

MAY-be WE   12
        WRITE
                                      ~~because~~
WE . . . like the *POWER*
that comes- in our {[(organization)]}

of; *the ability* to create strange meaning by punctuation:
fonts, and
size. . . ?

I've been asked to give my opinion on the subject of 13 why people write. I know why we write. My way is clear, log-ical and the exact definition while your way is poorly formed and utterly wrong. The Bible clearly supports my statements, ideas and theories. Have you read the Bible? Obviously not from reading your opinions. God and I say we write because we need to communicate. He wrote the Ten Commandments to show us how to live. He wrote the Bible to teach us. We write to communicate—that is what God says, that is what I believe. Anyone, like yourself, who says anything to the contrary is obviously sinning and of the Devil.

Learning about why we write is an important thing to 14 do. We should all learn about why we write. It will help us live our lives better.

Firstly, we write to express our inner tensions. As 15 humans, we need to express ourselves. Without expressing ourselves, we would explode. Not literally, of course, but it would still be bad.

Secondly, we write to communicate. We write to tell 16 other people what we feel. We also write to teach other people things. Without writing we could not communicate as well.

Thirdly, we write to communicate our inner tensions to 17 others. How would anyone ever know what we are feeling inside unless we write or tell them. Since we are not always near another person, we may not have the opportunity to tell them. So we must write.

In conclusion, writing is good and important in each of 18 our lives. We should do it a lot because it is good. Without writing there would be little communication in the world besides talking.

"Oh, Dan!!! You *must* tell me," she cried out.   19
"No," he said flatly.   20
"But why not? You simply must tell me," she pleaded.   21
Dan looked her straight in the eye, "No."   22
"You tear my soul apart with your secrets. Tell me now 23 or I shall end it all!!!" she screamed in a fit of passion.
"No."   24

Why do we write? We write for hundreds of reasons . . .   25
"Why do I write?" you may ask.   26

I write for the process of creation, the fevered banging 27
at the keyboard, the adrenalin rush at the sound of my print-
er . . . **I write because of how I write**.

Thinking About Writing

Often discussions in writing classes explore the many reasons
why people put pen to paper. Usually, the class will come up with a
list: to supply information, to satisfy requirements in school, to
express our thoughts, to communicate, to persuade, to earn
money. Van Brunt has essentially done the same thing; he has
given a list of reasons. But each reason takes on a life and style of
its own and he explains the reason and illustrates the style at the
same time. Notice how the writing changes as he moves from legal
style to dialogue to formal letter, etc. Why do you think he decided to answer the question of why in this way? Why is it effective in
communicating his personal answer to that question?

Writing Assignment

Why do you write? Is it only because writing is assigned in
classes, or do you keep a personal journal or perhaps write poetry
or letters or stories? For this assignment, answer that question for
yourself. You might also wish for the style you use to reflect the reasons you choose, as Van Brunt did.

APPENDIX

RESEARCH STRATEGIES

In many classes your teachers will ask you to research your topic. This may be a request for you to do *original research* or *library research*. Original or field research involves your collecting your own data through such things as observations, interviews, or surveys. Library research involves finding support from written sources to back up your own ideas and opinions.

GUIDELINES FOR ORIGINAL RESEARCH

Many disciplines will ask you to conduct original or field research. Future teachers must do observations in the schools, dieticians must observe in health institutions, environmentalists must observe changes in our natural surroundings, social scientists observe human behavior.

The success of original research depends on two things. First, you must have a clear *research question*—what do you want to discover through your observations, interviews, or surveys? As we discussed in Chapter Thirteen, you should not go into your research already knowing the answer to this question because this will bias your observations and your reading of the data. You will only see what you want to see, what supports your answer. Striking this balance between knowing what you are looking for and being open to whatever you might find takes careful preparation.

Second you must be certain that the information you collect will actually allow you to answer your question. Many times students will collect survey responses only to discover that in order to draw conclusions from these responses they needed to have asked one more question which was not included. Thus, although they now have a good deal of information, it is not the kind that will really help them create a strong paper.

In order to help you be prepared and achieve the results you need, we have provided some guidelines for helping you conduct successful original research.

Step One: Be Prepared to Collect Your Data

Think through exactly what it is you want to know and formulate this into a clear research question. For example, it is not enough to say that you want to know about the recreational activities provided for residents in a local nursing home. That is a good topic, but the question remains: *What* do you want to know about them? Do you want to know how often they are provided? How much variety there is? If the residents are satisfied with these activities? If they provide the proper amount of physical and mental exercise that residents need? Each of these questions narrows your topic down and focuses your observation, interview, or survey.

Step Two: Select Your Site, Person, or Sampling Carefully

If you are doing field research, visit your site ahead of time and make sure you will find what you need there. If you are going to observe an elementary school classroom, for example, to find out about current disciplinary techniques, visit the school and the teacher you have arranged to observe before you actually start your data collection to be sure that discipline plays a role in that environment.

If you are conducting an interview, ask enough questions at the time you set up the interview to be sure this person will be able to provide you with the information you need for your paper. Is this the expert you need for your topic? And don't be shy about asking for what you need. If the person is not cooperative at this initial stage, you might wish to seek out a different source. Be polite and clear about your goals. Neither you nor the interviewee want to waste time with an interview that won't help you.

If you are doing a survey, decide what group you want to answer your questions and how you are going to insure that you get as much information as you need. For example, if you were doing a survey on how students felt about their first-year writing class, you might ask your teacher to help you arrange to distribute your surveys in classes that will cover a wide range of the student population. The class format also makes distribution and collection easy.

Step Three: Know What You Are Looking For

If you are doing field research, you will need to decide what you are looking for, as well as how long it will take you to be able to draw some conclusions from the site. You will also need to make sure you are prepared to start the observation and have completed any preliminary data gathering you might need. For example, if you were observing that nursing home, watching a scheduled Bingo game for one day would not give you much information. While observing a recreational activity would undoubtedly be necessary, you would also need to find out what all the scheduled activities were, how often they were offered, and how well each was attended.

If you are doing an interview, practice. Ask someone to pretend to be the person you will be interviewing so that you can hear how your questions sound and also begin to anticipate answers that will lead to follow-up questions. Practice how you will begin the interview—how you will introduce yourself and explain what you are doing. These sessions will also give you time to practice listening and taking notes at the same time—a challenging skill. Make sure you have something solid to write on and a writing implement that won't run out of ink just when you need it most. You might also consider asking the interviewee if you may tape the interview. The tape frees you to listen more carefully, to ask better follow-up questions, and to be sure you have recorded exactly what the person said.

If you are doing a survey, make sure your questions will yield the information you need by testing your instrument first. Ask someone from the group you are surveying to fill out the questionnaire. Then examine the answers you get to make sure these will yield really useful information for you. You will also need to decide if what you are looking for from your surveys are statistics or comments. If you want to be able to tabulate your information, you should use yes/no or scaled questions (in which responders may choose a point on a range from most to least or best to worst). If you are instead looking for comments about your topic, then you need to be careful *not* to ask yes/no questions so that your responders are forced to write out their opinions or reactions. Remember that comment surveys are much more difficult to draw conclusions from. It's much easier to say that ten out of thirty students surveyed said that "Yes" they enjoyed their writing class, then to interpret thirty individual comments about the class.

Step Four: Be Prepared to Collect the Data

In the field, this means that you are prepared to collect your data efficiently. This may involve some preliminary research or the creation of charts or checkoff lists. For example, if you were observing discipline in that classroom, you would need to go into the field with some knowledge of what discipline is and what the different kinds are that you might see. You could then have a list of possible techniques to check and then simply add new ones as you observe them.

In an interview, efficient data collection means knowing your own questions and what you are looking for so thoroughly that you can be really listening to the person's responses and do good follow-up questions. An interview should not be like an oral quiz of the interviewee, but more like a conversation.

Surveys are hard work. You will need to draft your survey, test it out, revise it, copy it, distribute it, and collect it. Surveys that are simply left in mailboxes are seldom returned, so you need to make sure you have a way to insure that you will get some data out of this process. Look for opportunities when you can distribute the surveys, have people fill them out immediately, and then collect them. If your sampling involves students, for example, asking for a few minutes of class time or for a few minutes during a residence hall meeting would be more reliable than stuffing mailboxes.

Step Five: Analyze Your Data with Your Research Question in Mind

After all the data are collected, you will need to take the time to analyze them and reflect on the implications of what they say in relation to your research question. You will probably find it helpful to categorize your findings. These informational units can then help you organize your paper and use your findings to support what you want to say.

And that support is the ultimate purpose of doing original research. You have answered your research question and now you need to explain your findings to your readers. They will want proof of what you say and you have it in the observations, information, or statistics you gathered.

GUIDELINES FOR LIBRARY RESEARCH

When a teacher says that you must find sources for a paper, your initial reaction may be negative because you have found this process boring in the past and you can't see why you need them. Just as knowing the purposes for reading and writing makes those jobs easier, it is also valuable to consider the purpose behind source material so you know why it's worth the effort.

Supporting Your Ideas

Most often writers use sources to back up and support their own ideas and opinions. We may feel that something is right or a particular action should be taken and we may be able to express our opinions well. However, if we can find a study that was done that proves that our solution works or an expert in the field who agrees with us, it makes our ideas stronger.

In this case, you may not need to find sources until *after* you have finished a draft. Then you can decide which of your ideas could use more support and seek to find it.

Participating in the Dialogue

Another common use of source material is as background. Since there is nothing new under the sun, any topic that you choose to write about has likely been written about before. In fact, in most cases, there is a dialogue that has been going on for years, sometimes centuries, about this topic. Your paper is your contribution to this ongoing conversation, what you think about the issue or what you know about the subject.

However, to increase your credibility and authority you need to acknowledge that your voice is not the first to be heard on this subject—that you are aware of the ongoing issues. For example, if you wanted to write a paper on abortion and simply stated your opinion and why you felt this way, your readers' response would probably be that dreaded "So what?" Everyone has heard all the arguments on both sides and most people don't really care what yet another person thinks about it. However, if the current debate about abortion has taken a new turn (as happened recently in the rights of the workers in abortion clinics versus the rights of the unborn children debate) and you have a contribution to make to this particular part of the dialogue, then you enter into the debate with something others are more likely to listen to. You have acknowledged that this issue matters enough to you to keep up on its current developments and to formulate ideas about the issue. You acknowledge these developments by summarizing the current debate as it has been framed by other writers and then stating your position or adding your understanding to that debate.

This contribution may take the form of refuting what someone has said or of supporting an idea but taking it a step further and adding a new insight to it. In either case, you must summarize what others have said first and then add your contribution.

Adding to Your Knowledge Base

Sometimes you will be asked to write a paper on a topic you know little about. Perhaps the topic was touched on in a textbook chapter or lecture, and has now shown up as a possible topic for a research paper for the course. Your understanding of the topic has been increased by the course, but not enough to write a paper about it on your own. In this case, the purpose of your research is to increase this small knowledge base you already have.

You will find your research to be greatly aided if you know which aspect of the topic you wish to write about. Remember the advice you have been given throughout this book about narrowing your topic and selecting a focus. "Rainforests" are an interesting subject, for example, but the topic is huge and cannot be covered in one paper. If your knowledge base is such that you can narrow the topic down before you start your research, you will have an easier time finding sources that are relevant.

As with original research, start with a research question that you want to answer. Is the world's diminishing rainforest area harming the health of trees in the Pacific Northwest? What species are being endangered by the decreasing rainforests and what is being done to save them? From these questions you can focus your research and use what you find to increase your understanding of these topics.

Creating a Knowledge Base

Sometimes you will be assigned topics to write about that you know nothing about. This is a very difficult task because it often leads to *plagiarism.*

Plagiarism is stealing. It is taking someone else's ideas or words and using them in your paper without properly citing them. The difficulty with a paper on a topic that you know nothing about is that *everything* you say will have come from someone else. Since you had no knowledge about the subject to begin with, all of the ideas in your paper will be someone else's.

What is your responsibility in this situation? First, you must read your sources carefully, taking notes as you learn about the topic. After you have completed forming your knowledge base from the sources, you need to reflect on what you have learned and formulate a thesis about what the material says. Third, you should write down in your own words all that you now know and understand about this thesis from the material you have read. Finally, you need to go back to the sources and pull material which will support what you have learned and explain it more thoroughly than you can do on your own.

The crucial element of this activity is that you read and understand first. If you simply start recording what one source says and then do the same with the next, you are writing a series of book reports without doing any of the analyzing and synthesizing work that is needed to formulate a thesis about the subject. And if you don't understand what you are saying, you will likely borrow phrasing from the texts in a way that may lead to plagiarism. This kind of paper demands great care with your use of source material and often a conversation with the teacher to make sure you are doing exactly what is required.

CITING SOURCES

You have already been introduced to the two major documentation forms you should know through the essays in this book.

The MLA (Modern Language Association) style, which is used primarily in the humanities, can be found in the following essays:

1. "Multiculturalism and Education" by Sally Clark (Chapter Eight)
2. "Support the Children" by Sara Carter (Chapter Eleven)
3. "Minority Underrepresentation Among Police Is Dangerous" by Lonnie Martin (Chapter Eleven)
4. "Buying the Right Bicycle Helmet" by Louis Carparelli (Chapter Fourteen).

The APA (American Psychological Association) style, which is used primarily in the social sciences, can be found in the following essays:

1. "To the Other Side of Silence" by Mary Field Belenky et al. (Chapter Fourteen)
2. "Environmentalism Matters" by John Shepardson (Chapter Fourteen).

The difference in the two forms is that the humanities emphasize who wrote the piece, the *author*. In the social sciences, it is often very important when a particular study was done since developments happen very fast in these disciplines. So, the citation form emphasizes the *date* of publication.

For a more thorough discussion of documentation, see:

American Psychological Association. *Publication Manual of the American Psychological Association.* 4th ed. Washington: American Psychological Association, 1994.

Gibaldi, Joseph, and Walter S. Achtert. *MLA Handbook for Writers of Research Papers.* 4th ed. New York: Modern Language Association of America, 1995.

You should also keep in mind that while these are the two major documentation styles, there are other formats which writers use. Occasionally, in the essays in this book you have encountered other ways of acknowledging sources. See, for example, "The Psychopharmacology of Chocolate" by Diane Ackerman, "On Society as Organisms," by Lewis Thomas, and "The Hunger for the King in a Time with No Father" by Robert Bly, which can all be found in Chapter Fourteen.

MLA

As you will see if you look at the essays listed above, sources you use need to be cited in two places: within your text and at the end of your text. Within your text, you need to list the author and the page on which your quotation or paraphrase is located:

> Spencer Tracy's wife "could not settle for the fact that her marriage had been a failure" (Hepburn 421).

If the author is mentioned in your text, then only the page is needed:

> Hepburn felt that Tracy's wife "could not settle for the fact that her marriage had been a failure" (421).

If the author is unknown, substitute a shortened title:

> A stiffness in the helmet "is needed to protect against piercing" ("Better Bicycle" 6).

If there are two or three authors, use both or all three names.
If there are more than three, use the first author's name and then "et al." (meaning, "and others"):

> The study described "five different perspectives from which women view reality" (Belenky et al. 3).

Works Cited Page

At the end of your paper and on a separate page, all the sources you used should be listed alphabetically by author or by title if the author is unknown, using hanging indentation. Double space within and between entries. Below are some of the most commonly used types of citations.

BOOKS

For books with a single author:

> Hepburn, Katharine. *Me: Stories of My Life.* New York: Ballantine Books, 1991.

For books with two or three authors, the names are separated by commas.

For more than three authors use "et al."

> Belenky, Mary Field, et al. *Women's Ways of Knowing.* New York: Basic Books, 1986.

For an edited book, use "ed.":

> Christ, Carol P., and Judith Plaskow, eds. *Womanspirit Rising*. New York: HarperCollins, 1992.

For books with an unknown author, begin with the title.

For a work in an anthology, such as a reader:

> Fuchs, Lawrence H. "The American Way of Families." *Face to Face: Readings on Confrontation and Accommodation in America*. Eds. Joseph Zaitchik, William Roberts, and Holly Zaitchik. Boston: Houghton Mifflin, 1994. 337–339.

ARTICLES

For articles in weekly magazines:

> Clinton, Hillary Rodham. "The Fight Over Orphanages." *Newsweek* 16 January 1995: 22–23.

For articles in journals paginated by volume, begin with author's name. If author is unknown, start with title:

> "Bike Helmets." *Consumer Reports* 56 (1991): 331–4.

For articles in a newspaper:

> Tomlin, Michael. "Guilty in L.A." *Chicago Sun Times*. 18 March 1993, sec. 1: 1.

INTERVIEWS

> Davis, Billy. Telephone interview. 15 April 1993.

APA

As with MLA, sources you use need to be cited in two places: within your text and at the end of your text. Within your text, you need to list the author and the date of publication. For direct quotations, the page is also listed:

> Spencer Tracy's wife "could not settle for the fact that her marriage had been a failure" (Hepburn, 1991, p. 421).

If the author is mentioned in your text, then the date is given immediately after the author's name and the page follows the quotation:

> Hepburn (1991) felt that Tracy's wife "could not settle for the fact that her marriage had been a failure" (p. 421).

If the author is unknown, substitute a shortened title:

A stiffness in the helmet "is needed to protect against piercing" ("Better Bicycle," 1991, p. 6).

If there are two authors, use both last names in all citations connected by "&":

(Cunningham & Saigo, 1992)

If there are three to five authors, identify all the authors the first time you use the source. In subsequent references use only the first name and "et al."

The study described "five different perspectives from which women view reality" (Belenky, Clinchy, Goldberger, & Tarule, 1986, p. 3).

If there are more than six authors, use the first author's name with "et al.":

References Page

At the end of your paper and on a separate page, all the sources you used should be listed alphabetically by author or by title if the author is unknown, using hanging indentation, and double spacing within and between entries. But there are major differences between APA citations and MLA:

Use initials instead of first names for authors.
Use all authors' names instead of "et al."
The date follows the author's name.
In the titles and subtitles of books, only the first word is capitalized (and proper nouns).
Titles of articles are not in quotation marks.

BOOKS

For books with a single author:

Hepburn, K. (1991). *Me: Stories of my life.* New York: Ballantine Books.

For books with two or more authors, the names are separated by commas and "&." Use only initials for first names.

Halliday, M. A. K., & Hasan, R. (1977). *Cohesion in English.* London: Longman.

For an edited book, use "Ed.":

Christ, C. P., & Plaskow, J. (Eds.). (1992). *Womanspirit rising.* New York: HarperCollins.

For books with an unknown author, begin with the title.

For a work in an anthology such as a reader:

> Fuchs, L. H. (1994). The American way of families. In J. Zaitchik, W. Roberts, and H. Zaitchik (Eds.), *Face to face: Readings on confrontation and accommodation in America* (pp. 337–9). Boston: Houghton Mifflin.

ARTICLES

For articles in weekly magazines:

> Clinton, H. R. (1995, January 16). The fight over orphanages. *Newsweek,* 22–23.

For articles in journals paginated by volume, begin with author's name. If author is unknown begin with title:

> Bike helmets. (1991). *Consumer Reports, 56,* 331–334.

For articles in a newspaper:

> Tomlin, M. (1993, March 18). Guilty in L.A. *Chicago Sun Times,* p. 1.

INTERVIEWS

For APA, interviews are cited in the text only.

INDEX OF AUTHORS AND TITLES

~W~

INDEX OF MAJOR CONCEPTS